Justice DENIED

The Unsolved Murder of Peggy Reber

Michelle Gooden

NATIONAL CHILD ABUSE HOTLINE
1-800-4-A-CHILD / 1-800-422-4453

NATIONAL SEXUAL ASSAULT HOTLINE
1-800-656-HOPE / 1-800-656-4673

U.S. NATIONAL DOMESTIC VIOLENCE HOTLINE
1-800-799-SAFE / 1-800-799-7233

Shortly after 3 a.m. on the morning of May 25, 1968, Mary Reber entered her third floor apartment to find the electricity was not working in her unit. City streetlights offered the 33-year-old divorced mother limited lighting as she fumbled through the flat she shared with her 14-year-old daughter, Peggy. Mary was surprised to enter an empty apartment because normally Peggy was there with her boyfriend, Ray, and on this particular night Peggy's friend Pinky was supposed to be moving in with them for a couple days. Mary could see a suitcase just inside the doorway of Peggy's room, so she assumed Pinky managed to get some of her things moved in that day. She struggled to look around her daughter's dark room, and she was baffled by the fact no one was there at such a late hour . Mary was about to exit the room when she caught a glimpse of something odd on the bedroom floor. In the poor lighting it looked like it could have been a stand-up doll. Did Pinky bring a doll with her? Mary scoffed at the idea because18-year-old Pinky was a little old for dolls. Mary knelt down on the floor of the darkened room and she immediately knew it wasn't a doll she spotted across the room. She was certain Pinky simply passed out and fell on the floor, so she called her name and started to shake her to wake her, but the minute she touched the young girl's flesh she knew something was very, very wrong. The girl's skin was clammy and cold to the touch.

Mary Reber choked back a scream and fought tears as she stumbled out of the room. She ran across the hall and pounded on her neighbor's door begging for help. Jewel Beard opened her door to find a frantic Mary Reber talking at a rapid pace about thinking Pinky was passed out, but she's dead. She's dead on Peggy's floor. Jewel wasn't sure who Pinky was, but Jewel knew it was not uncommon for Mary to have a wide variety of visitors to her apartment and at some of the strangest hours. Jewel's boyfriend Walter stepped into the hall and attempted to calm the hysterical mother. Mary wasn't making too much sense as she kept repeating "Oh my God! She's dead!" Neighboring apartments were disrupted by the commotion in the hall as Walter entered Mary Reber's apartment to see exactly what had her so upset. It was almost impossible to see without the benefit of electricity, so Walter and another neighbor moved the furniture enough to allow them to open a door to the hall. Walter dropped to his knees to administer first-aid to the girl on the floor, but a simple touch confirmed not only that she was dead, but rigor mortis had set in on her body. He looked up at the crowd gathering at the doorway and yelled "Somebody call the police!"

While standing in the doorway, Jewel wrapped her arms around Mary and tried to comfort her, yet the shock and confusion was running deep. Meanwhile, someone made their way to the building's main fuse box, broke the flimsy lock and restored power to the Reber apartment. The lights revealed a severely beaten and brutalized corpse propped up in the corner of the room.

Jewel let out a gasp. "Dear God! That's PEGGY!"

Mary started to scream and just kept saying, "No! No! No!" The neighbors in the hall struggled to catch a glimpse of the morbid sight and some were not sure if it was Peggy at all. The young girl had literally been beaten beyond recognition. Her small lifeless body donned an orange garment and a small pool of blood could be seen on the floor between the girl's thighs.

Jewel Beard was a mother and she went to check on her own children in the midst of the chaos. Jewel was also an immaculate woman with her appearance and her home. She took great pride in always looking her very best and she would smile at young Peggy because she did, too. Jewel returned from her apartment and shook her head in disgust at the number of people gazing at Peggy like it was a freak show. Jewel entered the Reber apartment, picked up a lavender blanket and covered the lifeless body of her teenage neighbor. Jewel knew Peggy would never want to be seen looking like that and it was the respectful thing for her to do.

By the time police arrived at 770 Maple Street that fateful morning the third-floor hall was crowded with tenants from the entire three-story building. Officers pushed their way through the crowd and entered the Reber apartment still unaware of the horrors under the lavender blanket. Oh, local police were quite familiar with the reputation of The Maple Leaf Apartment Building and not one of them was spared the rumors of Mary Reber's wild lifestyle. Yet none of them were prepared professionally, or personally, for the truths they were about to uncover.

Police removed the lavender blanket covering Peggy's body and immediately realized they were dealing with a crime unlike anything Lebanon, Pennsylvania had ever seen before. A photographer from the local newspaper was called to take crime scene photos, while a substitute coroner was called to pronounce the body dead because the regular county coroner was out of town. The district attorney was also out of town at the time, so police alerted the assistant district attorney. It wasn't long before the State Police showed up, too.

It was obvious 14-year-old Margaret "Peggy" Reber was dead, but it wasn't until her body was removed from the scene merely six-hours later that the true nature of the crime would come to light. Peggy's autopsy would reveal she was beaten. She suffered a barbaric bite on her left breast. She was strangled in excess of four minutes with a cloth dress belt causing a laceration to her throat. And perhaps most disturbingly of all, she was rectally assaulted with a 5-foot recurve hunting bow. The killer thrust the bow in Peggy's rectum a minimum of 16 times. He savagely rammed the bow into her lower body wounding all her internal organs. His rage-filled assault reached so deep it perforated her lungs 11 times and her heart 5 times. The news reported the point of the assault was the size of a man's fist by the time the monster was done brutalizing Peggy. There was no indication of a vaginal assault, rape or sperm present.

In 1968 it was not acceptable to discuss such things as one's rectum, so countless individuals failed to truly understand what was done to Peggy Reber, yet a sharp newspaper reporter made the fact available even way back then. A local reporter told his readers Peggy's exact time of death could not be determined because the orifice commonly used to take a body's temperature was the focal point of the assault. Young mothers throughout the county were still using glass mercury-filled rectal thermometers to take their babies temperatures, yet they failed to make the comparison when reading the news about Peggy. The orifice commonly used to take a body temperature was the rectum. Peggy Reber was beaten, bitten, and strangled. Then the monster rammed a hunting bow up her rectum so far he punctured her heart 5 times.

Peggy Reber's killer unleashed his evil fifteen months before the nation would even hear the name Charles Manson, yet he was just as sick and just as twisted. Manson never killed anyone; rather he orchestrated evil acts in California, while Peggy's killer was a sadistic killer walking freely and unidentified on the streets of Lebanon, Pennsylvania.

■■

I drove through the well-manicured cemetery without saying too much. I reflected on the areas that hosted my own family's graves.

"You know," I opted to share a bit of my thinking, "When my grandfather bought space in this cemetery, he did so because he liked the fact that it donned nameplates instead of actual tombstones. He liked the thought that all people appeared equal, and if the family grapevine serves me well, this isn't exactly the cheapest cemetery in town." We moved at a snail's pace through the winding road that covered the grounds.

"Susan," I almost stopped the vehicle, "How did a poor girl that died in an apartment without electricity end up in such a nice cemetery?"

"Good question." She pointed toward a small building with a few cars parked outside. "Let's go and see if we can get an answer." We quietly entered the office and a bell alerted those within of our presence. I was a bit startled as the unexpected chime echoed throughout the foyer as we came face to face with a display of grave markers.

"Hello, may I help you?"

A soft voice attached to a small woman greeted us from behind the counter. The counter was exceptionally high and I was growing increasingly uncomfortable as I thought of my surroundings. I had many questions, but perhaps a visit to the cemetery was venturing a little too far.

"May I help you?" The woman repeated her question.

"Well," I stammered, "I am not sure if you can help me." I was truly at a loss for words, I could feel my face get flushed, and I looked out the window that offered a view of the many graves.

"I found the Hawley file!" A bouncy voice floated into the room followed by a larger woman with a legal-size file in her hand,, and she just seemed to ooze with energy.

"Oh, I am so sorry." She was immediately embarrassed "I didn't realize there was anyone here, Please forgive me." I was suddenly aware that I wasn't the only one uncomfortable, but our reasons were different, so I tried to put the woman at ease.

I smiled and took a few steps closer to the counter. "You are fine, just fine." I assured her.

"How can we help you?"

"Well, I was just saying," I cleared my throat. "I am not even sure you can help me." I looked toward Susan for support. "I am looking for a grave."

I managed to say the words, but I wasn't beyond the discomfort zone. "It's not a family member, and I don't even know if it's legal for you to give me the information." I was in over my head.

"What's the person's name?" The first woman asked so compassionately, I almost felt guilty, as though I was violating some sacred territory.

"Her name is." I hesitated before I continued. "Peggy Reber."

I turned toward Susan and rolled my eyes in question. I had no idea what to expect after I said Peggy's name.

The kind woman started to approach a filing cabinet when the second woman said, "Christ is looking over her." A silence embraced the room that can never accurately be articulated. The second woman, Daisy, silently walked across the room and opened a drawer without saying another word.

It was too much for Susan, and she broke the silence. "I beg your pardon? Christ is looking over her?" Susan's voice gave hint to irritation as if the woman were making light of the mention of Peggy's name.

"She is buried in the area of the cemetery known as Sermon on the Mount." The woman pulled a file from the antique drawer and walked toward the counter. "There is a statue of Christ there and she is buried at the foot of the statue, so," the woman looked Susan in the eye as if to match the suggestion of disrespect, "Christ is looking over her."

She placed the file on the counter and opened it for review. "Let's see," she licked her finger to page through the contents. "Margaret Lynn Reber."

I felt foolish as she said Peggy's name because while I had known her legal name was Margaret for more than thirty years, she had simply been Peggy to me.

"Died May 25, 1968." The woman stopped and made an inquiry as to why we wanted the information.

I stood numb as I looked for just the right words to explain myself. "I grew up here. I remember seeing her on the evening news. I don't know her, or her family." I was stammering like a damn fool. "And I considered writing a book about her, but the truth is I really just need to answer my own questions."

"That's *too* weird." The woman propped her elbows on the counter. "There was a man here last week that was looking into writing a book about her." She looked puzzled. "Are you working together?"

"Oh no," I quickly arrested her thoughts, "Not at all." I was floored by her words. "I have no desire to step on anyone's toes; I just had this silly idea about answering my own questions and perhaps writing a manuscript." I was speechless.

"Do you know the man's name?" Susan took the conversation back to reasonable. "And where exactly would we find the statue of Christ?" I glanced toward my friend and trusted her lead. "If you could recall his name we will gladly share any information that we have with him, but right now we would just like to pay our respects."

"You know, he told us that terrible things were done to that girl." She wanted to discuss the crime. "I had no idea, and I lived here during that time." She played with the corner edges of the paper that made up Peggy's file.

Susan wasn't going to miss an opportunity to learn something. "Well if you lived here then do you know how Peggy ended up in such a nice cemetery?" She was pouring on the flattery. "The child died in an apartment without power, but earns a final resting place here?"

"Well, let's see." Daisy dropped her eyes to the pages before her, "That's a rather good question." She studied the sheets before lifting her head and saying, "It appears Herman Reber bought this lot in 1957, and it was awarded to him after the divorce." She lowered her eyes again, "And he returned a few years after Peggy died and bought her a headstone."

"Bless his heart," I thought aloud. I knew enough about Peggy Reber to know that Herman Reber was not her biological father, but her stepfather, and he was divorced from her mother at the time of Peggy's death. "There's an angel in this picture after all."

"Says here," Daisy turned the file to its side and looked at a blue index card stapled to the worn folder, "Her mother was asked to leave town after the trial, and Herman Reber has all rights to the burial space." She seemed to catch herself and became aware of her prose. "Of course I didn't just say any of that."

"Of course you didn't, Daisy," Susan assured her. "Now," she winked at the visibly nervous woman, "Where would we find Peggy?" We left the office with a map in hand and a mission to find Margaret Lynn Reber's grave.

Susan and I searched the graveyard almost an hour before voicing frustration. "We have a map, the poor girl has been here over thirty years, and we still can't find her?" I threw my hands up in the air. "And who is this guy that's writing a book?"

"Michelle," Susan walked toward me. "Obviously we're doing something wrong here." She put her arm around my shoulder. "And I have always believed that two heads are better than one, so let's do this together." She guided us toward the statue of Christ.

"Susan, I love you dearly, but we have searched this cemetery for an hour." I started to walk toward the road. "I don't understand what's going on here, but this is strange even for me." I stood still for a moment and opted to walk toward my family's graves instead of the road. I moved toward the tree that shaded the names of my beloved, and I stood utterly confused.

"Hey Toots!" Susan called for me from the short distance between us. "I found her." I approached Peggy's grave with such a feeling of emptiness that I held my breath. Susan and I stood together for a long moment in total silence looking at the young girl's headstone and a bouquet of beautiful pink flowers in her vase. I uttered a few words. "Peggy I don't know who put you here, or why, but when I come back I will know the truth, or I will never return."

"Am I crazy, Susan?" we were driving away from the cemetery "Did I just ramble over the grave of some kid that I never met?" I wasn't sure of myself, and I didn't like what I was feeling.

"Michelle, you said the words, but I echo the sentiments." Susan touched my hand. "Neither one of us knew her, yet oddly we are both changed by her many years after the fact, so she must have been incredibly special."

"My dear friend," I was touched by her support. "You are worth more than gold, but this is so much more than anything we have ever ventured into." I didn't even know where to introduce rational thinking. "Peggy," I paused, "Well, Peggy was killed, and for some stupid reason I remember her, but how in the hell are we ever going to really know what happened to her?"

"We are going to know because," Susan giggled a moment. "Because we are stubborn determined women and Peggy didn't want to be forgotten." She adopted a note of seriousness and said, "That is why she tapped you on the shoulder so long ago."

It sounds so insane, but it was at that moment as we left the cemetery that the three of us seemed to form a pact: my best friend Susan, Peggy, and myself. I don't think we ever doubted Peggy's presence, but we knew better than to depend on her for too much. Yet somehow we set out to explore the life, death, and tragedy surrounding Margaret Lynn Reber, and we almost knew she would accompany us in our search for the truth.

"So who is this mysterious author that was visiting the cemetery?" Susan interrupted the eerie drive with a valuable question. "I can't help but wonder if someone with credibility is actually going to give Peggy her moment in the sun?" I raised my brows and shrugged my shoulders because I wasn't quite sure what to make of it either.

"I haven't a clue my friend, but I trust that you know me well enough to know that I wouldn't get in anyone's way or compromise Peggy's killer being brought to justice. I guess we will just have to wonder until Daisy remembers his name, but my gut feeling is that if it was anyone worth remembering, she certainly wouldn't forget their name. I don't think too much slips by good ole Daisy."

"She was a pretty sharp cookie." Susan and I agreed. "What do you make of the little blue index card stapled to the side of the file noting that Peggy's mother was asked to leave town? Odd notation even for a cemetery isn't it? Damn Michelle, the poor woman's child is killed and then she was asked to leave town?" I could hear the irritation in her voice.

"Make a list." I sat up straight and put on my business cap so-to-speak. "Seriously."

I reached across the front seat to open the glove compartment to retrieve a pen and paper. "We don't have all the answers, but we're definitely composing some questions, so let's make a list. I don't know that we will ever be able to answer all of our questions, but if we tackle this in small portions as opposed to a huge pile we might be able to understand a little better than we do right now. When I was growing up I remember having to take weekly spelling tests when I was a kid in grade school and my mother always had me learn three words at a time so the list wouldn't overwhelm me." I started to chuckle. "Maybe mom wasn't so dumb after all." It was an ongoing joke that Susan and I shared about how the older we became the smarter our parents were becoming. "We are far from detectives, and it doesn't appear that anything concerning Peggy is going to make perfect sense upon a first review, so let's just do what we do best." I broke out into laughter. "Let's be moms."

"God help the world, Michelle." She began to laugh as well. "If we apply our motherly strategy to this you just know someone is in for one hell of a punishment when this is all over!" We laughed like two schoolgirls for the remainder of the ride, but we almost silently understood that maybe a mother's instinct is just what the situation needed; maybe a mother's instinct was just what Peggy needed then *and* now.

"Susan, I might want to point something rather silly out to you before we go any further." I wasn't sure what we were embarking on, but she needed a clear understanding of the stage set. "Shortly after I arrived in North Carolina, my sweet little home town made the papers across the country." I paused, merely for effect. "Seems a janitor, cleaning lady, maintenance person . . . Hell, I don't remember. But a city employee found, oh, ten, twenty, thirty thousand dollars cash in a closet at the main municipal building. I can't tell you that I remember the details at all, but it was enough to tell the nation that something was amiss in good ol' Lebanon, Pennsylvania simply because most government offices keep their money in banks and not closets."

"A large quantity of cash in a closet?" Susan started to rub her chin as if she were concocting a reason for such an odd procedure. "Why in the hell would anyone keep cash in a closet, much less a government office?"

"Exactly," I started to nod my head, "If you can understand *that* then maybe you can understand why a slain teen's mother would be asked to leave town. I love this place and I will always be grateful that this is where I grew up. I can't put my finger on it at this point, but this story just stinks beyond the death of a fourteen year old kid. Peggy was alone that day because three factors were in play: her twin sister moved out of the adjacent apartment with her husband and newborn child, her mother made an unscheduled overnight run to New Jersey, and Peggy's boyfriend was picked up on an outstanding warrant for overdue child support. Her mother comes home from her trip and enters the dark apartment to find a body in Peggy's bedroom, but according to the newspaper article, she didn't think it was Peggy. Now I may be stupid, but if I enter my son's bedroom and I find a dead boy, my first thought is going to be the very worst. But for this particular mother at this particular time, that is not her first thought?"

"Hey," Susan replied. "I have a house full of kids, and at 3 AM, I am never quite sure which set of feet belong to my income tax deductions. I only claim four on my taxes, but on any given Friday night I may have eight or ten kids that just seem to sleep there, so maybe mom was not being unreasonable, and as a nurse I have to say that she may have been in denial."

"The news reports that Mary Alice Reber went across the hall to get a flashlight from the neighbor upon discovering a body in Peggy's room." I waited for Susan to explain that away for me, but she sat silently looking to *me* for an explanation. "Susan," I took a pen and underlined a caption of the article as I handed it to her. "Peggy died in an apartment that had been deprived of electricity, so why did her mother have to ask the neighbor for a flashlight? Wouldn't that have been a part of their norm if the landlord was trying to evict them by denying them power?" I wasn't about to go any further without some food for thought from my friend.

"Michelle, she just found a corpse, and while we can sit here three decades later and scrutinize her actions it's not realistic or fair for that matter. I'm not saying that there shouldn't have been an immediate panic on her part that the body was that of Peggy, but I also cannot say that her reaction was unreasonable. The flashlight is an interesting question, but maybe in her panic she just couldn't find one. Do you think there is something amiss with her mother?"

"Let me ponder that a minute." I placed my forefinger at my temple and said, "Yes! We are mothers, my dear, and when is the last time we just took off on a Friday night leaving our offspring in a dwelling without power? Oh, and then don't forget the part how the poor kid ends up dead." I threw my hands up. "My heart breaks for the poor woman."

I tried to make a quick recover because Susan was definitely not impressed with my outburst.

"Forgive me for repeating myself, but this is not normal behavior in this area. My mother didn't set the standard, but she definitely fell under the definition of the norm and this just isn't right for this area and especially not for that time frame. Peggy Reber was fourteen years old, the product of a divorce that didn't even father her, and she was involved with a married man. I hate to tell you, but all of that was almost unheard of in 1968. Hell, even now that's stretching it for this community. I won't say that this is the land that time forgot, but I will tell you that this has always been a very conservative community. Family values are at the core of everything the folks of Lebanon hold dear, and it is obvious at a glance that Peggy did not have that benefit. The first few articles reporting this crime tell us that Peggy was living in less than desirable conditions, no electricity, no food in the apartment, a high traffic of male visitors to the dwelling, she missed over thirty days of school, and child protective services was aware there was an issue within her household. I am not going to say that any of that justifies a murder, but her mother was breaking all the understood rules of motherhood at the time, and sadly she seems to pay the ultimate price."

"As a mother I have to agree that she paid a price, but I think it was Peggy that paid the ultimate price." Susan made mention of one of the few newspaper articles we had already read. "The reporter almost made an attempt to be polite as he described the amount of men that had access to the apartment, the possibility of marijuana being used there, and the probability that Peggy lost her life resisting advances by a prior visitor to the dwelling. Peggy's mother found her around 3 a.m. and went across the hall to the neighbor to get a flashlight and assistance. The neighbor said she moved Peggy's bed to have the benefit of the hall light to better see the crime scene, and after realizing Peggy was dead, she covered her with a blanket from the bed."

"That whole electricity thing just drives me wild. Do we know exactly what would prompt a landlord to take such measures? I can't imagine that even being legal." I was baffled.

"If I understand things correctly Peggy's mother was behind in the twenty dollar a week rent, and the landlord did not approve of the number of men that were being entertained in the apartment," Susan began to theorize. "When I was a kid my brother fell behind in rent on his apartment, and I want to say that the landlord put a padlock on the door until he received the money owed to him, and if that's the case, terminating utilities was probably another tactic used during that time frame. We'll just have to add that to our list of questions. I don't know what you have planned for today's activities, but why don't we stop by the apartment building and see whatever there is left to see?"

"That's a great idea, but in case I forgot to mention it, the apartment building was torn down years ago. I remember that too, but not in terms of a date; I simply remember my uncle's excavating company was involved in the demolition. When I was a little girl my aunt would sometimes take me along when she took my uncle lunch on his job sites, and I remember accompanying her to that particular site" I remembered hearing Peggy's name mentioned again during that quick visit to the demolition site.

"Well, so much for that idea." Susan let out a deep sigh. "Did Peggy's death have anything to do with the fact the building was destroyed?"

"I have no clue." I hadn't really thought about the possibility that the young girl's death could have resulted in excavation of the building. My youthful age at the time of the crime didn't provide me with too much insight to the details of the crime, much less the effects that the murder had on the community.

■■■

"Susan, you have just got to taste this bologna." I ran to the country store's deli display case like a small child in a candy store. "This is unlike anything you have ever had before, and anything you will ever have again. It's heavenly."

The woman behind the counter laughed at my excitement and instinctively knew which selection to remove from the deli case. She was kind enough to offer Susan a sample of the popular lunchmeat.

"Delicious." Susan voiced her approval while still chewing, and with all eyes on her it wasn't surprising because one almost knew better than to express a dislike for the county's signature delicacy. Lebanon Bologna was the pride of the county, and anything less than a roaring approval would have probably been grounds to run her out of town.

"I miss the food here so much that I can't even begin to explain it." Susan and I were strolling the aisles of the small run-down store. "If I lived here I would probably weigh a hundred pounds more than I do and die young due to clogged arteries." I filled my small cart with a wide variety of unhealthy treats only available in the Central Pennsylvania area. "Some of these things I can order by phone, or on the internet, and have them shipped by express delivery, but there are a few items one can only get by actually making a trip here." I continued to shop like a person that hadn't eaten in days.

"I didn't know that stores like this even existed anymore." Susan commented on the narrow rows of goods and deeply worn hard wood floors. I had never devoted any thought to the quaint shop because it was as much a staple to Lebanon as city hall, but Susan's words made me see its rustic charm for the first time.

"It's a pleasant reminder of a different time, isn't it?" Susan and I both shopped at a huge grocery store that was one of many in a national corporate chain. "There's no need for a broadcasting system when there is a spill in aisle three because everyone in the store will hear the jar break." We both laughed at the thought, and we both enjoyed the reminder of how simple life once was for everyone.

I loaded my goodies into the back of my vehicle and I smiled as I remembered the many times I had assisted my mother with the same task, at the same store. It had been years since my mother passed away, and a trip to Lebanon always reminded me of little things we shared. It made her seem to be just a little bit closer at heart.

"This really is a gorgeous little place." Susan commented on Lebanon as I gave her the scenic tour of the downtown business district. "I just love the grass islands in the middle of the streets."

The tree lined sidewalks and grass islands were again, points of beauty I overlooked, or took for granted over the course of my life. "I'll bet this is breathtaking when it snows."

Susan missed living in an area that was privileged to the beauty and hazards of any amount of snowfall. We lived an hour from North Carolina's coast, so snow was not a part of our norm during winter months, and Susan always joked that a winter without snowfall was child abuse for our children.

"I've been thinking about those articles and something is bothering the hell out of me." I interrupted the moment and steered the conversation in a completely different direction. "Peggy Reber's boyfriend was picked up on an outstanding warrant early on the day that Peggy was killed." I took my eyes off the road just long enough to make eye contact with Susan.

"Yeah?" she looked at me with a puzzled expression on her face. "And your point is?" She anxiously waited for me to continue with my train of thought.

"It was a Saturday." I started tapping my fingers against the steering wheel as I rolled the thought around in my mind. "I have to wonder how common it was to apprehend someone on a Saturday way back when?" I tilted my head and glanced at my companion. "Court dockets didn't know the overload that they do today, and according to the newspaper that guy had a job, so why was he picked up on a Saturday? Why not pick him up during the week at his place of employment? Do you get my point?"

I wasn't sure if my thinking was reasonable even to my friend. "I am not sure what doesn't feel right about the boyfriend being picked up on that particular day, but something just doesn't feel right." I knew that Susan would definitely understand that my words were inspired by intuition more than facts.

"I understand what you're saying." It was Susan's turn to ponder the topic. "Wasn't it the Memorial Day weekend, too?" Her voice trailed off as she weighed the possibilities out in her mind. "No, what was I thinking? That was before the Monday Holiday Law went into effect, wasn't it?"

"Susan, Memorial Day was always an event that was celebrated in a big way in Lebanon. Weekend cookouts, sidewalk sales and a parade attended by everyone within a twenty mile radius." Again, I was reminded of one of the many characteristics of the town that I called home that faded from my memory over the years.

"Someone took the time out to pick a guy up for delinquent child support because he was three weeks in the rears?" I resumed tapping my fingers on the steering wheel. I wrinkled my brow and contemplated the inspiration behind apprehending Ray Boyer on that particular day.

"Michelle, before we embrace any foolish thoughts, we would have to know exactly how many men were picked up for failure to pay child support for that entire year. Perhaps that was the standard procedure at the time, but I have to admit that his apprehension does seem slightly odd to me, too."

11

We enjoyed a period of silence as we both digested the questions related to the imprisonment of Peggy Reber's boyfriend, her only real constant companion, and the ultimate effect of his absence in her life on that fateful day.

I broke the silence. "Her twin sister lived in the apartment next door to her, and moved out of the building that weekend. Moving is not exactly a spontaneous act, so I trust that move was planned in advance to some degree. Peggy's mother skips off to New Jersey, and I don't get the feeling that it was out of character for her mother to vanish without notice."

I could see out of the corner of my eye that Susan was nodding in agreement. "Then we hit the issue that the boyfriend was picked up on an outstanding warrant, and if that isn't the standard operating procedure for the Lebanon municipality at the time. . ." My voice trailed off.

After a moment of silence, Susan finished my thought.

"Maybe Peggy's vulnerability was not necessarily a coincidence at all."

I didn't like the thought, and yet, I couldn't push the possibility out of my mind. The brutality that the teenage victim endured during her last few minutes of life was beyond understanding in itself, and to think of it as anything more than an outburst by a crazed maniac was hardly an option.

Or was it?

"Michelle, I'm not quite sure what we expect to find when we pull up the remainder of the news articles, but it will definitely provide food for thought. I think we are going to have to read them a couple times before we form any opinions."

Susan was being practical, and not a moment too soon. "We have to view everything on its individual merits, or it's all going to run together."

Truer words could not have been spoken.

"You're not going to get an argument here." I gave a deep sigh. "I can't put my finger on what is bothering me, but something just isn't resting well within me. I know I sound crazy, and I apologize, but something is wrong with the whole picture. I am probably not going to have any rest in my ass until I figure out what is wrong."

I was apologetic for my inability to articulate what was taking place in my head. I pulled to the side of the street, and parked my automobile in front of a coin-operated parking meter, yet another icon from yester-year. The thrill of small town simplicity was being shadowed by my distraction with Peggy Reber's fate, so it was just a matter of buying enough parking time from the mechanical parking attendant.

The afternoon traffic on the main street of Lebanon was relatively light compared to most cities, and the fact that vehicles were only permitted to travel in one direction eased the challenge of dodging cars. Potted plants hung from cast iron fixtures along the city's streets, and Susan and I were both amused that the decorations didn't fall victim to theft, or vandalism.

The complexion of the merchant lined street reminded one of a time before gigantic shopping malls, a time when cash was the primary means of tender, and all too often the cashier was the owner of the store. However, the pressures of modernization gave hint by a few businesses that had been closed; display windows that had once been illuminated and filled with merchandise were covered with wooden boards. A tattoo parlor had staked a claim on the block, and advertised a large selection of body alterations with a bright neon sign.

"My parents went to their grave convinced that George served the best hot dog in the world." I pointed toward an aged building on the corner of the street. "I couldn't possibly bring you to the thriving metropolis of Lebanon, Pennsylvania without introducing you to one of

George's hot dogs." I took my friend by the arm, gave her a playful wink, and guided her into a staple of home.

"Well by all means," Susan began to giggle. "I can hardly wait." We entered the dark tavern, and hesitated at the entrance as we waited for our eyes to adjust to the dark room with a long bar, jukebox, pool table, and a shine on its tile floor that would impress any military officer. We claimed two stools at the bar while a gray haired gentleman stocked a beer cooler at the other end of the bar. I shared a few treasured memories with Susan as we waited for service in the historic luncheonette.

"What can I get you ladies?" George approached us with a pleasant smile, his lined face hinting at the many years which had passed since the last time I saw him. The gleam in his eye was as youthful as ever.

"My, my, my," George placed a hand on his hip, took a good long look at me, and offered an even friendlier smile as he basked in the recognition. "Look what the wind blew in." He grabbed a bar towel and proceeded to wipe down the counter in front of us.

"Little girl, it's been a long time since I've seen you in this neck of the woods." I had known George as long as I could remember, and having a hot dog at George's was as much a part of my childhood as depositing a dollar a week in a school-sponsored savings account. I fondly recalled the school's banking procedure, and once again, a small piece of my history sparked pride in my community of origin and the values it instilled.

Elementary schools and local banks throughout the area had a program that promoted the importance of savings to children. The process was pretty simple, far too simple for modern technology, so like street side merchants, it fell to the wayside. Grade school students were provided wallet-sized bankbooks to record even the smallest of deposits to be made on a weekly basis. Each week it was an elementary classroom ritual to deposit one's bankbook into a canvas bank bag to be taken to a local bank for depositing into a student account. I remembered the pride of dropping my bankbook in the cloth bag. Once the tiny sum was delivered to the bank, recorded by the tellers, the small books would be returned to each student, to repeat the process the following week. It was a simple staple in being a native of Lebanon; another touch of small town charm that I had taken for granted on my way to adulthood.

After making the necessary introductions, and telling George I couldn't possibly pass through town without one of his famous hot dogs, I carefully brought up the subject of Peggy Reber. I knew the subject of Peggy was not a welcomed topic in Lebanon, even after more than three decades, but I knew that Peggy's mother was a regular patron of George's during the time of the crime. I also knew that if anyone knew anything in Lebanon it would be George. "Do you remember the murder of Peggy Reber?" I tried to be casual in my approach, but I was smart enough to know that such a brutal slaying would never fall into the category of idle small talk.

"Sure I do." George didn't hesitate with an answer.

It was almost as if I had tested his memory, and he had to meet the challenge, but in an instant his smile faded from his face. "That was a terrible thing." He started to shake his head. "Just terrible," he repeated.

He placed his towel on the bar and began to clean an area that didn't show the slightest hint of dirt, and I assumed it was merely a habit. "She was just a kid." He shook his head and was obviously recalling the person behind the name I just mentioned. I didn't want to be disrespectful, but I had to pursue the subject at hand.

13

"I remember seeing her mother here when I was a kid." I turned my head toward the door. "I was just a kid myself, yet I remember seeing Peggy's mother standing in front of that door as if it were yesterday."

I turned to look at George, and I waited for him to give some indication my memory was truly worth something. It was only after I embarked on researching Peggy's death that I realized just how young I was when Peggy died. I was stunned to learn that while I was only five years old at the time of the crime, Peggy found a solid place in my memory.

"Sure, she was a regular here." George stood upright and dropped his hands to his sides. "Everyone was a regular here back then."

I wasn't sure if he was escaping the issue, or bragging. "Back then, it took about fifteen of us to keep this place going." He looked across the room as if he were remembering the past. "Now, my wife and I can handle things."

He rested his hands on the edge of the bar. "Before all the schools had cafeterias we would feed all the kids during their lunch breaks." I remembered only too well having to go home for lunch when I started school because the school system did not offer a lunch program, so he was probably right about feeding scores of students on a daily basis.

"I clearly remember seeing Peggy's mother here," I repeated. I enjoyed the trip down memory lane that George was hosting, but I really wanted to know about Peggy, her mother, and the events that inspired my interest. I had a picture of a teenage girl in my mind, a few facts, and a ton of questions concerning Peggy Reber.

"That's just not a good thing to talk about, little girl." He shook his head in apparent disapproval, and it was all too clear that the conversation was over. Almost as if on cue, a customer entered the front door giving George the perfect opportunity to slip away without explanation.

"'That's just not a good thing to talk about?'" Susan repeated George's words, but sarcasm dripped off her translation. "Have we stepped on sacred ground?"

Susan was quickly getting a lesson in the closed ranks that engulfed my hometown. I knew that while Susan was from a completely different state, her own small town roots equipped her with an understanding of what was taking place. Peggy Reber's murder was a blemish on the history of the town I called home. It was an unsolved murder, and so many years had passed that it would be considered distasteful by many to dig up the past.

"Truth is that I have known George a long, long time." I put my hand on my friend's knee, "And I have never heard him utter a word about anyone on a negative note." I smiled into her blue eyes and let my words register for a moment. "George has been a successful bar owner for half a century, and I guess that kind of success doesn't find one with loose lips." I smiled almost instinctively because George reminded me so much of my own father, and one of the most admirable traits that my father possessed was to never say an ill word of any kind about another individual.

"I just don't see the harm in discussing something that took place thirty years ago. I don't think there is any great betrayal involved in something that aged." Her point was valid, but again, it was part of the beauty, and mystery, of central Pennsylvania. It was just *understood* there were some things that just shouldn't be discussed, and obviously Peggy Reber's death was falling into that category.

Susan and I ate our hot dogs in silence as I thought of the little bit that I actually knew about Peggy Reber.

May 25, 1968 I was a rather happy five-year-old living a pretty normal existence in central Pennsylvania. I didn't have too many cares in the world beyond my daily expense of six cents for a half pint of chocolate milk to be consumed during recess at school, or finding just the right container to store lightening bugs I captured in my back yard on a nightly basis. I lived the typical life of a five-year-old child. I didn't have the slightest clue that evil existed in the world.

"Oh my God!" My mother's tone of voice caught my attention instantly. "That poor girl." My mother wiped her hands on her apron, slid into the nearest chair, and gave the local nightly news her undivided attention. I think I may have attempted to speak, but my mother waved her hand at me with that understood gesture between mother and child and I just knew that I was to remain silent. I followed my mother's lead and directed my attention to the television screen, and sat silently waiting for my mother to return to her normal state of being.

Our black and white television screen displayed a photograph of a young girl, a pretty girl with dark hair falling past her shoulders wearing a gray blazer with some type of embroidered patch over her breast, and a radiant smile. While I didn't understand much of the report delivered by the news anchorman, I did hear him say her name: Peggy Reber. I understood from his tone of voice and my mother's reaction that something was wrong with Peggy. I studied the happy face that appeared on the small television screen because while I could tell something was wrong, she looked so happy in the picture displayed on the evening news. I never heard of anything bad ever happening to anyone, so she definitely had my attention.

I remember wondering if a car had hit her, because at my ripe old age my mother constantly warned me of the danger of running into the street without looking for cars. I stared at the photograph on the small television screen, and I wondered what really happened to Peggy Reber. More than thirty-three years passed, and I was still asking the same question, only this time I sat as an adult being told it was not a good thing to talk about.

Naturally, Peggy's fate didn't involve an automobile, and no one was willing to tell a five-year-old exactly what happened to the smiling face on the TV screen, so my curiosity mounted over the years. I understood enough that Peggy was dead, and a horrible person did terrible things to her, but beyond all the vague descriptions I didn't have a clue as to what actually happened to Peggy. Years passed and while life for me was nothing less than normal, I never forgot the young girl's face on the nightly news and my mother's reaction to whatever was said about her fate.

My childhood was pleasant, and I was blessed with parents that truly had a gift in communication. My parents hardly ever raised their voices, and they would discuss such a wide variety of topics with me that nothing ever seemed to be off limits in the arena of conversation. Equally, I was encouraged to explore all my interests in print format, so I was a regular at the local library. I was fourteen years old and a freshman in high school when I mentioned that I was going to the library and while I was there I intended to research the articles reporting the death of Peggy Reber.

My perpetually calm dad went into an immediate panic. "NO! You can't do that!" He raised his voice at me for the first time in my life. "There's a lot of money and power behind that, and those people aren't dead."

I could almost sense fear in his voice. "Shelly, they will find out if you start stirring that up." He gave me the strangest look. "There have been a lot of suicides attached to that case, and the only way they are ever going to really know what happened is if someone confesses on their death bed."

He almost seemed to be concerned for my safety simply for having a desire to research a few news articles. "Hell, no one is ever going to talk about that case, not the judge, not the lawyers, or anybody else. Leave it alone." He was giving a direct order, but his facial expression was one of fear. "Promise me that you will leave it alone."

I was stunned by his reaction, but I agreed to leave it alone. My intelligent, even-tempered, and normally very supportive father hit such an emotional state at the mere mention of researching newspaper files on Peggy Reber that it arrested my actions, but fueled my curiosity.

At that point in time it had been almost ten years since I had seen the young girl's picture on the evening news, and it was still a very excitable subject within my own home. I wondered about Peggy Reber, and why was she such an explosive topic?

Idle gossip taught me that Peggy Reber was a fourteen-year-old girl found dead on her bedroom floor in an apartment she shared with her mother just a few blocks from city hall. I didn't know all the details, but I knew Peggy was assaulted with an archery bow.

I remembered seeing her mother at George's Place, and I don't think anyone even gave me a second thought when they started to gossip about the slain girl's mother. I remembered studying the platinum blonde donning a leather jacket and jeans. I was surprised that a mother would dress in such a manner because my mother had yet to buy her first pair of slacks. Peggy's mother was dressed like the local teenagers wearing tie-dyed shirts and patches with peace signs. Peggy's mom was laughing when I saw her at George's Place, and talking to a leather craftsman that shined my dad's work boots each and every Saturday. I remembered wondering how she could laugh so hearty if something terrible had happened to Peggy, but I was questioning her actions through a child's mind.

"Your parents were right." Susan's voice brought my thoughts back to the present. "This is the best hot dog that I have ever had in my life." I gave my friend a weak smile and nodded in agreement. "You're right about one thing."

Considering that I had said very little over the course of the last few minutes I wasn't quite sure what to expect. "Between the bologna, this hot dog, and Goodness knows what other treats this place has to offer. I could never live here and maintain any type of a girlish figure." We both began to laugh.

"Well, now that we have all the important stuff out of the way," I giggled as I teased Susan, "Perhaps we should set out to do what we are here to do."

George refused to take any money for our lunch, so I left a more than reasonable tip as a regular customer pointed out that George didn't accept tips. I smiled again because I thought of the many times that George himself would give me a dollar to deposit in my little savings book for school, and it was an odd twist that I would be giving him an extra buck or two.

"Where are we going now, kiddo?" Susan had obviously gained a second wind of energy because there was a bounce in her voice.

"Considering the local newspaper told me on the phone that the file on Peggy has been viewed so much that it is almost impossible to print, and follow that with their equipment to view the file has been broken for almost three months," I let out a sigh, "That leaves but one place to go to research newspaper archives, The Historical Society."

A short distance down the street, another parking meter, and we were on the steps of the Historical Society in a matter of minutes.

"This is absolutely beautiful." Susan was impressed the minute we entered the restored historical landmark. I absorbed its beauty only briefly because I was anxious to get to the files that I hoped would answer the questions that haunted me for so many years. After paying the nominal fee to utilize the facility as guests and getting the briefing on how to access the files, Susan and I split up to expedite our search time.

The hours just seemed to fly by as we removed one small film after another from a file drawer, and as each page was printed I was convinced that we would truly know everything that happened to Peggy by the day's end.

It was difficult to pull up one article after another on the small screen and resist the urge to read them through, but time was of the essence and there seemed to be a never ending list of dates that needed to be researched and printed on a less than speedy copier.

After a few hours we took a break to grab a soda outside on the sidewalk.

"Did you ever get that feeling you were being stared at?" Susan raised her brows and rolled her eyes toward the window of the building. I didn't want to be too obvious as I looked at what she was referring to, so I faked a sneeze enabling me to quickly dart my eyes in the direction of the window without arousing suspicion. Sure enough two employees of the famed establishment stood at the window staring at us, and it was almost like something out of a movie.

"Guess it's pretty obvious that we aren't exactly residents." I sort of threw my eyes toward the North Carolina license plates on the back of my vehicle. "I wouldn't think that they get too many people that travel five hundred miles to visit their humble establishment." I was joking, but yet I was being somewhat sincere at the same time.

"Michelle," Susan's voice took on a very serious tone, "It's really hard to avoid reading those articles as I pull them up, and I am trying to get as much printed as possible, but I saw something that really surprised me." I gave her my undivided attention. "Did you know that there was a man arrested for the murder?" Her words hit me like a ton of bricks.

"No." I was stunned at her revelation. "What do you mean someone was arrested? Who was arrested?" I always understood the murder of Peggy Reber to be unsolved. I never heard that someone was actually suspected of the crime, much less charged with committing the murder of the teenage girl.

"I think his name was Art Root, but I'd have to go back and check it." She put her soda to her lips. "I have just been pulling up anything and everything that I can get my hands on, and I figured we would sort through it later." I was left speechless by her dialogue. I could have literally been knocked over by a feather.

"So what happened? Was he found guilty?" I started shooting questions out like bullets. "I know Art Root." I was too stunned to explain it right there on the sidewalk, but I knew the name she mentioned only too well.

"I don't know." She looked just as confused as I felt. "I just caught a glimpse of a name and a mention of charges being pressed against him." She started to walk toward the door of the small town museum. "But if we're going to answer these questions we had better get back in there and find the rest of the articles on this case, because I saw a sign that stated this place closes early this evening."

I followed her lead as I glanced at my watch, and time was becoming increasingly more valuable. We both knew we only had one day to devote to this type of research before we returned to our normal day-to-day living in North Carolina.

I resumed my spot in the research room and continued with my quest to obtain facts, but I couldn't prevent my mind from playing his name over and over again in my head. Art Root was a local merchant who owned a leather shop next to George's Place, and I would accompany my dad to his shop every Saturday like clockwork for my dad's weekly shoe shine. I remembered the man's face so vividly, and what I remembered even more was that the memory I had of Peggy's mother at George's Place included Art Root.

Peggy's mother was standing at the front door of George's Place and she was laughing with Art Root. I had been fascinated by her gay mood as a child because I already knew something terrible had happened to Peggy, and I didn't understand how she could even smile after such a loss. As an adult I was exasperated that she could laugh with any man possibly connected to the death of her teenage daughter.

What in the hell happened to Peggy Reber?

What did Art Root have to do with the death of the slain teen?

How could a mother be so jovial in light of such an event?

My mind was producing questions faster than the primitive printers could put the news on paper, but again, I trusted I was rummaging through all that would provide the answers about Peggy Reber.

■ ■

Susan and I successfully beat the clock in our research and managed to walk out the doors of the Historical Society a few minutes before they were scheduled to close. Exhausted, we drove to a nearby military installation in almost total silence. Susan and I were both married to soldiers, so it just seemed prudent to take advantage of our military benefit and use military lodging rather than a local hotel. We checked into a small military cottage that once served as on-post housing for a military family, and while the accommodations were quaint it was truly cozy with a small parlor, kitchen and two bedrooms.

We quickly took turns enjoying the benefit of a hot shower and settled down in front of the television with a cup of tea and all the information we had obtained that day. Few words were exchanged between us as we read through the many pages of news reports. While we were both incredibly tired, the desire to learn about Peggy proved to be far greater than our fatigue.

"Oh my God!" Susan broke the silence with a burst of horror.

I dropped the articles I was reading onto my lap and looked at my friend. Susan raised her eyes from the articles that she had in hand. "It was a rectal assault."

"You have got to be kidding me!" I got up from the chair and took a seat next to Susan on the sofa.

"Look at this!" She ran her finger across the print and read it aloud. 'The time of death could not be determined because the orifice normally used to determine a body's temperature was the point of assault with the five foot archery bow.'"

I stared at my friend and shook my head in total disbelief as tears welled up in my eyes.

Having been a nurse for twenty years, Susan did not need any explanation regarding the statement, rather it just crossed a line that we weren't necessarily prepared to cross.

"Bless her heart." Susan wiped a tear from her eye, and I knew she was thinking of her own fourteen- year- old daughter. We sat side by side and read the remainder of the report that truly epitomized the horror that Peggy encountered.

Fourteen-year-old Margaret Lynn Reber, known as Peggy, was found dead on her bedroom floor in an apartment that she shared with her divorced mother on May 25, 1968. Peggy had been beaten, strangled with a dress belt, and she was assaulted with a five-foot archery bow. Peggy died in an apartment that had been stripped of electricity by the landlord in an attempt to evict her and her mother. The newspaper reported that there wasn't any food found in Peggy's stomach at the time of the autopsy. Further reading of the articles taught us that Peggy had a bite mark on her breast, and there were other items used in the slaying, but testimony by the coroner and other experts never identified the other weapons used in the attack. Susan and I sat in complete silence for a long while digesting the gruesome facts that were unfolding before us.

"One has got to love the skills of that newspaper reporter." Susan broke the mood. "His play on words is better than my eight year old when he's been caught in the cookie jar just before dinner." I tilted my head and waited for an explanation.

"Think about it Michelle. Thirty years ago that man managed to get details of a rectal assault on the front page of a small town paper, and yet he never used the word rectum."

She made a great point. I was almost too tired, and far too stunned, to really appreciate the journalistic skills at hand.

"Point well taken." I loved the intelligence that Susan brought to the table. "But please tell me what kind of animal rams an archery bow in a fourteen year old girl's rectum a dozen or more times?" I got up from the sofa and went to the kitchen to trade my mild-mannered cup of tea in for a glass of wine, and returned to the parlor. "She died in an apartment that didn't even have electricity." I took my place back in my chair. "She didn't have any food in her stomach." I reached for my cigarettes, and stared across the coffee table at my traveling companion.

"I grew up in this damn town, and I don't ever remember my parents ever locking our doors, and yet something this horrendous took place here?" I just couldn't imagine my home town playing host to such an evil act. I looked at the stack of articles that we had yet to read and I threw my hands up. "Let me guess," I was oozing with sarcasm. "We'll read the rest of that crap and find that I actually knew the man that did this." I hadn't forgotten Susan mentioning the name Art Root when we were in the midst of our fact finding mission. I reached for the pile of pages that we had yet to review and started paging through them on a mission.

I found a front page article that sported a large picture of a young man in handcuffs and as I read the caption I almost felt a sense of relief, Arthur M. Root, Jr. was charged in the death of Peggy Reber. "Forgive me." I tossed the papers down in front of me. "The man charged was not the shoe shine man after all, but I'm assuming, his son." I was feeling slightly confused, betrayed, and frustrated by the truths that were coming to light.

"Michelle," Susan's tone suggested she was about to offer some sort of reason to my rather emotional train of thought. "We're both tired. It's been a long day, and we have the information sitting here, but maybe after a good night's sleep it will make more sense."

I gave in to the truth in her words, but not without an argument. "I grew up here, and I grew up with this kid's picture carved into my mind." I ran my fingers through my hair. "How could I feel so safe in a place where Peggy met such evil?" I knew I would never see my hometown the same way again.

■■■

"Housekeeping!" The muffled voice was obviously attached to the banging on the cottage door. I rubbed my eyes and looked around the room before it sank in where I was and what the commotion was all about.

"Housekeeping!" I threw the blankets on my bed back and stumbled across the floor to greet the cleaning team that was knocking on the door. I could hear the sound of water from the bathroom and the smell of coffee filled the small cottage, so I knew that Susan had already greeted the day. I opened the door enabling the cleaning crew to enter and embark on their duties as I took a seat at the kitchen table. I was still stretching and rubbing the sleep from my eyes when Susan emerged from the bathroom in a robe with her hair wrapped in a towel.

"Good morning, Toots!" She was just too damn cheerful early in the morning.

"Sorry they woke you, I was going to let you snooze for awhile." She was as pleasant as ever. "Want a cup of tea?" She knew I wasn't worth a damn without a cup of tea or two in the morning. Two women scurried about picking up anything that appeared to be trash, dirty linen, or something out of place, and I held my hands between my thighs as I rocked back and forth in my chair saying nothing.

"So are you going to be stationed here?" One of the cleaning women initiated a conversation, and her words caught us off guard. "We don't get too many regular army people here, and the reservation says that you are sponsored by regular army service members."

The housekeeper was obviously in search of an explanation for our presence. Susan and I rarely viewed ourselves as military wives, and the rank of our husbands alone pretty much summed that up. Susan's husband was an officer and my husband was enlisted. We were friends because we were neighbors in a civilian neighborhood and we didn't bring the army into play in the course of our relationship, but we were quickly reminded that we were in military territory as this woman questioned our purpose for being there.

The housekeeper ran her eyes across the room and spotted an article with Peggy's picture clearly displayed and her facial expression took on a look of surprise and question. Suddenly, I was very alert because I could tell she knew the picture, and I trusted she knew Peggy's name, and I wanted to hear about anything that she may have known or remembered about the events at the time of the crime.

"Do you remember Peggy Reber?" I threw my question out as she still had her eyes glued to the picture of Peggy on the coffee table. The woman was instantly uncomfortable with my question.

"Sure." She cleared her throat giving hint to a smoker's ability to cough at will. "That was just terrible." I watched her face and it took a moment before I made the connection that she was utterly confused that her reservation sheet listed two army wives from Fort Bragg, North Carolina, and she was looking at articles about a local murder that took place over thirty years ago.

"I grew up here." I knew I needed to find common ground quickly or the housekeeper would be spooked just by the mere look on her face.

"Oh really?" She was skeptical. "Where?"

Mentally I laughed at her challenge even through my sleepy state because I could speak fluent central Pennsylvanian even though I had left the area almost twenty years prior. I entered into the exchange enough to prove I was legitimate, and it obviously passed the housekeeper's scrutiny because she went out to her vehicle got her cigarettes and returned to discuss Peggy Reber.

"I lived right down the street from her." The middle aged woman stood leaning against the doorway holding a leather cigarette case in her hand. "God, I wish I had seen her that day, I would have taken her in."

She shook her finger and said, "No kid should have to live like that." She wasn't going to get an argument from us on that matter. "I knew damn well the minute that I heard that on the news that the Boyer brothers would be involved with that somehow."

20

"The Boyer brothers?" Susan jumped on her words quickly and made an even quicker recover. "You will have to forgive me, but I am not a native." One just had to love Susan's style as she extended her hand to the chambermaid.

"I am Susan Chaffin, and I didn't have the benefit of growing up in this beautiful area. I am, however, blessed to be a mountain girl from West Virginia, so allow me to offer you a cup of coffee." Susan moved toward the kitchen and without a care said, "You mentioned the Boyer brothers, forgive me for asking, but who are they?"

"Oh, they were bad news." The woman shook her head in disapproval. "I remember them from the old Casino Roller Skating Rink, and everybody just kind of knew to stay away from them. The minute I heard that poor girl was killed I just knew they were going to be involved somehow. Why do you have all this stuff?"

She made a hand gesture toward the articles scattered about the bungalow, and before we could offer an explanation she said, "My husband and mother would have a fit if they even knew I was talking about this with you. We don't talk about this around here because sometimes it's best to leave the past in the past." It was obvious she was growing uncomfortable and she was out the door in a matter of seconds.

"What is it with your hometown?" Susan sat down at the small dinette set with her morning coffee in hand. "George serves a great hot dog offers a smile and a joke, but the mere mention of Peggy and he says, 'That's just not a good thing to talk about'. Now a housekeeper says, 'We don't talk about that because it's best to leave the past in the past."

"I told you this subject has met that same reaction my entire life." I rubbed my face with both hands and then stretched both arms over my head before letting them drop on my lap. "We need to pack our things and get on the road or we will be caught in the beautiful thing known as gridlock traffic surrounding our nation's capital."

"I am not going to lie to you I am anxious to get back to my children, but I also want to make sure that you have the answers to your questions before we leave here." Susan winked at me and smiled, and I knew I was truly blessed to have such a supportive friend.

"I don't know about all the answers to my questions, but I do know that for over thirty years I have carried a memory of a smiling face from the evening news and while I was too young to understand her fate then I almost need to know what happened to her now. We could probably stay here another week and attempt to learn as much as possible, but I have to believe the bulk of the answers to my questions and the truth rest in the articles we have researched, so we will take what we have and go home and read them without any distractions. Let's face it, we have both just lightly skimmed over the contents of a few articles and I trust that if we read all of them in their entirety and absorb it slowly we will understand far more than we do right now. I am trusting that our questions will answer themselves as we get through that stack of news reports." I felt confident that the answers to any questions I had about Peggy were right in front of me.

"There's no doubt that it's a lot of material to read and we just scratched the surface with a few headlines and a couple details, and if you are content with what we have then let's wrap it up and hit the highway."

We were on the road within the hour.

"Is this not the prettiest place?" I gazed at the beautiful horizon as we exited a diner after having breakfast. "Pennsylvania is truly a magnificent state." I was proud of my roots. I grabbed a newspaper from a coin-operated machine tossed it in the back seat and headed toward the interstate.

21

"I should have probably fit in a quick visit to see my uncle, and my cousin, while we were in town." I was suffering from a touch of guilt as we started our trip to return to North Carolina. "Anne was kind enough to entertain my bizarre request for news articles about Peggy, before we ever even considered a trip to Pennsylvania."

I thought of the day I called her at work and hit her with the strange twist of my curiosity surrounding Peggy Reber. Anne was only three months old when Peggy met her fate, and I probably appeared to be quite insane, but Anne was receptive to assisting me.

Anne worked at a popular candy factory during the day, and took college classes by night, so I was hoping that she could stop by the college library and squeeze in a little research to answer my silly questions. I was thrilled the day the over-sized envelope arrived in the mail, and read its contents over my evening meal.

I was convinced that once Anne sent the initial articles reporting the crime I would have a clear understanding as to what happened to Peggy. I thought I would be able to put the subject to rest, but the articles she provided only told part of the story. The little bit of information fueled my curiosity even more.

Anne had more than enough personal projects on her plate, and her free time was very limited, so researching the articles was a challenging process for her. She sent the articles as she managed to find the time to research them. It was the handful of articles that Anne initially sent to me that inspired the trip Susan and I made to Pennsylvania to obtain the remainder of the news reports. I was not about to appear ungrateful for my cousin's efforts, but the bits and pieces of news that she would send just puzzled me more and more. I eventually just decided to return home and obtain the rest of the story on my own.

"I'm sure they will both understand that we didn't have much time while we were in town." Susan tried to ease my feelings of guilt. "Anne knows only too well that she doesn't have the time to sit down and go through the files, and films, like we just did." Susan reached across the back seat, and grabbed the folder bulging with the many copies we printed while we were in town.

"Bless her heart, between work and school she barely gets time to take a deep breath, but I wouldn't hurt her feelings for anything." I truly loved my late aunt's only child, and I was very appreciative of her efforts. "I love my uncle, and I know better than anyone that he tickles odd, so it won't faze him that I slipped into town and back out without as much as a phone call, but Anne might be offended." I let out a deep sigh. "I will call her when we get home, apologize and try to explain."

"Michelle," Susan had that comforting tone in her voice again. "So much time has passed since she sent those first articles that she has probably forgotten all about this by now." It was quite awhile since I first opened the envelope that arrived in the mail. I had read the first news reports with such zest, and sadly, disappointment, when I realized I didn't have all the reports. I voiced my frustration and confusion over and over. My teenage son almost touched my soul when he wanted to know if my goal was to learn about the crime, or solve it. I didn't have an answer for his question, so I put the articles to the side until I could truly answer that question honestly, and the months just seemed to slip by as the envelope collected dust.

I certainly wasn't a detective, but Peggy never strayed too far from my thoughts. By the time I was equipped with an answer to my son's profound question, I knew in my heart that my only real desire was to learn about Peggy. The articles my cousin researched were simply the tip of the iceberg, and I needed the rest of the story, so Susan and I embarked on a trip to Pennsylvania.

"Well, thanks to Anne's articles we knew that it was weird that a girl that died in an apartment without power was buried in a better than average cemetery, and our trip has cleared up the pocket of curiosity surrounding that." I reflected on our brief visit. "We learned Peggy's stepfather must have been a pretty good guy and he obviously loved her."

"I wonder if he is the one that placed the flowers on her grave," Susan thought aloud. "Michelle, I was just so surprised by those flowers. I guess I just assumed after all these years that her grave would almost go ignored." I had to agree that I shared my friend's opinion.

"Susan, the articles report Peggy's boyfriend was picked up on an outstanding warrant for failure to pay child support, and the reporter mentioned that the boyfriend's wife was pregnant with a second child." I paused for a moment. "My God, think about that Susan! She was fourteen years old and involved with a married man. How in the hell did that happen? That's pretty powerful for this day in age, but thirty years ago such actions were almost unheard of."

"Michelle, it's pretty clear she wasn't being raised in the healthiest of environments, and while we don't know everything right now, we certainly have a clear view that Peggy's mother was marching to her own drum, and obviously taking Peggy along for the ride. Peggy's mother said the boyfriend had been staying at the apartment for almost two months. Yeah, like I am going to allow my fourteen-year-old's boyfriend to stay at my house for two months." Sarcasm dripped from Susan's words.

"Work with me for a moment, and don't say a word until you take a minute to think about what I am going to say." I collected my thoughts. "One look at this crime and one immediately thinks it was a man, but what if it was a woman, a jealous woman? Peggy wasn't exactly playing hopscotch with the girls in the neighborhood; she was playing in the big league, and perhaps she pushed one woman a little too far. Judging by the things we know to date there is no proof of a sexual assault on Peggy. What if the killer is female? There was a movie a couple years ago, the title escapes me, but the mistress is killed and semen suggested a male killer, the cheating husband was the main suspect, and the wife is never once considered as a suspect because of the semen, yet the ending reveals that the presumption of her innocence allowed her to get away with murder."

"I remember the movie, and its name is on the tip of my tongue." Susan was a true movie buff. "I don't know. You could have something there, but it seems like a pretty brutal act for a female to commit. The amount of force needed to penetrate the human body with an archery bow would be tremendous. We aren't talking about arrows, Michelle; we are talking about a five-foot archery bow. How tall are you?" She stopped talking on that note.

"I am sixty three inches tall. . ." My voice trailed off as I thought of the comparison of my height to that of the bow used to assault Peggy.

"My God Susan what kind of animal could do such a thing?" I didn't surrender my thought of a female assailant, but I was wise enough to know that it took a powerful force to commit such a crime.

"I have read more than my share of true crime books because I am just weird like that." I made a light attempt at humor. "But this is almost a crime before its time. Susan, this happened before Charles Manson orchestrated his horror on the world, before the profiling of killers was even a science, and yet just on the coat tails of the Boston Strangler. The person that killed Peggy Reber is a sick and twisted human being, and unless those articles are concealing the conviction of a killer, it scares the hell out of me to think the lunatic got away with it. How does one commit such a crime and go about life after the fact?"

"That's an interesting thought." Susan answered my question with her own puzzlement. "One brutalizes a teen, and does what? Combs his hair, dusts himself off, and goes to the movies?" Susan stared out the window apparently in deep thought with the pile of articles still resting on her lap. Silence engulfed the automobile for quite awhile as we both traveled our own paths of thought.

"She had a twin." I broke the silence. "The twin was married with a newborn baby." I waited a moment until I was sure I had Susan's attention. "And if I understood the article correctly Peggy's boyfriend and her brother-in-law were brothers. Isn't that cozy?" I offered a bit of my own sarcasm to the debate. "So, Peggy has a married boyfriend, and her twin is married with a child at the ripe old age of fourteen. I still have to keep reminding myself that this took place in my sweet little conservative hometown. I had teenage babysitters during the time of this crime, and I know for a fact they would have received a damn good beating for even thinking about being sexually active at such a young age, much less sleeping with a married man, or being married with a child. I must have grown up in a bubble."

"Or, Peggy was raised outside the traditional bubble." Susan offered an alternative thought. "You and I both had the benefit of growing up in the bubble so-to-speak, but obviously, not everyone was as lucky as we were." Susan started to giggle. "Remind me to send my mother some flowers when we get back home."

We shared a laugh as we thought of Susan's mother.

A few moments later, Susan looked up from the articles, shocked. "Supposedly, Peggy's twin sister attempted suicide within a few hours of the discovery of Peggy's body. She was rushed to the hospital, and they pumped her stomach because she had taken an overdose, but the article didn't identify the drug she ingested."

"Really? One twin is murdered, and upon learning the fate, the other twin opts to join her in all eternity? We apparently have either two very close siblings, or a really horrible reality on the table." A suicide attempt wasn't shocking as one considered the oddities already in place, and nothing touching Peggy appeared to be anywhere normal to date. "Kind of hard to think of a new mother attempting suicide, isn't it?"

We knew through news reports Peggy's sister gave birth to a baby girl just a few weeks prior to the murder. "It's hard enough to think of a fourteen year old killed in such a manner in her own room, so why should it surprise us that a new mother would choose to check out on life?" We were learning at a rapid pace that each new piece of information uncovered was more curious than the last.

"I can't imagine my daughters being that close because God knows I break up enough fights between them, but it is believed that twins share a mystical bond." Susan was looking for logic. "And perhaps she was suffering from guilt because she moved out of the apartment next door, the day before the crime. Remember that was one of the three factors that left Peggy vulnerable. I wonder where she is today." The thought of finding Peggy's twin today was simply mind-boggling.

"I wonder where most of these people are today." I paused to hit the horn as the sign marking the North Carolina state line appeared on the horizon. Our conversation took on a new focus as we anticipated seeing our children, and pets, and the mountain of housework that accumulated during our absence. We pulled into the driveway with a half dozen children charging the vehicle before we even came to a complete stop. "There's no place like home!" We broke out into hearty laughter as we opened the doors to greet the children's smiling faces.

Day to day life did not allow Susan and I to devote a great deal of time and energy to an unsolved homicide from over three decades prior, in a land over five hundred miles from us. We were active PTA moms, and with the exception of my memory of Peggy, we led a rather normal humdrum existence. I longed to write a book of some sort, but it was little more than a fantasy, and Peggy didn't really start out as a topic for a book, but rather a memory that nagged at me. Laundry, grocery shopping and school activities took their place on the front burners of our lives upon our return, and Peggy dusted our conversations over morning coffee.

"Uncle Eugene," I gave the man a moment to recognize my voice. "Is Anne home?" I made the dreaded call to my cousin after my return to North Carolina. I still hadn't overcome the guilt for not visiting her when I was in Pennsylvania.

"Is this Michelle?" He wasn't sure of himself, but he continued just the same "She's at the library."

"Yes, Uncle Eugene, this is Michelle." I was almost relieved that I didn't have to explain to my cousin that I made a trip home, and didn't get a chance to see her.

"Michelle, have you been talking to the police?" he sounded queer as he asked the strangest question, and my mind raced as I wondered what he was thinking.

"No." I wasn't even sure how to respond other than with raw curiosity. "Why would you think I was talking to the police?" I held the phone away from my face and looked at it as if I were dreaming.

"They're opening up the Peggy Reber murder case, and I thought maybe you had been talking to somebody because Anne told me how you wanted some articles awhile back. It's just kind of weird after all these years that everybody's talking about that again." He waited for me to respond, but I was almost at a loss.

"Peggy has been in the headlines recently?" I slowly approached his declaration.

"Slightly." He started to laugh. "They fired some lady cop for taking the file home and then there was a big article in the paper about some cop opening the case again. I just thought maybe you stirred everything up, and started all of this." I could hear a devilish tone in his voice. My uncle thrived on good old-fashioned drama in any form, but I had made no attempt at breeding drama on any level.

"Peggy Reber has been in the news recently." I repeated his words. "A female police officer took the murder file home, got fired, and some cop is going to look into the case again?" I wanted him to confirm that I heard him correctly.

"That's it in a nutshell." He was pleased with himself.

"When did all of this take place Uncle Eugene?" I was utterly baffled.

He knew I was skeptical. "This was just last week. I knew I should have saved the damn paper." My mind started racing and I asked him to hold on a minute, and I ran out to my car. I remembered the paper I bought when Susan and I were leaving town. Sure enough, I opened the paper to see Peggy's name on the front page, and I stood numb for a moment.

"Uncle Eugene, you're right." I returned to the phone with the paper in my hand. "I just happen to have the paper in front of me." I stared at the news report as he rambled on about his accuracy, and how he was on top of current news. "Uncle Eugene, please let Anne know that I called." I hung up totally confused.

I carefully read the report in front of me. I learned the town's *only* female police officer was apparently terminated for taking Peggy's murder file home. It appeared her motivation was to obtain information to write a book. I could barely believe the words in print right before my eyes. I read the article over and over as my mind weighed out the scenario-taking place.

"He said a cop was opening the case again." I called Susan and within minutes she was seated at my kitchen counter reading the article. "It doesn't say anything about the case being investigated again, but he also made mention of a second article, so I am thinking that if I call the local paper maybe they can tell me about the other article." By the time Susan could even acknowledge me, I was on the phone with the newspaper. "Of course you can fax it to me." I tapped Susan on the shoulder in sheer delight. "I would be thrilled if you could do that for me." I hung up the phone and waited for my fax machine to supply me with the rest of the story. Sure enough within a few minutes I was provided with a blurred copy of an article featuring a local law enforcement officer, and his desire to review the case of Peggy Reber's murder.

"Peggy is rather popular after all this time." Susan read my mind. "I wonder if we suffer from poor timing, or if we are right on time."

"I wonder a lot right now." I placed the article on my kitchen counter and leaned back on my stool "I will abandon any pursuit we have begun if professionals are going to step up to the plate, but I really have to wonder what's going on here. We learned at the cemetery that a man had visited recently with the intentions of writing a book, there is a police officer released from the force because she apparently took the file home because she wanted to write a book, and now the city wants to stage another investigation. I have to wonder if it's all related, or do these people and incidents stand isolated?"

"Michelle, has anyone written a book about this murder yet?" Susan looked a little puzzled herself.

"Not that I know of, or we would have just bought the book and spared ourselves all the research we just did." I never heard of any book written about Peggy which was one of the reasons I considered her fate as a subject for a manuscript. I didn't know the details of her life, or the crime, but with the amount of time that had passed since the event I trusted it was something that could be explored without causing anyone too much discomfort.

"Isn't it odd that suddenly everyone wants to write a book about the poor kid?" Susan had a point, and I wasn't equipped with an answer.

"Well," I picked up the cordless phone. "It's not going to hurt anything to call this detective and see if he has anything worth saying." I giggled a little bit. "I can't believe I am about to call some complete stranger, a professional law enforcement officer no less, and ask about a murder that I have no business asking about." I could almost hear my father's warning from yesteryear echo in my head as I dialed the number.

After a light introduction on the phone I found myself stumbling over the words: I was considering writing a book about the murder of Peggy Reber.

"You aren't the only one" the detective on the other end of the phone chuckled as he commented on my desire. "You say you're from the area? Well, I am very interested in talking to you because I truly believe that the case is worthy of a book. You must understand that there are some things that I just cannot divulge to you because this is an open investigation, but feel free to email me and we will take it from there."

I grabbed a pencil and wrote down his contact information and hung up the phone with a strange feeling of optimism.

"Detective Donald Hall* was nice enough."

Susan sat eagerly waiting to hear the outcome of my phone call.

"He laughed when I said I wanted to write a book, but he opened the door to entertaining any questions that I may have with a quick disclaimer that there are some things he just can't say because it is an ongoing investigation." I tapped the pencil that was still in my hand on the counter as I stared across the room.

"This is a little bit more than I had in mind, Susan. Nowhere in my plans did I ever intend to contact any police officer."

"Before you go into a panic," Susan reasoned, "You didn't exactly act on a wild urge. You simply followed the path set before you, and if it helps answer your questions there's no harm done."

I was feeling less than comfortable. "I am not qualified, nor do I have any legitimate business bothering a police officer that is trying to solve Peggy's murder. I may be dabbling in an arena that is well over my head."

"Everybody has to start somewhere, and this may be where you have to start." She didn't seem to be the least bit intimidated with the stage set. "If Detective Hall thought you were crazy, I think it is safe to say that he would have probably hung up on you, but he didn't. So just go with the flow." She patted my hand. "I don't think there is anything wrong with you asking a cop a few questions, but I think it would be terribly wrong if you just stopped pursuing this because you aren't comfortable. Peggy Reber has danced in the back of your mind for a long, long time and we may both be crazy, but I think that deserves some consideration in itself."

"I just don't want to waste anyone's time, and I certainly don't want to interfere with anything that could bring closure to the case." I looked at my friend quite seriously and breathed out a deep sigh. "You stood on that grave with me." I lowered my eyes as they welled up with tears. "This isn't a game."

"And it is that sincerity that gives you every right to talk to anyone about this case, Michelle. Your heart is in the right place and as long as that is your inspiration, you can't go wrong. Personally, I think you are making a bigger deal of this than necessary." Susan got up from the counter. "He is just a man, Michelle. Puts his pants on one leg at a time like everybody else, and if he really had all the answers it wouldn't be an open case, but a solved case. You might not be the professional that you think you should be to review this case, but judging by the articles that I read, the professionals that have handled this case missed a few little facts like bringing the killer to justice. So asking a few questions thirty years after the fact isn't going to hurt anyone." She moved toward the door. "I have got to go make dinner for my troops, but call me if you need anything. Quit thinking so hard, and just take it one step at a time."

I sat at my breakfast counter for quite a while after Susan left and I did just what she cautioned me against. I thought far too hard on the subject.

••

"Hey Mom!" My son bounced into the room. "What's for supper?" He slowed down just long enough to throw the day's mail on the counter as he breezed through the room. I didn't get a chance to answer him before he was out of sight on his way to the television. I mumbled something ridiculous as an entrée just to see if he was listening as I picked up the mail from the counter. I read my maiden name on an envelope and saw the Pennsylvania postmark in the corner. I changed my name legally over fifteen years prior, so it was a real attention getter to see my maiden name in print.

"Susan," I waited for my friend to respond to me on the phone. "I may not want to follow these paths leading to Pennsylvania, but I have a feeling Pennsylvania wants me to follow these paths set forth." I barely gave her a chance to question me before I continued. "I got a letter in the mail today addressed to my maiden name and once I got over the shock of that, I opened the envelope." I let a moment of silence lapse just for effect. "Well, it was an invitation to my class reunion."

"Oh joy!" She let out a sigh. "I hate those damn things!" She started to ramble about the horrors of reuniting with old classmates.

"Susan," I interrupted her. "This invitation is for my twentieth reunion and while that's all well and good. . ." I paused again. "My reunion is not due to take place until next year, and this invitation is dated for this summer." Silence found its way on the phone line. "Let me add to the oddity of it all." I paused long enough to collect my thoughts. "I have lived in this same house for over fifteen years and though my graduating class has reunions every five years, this is the first invitation that I have ever received."

"Are you serious?" Susan's voice was suddenly sober. "Michelle this is just too weird." Her children's yelling was providing far too much distraction in the background. "I'll be right over." I hung up the phone and waited for my friend to walk through the door as I stared at the invitation in my hand.

"Don't you see?" Susan waved the invitation in front of me. "You can't just walk away from this, or that cop, or Peggy."

"That invitation has nothing to do with Peggy Reber." I reminded her.

"No," She didn't hesitate. "But it has everything to do with Pennsylvania, and it's safe to say that you are being called home. How much more do you need to read the writing on the wall? Aren't you the woman that believes God talks and we simply have to slow down and listen? Open your ears, girlfriend!" She was determined. We must have talked about the invitation for over an hour before the subject embraced exhaustion, and we both retreated to our domestic duties.

■■■

I harnessed my nervousness and composed a letter to Detective Hall.

■■■

Before I could even tell Susan that I had succumbed to the challenge of writing to the detective, she shipped off her own electronic correspondence to someone in the Lebanon's local government inquiring about information on the Reber case. She received such a professional response that we both sat overwhelmed.

Susan's email was quite simple:

I am researching an unsolved murder that took place in Lebanon on May 25, 1968. Margaret Lynn "Peggy" Reber, a 14 year old girl, was brutally murdered in an apartment building located at 770 Maple street. Any information or direction you could give me would be greatly appreciated.
Sincerely,

Susan's email received a blunt response in bold print:

THAT WAS THE YEAR BEFORE I GRADUATED FROM HIGH SCHOOL. SORRY, BUT I DON'T REMEMBER OR KNOW ANYTHING

We met later in the day, both unaware of the others activities. After swapping stories, we sat baffled by the response that Susan had received on her correspondence. We were both starting to realize that Peggy was far from a forgotten topic for local officials. The mention of Peggy's name was starting that whole strange reaction thing all over again.

"I didn't mean to step on your toes." Susan apologized. "I just thought I would make an attempt to see if we could learn anything else. So I looked up Lebanon's local government on the internet and gave it a shot."

"Let's get something straight," I looked at my friend with the utmost of sincerity. "There is nothing about this that can cause any hardship between us, got it?" I raised my hand and she placed her hand against mine. "If the silly woman at the courthouse doesn't want to help, so be it. If a letter to Detective Hall was a waste of time, that's fine too. But we are going to handle this just like you said." I winked at her, "one step at a time."

"But we *are* going to handle it, aren't we?" She was looking for an answer that I didn't have. "I just have a feeling about this Michelle." Susan was almost on a crusade.

"What in the world have I started?" I tried to be humorous, but I was concerned about what was starting to unfold.

"I am not so sure you started this, but I want to point something out to you that is really strange, and I just realized it last night." She baited a hook and naturally I was going to bite. "What is my youngest daughter's name?" She quizzed me like I was a stranger.

"Blondie," I answered the silly question like she had lost her mind.

"What's her legal name Michelle?" She obviously wasn't content with the nickname we used on a daily basis. "Her full name."

"Margaret Katherine," I said it quickly and stopped. "Margaret Katherine," I repeated it again slowly because I got the point loud and clear. I felt a chill rush through my body. "This is getting weird."

"No, it's not weird." She was oozing with confidence. "At first, it appeared to be a bit strange, but it's taking on its own form, and if you refuse to see it," she stopped in the middle of her sentence, "Well, that would be a shame."

"Margaret Katherine, huh?" I was still spinning at the thought "What are the chances of that?" Peggy's first name was Margaret and her twin sister's name was Kathryn, so it was just the slightest shade of queer that Susan's daughter's name would be Margaret Katherine.

"I don't know what the chances are that the names just seem to tap me on the shoulder anymore than I know why your class reunion is scheduled a year early, but my inner voice is telling me that this isn't all merely coincidence." Susan said.

"Susan, are you suggesting that there is something spiritual behind all of this?" I was skeptical. I was so skeptical that I was regretting having ever even brought the subject up.

Susan's blue eyes never looked more serious. "Michelle, it's just not natural for a five year old child to remember a crime victim thirty years after the fact. I love you but that's just not normal. I accompanied you home because you deserve answers, and this is evolving into a bit more than that at this point." I listened to her but she knew I was not convinced of her argument, "What if?"

I stopped her. "What if what?" I sprung to my feet and started to pace about the room. "What if we are both crazy? I knew I was dabbling in strange when I first brought this subject up. But I didn't intend to take anyone along with me, and I think you're right, this is getting weirder by the minute. We can't solve this crime! Hell, we don't even know all the facts, but there's something about Peggy that just seems to. . ." I hesitated, ". . .linger. She's been lingering in my mind for a long, long time."

"I'm not sure Michelle, but there are too many strange things in the air to just accept everything as mere chance. I am not going to be any more dramatic than the situation calls for, but given the status quo I have to say that I think we have to keep an open mind and be creative in our thinking." She chuckled a bit.

"I agree to keep an open mind, and I can be as creative as the next person, but I also think we need to be realistic in our thinking. There is no denying the fact that any mention of Peggy inspires strange reactions and it is strange, but it doesn't really mean anything. I think it is slightly amusing that I finally receive an invitation to a class reunion after all these years and oddly enough it is going to take place a year early. I guess I am surprised that Peggy is once again front page news just as we start to embark on a little research" I rolled my eyes on that note.

"The cute little thing with your daughter's name being Margaret Katherine and the twins in this case being named Margaret and Kathryn?" I allowed my voice to trail off. "I think it's. . . I think it's interesting."

I didn't want to embrace an angelic guidance, but I couldn't deny that I, too, thought it was an interesting little point. "I also think we have to constantly keep in mind that we are not detectives. We are two completely ignorant individuals that just have a bunch of unanswered questions about an ancient crime and if we read everything that there is to read thoroughly, we will probably have all the answers to those questions."

"Michelle, I don't ever want to be the one to rain on a parade, but I beg to differ with you. Peggy's murder is listed as unsolved, so all the answers aren't sitting at our fingertips. If the answers were just sitting there waiting to be found someone would be convicted of the crime and that is not the case. I am simply suggesting that we be thorough in our reading, research and thinking because surely something was overlooked or justice would have been served." Susan's mild-mannered nature was being replaced by an aggressive desire to go on a fact-finding mission, and I had to respect her for that.

"I guess you're right." There was no arguing the fact that no matter how much we read about Peggy, the crime and the process the bottom line was still the same: the murder of Margaret Lynn Reber is listed as an unsolved homicide. "So what do you have in mind?" I got the feeling my friend had a plan.

"Let's send all the children to the skating rink and sit down and read everything that we have on this. We can each list our own personal questions as we read through the articles, and when we're done we'll compare notes." She had put some thought into her plan. "I am willing to bet that we'll be able to answer a good part of our curiosities just by tossing our own questions at each other after reading everything, and whatever we can't answer is what we'll focus on just a little bit more than the rest. Do you understand what I am trying to say?" She doubted herself if only for a moment.

"I understand completely and I think it's definitely worth the effort." The time had come to clear the table and spread everything out, so we could see the whole picture from beginning to end.

Peggy apparently got up the morning of that fateful day and shortly after noon found a constable on the doorstep to apprehend her boyfriend on an outstanding bench warrant for not paying child support. Supposedly a male Hispanic neighbor and a female friend of Peggy's were at the apartment at the time of the arrest. Peggy and her girlfriend went to a local café looking for her mother, and when Peggy failed to locate her mother, she walked her girlfriend to work at a diner on the opposite end of town.

I was never strong in measuring distance, but even I knew the girls traveled several miles on foot one way. Peggy had a burger at the diner before she left her friend, the only meal Peggy would have that day, and sadly what would be her last meal ever. Peggy walked with her girlfriend to the diner, but the paper made no mention of anyone walking back to town with Peggy. Several people reported seeing Peggy on the streets of Lebanon that afternoon, so it leaves one to wonder if Peggy's killer saw her walking alone that sunny afternoon in May as well. A classmate said she saw Peggy down town and they exchanged salutations across the street while others reported seeing Peggy walking toward her apartment building tearful and distressed carrying a paper bag.

The coroner reported that the time of death could not be determined accurately because the orifice used to determine the body's temperature was the point of assault with the bow, but Peggy was killed in an apartment without electricity, so surely the slaying had to take place before dark, or how would the killer be able to see what he was doing?

Art Root Jr. dated Peggy's mother, Mary, the weeks prior to the crime, and he admitted to seeing Peggy alive at the apartment at 6 p.m. on the day of the crime. Arthur Root Jr. said Peggy was very upset because she didn't know the whereabouts of her mother, and she was packing in preparation of the eviction by the landlord. Another news report had Peggy alive as late as 8 p.m. at a public restroom located downtown, and she was with a couple other girls her age. A couple of employees of the public restroom testified to talking to Peggy after 8 p.m. They recalled her vividly.

If the latter report was accurate, Peggy had to have entered an apartment with limited lighting because even with daylight savings time 8 p.m. would not afford one too much natural lighting, and not for a long period of time. However, if Peggy met her demise after Root admittedly saw her for the last time, there was plenty of lighting for a killer to see exactly what he was doing.

Then there is the issue a killer went unnoticed in the middle of the day just a few blocks from downtown Lebanon on a Saturday afternoon. Perhaps Art Root Jr. did see her at 6 p.m. as he said, and Peggy went on to leave the apartment after that encounter and that explains her presence at the comfort station a couple hours later. I wasn't sure of the importance of the conflicting reports, but a few hours mattered in the big picture on some level; I simply wanted an idea of the course Peggy traveled during her final hours.

Somewhere around 10 p.m., Pinky, the friend that Peggy escorted to work earlier in the afternoon, knocked on Peggy's door, and she thought she heard the shuffling of feet on the other side of the door, but no one answered her knock. The apartment building had over twenty apartments and all but a few were occupied and it was a known fact that the walls within the building were paper thin, yet no one heard a thing when questioned about the crime. Did Pinky hear the footsteps of a killer?

Shortly after 3 a.m., Peggy's mother returned home from her trip to New Jersey, and she entered the dark apartment to find a young girl's body on Peggy's bedroom floor. Mary Alice Reber went across the hall to a neighbor to get a flashlight after discovering the body and the two women returned to the Reber apartment. The neighbor moved the bed in order to open a door leading to the hall so they would have the benefit of the light from the hall, and it was then that they both realized it was indeed Peggy on the floor.

The neighbor took a blanket from the bed and covered Peggy's body until police arrived on the scene. The horrific crime apparently overwhelmed the small police department and chaos unfolded from that point. Peggy Reber's murder was not simply a shocking crime in a small conservative town, but an act so bizarre it would have shocked the nation.

The weeks that followed were filled with interrogations, pleas by the district attorney for any information possible and strange behavior by the strangest cast of characters. Six months after the crime an arrest was made and the Commonwealth of Pennsylvania charged Arthur M Root Jr. with the murder of Margaret Lynn Reber. Sixteen months after the arrest Root was put on trial for his life and the news accounts of the court proceedings were far too much to absorb in one reading.

It was amazing to view the judicial system thirty years after the fact because we quickly learned the Miranda Rights were relatively new at the time of Root's arrest and jurors names and addresses were published on the front page of the paper for all to see. The jury took less than two hours to find Arthur Root Jr. not guilty for the death of Peggy Reber, and it was at that point that the case found its spot on the list of unsolved homicides for decades to come.

■■

"Okay, my friend, we have completed the crash course on the murder of Peggy Reber. We now know the whole story and we both have our list of questions, but I want to throw another idea out at you before we go any further."

"By all means."

"We have read everything from beginning to end, and while we can't quote details off the top of our heads we have the general idea of the events that took place." She nodded in agreement. "Before we take these pages of questions that we have composed and start driving each other crazy bantering back and forth about events that span over two years, I think we should now tackle each article individually."

"What do you mean?" I could tell by her facial expression that she was confused.

"We just bit everything off in a big chunk and that gives us the big picture. Let's slow down and take this just the way we said we would." I waited for her to think about what I was saying. "Let's take this one step at a time." I reached for an article that reported on Peggy's funeral.

"Do you remember when Anne sent those first few articles long before we ever made the trip to Pennsylvania? We read them slowly and carefully to the point we came up with a dozen different questions based on one article alone?' I sat up straight and looked at the article in my hand. "Just on the report of the funeral alone we questioned how Peggy found her way to that particular cemetery and who paid for the funeral of the poor girl that died with an empty stomach in an apartment stripped of basic utilities?"

"I remember." She almost whispered her response as I continued with my point.

"Would we have asked such a silly question if we had the benefit of all of this knowledge then?" I wasn't going to stage a campaign. I just had to hope she would understand my reasoning.

"That's a tough question, Michelle. I don't know what we would have thought if we had all of this information from the onset, and I kind of understand what you're saying."

"Well, let me present another approach." I paused long enough to collect my thoughts. "We just sat here and had a mini-history class, but the Lebanon community didn't have that benefit at the time of the crime. Almost every article that we read was published on a daily basis and that is how the general public received it. We just had a news buffet in regards to the many articles we have access to in one reading. The point I am trying to make is Sunday, May 26, 1968, Lebanon, Pennsylvania woke up to a shocking crime, and I am certain the gossip spread like wildfire. But the first actual news report didn't hit the headlines until Monday, May 27, and then the general public waited until Tuesday to read the next bit of news, and then Wednesday, and so on. I don't think we can truly understand the mood of the town or the emotional impact unless we attempt to digest it the way the local community did back then."

"So what exactly do you have in mind? We can't exactly roll back to complete ignorance at this stage of things." She was correct about that.

"We both needed to read everything we had if for no other reason than basic human curiosity. Now that we have a feel for everything that happened, I think we should slow down and take each article, or each revelation, on its own merit. Rather than have all the articles tell one story I think we should approach each news report as a freestanding source of information. I want us to really read each article as if it were all we had for that day just like the community did back in 1968. I also want to question everything as much as we did the first few articles we read." I wanted to know what happened to Peggy and the investigation, but I also wanted to truly understand everything as well, and that included how the public learned about Peggy in 1968.

The evening closed with a silent agreement that we would sleep on all that we learned that night and all that was left to be explored. There was no need to rush on the issues concerning Peggy because nothing was going to change in terms of the facts. We just needed to open our minds to host a clear perception of all the information that was available.

"Are you ready?" I asked Susan as I stood with my hand on the light switch. "Here goes nothing." I hit the switch to turn off the only light remaining on in my house at 6 p.m. on the anniversary of Peggy's death. "Walk with me."

Silently we walked through each and every room of my house to get an idea of what kind of lighting would have been afforded a killer at that time of day.

"What direction did her room face?" Susan was looking for precision. "If the window was facing south there would be more lighting than if it were facing east."

"I haven't a clue." I remembered the apartment building, but it had over twenty apartments, and I wasn't sure of the direction that Peggy's bedroom window faced. "The newspaper had one of those arrows pointing down at a picture of the building, and it was identifying which window was Peggy's, but the picture doesn't give hint to any direction that is familiar to me."

"It doesn't take a scientist to realize that under these conditions there is barely enough lighting to see what one is doing, but the theory of anything happening after 8 p.m. is placing a killer and Peggy in the dark." Satisfied with what we saw, Susan turned the lights on again.

"Want to try it again at 8 p.m. just to be thorough?" She knew me well enough to know that I couldn't do anything half way.

"You've got a date." I looked at the sun setting in the back of my home and I thought of Peggy and her last sunset. "I wonder if anyone placed flowers on her grave today."

Susan and I repeated the same process of testing the lighting two hours later, and we weren't surprised when we found most of my home engulfed in total darkness at 8 p.m.

"Received any word from the detective?" Susan and I shared a soda after our little experiment and sat on the front porch enjoying the warm Carolina evening. "I would have hoped he would respond by now."

"No, as a matter of fact I haven't heard from him, and I just may need to follow up on that one more time." I almost forgot about the email that I had sent to the detective back home. "I have been so busy reviewing the articles that we recovered that I haven't given much else a lot of thought lately." I had seriously devoted a great deal of time trying to form an understanding of what unfolded on May 25, 1968 in Lebanon, Pennsylvania.

"Good for you." My friend began to clap her hands together in an obvious display of approval. "The woman that was so uncomfortable writing to him in the first place is going to follow up on his failure to respond." She started to laugh. "I'm very impressed."

"Look, I am still not sure that I have any business doing this, but it's not going to hurt to try to contact him one more time because for all we know, I screwed up his e-mail address and my letter is out in cyber space somewhere." I chuckled a bit at my lack of computer skills, and after Susan left for the evening, I composed my second email to Detective Donald Hall.

Detective Hall,

I sincerely have no intentions of being a thorn in your side, and I will direct my questions elsewhere if you have opted not to talk to me. During our conversation last week you instructed me to email you and prove myself legit. I attempted to provide enough information about myself to answer any of your questions or concerns.

My mail has gone unanswered, and I am not sure if that is due to a choice on your part, a hectic schedule, or an incorrect e-mail address. I am sending this in hopes of at least receiving a response to confirm that I did not make an error with your e-mail address, and you have received my correspondence.

I appreciate your time and effort,
Michelle

I wasn't quite sure what to expect as I hit the button on the computer to send the document. I just knew that I had to make one more attempt at contact with someone with answers about Peggy. I didn't have a tremendous amount of questions, but I also didn't possess a clear understanding of everything that took place either.

Two days later I found an email on my computer's monitor from Detective Hall and I could feel my heart race as I read what he wrote:

Michelle,

I just got your email today. I don't know why there was such a delay. You can ask me all the questions you want, but please bear in mind that certain aspects of the case I cannot divulge to you or any non-police investigative personnel.

I really like the idea of this becoming a story. I would have to think that the killer is dead or in prison. There is one local suspect that was never talked to by the police but I have my doubts if he is the man that did the killing. This killer would have gone on to do more killings and other types of crimes. At some point he would have been caught. This man was never arrested for anything. Also he is not very intelligent. I don't view him as a smooth talker who outwitted police officers. Although I would not consider all police officers to be very intelligent either and most are extremely lazy.

Write soon – we'll talk,
Donald

I ran to the phone and called Susan immediately "You are never going to believe what I got today!" I teased her, but before she had a chance to answer I blurted it out. "I got a letter from Detective Hall."

"Oh really?" Her voice rose with obvious curiosity. "And what does the honorable law enforcement officer have to say?"

"I don't know exactly. I was so excited I can't remember a thing. There is plenty of time for that. I can print it out, frame it and put it on the wall, but I wanted to tell you that he finally replied to my letters." I was excited. Donald Hall's mere acknowledgement of me left me feeling somewhat legitimate in my pursuit to write an honest account of Peggy Reber's life and death. Susan and I talked a short while before we hung up, and I returned to the computer to read the letter one more time.

I went about my normal routine the remainder of the day, but the letter was never far from thought. All my life I wanted to know about Peggy Reber and finally someone was willing to discuss it with me.

My response to the law enforcement officer was lengthy and scattered in thought, but I attempted to open a door, any door, to embark on an exchange of information with the detective. I knew that I was taking a chance of frustrating the police officer by writing so much with such ignorant views, but it was a gamble that I was willing to take.

The next couple of days I concentrated on a report that focused on Peggy being at the city's public restroom known as the comfort station on the evening of the crime. An attendant that had complimented Peggy on her beautiful long dark hair supposedly saw Peggy there. The attendant remembered that Peggy was with a friend at the time, and the attendant further recalled that it was 8 p.m. when she saw Peggy and her friend. The news reported that there was a desperate search to locate the young girl that was with Peggy that evening, and the parallel efforts in the investigation included sending all the tenants in the apartment building a letter pleading for any information about the day of the crime. The district attorney included self-addressed stamped envelopes with each letter sent to the tenants in hopes of obtaining information about that day's events.

■■■

"Hello?" I answered the ringing phone on the wall in the hall of my home.

"How is my favorite cousin?" Anne's perky voice was on the other end of the phone. "I haven't heard from you in awhile so I wanted to make sure you were still kicking."

I filled her in on my current status, and naturally we ventured onto the topic of Peggy. I told her how I was stumped by the search for the girl that was with Peggy that day.

"How much do you love me?' She started to toy with me. "Do you love me a little bit or a whole lot?" She was being quite the jovial one. "I not only know the young girl that was at the center of that search, but you do as well." She was pleased with herself.

"Say what?" I was stunned. "I know the girl that was with Peggy that night?" I couldn't imagine knowing anyone personally that actually knew Peggy.

"You sure do." Anne was having too much fun. "You have known her all your life." I waited for her to share her little secret. "That girl would be none other than Ruth*."

She gave me a minute to think about her words. "I brought up your project at a family gathering a couple weeks ago, and Ruth started to tell me all about it. Ruth was with Peggy that night. She was the girl at the comfort station, and she refused to step forward when the police started looking for her because she knew her Dad would kick her butt for being at the comfort station. Anyhow, Ruth told me that Peggy was scared to go home that day, and Peggy wanted Ruth to spend the night with her at the apartment because she didn't know where her mother was, and her boyfriend was locked up. Ruth was going to sneak out of the house to be with her later that night, but I guess Ruth got home and was in enough trouble, so she didn't meet Peggy later that night. How is that for some drama?"

"I don't even know what to say." I shook my head in disbelief. "I can't believe I have actually known someone all these years that knew Peggy, much less to be one of the last people to see her alive."

"Eventually the police showed up at her house, and she got her ass kicked again because her name was even mentioned in the midst of all the murder hype." Anne reminded me of how strict Ruth's parents were with her when she was growing up.

"Michelle, it sounds like Peggy was allowed to visit Ruth's house, but Peggy's apartment was off limits for Ruth, and judging by its reputation that would be about right for the times. It wasn't exactly the type of place that parents wanted their teenage daughters to frequent." Anne definitely had the right perspective on the place that Peggy called home. "When all was said and done, it sounds like Ruth's mom went looking for Ruth that day and found her walking down the street with Peggy. She loaded Ruth into the Cadillac and drove off, leaving Peggy standing on the sidewalk."

I thought of Peggy being left alone that day and it broke my heart.

"Michelle, can I remind you of something else while we are on the subject?" I was surprised she would ask such a silly question. "Do you remember mom's insurance salesman? I don't remember him, but I remember her talking about her insurance salesman coming to the house on a Friday to pick up her premium payment. I don't remember what was said, but he freaked her out by saying something about the Reber murder, and that afternoon he blew his brains out."

"You are just a wealth of information, aren't you?" I didn't even have to leave the house, and I was learning more and more about Peggy with each day that passed. I didn't necessarily have any answers, but I had a different perspective on that day, and I had a few more questions that I didn't have earlier.

After hanging up the phone I pulled out the articles that headlined the police department's search for the young girl with Peggy that day, and sure enough the young lady was eventually located but never identified, or was she?

The young girl's name would rest safely within the police file, a file that I would never see, but to which Donald Hall was privileged. He couldn't share information included in the murder file, but I had to wonder if he could confirm what Anne had shared with me. I wanted to run to the computer immediately and email Donald Hall with my questions. However, I had yet to receive a response to the lengthy email I composed, so I waited patiently to hear from the detective.

Michelle,

First, yes that is a lot to digest quickly. I need to think before I respond to everything that you are pondering.

Boyer had a brother. He was a suspect also because it was his bow in Peggy's room, not her boyfriend's. Boyer, Dick, was married to Peggy's twin sister and she was pregnant at the time of the murder. Dick did have a polygraph and it was said that he passed.

One note: polygraphs are not conclusive more to the proof operators are not fail proof. I did not see the polygraph on Dick Boyer so I cannot comment on it. I don't think it even exists.

He is also a good suspect. I will answer all your questions shortly. I just don't have time right now.

One last thing: never project your emotions on someone else. What you may feel for your children should not be projected on whether or not Peggy's mother gave a damn about her children.

Keep thinking, the key to the suspect should be narrowed to several elements

1. knowledge of Peggy's coming and going
2. position of the body
3. lack of defense wounds
4. type of death....strangled and then brutalized
5. position of the clothing, and there are more

Does the bow mean anything? In my opinion it does not. It was just there.

Donald

My brain started to move at a rapid pace, and though I didn't realize it at the time, my thoughts wouldn't really slow down for a long, long time. Peggy was starting to generate a tremendous amount of energy in my world, and I wasn't sure where the path was leading, but I had to follow it one step at a time.

■■■

"What's your feel for this, my friend?" I quizzed Susan over a glass of iced tea. "Are things getting a little strange, or am I imagining things?" Everything involving Peggy was taking on such an eerie feeling, and I wasn't sure if it was my imagination.

"It's not your average walk in the park, no doubt." She put Donald's email to the side. "But the good detective is in error on a few things if the newspaper reports are correct, because according to the news Peggy's sister was not pregnant at the time of the crime as he just said. I don't really doubt the report because it actually gives the baby's name, and somewhere I read that the bow used in the assault was the property of the boyfriend, and he is attaching it to the brother-in-law." Susan's eye for detail was as focused as ever.

"Okay." I let out a heavy sigh. "So what does it mean? What's it all worth? Forgive me, but I am slightly confused." I was frustrated by the conflict presenting itself. "We either have one hell of a good reporter and a poorly informed cop, or an inaccurate news report and a sharp cop." I threw the options out for consideration.

"Let's not be too quick to make that decision, and let's not be too quick to place all our trust in any one source. Remember, we agreed to take this one step at a time and today the stepping stone is a little shaky, but maybe tomorrow it will all make sense." Susan was wrestling with reason.

"We know that there was a trial, so let's fast forward a little bit, scan through the articles and get enough information to pursue getting a copy of the trial's transcript." I left the room long enough to get the file we had created with all the information we had pertaining to Peggy. "By the time we submit a request for the transcript and get the wheels of production moving, we will be ready for all the information and an actual court document should clear up any confusion we may have."

"My Dad mentioned suicides involved in this case when he cautioned me about looking into these articles when I was a kid, and Anne mentioned that my aunt's insurance man committed suicide after talking about this case." I started to wave an article in the air. "Guess what I have here."

Susan picked up the pen and tablet, and I started to read the article to her. "Anne may not be not too far from the mark according to this report because it identifies a young man that sold life insurance, and based on a description that he provided police they came up with a composite sketch of Peggy's assailant. The young insurance man was allegedly in the neighborhood the night of the crime and he may have seen the killer. But surprisingly enough, the day the composite was released in the paper, a Friday by the way, just like Anne said, the young man went out to that same military reservation that we stayed at and blew his brains out in front of two military policemen."

I pushed the article across the table so Susan could see the young man's photograph as well as the composite that was put out by the police in an effort to apprehend the killer.

"That's too weird." Susan started to read the article, and I remained silent to avoid distracting her.

"It gets better, if that's even possible." I had continued on to the next article while Susan read the first one. "Almost the next business day it was confirmed by the FBI that the insurance salesman was cleared of any suspicion of being Peggy's killer. Hair and fiber analysis came back from the FBI laboratory and excluded him from any possibility of being Peggy's attacker. The same article detailed that at least four men were jailed for unrelated charges after being questioned about Peggy's murder and it's at that point I think we get a clear picture of the caliber of people surrounding Peggy."

"I think I remember seeing something about a couple of guys being picked up on outstanding warrants when the detectives went to talk to them. It caught my attention because those guys just seem to be picked up because it was convenient for the officials as they were questioning them about Peggy, but Ray Boyer, Peggy's boyfriend, managed to get picked up that Saturday afternoon on civil charges, while the others apprehended after-the-fact all had criminal charges." She was right.

"Amen on that one." I agreed with my companion. "Now we know it to be true that Ray Boyer was not the only man in the city that had an outstanding warrant, but he was the only man in this picture that received that specialized attention to see justice served in the middle of a weekend, and that just smells bad to me."

"Michelle, I don't want to bet the farm on it, but I think if you check the names of those men picked up during the course of questioning after Peggy's murder and then check back to the name of the Hispanic male that was present when Ray Boyer was picked up at Peggy's apartment that day you may have a match."

"Are you saying that there were two men in the same apartment that day and both had outstanding warrants against them and only one was picked up that day?"

Susan nodded her head to confirm my thoughts.

"And Ray's charge of failure to pay child support was the worst offense on the books that day in good old Lebanon, Pennsylvania? Forgive me for being skeptical, but I don't buy it for a minute. That doesn't even make good common sense, and one doesn't have to be in law enforcement to explain it away." I snickered a bit. "Ray Boyer either had an enemy in the man that apprehended him, or that constable was sent there to specifically pick up Ray Boyer and get him out of the picture that day, but either way that representative of justice was not looking to pick up all the bad guys on the streets of Lebanon that day, rather just Ray Boyer."

"Here it is." Susan sifted through the articles on the table. "Chico Reyes was in the apartment with Peggy when Boyer was apprehended and Chico Reyes was jailed after being questioned concerning Peggy's murder on an outstanding warrant." She placed her index finger on the young man's name so I could clearly see her memory was correct.

"I don't know if I ever bothered to mention it because it never really mattered to me, but when I was growing up I had the greatest babysitters in the world, and I might add that they were Puerto Rican." I sat back down at the table with my friend. "My parents never saw ethnic origin so I never saw ethnic origin. I think that is truly one of the greatest gifts my parents ever bestowed upon me, but the rest of the community definitely saw ethnic origin. And let me tell you that Puerto Ricans in Lebanon were second-class citizens back in 1968. Our families were unconditional friends, and it has proven to be a friendship that has lasted many decades, a generation or so, and a whole lot of miles in between. We share tears over cradles and graves and if that isn't real than nothing is."

I choked up at the thought of my second family. "If I remember anything during that time frame, I truly remember the community's dislike of Hispanics, and that just fuels my suspicion even more concerning the apprehension of Ray Boyer over a Hispanic male with an outstanding warrant."

I could feel the hair on my neck start to stand up.

"Maybe the constable didn't know about the Hispanic male when he picked Ray Boyer up that day?" Susan was being diplomatic.

"Right." I volleyed her reason with sharp sarcasm. "He was on top of his game so much so he just had to settle the issue of Ray Boyer being a menace to society and loose on the streets. He was sharp enough to locate Ray Boyer somewhere other than Boyer's legal address, but he overlooked the Hispanic male with an outstanding warrant of a criminal nature? Yeah, Boyer's delinquent child support took priority?" I shook my head with determination.

"Bull." I could feel myself getting angry. "I don't know exactly what's wrong with that picture, but something's just not right, and sadly the detention of that one particular man leaves Peggy alone, vulnerable, and ultimately dead. Was that a tragic coincidence, or orchestrated in advance?" I really didn't like what I was thinking of that constable and his motives.

"Let's not be too quick to form any opinions." Susan waved her hand across the table. "I am inclined to think that Ray Boyer's arrest was a little too convenient for somebody, but we have a lot more to cover before we get too comfortable. Let's keep reading and maybe it will all start to make sense." Susan picked up another stack of reports and continued reading.

"I'm with you, and I apologize for losing focus." I started tackling the pile of paper in front of me as well. Susan and I sat in silence for what seemed like hours as we carefully read about the events surrounding Peggy that day. I knew we were both resisting the urge to share each bit of information as we discovered it, but we pushed forward quietly because there was a shared hunger to learn the truth.

"After awhile these words all start to run together." Susan broke the silence. "I need a break."

Susan excused herself to visit the bathroom while I got up to prepare us two cold glasses of lemonade. I carried our drinks outside to the patio so we could enjoy a break from the clutter spread across the dining room table and get a breath of fresh air.

"There you are." Susan poked her head out the sliding glass doors in search of me. "What a great idea!" She took a seat next to me at the patio table, and propped her feet up on an empty chair. "Do you realize that we have been at this for hours, and we still haven't knocked a dent in all that stuff?"

"It's kind of discouraging, isn't it?" I knew only too well what she was saying.

"Michelle, I just think it is a very sad story." Susan put her glass to her lips, and I saw a tear trickle down her face. I looked at the pine trees that accented our neighborhood scenery, and I thought of Peggy. Peggy never had the benefit of growing up, owning a home, or enjoying a summer evening as a middle-aged woman.

"Peggy's death was very sad." I echoed her words. "But the events that came to light before and after the crime are just tacky for lack of a better word. I remember when I was a kid I would get so embarrassed because my Dad would spend a little too much time at the corner bar, but after reading about this cast of characters I only wish I could take my Dad to the corner bar to have a few too many for all of Lebanon to see. I am almost proud of the skeletons in my family closet."

"Peggy would have been blessed if the biggest demon she had to battle was a parent that tilted the bottle a little too much." Susan dropped her feet to the green grass below the table. "Remember how I said that I had read where a couple guys had been jailed for unrelated charges during the course of questioning after Peggy's murder?" She was ready to talk. "Well, make that five men so far, and we aren't done reading yet."

"Yeah, I didn't bother to count them, but I got the picture that we weren't dealing with society's finest, and these would be the men that frequented that apartment on a regular basis. The police and the newspaper reporter didn't hesitate to point out that Peggy's mother entertained a large quantity of men, and that created a huge list of possible suspects. Mom was a popular lady, but judging by all the arrests she wasn't necessarily a good judge of character and in the midst of all that was Peggy. There is a little paragraph about a man being brought up on charges of assault with intent to ravish and corrupting the morals of a minor. According to that silly paragraph the charges were reduced to two counts of assault and battery. That event took place in April 1967, but went before the court during the February 1968 criminal court session three months before the murder.

"I missed that." Susan's face took on the strangest expression. "You mean this kid was corrupted, or whatever the exact charges were, and just a few months later she's brutally murdered?"

"It appears so." I nodded my head. "In fact, school officials admitted that Peggy had missed thirty days of the current school year, and to add insult to injury the director of the County Child Welfare Department *was aware* of the family prior to Peggy's murder. Of course the director refused to give out any information about the complaints received or the agency's involvement because all those records are confidential. I think he was asked something about if his agency should have involved the police, and he gave some weak answer like he didn't want to commit himself at that point."

I threw my hands up in a gesture of surrender. "No, I wouldn't want to commit myself either after there's a dead teenager on the floor of her bedroom. Yep, keep those damn records confidential because we don't want to hurt anybody's feelings, now do we?" I was disgusted.

"This is just unbelievable." Susan stared into space with a blank expression. "That kid never really stood a chance, did she? The killer was just the last monster she had to face, but she was surrounded by evil in various forms, and that, for the record, just pisses me off."

"Remember," I cautioned her. "We must limit just how personal and maternal we become, or we will cloud our pursuit of collecting facts. A friend of mine once told me that logic beats emotion every time, so let's gather the facts and we'll go from there." It was funny how we constantly reversed the role of anchoring each other.

"There were two Hispanic males that hung out at the apartment that were picked up after the murder. One of them being that Reyes that we discussed earlier and the other was some guy named Rivera." She got up from the patio table and darted into the house returning almost instantly.

"Reyes was jailed on charges of burglary, larceny and receiving stolen property while Rivera hit the lottery with disorderly conduct and using indecent language, oh and by the way, he failed to appear for his hearing."

"Add to that Art Root being incarcerated for violating his state parole, a few charges of vending machine larcenies, and forgery charges for allegedly cashing a few checks made out to none other than Peggy's mother." I tried to laugh, but it was a weak attempt. "What a lively group of people!"

"Michelle, it doesn't stop there." Susan managed to laugh. "The last two players are probably the most entertaining in the lot." I vigorously began to rub my face in total frustration. "There is a real joker in the bunch that decides to earn himself a charge of perjury for sending the cops on a wild goose chase looking for Peggy's killer, and he throws a forty-eight hour delay in the whole investigation thanks to his creative story telling. I can't remember his last name, but his first name was Paul."

"I remember seeing his picture on one of the front pages we pulled up, but I didn't get a chance to read what exactly got him his claim to fame." There had been so many faces splattered on the dozens of articles relating to Peggy.

"Do you remember seeing the picture of the other guy questioned about this case that committed suicide? He's a novel in his own right." She just shook her head in amazement.

"Oh, you mean the second suicide? The guy that killed himself after my aunt's insurance man checked out? Yeah I read about him and it almost blew my mind." I lit a cigarette of my own and watched the smoke float easily up and away. "Let's see if we both read the same thing." I leaned back in my chair. "A young outpatient from the local Veteran's Hospital was questioned about the murder. When officials showed up at his room, rather than answer the door, he bolted out the second story window, walked around some ledge on the outside of the building, and when the police entered his room they found a bunch of goods stolen from local residents during a recent crime spree. Morris, I think that was his name, takes off on foot and it takes a couple days to find him again. Somewhere in the course of looking into the burglaries the cops learn he had a female accomplice that was a nurse at the Veteran's Hospital."

"Hold it right there." Susan raised her index finger as if to scold me. "The police later learned that she was not a licensed nurse at all. I have to defend my profession on this one," she giggled.

"Consider it duly noted, my dear." We both had to smile. "Anyhow, they catch up with Morris a couple days later, and the poor guy is so spooked that he kicks out the windows in the back of a patrol car. Now Morris doesn't appear to be anywhere close to guilty in Peggy's slaying, and the only reason he was being questioned was because he was known to frequent the apartment, but he was definitely a few cans short of a six pack."

"So much so," Susan picked up the story from there, "That he manages to escape from the local jail, steals a car and when he wrecked the car the police arrived on the scene to find him sitting behind the steering wheel bare-ass naked. The poor guy is taken back to the local jail and placed in a solitary cell so the guards could keep an eye on him, and sure enough the young man manages to unscrew the light bulb that acted as a spotlight on his cell, hung up his sheet to obtain some privacy, and he was found hanging when the guards checked his cell. Don't forget your aunt's insurance salesman blew his brains out in front of MPs on Fort Indian Town Gap, too."

"And all of this happened within four weeks of Peggy being killed? I was on the other side of town living a nice normal little existence, and the rest of the town was going absolutely crazy. I have to pinch myself and remind myself that this is the same tranquil community that I grew up in, and I have to tell you that none of this is a fair representation of that town."

■■■

The days that followed did not afford Susan and me the time to review the data on Peggy because there were still children to care for and daily responsibilities that required our attention. However, Peggy was never far from thought, and Donald Hall provided bits and pieces of information with each new correspondence, so the learning process was never idle, just pregnant at times.

Each morning I would check my email hoping that there would be a letter from the detective that would finally put my questions to rest, but each correspondence, much like each new fact discovered, manufactured even more questions on my part. Late at night after most of the world embraced sleep I would sit at my computer and articulate my confusion about Peggy's death, the investigation that followed and the chances of securing justice for Peggy three decades later and email it to Detective Hall.

Shortly before midnight on a Saturday night I received an email from an unfamiliar recipient, and though my normal response would be to delete it the subject title of *Same Page* captured my attention.

Hello,

You don't know me, but I think we are working on the same story. If you are interested in corresponding with me please send a reply to this message.

Hint:...the root of all evil.

I could feel chills run down my spine as I read the strange message on my computer monitor because though it was vague the mention of root had two-fold meaning and I knew that someone other than Donald Hall wanted to discuss Peggy with me. I don't spook easily, but one could never lose sight that the murder of Peggy Reber remained unsolved and that always opened the door to the possibility that the killer could learn of my inquiry into the case. Thirty years may have passed since the crime but nothing guaranteed that the killer had died or left the immediate area, so anything was possible, and there was a stranger tapping me on the shoulder electronically. The queer note caught me by such surprise that it took several readings before I even noticed the sender's actual name in parenthesis next to his screen name.

"Susan, I apologize for calling at such a late hour, but go to your computer. I just forwarded an email to you, and you're not going to believe it when you see it." I waited for her to get a chance to grab a gander at the strange note before I said anything else. "Is that not the weirdest thing?"

"The root of all evil?" She pondered over the words. "If I recall correctly the root of all evil is money, isn't it?"

"Money is the root of all evil in the real world, and in the Bible, but in Lebanon, Pennsylvania, I am willing to bet that the root of all evil is a murder defendant from a long time ago." I let my voice trail off. "Identifying the root was easy compared to the author of the email."

"You think the root of all evil is Art Root?" She questioned my theory. "We know he was charged with the crime but we also know that he was found not guilty." She was answering her own questions. "Michelle, we have got to take the time to read everything pertaining to that trial because every time this guy's name comes up, that's about all we know."

"I know, I know" I agreed with her, but we don't have time to get current in a flash, so we'll make it a priority, but in the mean time we have someone wanting to talk about the case and in the most mysterious manner. I am just not sure what to make of it."

"Well, who is Larry Kelly*?" Susan spotted the sender's name a lot faster than I had initially. "Do you know him?"

"I never heard of the man." I printed the email as we continued to talk. "But somehow, some way, Mr. Kelly has learned that we are reviewing the case and obtained my email address, yet he wants to attempt an anonymous approach. I'm not sure that I am feeling all warm and fuzzy." I was being playful, but the unsolicited email made me distinctly aware of some risks involved in seeking out the truth about a crime.

"Let's see what we can come up with on Mr. Kelly." I wasn't sure exactly what Susan meant, but there certainly weren't any limitations on educating ourselves. "Just give me a couple minutes, and I'll meet you on the porch."

I hung up the phone and smiled because I had such a wonderful friend in Susan that she didn't complain about a midnight call about something so absurd, and she bounced back with an invitation to discuss it with me at a rather late hour. I wasn't going to be able to sleep peacefully after reading the contact from afar, so I welcomed the opportunity to chat with her, and weigh out its meaning. I picked up a few stray toys, fed my dogs and tried to busy myself waiting for Susan to stroll across the street. Susan finally walked through the door with a radiant smile on her face.

"Sorry it took so long, but I wanted to check out this Larry Kelly person before I came over." I still wasn't sure what my friend was referring to, so I opted simply to listen.

"I didn't take the time to dig up everything I could because after I made the first find I couldn't stop laughing long enough to go any further." Susan broke out into a hearty burst of humor. My curiosity was all but killing me. "Michelle," Susan attempted to stop laughing long enough to share the joke, but she held her side and almost rolled on the floor as tears streamed down her face. Several minutes passed as Susan attempted to gain her composure.

"I'm sorry." She wiped the tears from the corner of her eyes. "I ran a check on other screen names for this guy because it freaked me out that he just emailed you out of the clear blue, and after a little bit of digging around on the internet I found that Larry Kelly's other screen name is The Force is in My Pants." She giggled a bit. "There. I managed to say it."

"The force is in his pants?" I didn't understand.

"Yeah, the force is in his pants." She picked up on my confusion. "There is a way to cross reference people and their names on the internet and find all the screen names listed under a person's name, and when I did that check on Larry Kelly I found The Force is in My Pants as his alternate screen name."

"Great." I nodded my head in affirmative agreement. "I have a pervert emailing me about an unsolved murder." I was shooting for humor, but it really wasn't that funny. I didn't know anyone named Larry Kelly, and judging by Susan's revelation I didn't appreciate his frisky side. I was a little concerned as to how the man even knew about me. "So who in the hell is Larry Kelly?"

"I don't know, but do you remember the woman at the cemetery said there was a man that was writing about Peggy as well?" Susan reminded me of the man that visited Peggy's grave a few weeks before us. "I think he is a good possibility to consider, but who knows for sure? I don't think it's going to hurt anything to respond to the strange little man. Michelle, he's not a force to fear." She giggled at her play on words. "He left himself too exposed. No pun intended, of course."

Larry Kelly was indeed the aspiring author that had visited Peggy's grave, and he obtained my email address from the ladies in the sales office at the cemetery. After a brief exchange of electronic mail, Larry and I talked on the phone.

"Before we go too far I want you to know that I have no desire to interfere with any project that you have begun. I am nowhere near close to being a professional writer, and I am just in the exploratory stages of collecting information for a manuscript. I grew up in Lebanon, and I was just a kid when this happened."

"Exactly." Larry interrupted me with obvious excitement in his voice. "Anyone that lived here at the time remembers Peggy. How could anyone ever forget? I drive by the location where that apartment building stood almost every day, and I think of her every time. I am amazed that no one has written a book yet, but it almost makes sense because there are so many brick walls."

"Excuse me." I interrupted the male voice on the phone. "What do you mean by brick walls?"

"I have been working on this about six months, and every time I ask a question it just hits a dead end. I'll tell you what though I am fortunate enough to be friends with one of the first police officers that arrived at the scene of the crime, and I can't guarantee anything, but maybe he would talk to you, too. If we worked on this together maybe we could get a big name, or one of those crime solving shows to come to town and look into this case. I don't understand why someone hasn't sold this story."

"Mr. Kelly, I don't have any desire to really sell the story because I don't know the whole story, and it is not mine to tell or sell at this point. I am probably using the word 'manuscript' prematurely. I don't know that I am capable of writing the book, or if the story is even worthy of a book because it is after all an unsolved murder. We don't even know who killed Peggy."

"Sure we do." He quickly interrupted. "Art Root Jr. killed her."

"Mr. Kelly, I don't mean to be disrespectful, but Art Root Jr. was found not guilty by a jury in less than two hours time. I have learned enough to know that the community definitely wanted to solve this case, and the charges against Art Root didn't provide the closure necessary to put this issue to rest. How could a jury come to such a rapid conclusion if he was truly guilty?"

"Oh that's pretty simple to figure out." I sensed his sarcasm. "The evidence was too complicated for them to understand, so they let him walk." He rambled on about hair and fiber analysis, but I kept thinking of the recent trial of the century viewed by an entire nation courtesy of television, and the many, many public debates about a jury being overwhelmed with complicated forensic evidence. Larry Kelly's revelation was almost an echo of that controversy. "Art Root was one of the lowest forms of life."

"Where is he now? Does anyone know what happened to Art Root?" I was curious about the former defendant's whereabouts. "And you may be right about Root being a less than upstanding citizen, but he wasn't the only wild child in the picture because Peggy's mother wasn't winning any awards."

"Michelle, I don't know you at all, but how could you say such a thing when that poor woman lost her daughter at the hand of Satan himself? She suffered the greatest loss any mother could ever endure and my heart breaks for her." He was obviously a compassionate soul.

"Mr. Kelly," I paused a moment to collect my thoughts because I knew I was about to anger him to the point that he would terminate the conversation, and I wanted to ask him a few more questions. "I can't imagine losing my child, much less in such a truly evil manner, but one cannot lose sight that Peggy was left alone in an apartment without the benefit of electricity, food, or adult supervision. I don't want to be anyone's judge or jury, but Peggy's basic needs were not being met her last few days on this earth. I don't know enough about the whole story, I am still just learning, and that's why I asked if you know where Art Root is today."

"That was one of those brick walls I told you about because he died out at the veteran's hospital a couple years ago, so he's not talking anymore. I went to the historical society and I spent hours and hours researching the newspaper articles, and I studied each and every word. I have some friends that have a band in the area, and I asked one of the musicians to write a song for Peggy because she deserves to be remembered, and that's why I think we should take this story to New York and attempt to get someone that knows what they're doing to come into town."

"Mr. Kelly, we are both natives of that area and that gives us both the benefit of knowing that the local community is not going to discuss this with total strangers. The nature of Peggy's death alone is enough to inspire silence. The poor girl endured a rectal assault with an archery bow that penetrated her heart almost a half dozen times, and I just don't ever see the community discussing that freely. Do you know where Peggy's mother is today, or her twin sister?"

"I have often wondered about her sister and what she looks like today." His voice trailed off. "I don't know that I could handle seeing her because that's what Peggy would look like today since they were identical twins, you know? I heard her mother left town years ago, and who could blame her? Surely she was devastated after her daughter died. I told you, it's nothing but a bunch of brick walls. I have heard her dad will discuss it and I just could never bring myself to bother him."

"Mr. Kelly, I am just learning, but the man that killed Peggy was far ahead of his time, and on the chance that Art Root Jr. truly is innocent, someone got away with a horrendous crime. I have lightly researched murder, sexual assaults, strangulation and keeping in mind that Peggy was not sexually assaulted, the anal assault with the bow gives this killer a unique twist."

"Stop right there!" He was almost shouting at me. "You have said something about a rectal assault twice, and I want to know where you got such an idea. I have spent a lot of time learning about Peggy, I have talked to the cop that was at the scene, and I have never heard anything about a rectal assault."

"Mr. Kelly, it is right there in the articles." I tried to be tactful. "I got my articles at the same historical society that you got yours." We were working with the same information, but he apparently missed a vital point.

"Where?" He was anxious. "I have every article published about Peggy. Let me get my book, and I want you to tell me where it says it was a rectal assault." He put the phone down without waiting for my response. I got lost in my own thoughts because Larry Kelly obviously went the extra mile to learn about Peggy, and even with all his research he missed the simplest of details. "Now you tell me where it says that bow was thrust into her rectum." He was highly emotional.

"I'm sorry Mr. Kelly. I didn't mean to upset you." I almost felt guilty for ripping his blinders off. "It isn't clearly stated that it was a rectal assault. One must be familiar with the definition of the word 'orifice'."

"I know what 'orifice' means." He was clearly angry, and I wasn't winning a popularity contest with the man. "Now tell me where it says it was a rectal assault."

I took a deep breath and began to read from the article: " 'The coroner reported during the trial that the time of death could not be determined because the orifice normally used to determine a body's temperature was the point of the assault with the five foot archery bow.'"

I waited a few seconds before I continued. "Mr. Kelly that is an exact quote from the newspaper, and while a living person would have their temperature taken orally, with a corpse it is done rectally." I didn't even attempt to utter another word because I knew he was in shock.

"Dear God in heaven." He broke the silence. "That poor, poor girl."

"Mr. Kelly, I really don't know what to say to you." I felt bad for the kind heart that was wounded by learning the truth. "I just assumed that you were aware of that detail of the crime."

"Michelle, I haven't had all the help with this that you have had. I have been doing all my research alone." His tone was bitter. It didn't require a degree in psychology to recognize a wounded ego at work.

"You're right Mr. Kelly, I am fortunate enough to have my best friend's assistance, and that does help me a great deal." I made every attempt to be considerate of the man's feelings, and I knew when the conversation ended Larry Kelly and I would probably never talk to each other again.

Larry Kelly was not a professional writer, though he had every desire to write a book. Rather, he was a kind individual that never forgot Peggy, and so in many ways we weren't very different. Larry's oversight in regards to Peggy's actual cause of death wasn't due to ignorance, or stupidity, but instead of reading with his mind his heart was in play, and I had to wonder how many others missed that one single sentence in the midst of such drama. Did the people in Lebanon even realize how Peggy Reber met her death, or did it slip by the community at the time of the crime just as it slipped by a man thirty years after the fact?

I could almost envision the excitement in the air as the papers would hit the streets for sale the days following the murder, and I could fully understand how one simple sentence could get lost in the mass of words and emotional hype surrounding the crime.

I didn't want to correct Mr. Kelly anymore than necessary, but when he told me that Art Root Jr. died in the local veteran's hospital I had a few doubts. I knew that Art Root Sr. had been in that same hospital when my own father was a patient there. Only veterans with honorable discharges from the military were eligible for treatment at the veteran's hospital, and I didn't know enough about Art Root Jr. to even know if he served in the service, but I was going to find out. I wanted to know what course led Art Root Jr. to Peggy Reber's doorstep, the courtroom, and beyond.

Art Root Jr. was Mary Alice Reber's most recent steady boyfriend prior to Peggy's death, and equally it was no secret that he was married with two small children at the time of the affair and the crime. He was never going to be the poster child for a model citizen and though the community held on to the thought of his guilt, I had to respect the verdict rendered by his jury.

Root had a handful of siblings; he grew up in the Lebanon area, and though his childhood wasn't perfect it wasn't exactly a breeding ground for murder.

But Peggy's murder was so absurd that it was impossible to know where such evil was incubated.

▪▪▪

Donald Hall confirmed in an email to me that he had indeed seen Ruth Winters name in the police file of Peggy's murder. I understood quite clearly that he was limited as to what he could share about the contents of that file, and I had the utmost respect for the limitations set. I simply assumed his confirmation of the name and lack of opposition on the subject meant Anne was correct when she told me that Ruth was the unidentified girl last seen with Peggy the day she met her killer. I wanted to talk to Ruth, but Anne already warned me that like most everyone else I encountered, Ruth didn't welcome the topic of Peggy's final hours as a topic for discussion.

Donald Hall and I shared correspondence almost on a daily basis, and while I enjoyed being able to discuss the crime with someone with some real knowledge, Donald was very reserved in his approach. I resisted the urge to get frustrated because I knew that he couldn't tell me things, so I carefully read the news reports formed my questions and attempted to present them to him in a manner that he could answer. Donald, however, managed to throw out a few questions of his own and it would inspire my thinking.

"Where is Art Root Jr. today? Is he dead? How did he die? Who was with him when he died?" He tossed out a series of questions and though I was hoping he would answer such inquiries, I credited his reverse approach to the fact that he couldn't share all that he knew, and he was trying to assist by pointing me in the right direction.

I called the Lebanon County criminal records department and attempted to obtain a copy of Arthur Root JR's criminal record. I was slightly disappointed when the young woman on the phone told me that Root's records were "retired". I questioned her as to the meaning of a retired criminal file, and she told me it meant that he was deceased.

I didn't understand why Donald Hall would produce such questions about Root if he knew he was dead. I looked at the questions Donald asked again, and once I got past the first one, it appeared that my goal was to learn the details surrounding Root's death. I questioned Donald about his motives for asking such questions of me and he responded:

Michelle,
Firstly, you must find the location of Root's death and the local paper will be able to help you with that. A simple search of Art Root Jr.'s file name will reveal the location and type of

death. He was famous in Lebanon so when he died I am sure they covered it. Once you learn that, contact the newspaper in the area of his death and inquire as to the circumstances. The key is questions and then more questions. There are no stupid questions only stupid people that can't answer the questions. Also a good detective is a good thinker. My wife is an excellent detective and yet she never had any training.

    Donald

The task at hand didn't appear too difficult: I would simply place a call to The Lebanon Daily News and the answers would be mine within a matter of minutes. I learned rather quickly that modern technology had not yet found The Lebanon Daily News and its archives. The paper's librarian was so sweet, and I could hear in her voice that she wanted to assist me, but it wasn't as simple as typing one's name into a computer and accessing information. I needed a date to research and then it was a matter of going into an attic storage area and sorting through boxes to find that day's news reports.

Unfortunately, I didn't have a date to research, or a location, or even the slightest bit of information beyond the fact that I knew his name and his criminal records were retired. I decided to think like a detective and my next thought was to call the vital records office and inquire as to the date on his death certificate, but I got an education there as well. I was not a family member and in the state of Pennsylvania such information is not public record. I thought of Larry Kelly and the brick walls that he mentioned, and I realized I was meeting up with a few of those brick walls, too.

"I don't understand why Donald Hall doesn't just tell you what happened to Art Root Jr.?" Susan was not impressed with Donald's approach to helping us. "He is sitting right there with all the information at his fingertips, and it's not going to compromise national security for him to share a little information about a dead man."

"Susan, he made it clear when we first contacted him that there would be certain things that he couldn't tell us, and I trust that this is one of those things." I didn't have any other explanation for the detective. "It's probably not that difficult we are just at a disadvantage by being less than professional investigators and add to that we are five hundred miles away."

"That's my point, Michelle." She was visibly irritated. "We are not investigators, and we can't exactly run down to the court house in a matter of minutes, so I think he could share a little more information instead of a bunch of questions."

"Oh, we have never been the type to back down from a challenge, so why should this be any different? We just need to be creative." I didn't share my friend's frustration. "I have an idea." I got a little excited as my thoughts started to take form. "Isn't there a way to research deaths on the internet?"

"Yes, Social Security has a web site." Susan was a wealth of information on things that could be accessed online long before Google existed. "And I think I told you that I already looked for that joker and the only thing I came up with was his father."

"There you go!" I clapped my hands with delight. "That's it!"

"Okay, I may not be the sharpest knife in the box, but that's what?" She was not amused with my zest.

"That, my dear friend, is our starting point. We don't have a date for Art Root Jr.'s death, but we do have a date for his father." I could see she was lost. "If we research his death, we can research the obituary article that appeared in the local paper reporting his death, and that will give us a time line to start with where Root Jr. is concerned. Normally an obituary lists one's children living and departed, so we will find out if his son was alive when his father passed away."

"I see where you're going with this." She didn't share my excitement. "It's definitely going about it through the back door."

"But hey," I almost shouted with joy, "It is at least a door instead of a brick wall." We both laughed at my mention of brick walls. "If sonny boy is listed as deceased in the obituary, there is a good possibility that we could contact the funeral home and get the date of his death, and if he is listed as a survivor we know that we need only research years since the passing of his father."

"I'll try anything once, but I have to ask the obvious question, Michelle: What's the point in locating Root's grave? He was found not guilty, and I'm not sure what it's going to accomplish by finding the record of his death."

"I don't have the answer for you, but I guess it would help to know how one goes about life after being put on trial for killing a fourteen year old girl. I wonder how he died."

"Maybe he is another suicide, Michelle." She perked up at that thought. "Maybe Root is another suicide, and he left a note explaining everything."

"Wouldn't that be a queer twist of fate? I won't rule anything out, but I don't think it is that simple. I don't see Root as the man that got away with murder even though I know part of Lebanon's population still sees him as the real killer. If you think about everything we know about Art Root Jr., it just doesn't fit. Root was serving time in a neighboring county for petty crimes a few years before Peggy's murder, and he walked away from a work release program. He walked all the way to Illinois, so-to-speak, adopted a new name, got married and had a couple kids. He returned to the Lebanon area just a couple months prior to the killing, bringing his wife and children with him."

"Yeah, and then the husband and father started sleeping around with Peggy's mother." Susan was quick to interrupt with dark side of the truth.

"I think we both know that there is one hell of a big difference between being a cheating husband and being a killer. I am not defending his actions, and I realize that his moral bankruptcy is less than attractive, but it's still a far cry from murder." I didn't know Art Root Jr. personally, but I just wasn't convinced of his guilt in the slaying of Peggy Reber.

"Michelle," Susan was ready to do battle. "The paper reported that his wife showed up at the Reber apartment a few weeks before the crime to tell Mary Alice Reber to stay away from her husband. He ripped off a nearby Laundromat and put the money at the Reber apartment for safekeeping, and that was why he went to the Reber apartment the day of the crime: to get his stolen money. He admitted that he interviewed for a job that day and then stopped by the apartment to get his money. When he realized Mary Alice wasn't home he went to a nearby bar to drink a beer." She was thorough. "He returned to the apartment several times that afternoon and at one point took Mary Reber's stereo as collateral for his missing money with the help of a guy from across the hall of course, and let us not forget it was during one of those visits that he admitted to seeing a very upset Peggy."

"Yeah Susan, he admitted to seeing a very upset Peggy. Now think about that for a minute. Do you really think he is going to admit to even being in that apartment that day if he actually killed her?" I just didn't buy it.

"Michelle, he had no choice but to admit to being in that apartment that day because, after all, he took the stereo. He wouldn't be the first person to commit murder and admit to seeing the victim the day of the crime. His admission to being there explains away any fingerprints found in the apartment and any testimony by witnesses that saw him there that day. If you ask me, Art Root Jr. was pretty slick."

"Are you saying you think Root is the real killer?" I inquired incredulously.

"Nope." She started to laugh, and I knew the joke was on me. "I was just arguing one of the possibilities. I have no idea who killed Peggy, and I'm not sure that locating Root's gravesite is going to do a whole lot for us, but if that's what you want to do then that is what we will do."

"Let's toss this around a bit more before you go running off to find tombstones." I liked the way Susan would volley thoughts and possibilities back and forth. "Root is merely a petty thief and when he was questioned about Peggy's murder it was realized that he walked away from the work release program in Lancaster County a few years prior, so he was placed in jail as an outstanding fugitive. I think the original charge in Lancaster County was stealing a car, so again, there isn't an issue involving a violent crime. He sat in the Lebanon County jail six months before he was formally charged with Peggy's murder."

"There's two ways to look at that little factor, and the first one being that there was no rush to charge him because due to his incarceration. He wasn't going anywhere, and the officials probably just wanted to be thorough in their investigation before they actually charged him with murder. The other side of that is the possibility that they simply needed to charge somebody to comfort the community and after months of investigating, Root was the best suspect they had, so he found himself as a defendant in a murder case." Susan had the bases covered with her logic.

"What was the evidence against him?" My friend obviously spent some time with the articles detailing Root's arrest, and I was hoping she got as far as the trial because she had my curiosity aroused.

"Not as much as one might think. There were some pretty impressive experts called in to assist with this case. The killer supposedly inflicted a bite mark on Peggy's breast, and a dental expert from the navy was brought in to take dental impressions from several suspects, and it was discovered that Root's dental impression did not inflict the wound, so that wasn't a mark against him. The autopsy did not reveal any semen, so that's not against him either. Fingerprints didn't take center stage in the investigation, and it wouldn't be a major factor anyhow because he was shacking up with her mother on a regular basis, so it wouldn't be unusual to find his fingerprints in the apartment. His wife insisted that he was home early that evening and after dinner they took their children for ice cream, and they went shopping for a thimble. The revelation of him having dinner with his family and accompanying his family for some shopping creates a question of time in regards to Peggy being at the comfort station at 8 p.m. If Root killed her she would have been dead as early as 6 p.m. in order for him to be home with the family for supper, and then Peggy wouldn't have been alive to be at the comfort station with Ruth."

My lack of patience forced me to interrupt her. "You are telling me all the reasons Root couldn't commit this crime. Now would you get to the reason they charged him?"

"Hair and fibers." Susan cut through the chase. "His hairs were found in, about, and around the body and there was an exchange of fibers between his clothing and Peggy's clothing."

"That's it?" I was stunned "Hair and fibers?"

"Well Michelle, it looks like Mary Alice gave out more than a few keys to the apartment to several of her male friends, and Root was one of them. It was rather obvious that the killer did not force his way into the apartment, so that didn't help him, but there is one other huge factor in play." She paused solely for effect. "If you remember reading the first article about the night of the murder the neighbor placed a blanket over Peggy's body. Mary Alice testified in court to having sex with several men on that blanket one of them being Root, and that could possibly explain his hair being found at the scene."

"It's unbelievable, isn't it? Six months after the crime and the best they had on him was hair and fibers, the fact he had a key to the apartment, and he admitted to being there at some point in the day plus he told authorities he saw Peggy that afternoon. Was there any blood on his clothing? I would think there had to be some amount of blood on the person that committed this act."

"There was not a drop of blood to be found on his clothing." She nodded her head back and forth. "The case against him was weak from my perspective, and I guess it was weak for the jury as well because they returned their verdict in less than two hours. On an odd note, and not that it has anything to do with Peggy, the trial was the place to be because people stood in line to get a seat in the court room. The crime that shocked the conservative little community gave birth to a trial that captivated the local population and what is even stranger is the fact that most of the court room spectators were women."

"Oh you know the deal. Everybody just has to look when they pass an accident along the road, and this just brought out the curiosity in everyone. Let's face it, women were probably more inclined to have a desire to watch the proceedings because in many ways Mary Alice broke ranks from traditional parenting and she paid the ultimate price for it." I didn't allow myself to dwell on the questionable parenting of Peggy's mother.

"Funny you should say that because as far as Mary Alice was concerned everything from the new tattoo on her hand, her weight and the color and style of her clothing was newsworthy. I remember reading how her platinum blonde hair fell on her shoulders, and I thought it was pretty weird to use such wording while reporting on a murder trial."

"Okay, I think along with locating Art Root Jr.'s final resting place it is time to secure a copy of that court transcript, and I am certain that will make for interesting reading. I can't wait to hear the fee for a copy of the transcript because the last time I got something downtown I was charged $3.00 per page." I had no doubt that the trial transcript would consist of hundreds of pages, if not thousands.

"We'll just clip a few more coupons out of the paper and feed the kids a lot of peanut butter and jelly sandwiches." Susan was quick to offer a solution to the pending expense. "It's not exactly a shortcut we can afford to take."

"I understand the importance of the transcript, and I'll gladly bite off the expense, but I also think that is going to be a time consuming process because we know only too well that government offices move at a snail's pace. This is not going to hit a priority list, so we need to submit a request immediately or sooner." I was not versed in the process of obtaining such information, yet I theorized it would be decorated with a ton of red tape.

Art Root Sr. died January 31, 1992, and the obituary listed Arthur Root Jr. as a surviving son that resided in Oklahoma. Therefore, we knew his death occurred after that time, and Oklahoma provided a starting point to search for the former defendant. Assuming the younger Root passed away there was a slim chance he was buried in the Lebanon area, and that being the case I was confident the family used the same funeral home for him.

I placed a call to the undertaker in Lebanon that handled the senior Root's services. I was rather surprised when I recognized the name of the man that answered the phone at the funeral home because it was a guy I sat next to in high school homeroom for several years. We tickled memory lane a bit before I hit him with the real reason for me call.

"Michelle, I have no record of Arthur Root Jr. expiring or being handled by our organization, but I do have a few other family members listed." He was kind enough to recite the names and dates of what he did have available.

I hung up with a few more notes to add to the growing pile of information I was accumulating, but I still didn't have the answers I sought. I brushed off the feeling of discouragement that was starting to embrace me, and I decided to get a little crazy in my pursuit. I sat down at my computer and began a search for the state medical examiner in Oklahoma and within a matter of minutes I was placing yet another call in regards to Art Root Jr.'s passing.

The state of Oklahoma had no record of Arthur Root Jr.'s death and they assured me that all deaths within the state passed through their office on some level. I was starting to develop a few doubts as to Art Root Jr.'s alleged demise, and I wrote to Donald Hall and expressed my skepticism. I realized Lebanon's government listed his criminal file retired due to death, but my faith in Lebanon's legal structure was not the strongest, so I pressed Donald Hall for the information that caused his file to be retired. The local officials didn't just get a sudden urge to retire a criminal file, rather something lead them to believe Root was dead, but what?

Donald applauded my efforts to locate Root and the discovery that he resided in Oklahoma impressed him. He admitted his knowledge was weak, but apparently Root died somewhere out west and the local municipality was contacted requesting fingerprints, so his body could be identified. Out west when one resides in central Pennsylvania could be as far east as Pittsburgh or as far west as San Diego, California, so that didn't really narrow the search. Donald brought to light a point that I overlooked in my quest: Arthur Root Jr. adopted an alias years prior when he fled to Illinois, and it wasn't a great secret, merely an oversight on my part, so it was back to square one.

Meanwhile, Susan took the ten-cent tour of reading all the obituaries for the Root family based on the names we acquired from the funeral home. "I hate to say it, but if he died no one bothered to tell his family, because he is either listed as residing in Oklahoma, or address unknown. I saw the strangest thing, Michelle. His kid brother died a year to the day after Peggy was murdered."

"How did he die?" She caught my attention. "Don't tell me he was murdered, too."

"Not quite, but it wasn't a death due to natural causes." She handed me a fax. "I took the liberty of calling Lebanon and getting the story sent to me after I realized it was something out of the norm. The poor boy was just a teenager himself and he was swimming with some friends in a dam or something like that, and when he started yelling for help everyone thought he was kidding, so they ignored his cries only he wasn't joking. Sadly it looks like he went swimming with his sneakers on and the shoes weighed him down so much he couldn't save himself."

"Oh my God." Silence swept the room.

****

"Well, I keep telling myself that we are not detectives, and I am not sure what we hope to gain with our efforts. In the midst of all our efforts where Art Root is concerned, we forgot that silly little point that he changed his name long before Peggy ever took her last breath."

"That's right. He did change his name, didn't he?" Susan's face lit up. "And of course we are not detectives, but if you want to know about Peggy Reber we need to learn everything we possibly can so you can tell the whole story. I don't think the whereabouts of Art Root will make or break the story, but it would leave a loose end as to what happened to him in the years that followed the trial. Dead men do not make it a habit to move around too much, and we know he is dead because his criminal record is retired. So the biggest task at hand is finding his ultimate resting place and if we used the correct name it would probably make the search a lot easier."

"Susan, I am not so sure I believe that he's dead." I was coming out of left field with my unwarranted suspicion. "I can't explain it, but something just doesn't feel right to me. I know that his criminal record is retired, and I know Donald Hall is attempting to point us in the direction of finding out the circumstances surrounding his death, but something is just not right."

"We were researching the wrong name, Michelle." She sounded convincing. "Once we bird dog the alias a little bit, we'll be able to put flowers on his grave in no time, and we will know exactly what happened to him after the trial." The optimism in her voice faded. "I called about a copy of the transcript of the trial, and you aren't going to believe this, but there is no recorded transcript of the trial on public record."

"Say what?" I could feel my jaw drop. "What do you mean there isn't a recorded transcript of the trial? It was a murder trial, not a traffic violation! And the verdict rendered left the case just a wee bit unsolved, thus some of that testimony could be used in a second trial if ever they find the bastard that killed Peggy. You must have talked to a trainee or something like that, and they just didn't know where to look."

"I talked to the chief bitch in charge of the Lebanon County Prothonotaries Office, and not only was she proud to state her title, but she wasn't the most pleasant when I told her what I was inquiring about," Susan chuckled. "By now we should just immediately expect the cold shoulder response when Peggy's name is mentioned, and I have yet to figure out why."

"Isn't it a law that a trial such as that has to be transcribed?" I was still spinning over the possibility that a transcript might not exist. "How in the hell can there be such a horrendous crime, a verdict of not guilty, and no record of the testimony given during the proceedings?"

"There is no such law my friend. I knew you wouldn't be satisfied with a simple explanation like a transcript just doesn't exist, so I come prepared with a few more answers, but don't push it too much." She was trying to lighten the mood. "A court stenographer only transcribes a transcript if one of the trial lawyers requests it, otherwise it is not legally required that all testimony be recorded in transcript form. The defense attorney had no need for a copy of the transcript because his client was cleared of the charges, thus placing the burden on the district attorney to request that the trial be transcribed. Apparently, district attorney George Christianson was so convinced of Root's guilt that there wasn't any hope of ever trying someone else, so he didn't have it transcribed either."

"A hell of a lot of experts testified at that trial and now all that testimony is lost." I was growing increasingly angry. "It would be transcribed if Root was found guilty, naturally, because he would need it for an appeal, but since he was found not guilty and the district attorney was not allowing any consideration for error on the part of investigators everything said at the trial is just a mere memory. Do I smell ego or stupidity in the air? Which one is it, Susan? I don't like my home town very much right now." I could almost feel my blood boil.

"It is not going to accomplish anything by getting upset." Susan tried to calm me. "It isn't exactly what I expected to hear when I called to get the copy, but surely it's not that big of a deal." She stopped talking for a second. "Okay, it's a pretty damn big deal, and I think it is one of the most bizarre things I have ever heard, but standing around bitching about it isn't going to change anything."

"You'll have to forgive me, but right now I want to bitch." I slammed my hands down. "Experts from the FBI as well as the military testified at that damn trial not to mention little old ladies that have probably been pushing up daisies for years; the testimony given at that trial was priceless. For a district attorney to assume that a jury rendered a not guilty verdict in favor of a guilty man is one thing, but for him to forever silence the testimony of such experts based on his own opinion is pathetic. If the trial was transcribed, the testimony could possibly be used in a second trial against the real killer, but if he never requested that the testimony of the experts be recorded then it was lost forever, and any hope of ever prosecuting someone else for Peggy's murder is a fantasy. Well forgive me, but if he was so damn convinced of Root's guilt then why in the hell couldn't he convince a jury? A jury spoke and the district attorney didn't give their voice the credit it deserved. The jury's verdict told the district attorney he failed to prove guilt and perhaps that is because they put the wrong man on trial. Peggy didn't get justice, the Commonwealth did not get justice, a killer is walking free and the district attorney didn't bother to have testimony preserved with a transcript of the trial." I was fuming.

"It does appear that arrogance could be a factor in failing to have the transcript recorded, but if he truly believed in his case against Root maybe he walked out of that court room in a cloud of defeat." Susan was being fair and I wasn't having any part of it.

"Screw his clouds and his arrogance!" I was shouting. "I'll spare you the soap box about a slain teen and I will hold on cold hard facts. A not guilty verdict was just that for Root, but it didn't do a damn thing for Peggy, and it was the state's responsibility to secure justice for Peggy, so they were in error with their charges against Root. That doesn't give them the right to throw their hands up and walk away from the case. I don't sport a legal degree but I think the district attorney had an obligation to preserve any testimony, evidence and anything else that would nail the son of a bitch that decided to stick an archery bow up a fourteen-year-old girl's ass. Hell, the killer wasn't the only one sticking it to Peggy, was he? The judicial system failed her even after the fact." I could feel the tears welling up in my eyes.

"I don't think for a minute that the district attorney or any other officer of the court intentionally allowed Peggy's killer to escape justice, but damn if this girl's best interests don't get overlooked every time I turn around, and it really pisses me off."

There is no reasonable explanation that will justify the prosecuting office failing to have the murder trial of Peggy Reber transcribed. Time simply doesn't justify such an error. All expert testimony and testimony of various witnesses is forever lost because the prosecuting office did not secure it and protect it, while they failed to deliver a guilty verdict and solve the murder of Peggy Reber.

■■

The evening before Peggy was murdered her mother sat on the sofa in their apartment and playfully joked with her daughter. Mary Alice ventured out for a Friday night on the town and Peggy settled into an evening with her boyfriend Ray Boyer. Shortly after Mary Alice left for the evening the landlord cut off the electricity to the apartment in an attempt to evict Mary Alice from the dwelling. Ray Boyer quickly connected an extension cord from the adjacent apartment being vacated by Peggy's twin sister, Kathryn, and Ray Boyer's brother, Richard. The bootlegged power provided Peggy and Ray enough electricity to watch television and have the benefit of a lamp.

Ray and Peggy were a mellow duo and the evening was rather uneventful until the older Boyer male arrived at the neighboring apartment to finish removing the last of his belongings. Richard "Dick" Boyer and his wife, Peggy's twin sister, Kathryn, and their newborn daughter, moved into his parent's basement apartment the previous day. He was removing the last of their possessions.

Dick enjoyed a few beers with a neighboring male tenant from the building before he started moving the family's final items, and somewhere in the activity the Boyer brothers exchanged heated words. Dick responded to the sibling hostility by ripping the extension cord that provided power to Peggy's apartment from the wall, thus leaving her and Ray in the dark. The news reported that the couple went to sleep on the floor in a friend's apartment to avoid any further turmoil. Peggy Reber spent the last night of her life in a foreign apartment in an attempt to avoid darkness and to avoid a fight. Sadly, the following night Peggy would encounter violence in its darkest form.

That particular article epitomized things for me; Peggy was deprived of a basic need such as electricity by an adult, and in the midst of drama she walked away to avoid the turmoil. I realized she was fourteen years old and her companion was legally a married man estranged from his wife, and I also realized that if ever there was a poster child for victim it was Peggy Reber. Emotionally, I struggled to get past the way she spent her last night, but eventually I found comfort in the fact that Peggy escaped if only for a little while.

Peggy's mother didn't necessarily plan to leave town that night, or did she? I had to wonder. I wondered about everything relating to Peggy's final hours. I wondered for a long time if it wasn't a deliberate scheme to leave the young girl vulnerable for some sick self serving reason, but I resisted the thought that her mother knowingly left her vulnerable. Peggy was not completely vulnerable as long as Ray Boyer was in the picture because he protected her. Ray Boyer was Peggy's Mr. Wrong and yet in so many ways he was Mr. Right. I never forgot that he had a wife and child during his relationship with Peggy, and I questioned his motives until I actually talked to him. By the time my journey in the world of Peggy Reber would come to an end I would talk to two people that loved her so much that I could hear it in their speech and Ray Boyer was definitely one of those two.

■■■

I located Ray Boyer over thirty years after the crime living in the same home with none other than the woman to whom he was legally married at the time of the crime. Ray Boyer made it clear that he wanted nothing more than to see Peggy's killer come to justice and he was willing to talk to me, but never at the expense of his wife's feelings. I thought he was expressing remorse for his infidelity where Peggy was concerned, but that was not the case at all. Ray Boyer did not regret nor deny his relationship with Peggy Reber, but he was clearly aware of the anguish his sentiments caused his wife and he had no desire to hurt her anymore than she had already been hurt. I immediately respected his conviction to Peggy's memory and his wife's feelings.

Ray Boyer told me how he met Peggy after his brother married her twin sister, he almost instantly felt drawn to the fragile young female. Ray was barely eighteen years old and married with a child when he found himself not simply attracted to Peggy, but compelled to protect the teen living in the midst of chaos. I foolishly assumed I understood their relationship when I read a young girl was dating a married man until I listened to him talk about her. I heard things in Ray Boyer's voice that one just can't articulate and that was three decades after Peggy took her last breath. I never asked about their passion or romance because too much of Peggy's existence had been violated already and I could tell the man made peace with the loss years prior, so I focused my questions on facts surrounding the crime.

I also realized that he devoted years to regaining the trust of a woman he betrayed, his wife. Oh, he didn't go from Peggy's gravesite to the family dinner table, but somewhere in the course of the thirty years that followed, they found each other again and I respected the importance of that reunion. So did he.

Ray Boyer made a sick attempt at humor when he said, "I always said her life was worth $58.00."

I was speechless. "Yep, I was behind in child support to the tune of $58.00, and that cost her life because that would have never happened if I was there. And everybody knew that, but they got me out of the picture."

"Who got you out of the picture?" I waited to hear the name of the party responsible for Peggy's death, but it didn't come to fruition. "Mr. Boyer, you acted as Peggy's protector, but what were you protecting her from?"

"I would have fought to the death for that girl."

I didn't doubt his sincerity.

"I don't think you have any idea how many men went through that apartment, lady. Mary Alice had a hell of a lot of men coming and going at all hours. Peggy was beautiful and shy and she just didn't belong in that environment. I can't really explain it even after all these years, but I had to look out for her. I walked her to school in the morning, and I waited outside for her when classes were over at the end of the day. I encouraged her to go to a school dance with some guy from her home room. I didn't want Peggy to miss out on something so important because she was involved with me, and I knew I couldn't exactly take her to a school function under the circumstances."

"Did the male visitors to the apartment threaten Peggy?" I asked. He obviously sensed danger of some sort.

"Peggy didn't look anything like the picture plastered all over the papers when she died. Peggy was a knockout, and yet she was like a scared deer. No, there wasn't one guy that stood out and posed a threat to her because I wouldn't tolerate it, but the minute I was removed from the picture you see what happened. Hell, I had to run the damn landlord off because he was just a little too friendly, if you know what I mean."

I pushed him to explain about the landlord.

"He was a lawyer in town and he owned several apartment buildings and everybody knew he had an eye for the ladies, but when it came to Peggy, I put his eye in park. Not that I hit him or anything like that, but I made it clear that he needed to leave her alone."

"You were picked up on a Saturday for an outstanding warrant." I reminded him of the circumstances surrounding his apprehension "Did you have an enemy in the constable that would explain his pursuit to pick you up on a Saturday? How did he know where to find you?"

"Well, I didn't think he was an enemy the day he threw those cuffs on me, but after Peggy was killed he could never be anything but an enemy." Ray Boyer harbored bitterness toward the law enforcement officer that jailed him the day of the murder.

"Your brother was angry the night before Peggy died, so much so that he stripped you and Peggy of the only source of electricity that you had in that apartment." I wanted to talk about Peggy's last night alive.

"He's always been a little crazy; the guy would get into a car chase with police and then climb a tree and throw rocks at them. My folks always knew he was a little strange and they had him checked out a couple times and the doctors came back with some diagnosis like that's just the way he is."

I clearly asked the aged beau, "Do you think Art Root Jr. killed Peggy?"

"No I don't." He didn't hesitate "But when you find the son of a bitch that did I swore on her grave then, and I swear now I will kill him."

"Mr. Boyer," I attempted to show respect, "Too many years have passed for you to harbor such anger. I would never provide you any type of information to send you into a vengeful frenzy."

"Lady, you don't know me and I don't know you, but I swear to you that the day Peggy's killer is identified, with God as my witness, I will right the wrong."

I didn't doubt him for a minute.

∎∎∎

Personally, I still had trouble with a brother getting so angry with his sibling that he would deprive him and his teenage girlfriend electricity. I didn't have a full grasp on the cosmetics in play, and I trusted no one expected the outcome to result in a corpse of any kind, much less that of a defenseless teenage girl.

Research taught me Ray Boyer's brother, Dick Boyer, was an angry soul. Police responded to a call at the apartment building a few days before Peggy's death because Dick Boyer was allegedly assaulting his wife. The teenage mother gave birth to his daughter weeks earlier, and that didn't deter an angry and supposedly violent outburst. Dick Boyer possessed a key to the Reber apartment because of his connection to the family, and I trusted he was reviewed during the investigation, but I still found his behavior very peculiar. I wrote to Donald Hall and expressed my uneasy feelings concerning Dick Boyer because I wanted conformation that such an explosive temper and personality was not overlooked in the original investigation, and Donald assured me Peggy's brother-in-law did not escape scrutiny.

∎∎∎

My wheels starting spinning and I pondered the information about the landlord. I remembered the apartment building Peggy called home, but I don't think my youth ever crossed the threshold. I asked enough questions to learn the landlord owned rental properties throughout the town, and he was an interesting character. I gave him the same attention as any other questionable face in the picture, but oddly his colleagues and other professionals clammed up at the mention of his name. Years would pass before I would talk to most of the players involved and the reactions of two prominent attorneys would sum it up where the landlord was concerned.

One lawyer asked if our phone call was being recorded and the second attorney asked if the landlord was still alive and after I said he was deceased he told me point blank that he wouldn't discuss him. I don't think I ever truly embraced the theory that the landlord had anything to do with Peggy's slaying, but I definitely got a lesson in professional respect even post humus. The white collar world in Lebanon County and beyond was not going to discuss the late attorney, or his practices as a landlord in the small agricultural community. He was odd to say the least, and another strange twist in the life and death of Peggy Reber. Being the owner of the building, he also had a key to Peggy's apartment.

"Here read this." I pushed a news article in my friend's face. "Now read *this*." I pushed a second article in front of her. "Do you see it?" I didn't give her a chance to respond. "The belt doesn't match." I was beyond excited. "Peggy was strangled with a dress belt, but it doesn't match the dress she was wearing." I was certain I found the link to truth.

Susan didn't respond. She simply read the newsprint I placed in front of her. "You're right." She looked up at me. "A green dress belt and an orange dress."

"Susan I remember the earth tone fashions of the 70s like everyone else, but this crime didn't happen in the 70s, and a green belt does not match an orange dress." I searched for yet another news article. "It states Peggy made the dress she was wearing in a home economics class. "Oh yes," Susan reflected. "Good ol' home-ec!" She giggled at the memory. Susan was not only a nurse, but a talented seamstress.

"My dear, as I recall, home economics classes they taught us to be good homemakers because that's what the times called for, but nothing too complicated." I reminded her of past lessons learned. "A high school freshman class in home economics would never venture into the construction of a belt unless of course it was a wrap around belt." I rambled a bit. "But no high school freshman class is going to attempt a belt with a buckle, eyeholes, etc. The belt found around Peggy's neck does not match the dress she was wearing because we know for a fact she made the orange dress in a high school class, but a green belt didn't come out of that classroom." I was on a natural high. "Green and orange come into play somewhere in the 70s, but not in 1968."

"My mom had the ugliest green kitchen appliances." Susan broke out into a hearty laugh.

"When, Susan?" I pushed her for an answer. "When was your kitchen decorated in olive green?" I couldn't remember when the earth tones embraced the American culture, but Susan was a few years older than me, and maybe she could date the trend.

"Well I was the drum major in the high school band, so it had to be. . . "

I interrupted her on that thought because I knew it was long past the time of Peggy's death.

"If Donald Hall hits the evidence room, he is going to see for himself that Peggy was strangled with a belt that didn't match her dress." I was certain we were on the right track.

"You have a point" Susan agreed "The belt definitely doesn't belong with that dress." She took a deep breath. "Not for that era anyhow."

I didn't waste any time emailing the detective in my hometown, and I was certain what I uncovered would assist in learning the identity of Peggy's assailant. Donald was not near as excited by my discovery, but invited me to place a call to his home to discuss my finding. I was nervous about calling the detective because he appeared larger than life to me. He was a professional and I was just a fresh eye on an aged case, so I placed the call with a lot of apprehension.

"Great job!" He applauded my discovery of the belt not matching the dress. "But what is it worth today?"

He sounded sarcastic. "I am certain the original detectives missed that factor, so you did a great job, but what does it matter?" I listened to him and I could feel the sweat on the palm of my hand as I held the phone. Granted I realized Donald Hall wasn't a celebrity, but unlike me, he was trained to investigate crime and in the Lebanon community he was considered an authority on the Reber case, so I was intimidated by talking to him. He could not confirm or deny the mismatched coAnneng of the belt based on his memory alone and the dress, so I all but begged him to check the evidence in possession to confirm my discovery.

I brought up a second detail that caught my eye: a dust mop was found on top of Peggy's body and there was testimony relating to the dust mop and blood on its handle, but without a transcript the actual testimony was unknown "The killer committed a brutal assault with the archery bow, and then decided to mop the floor and toss the mop on top of her?" I couldn't envision the role of the dust mop. "Or was Peggy assaulted with the mop also? Or did someone find Peggy before her mother arrived in the apartment that night step in a pool of Peggy's blood and attempt to cover his footprints and in a rush to flee the premise tossed the mop on top of the girl?"

"The mop is an interesting point, Michelle." Donald didn't immediately respond. "The real question is the killer's association with the dust mop."

"It seems pretty clear to me." I was ready with a couple of possibilities. "The killer either put it there or someone else did, and if it was the killer, I will still sleep peacefully tonight. But," I paused simply for effect. "If someone else placed that mop there then that changes everything on the table."

"Very true." He chose his words carefully.

"We have a maniac so consumed with rage he does the unthinkable with the bow, and there's more than one vague mention that other items were used in the assault on Peggy, but at the last minute the monster suffers from a case of guilt and attempts to clean up his mess?" Sarcasm replaced my intimidation.

"You're thinking is good," He interrupted me. "Continue to question everything, and forgive me, but I must go right now because I have a family obligation." He said little else and terminated the phone call.

My investigative skills were nil, but if I could spot the mismatched belt and garment Donald's theory that the original investigators missed that fact was doubtful. Peggy's murder took place in a small town with a less than sophisticated police force, but the individuals involved in the case were skilled and intelligent professionals and it didn't take a rocket scientist to spot the contrasting colors. The dust mop was a huge issue and he didn't offer the slightest help in determining its exact worth, but there was little doubt it was a major factor in revealing the truth surrounding Peggy in its entirety.

The apartment Peggy shared with her mother was notorious for the large amount of traffic that frequented it; a fact investigators insisted was a detriment to narrowing down a list of possible suspects.

Peggy's mother found her body sometime after 3 a.m. Sunday morning, and according to the trial lawyers, Peggy either met her demise as early as 6 p.m. or as late as 10 p.m., but that puts that apartment at near abandonment from the time Peggy was killed until her mother found her body hours later. If Root was the killer, Peggy's death would have taken place early in the evening and that would have the teen laying there almost eight hours without being discovered. The apartment that hosted such a wild life style and according to the police, Mary Alice made accessible to male associates, sat completely, literally, lifeless on a Saturday night, and a murder went undetected until Mary Alice returned. It wasn't impossible for the apartment to go ignored on a Saturday night for so many hours, but that didn't support the claim to fame that it was such a party spot.

I didn't doubt the reputation that rested on the dwelling and that made me wonder if Mary Alice really was the first person to discover Peggy's body, or did someone else find Peggy and panic, thus altering the entire crime scene and hindering the investigation.

"That woman was raked over the coals and every detail of her life was put on public display and it all rested on the traffic in the apartment. One of the reasons Mary Alice and Peggy were being evicted from the damn building was because of the amount of male visitors that frequented the apartment, and one of the reasons the police couldn't narrow the list of male suspects was because so many keys were given out to the place, but on a Saturday night no one ventures into the apartment." I snickered "Well, no one except the killer. I don't buy it."

"It does sound a little strange" Susan was in agreement "They make it sound like there's a swinging door on the damn place and when the spotlight hits the stage there's no one to be found."

"I don't think Mary Alice was the first person to find that girl's body" I was running on a hunch "It doesn't make sense to me"

"Maybe the killer locked the door on his way out, Michelle" Susan was reasonable.

"Okay." I was being obstinate. "The jackass locks the door behind him after he kills the kid, and I will ask you again, what happened to all those men that supposedly had keys to the apartment on a Saturday night? Let me guess. One of the hottest party spots in town conveniently wasn't appealing on the same night a fourteen year old kid was slaughtered in that apartment. Damn Susan, we are racking up quite a list of convenient occurrences that day. We don't need to read the autopsy report to know that Peggy was dead way before midnight and that has her body on the floor a long time." I shook my head in disbelief. "I know it makes a great headline. Mary Alice came home and found her poor daughter dead on the floor, but think about that for a minute."

"I see where you're going and I guess that's possible, too, but damn, Michelle! Who is going to admit to entering that apartment and finding Peggy dead? Self preservation is everything, and only a fool would admit to discovering a body under those circumstances."

"I couldn't care less about the person or persons that actually found her, but what did they do to the crime scene? The slightest disruption in that crime scene could mean the difference between a conviction and an acquittal." I wasn't amused at the thought.

"Maybe that is where the original investigation found itself with a couple suicides." Susan was weighing out possibilities. "Maybe one of those poor guys actually found Peggy and couldn't live with it."

"Daddy always said dead men don't talk." I was being flippant. "Anything is possible at this point and we may never know the truth, but it's mighty strange that all the emphasis is on the body count in that apartment until there is a body to count."

"Maybe she was discovered by a third party and they used the dust mop to cover their tracks." Susan wasn't buying into my humor. "I recall reading they cut part of the floor out to use as evidence, and it was presented to the jury. Let's entertain this for a few minutes." She was serious. "Some dumb fool cruises in looking for a good time not knowing Mary Alice isn't home and finds Peggy at her worst and then he attempts to cover his tracks with the dust mop."

We hashed that through already, so I didn't share her thought pattern.

"If that's the case," she said, smiling, "Think about it!" Her blue eyes were glistening. "He was there during the day, Michelle."

I expressed a look of utter confusion. "There wasn't any power in the apartment, and we know that Mary Alice got a flashlight from the neighbor when she found Peggy, so if there is a third party he was there before dark, and that has Peggy dead before sunset."

"Got it," I nodded. "There was blood on the handle of the dust mop" I didn't have a point; rather I was replaying the information we knew to be true. "Was the source of that blood ever identified?"

"Nope, at least it was released to the public."

"Great." I was frustrated. "Donald doesn't think that the original investigators noticed that the belt used to strangle her didn't match her dress."

"You're kidding!" Mild-mannered Susan was shouting. "Didn't the seeing-eye dog point it out to them?"

I started to laugh at her witty comment. "No, I don't think the seeing-eye dog pointed it out to them."

The mood in the room relaxed. "Hey, I never claimed to be a professional, and I had no intentions of trying this at home, but I think the belt matters. I would bet a mortgage payment or two that the tracking of that dust mop matters too. How are we making out on finding my favorite defendant in a murder trial?"

"Well, Art Root Jr. is not legally or technically dead east of the Mississippi River, and the alias is holding with a pulse, too." Susan adopted the task of locating Root.

"Oh but I beg to differ," I interjected quickly.

"Oh yeah, that's right." She was oozing with venom. "Lebanon, Pennsylvania has apparently embraced his death because they retired his criminal file. I'll bet that same damn seeing-eye dog does their filing."

We couldn't resist laughing. "I can't find that bum, but when I do, I am either going to put flowers on his grave or buy him a beer because this shouldn't be this hard."

"Maybe he doesn't want to be found," I said sincerely. "Could you blame him?"

"Hell no, I don't blame him!" she exclaimed. "If I were jailed for two years for killing a fourteen year old kid, and I was innocent I would run so far no one would ever find me."

"I know I'm a hard sell, but I don't think he's dead." I couldn't shake the feeling that Art Root Jr. was alive and well, but the location of his existence was the challenge at hand.

"What does that cop in Lebanon have to say about Root?"

"He thinks he's dead and gone." I shared what I knew. "But when I ask the details about Root's death, he doesn't provide enough information to feed a bird."

"Michelle you are devoting time and effort writing to this guy, and he doesn't give us anything to work with. You are too damn bright to weigh out every word and be so articulate in your writing when you get nothing in return. He's sitting on the police file, crime scene photographs, autopsy report, the evidence and everything else that we're busting our asses to learn about the hard way. I think it's time to tell him to take a hike."

"We knew going into this that he was limited on what he could tell us," I said defensively. "And I probably put more time into my correspondence than I need to, but in many ways I am my own sounding board. I would love nothing more than for him to lay it out so it makes sense, but if it really made sense there would be a killer behind bars, and we know that is not the case. Maybe he's learning, too."

"Let him learn on someone else's time. Peggy's been dead over thirty years and her killer's free to walk the streets!" Susan's patience with the exchange with Donald Hall was nearing its end.

"Look," I reasoned. "He's all we've got. We can't exactly charge city hall and demand to see the file because this is not a closed case, so he is the closest we are going to get to that information. In light of the current political climate in Lebanon regarding this case, we are lucky to have him. If you recall, a female police officer was fired for taking this particular file home because she was considering writing a book about Peggy's murder."

Susan nodded.

I continued. "I pulled up my hometown paper online the other day and it appears that former officer is suing the good city of Lebanon for wrongful termination, and the city is claiming that due to her taking the Reber file home, the case has been compromised and thus it can never be solved."

"Say what?" Susan was shocked.

"You heard me correctly." I shared her disbelief. "The female officer single-handedly compromised justice for Peggy by taking the file home with her."

"That same seeing-eye dog is now chief of police?" she was poking fun, yet serious.

"I don't know all the details, and I am not sure I want to."

No truer words were spoken. "But because some female cop took this file home to review it, Peggy is front page news once again. I would have no problem with that at all if the goal was to pursue the truth, but since the city fired this female officer and they are accusing her of compromising the case, she is suing the city." I paused again. "Truth is that the last thing that city wants."

I let my friend catch up mentally before I continued; "Now it looks like that's where Peggy's case hit the news and the case was going to be reviewed again. But one must understand that if the city solves Peggy's case then the female officer cannot be held to blame for compromising anything, thus they lose her wrongful termination lawsuit, and if they actively review it and hit brick walls of course it will be the former officer's fault."

"Thirty years plus without justice and suddenly it's all her fault?" Susan was skeptical. "They are nuts!"

"Pretty much." I tossed my hands up in a carefree gesture. "I don't know this to be a fact, but I am trusting that Donald Hall probably can't even get close to Peggy's file right now because the former cop's lawsuit is front-burner news. I have a feeling Peggy's file, or the file the female cop took home which in this case is Peggy's, is precious stuff right now, and the city can't afford to jeopardize it any further"

"That's bull." Susan was disgusted.

"Oh, hell yeah!" I raised my voice in agreement "Peggy is getting screwed again and not to mention the female cop. She didn't compromise justice by taking a file anywhere. It looks like they wanted to run her out and they used Peggy's file to do it" local politics didn't support justice for Peggy at all. "I frankly don't give a damn about a lawsuit, but common sense will dictate that the best interests of Peggy are in question due to the almighty dollar. The city can investigate until the cows come home, but I will repeat it one more time." I took a deep breath. "The last thing the city of Lebanon wants right now is resolution to the death of Peggy Reber. They are holding this former officer responsible for breaking the chain of evidence and she is challenging their claim in court."

"What did you say?" Susan was perky again "The chain of evidence?"

"So they say."

"The file wouldn't be evidence." She shook her head in disbelief. "The bow is evidence, the belt, the dust mop, but not the file. Did she take the bow home?"

"No, Susan." I rolled my eyes. "She did not take the bow home."

"Then where is the evidence?"

"Relax." I tried to calm the beast within my friend. "I don't know the details, but I'm telling you that Donald Hall is the best we're going to get right now, so let's not walk away from all that we have, okay?"

"Okay," she agreed easily. "But Peggy's murder is being investigated again, and yet we know the last thing authorities want is to solve the case?"

"Susan," I scolded her. "You know damn good and well that you will never get a government official to admit to what you just said, so quit. But an unsolved crime of three decades compared to a multi-million lawsuit in modern day could equate into something less than a desire for justice"

"So Peggy sits in the middle of a bunch of bullshit again?" Susan wasn't amused.

"It looks that way," I admitted angrily.

"I'd love to talk to that female officer," Susan mumbled.

"Why?" I asked. "What does she have to offer? She read an aged file, took it home, and lost her job because of it." I wasn't impressed. "She has absolutely nothing to do with Peggy Reber. Peggy's killer didn't meet justice for thirty years and then suddenly it's the result of this cop, the only female cop on the force, but it's suddenly her fault. The lawsuit and her termination are just another injustice in the arena of the murder of a fourteen-year-old girl. If Peggy's case has been ignited you are welcome to use your own imagination, but I have to tell you I would kiss the ass of any official that legitimately sought justice for the slain teen and with modern technology. It can't be out of reach."

"Why aren't they reaching Michelle?" Susan was persistent.

"The issue is not about using modern technology now because I truly believe a multi-million dollar lawsuit is a key factor for local politicians, but why didn't they utilize modern technology a year ago, or two years ago?"

"I'm right there with you, and I have watched my share of television. This is a cold case file."

"Forgive me," I laughed. "My vocabulary isn't exactly current, so I trust you are correct, but the general idea is the same."

"Why aren't they researching cold case files, Michelle?" Susan wasn't convinced Peggy should find her place on a shelf.

I attempted to introduce reason. "The police force is in Lebanon nothing like we enjoy here." I reminded her of the size of Fayetteville, North Carolina's law enforcement team.

"Michelle, that is the point!" she said emphatically. "They aren't a huge police force, and how many crimes do they encounter of this magnitude? Why wouldn't they pursue this every couple years?"

"I don't know, I just don't know," I said, exasperated. "Let's assume that the officials believed they tried a guilty man and he managed to walk away, so they didn't pursue it any further. I don't have the answers, but I think that the day we locate Art Root Jr. we will have some answers."

"I get the feeling we're moving in circles." Susan didn't sound optimistic. "We stand a better chance of finding Jimmy Hoffa."

"Well when we're done with this, we can put Jimmy Hoffa on our list of things to do, but right now I think we need to see this through. We are limited on our knowledge of the green belt and dust mop, but the possibilities of Root's whereabouts are endless, and one doesn't need certification in law enforcement to find him; we just need to be thorough in our search."

"Detective Hall could put his name in the computer at the police station and offer that much assistance."

She was right.

"It's probably in our best interest to use the detective as a tool rather than a source. He is only able to help us so much and that's fine because if we do this together and we do it correctly we will know for a fact our information is correct. I don't think it is wise to trust anything that we can't confirm on our own. I don't ever want us to ever get so blind-sighted that we think we are detectives or we're staging an investigation, but we aren't crossing any lines by carefully reviewing everything we possibly can." I gave my friend a pep talk.

"I have no real desire to call Art Root's mother and ask her about her son, but I did a little bit of checking and she is still alive, so that is an option. The obituaries we read listed surviving siblings and thanks to the internet, I located what could be one of his brothers, again another consideration. Root and his family returned to Lebanon after living in Illinois."

I was on a roll "Illinois deserves some effort."

"Oh my friend, but I have researched Illinois," she said quickly. "I covered everything from looking for records recording their marriage, their children's births, and anything else I could think of, and I came up empty handed. I even contacted the churches in the town that was listed as their place of residence hoping to stumble across a church record of their nuptials. I took the time to focus on his wife solely, but after all this time it's safe to say she has probably remarried and has a different last name. I got so frustrated I paid one of those stupid people locator services to research both his known names and to date that was pretty much a waste of time and money."

"My apologies!" I teased. "I didn't know I was working with such a professional."

"There's nothing professional about it," she said with a frown. "I just don't think the guy fell off the face of the earth, and I've been racking my brains trying to find the little weasel, but that's easier said than done."

"Well," I thought hard for a minute or so, "Oklahoma is still an option because we know he lived there at some point."

"I've been there and done that too, and there is not one single record to be found there either." Susan didn't need my suggestions. She was thorough on her own accord. "I'm telling you, he is a ghost. The guy could be in the CIA for all we know."

"We both know his criminal history is not going to permit him to be a secret agent, but you might be making more sense than we realize."

I winked at my partner in research and said, "What if he's in the witness protection program? Damn, Susan! That would explain every obstacle to locating him including retired criminal records."

"That's really nice, Michelle. Now we're engaging in mission impossible."

"I don't know about that. I'm just considering all possibilities, and in light of the difficulty we're having in finding any trace of him, maybe that's because he had some help with his disappearing act. I don't think we can rule anything out until we know something for sure, and that is again where I will repeat myself by saying we can't take the word of any one at this point; we need to see it for ourselves before we actually believe it."

••

The headlines following the crime centered on locating the sex maniac responsible for the brutal slaying, and law enforcement feared the assailant could strike again. Peggy's death mustered the effort of scores of law enforcement officers from across the region and they worked around the clock to harness the evil that dwelled among them.

The community was beside itself with shock and fear at the same time.

The heinous nature of Peggy's murder is shocking even by today's standards, but in 1968 the sadistic twist to Peggy's death was bizarre. Law enforcement met a huge challenge toe to toe, but they weren't truly equipped to deal with a killer such as Peggy's.

Technology available did not include criminal profiling, DNA, or many of the other wonderful tools currently utilized to solve crime, so law enforcement officers battled the odds against a killer that did not stand holding a smoking gun. Officials pursued a sex maniac, and that thought danced on my mind until it drove me wild.

Police sought a sex maniac in a crime that did not really prove a sexual assault. The medical examiner testified that Peggy suffered brain damage due to strangulation by a dress belt. The left side of Peggy's face was beaten. Peggy's killer then took a five-foot archery bow and sodomized her, repeatedly puncturing her heart with the bow. Peggy's murder was brutal and violent, but it was not sexual in nature, yet police sought a sex maniac. It was a crime of mutilation and extreme violence, but I could not wrap my thoughts around a sexual deviant as the killer.

Strangulation causing brain damage could take up to four minutes. There is an old joke that goes, 'Five minutes can be a long time or short time. It just depends which side of the bathroom door one is standing.' Peggy was definitely on the wrong side of the door.

I took a deep breath and held it until I could not hold it any longer, and I watched the seconds tick by on the clock. I sat quietly in my own home attempting to deprive myself of oxygen in an effort to understand what Peggy endured, but that was a joke, because I was not fighting for air or in a struggle for my life during my silly little test. I was free to breath at will at any time of my choosing, and Peggy was not that fortunate. Four minutes devoted to depriving the victim of air translated into an eternity of torture for the teen, but the killer was a completely different story. Murder committed with a gun is rapid beyond one's imagination, and even a stabbing embraces speed to some degree, but strangulation along the lines of what Peggy endured was a time consuming act. Four minutes into the attack and the killer was not repulsed with himself and he was nowhere near done with her.

The left side of Peggy's face was beaten, and I immediately accepted the theory her killer was right-handed. She was beaten, but not to the point of death, and she was strangled, but in what order did those acts take place? It was a known fact that the walls in the building were paper-thin and tenants in the building could hear most all the goings- on in other apartments, yet no one heard anything that fateful day. Surely, Peggy would have screamed if someone struck her in the face.

The crazed lunatic then traveled a course that put him in a unique class among killers; he focused the remainder of his assault on the teen by means of sodomy with foreign objects, to include a five-foot archery bow. The medical examiner told the jury that the killer inserted and withdrew the archery bow at least ten times. Peggy's perforated internal organs included the left lung, stomach, bowel, liver and heart. Peggy's heart had five holes in it, and the bow protruded between two ribs and settled just under the skin in her chest area. The medical examiner stated Peggy suffered a puncture to her lower intestine the size of a man's fist. The bow was not the only weapon that mutilated Peggy's body, but court testimony never identified the other weapons. Failure to identify all the weapons left the jury ignorant concerning Peggy's final minutes. I understood the defense attorney did not want to enrage the jury with brutal details of the murder because his loyalty was to his client's defense, but I questioned why a prosecutor would not outline all the torture the victim endured.

The medical examiner testified that he could find no obvious evidence of a sexual assault during the autopsy examination. Everything detailing Peggy's murder oozed of anger not lust, yet the authorities pursued a sex maniac. The newspaper reports made repeated references to the assault with the bow to Peggy's lower body, but at no point did the paper literally report that it was a rectal assault, so I wondered how many people thought the sex maniac killer assaulted Peggy vaginally.

A U.S. Navy dental expert testified about a bite mark inflicted on Peggy's left breast. The oral pathologist testified Peggy suffered the bite a maximum of thirty minutes before her death, but he added he thought the time range was probably much shorter. The bite mark was a controversial factor in the pursuing Peggy's executioner. Eight dental impressions from males questioned in regards to the case provided the expert comparisons to attempt to identify the teeth that inflicted the wound. The Naval Captain stated he ruled out Arthur Root Jr. as a source for the wound because his teeth did not match the bite mark. He concluded his testimony stating Peggy's boyfriend had the dental impression with the closest match. However, Ray Boyer was the only man close to Peggy that had an ironclad alibi; he was in jail. Eight dental impressions and the expert placed his professional opinion on the one man jailed the night the crime occurred, but even that was not an exact match.

I was not familiar with all the names attached to the dental impressions, but something caught my eye instantly; Peggy's brother-in-law was not included on the list. The older Boyer was angry enough to deprive the teen bootlegged electricity hours before her death and he had a key to the dwelling that hosted the murder. I was not donning a badge, but he was certainly worthy of giving a dental impression, too. Ray Boyer's dental impression was a close match, and his brother did not submit a dental impression at all. The homemaker in me came to life because a female friend recently complained to me about orthodontic bills; her children both shared the same dental imperfections requiring braces and it was quite expensive. It was not unreasonable to think the Boyer brothers could share the same dental imperfections, too. I wasn't a genius and the police weren't stupid, but how did that happen? Why wasn't every man with a key to the Reber apartment subjected to dental impressions? Mary Alice listed Dick Boyer as a man that had a key to the apartment early in the investigation, so it wasn't an oversight, but it didn't make sense either.

"The more I learn, the less I understand," I wrote to Donald Hall as I vented my frustration. I had great difficulty understanding how a district attorney could campaign for the death penalty without revealing every weapon used against Peggy, and how the one person displaying anger toward the kid escaped submitting dental impressions. The more I learned the less I understood the case against Art Root Jr.

Donald Hall responded diplomatically, "I have to rule out any suspects including Root." Donald encouraged me to research the crime from scratch using the theory of good old fashioned police work, and he cautioned me about focusing on a suspect and having my facts confirm my suspicions.

"A good investigator collects facts and they identify the suspect, not the other way around."

Realistically speaking Donald was correct, but I wasn't trained or qualified to engage in good old fashioned police work. I was at best an aspiring author, not a cop. Donald could not reveal the other items used to mutilate Peggy, and he gave hint to Dick Boyer having an alibi and passing a polygraph test, so the dental impressions were not so important after all.

"This guy is really starting to work my last nerve," Susan said as she read Donald Hall's latest correspondence. "He doesn't give a single straight answer to any question asked and yet he wants you to share anything we learn along the way. I don't think he knows a damn thing about Peggy. He wasn't old enough to be on the force back then, so our guess is as good as his."

"Don't be ridiculous!" I was stunned by her outburst. "We aren't exactly real live law enforcement officers, my friend."

"Yeah, we're better." She was cocky. "We are intelligent, determined and we aren't restricted by the rules of the trade. We don't exactly know how to investigate a murder, so it is not as if we can do anything wrong, and it looks like the professionals took a few short cuts that we don't even know exist. Our stupid asses think Dick Boyer's teeth deserve consideration, so what was the worst thing that could happen if they made him chomp down on some play dough? Screw his alibi and his polygraph. Our ignorant minds scream ALL key holders need to bite the clay mold and if the powers that ruled missed that, we are already a step ahead of the world. Don't even get me started on the omission of details surrounding what was used to mutilate Peggy."

"I agree if the kid had to endure it then the state owed it to her and the jury to tell the whole truth during the trial. You're preaching to the choir, but we still aren't equipped to solve this crime." I knew my limitations.

"I want to remind you of something," Susan said solemnly. "We stood on that girl's grave and told her we would learn the truth or we wouldn't return. Well not only are we going to return, but we are going to place beautiful flowers on her grave. Of course we can't put a killer behind bars, but we can turn over every rock we encounter, kick down every brick wall that gets in our way, and together we will figure out what went wrong thirty years ago."

"I just want to understand what took place thirty years ago, and I'm not talking about the insanity that cost a young teen her life. I do not understand an entire apartment building and nobody hears a thing. I do not understand the brother-in-law's anger and he escapes dental impressions. I do not understand two people committing suicide in the midst of the investigation. I do not understand Ray Boyer's untimely apprehension. I do not understand mystery murder weapons lightly mentioned, yet not identified for the jury. I could go on and on," I said with frustration.

"Did that idiot ever answer the question about the belt around Peggy's neck not matching the dress she was wearing?" Susan was still bitching about the detective. I nodded my head indicating he did not respond to the question.

"What in the hell is he waiting for? I won't tell you what to do, but he can take a long walk on a short pier because he hasn't done anything to help us. I would love to see those crime scene photos."

I wrinkled my brow at the thought of the gruesome pictures.

"You forget I am a nurse and that stuff doesn't affect me the same."

"I don't ever want to see those photographs." I shook my head. "In fact, this is so much more than I ever bargained for. I just wanted to know about the girl from the evening news. I still want to know about that girl. Hell, what music did the kid like?" Peggy was getting lost and in many ways, that is what happened to her decades before. I was growing tired of all the questions and technicalities that surfaced almost daily.

"I would love to read the autopsy file and see the crime scene pictures. I think we would understand a lot more with visual assistance. I know the case sits protected from strangers' eyes because it is unsolved, and you just know Lebanon is going to solve it someday," Susan said sarcastically. "And until they do, the case is not free to be explored by anyone else, but I would love to get a gander at that stuff."

"You make a good point." I snapped back to reality. "All the weapons used escape public record because the prosecutor didn't have them identified at the trial. The trial escapes a complete transcript, and now the case and file collect dust because it's an unsolved crime." I laughed a little. "I'm not a suspicious woman, but if I was," I gave a long pause and then continued, "I might start thinking that the world in general or someone in particular wants everything about Peggy to just go away. Damn, if she had the protection that the facts surrounding her murder receive she could have lived to be eighty." I felt my skepticism mounting. "Too much is shady in this nightmare. I'll buy into one mistake and maybe two, but there is a whole lot piling up in the big picture, and I'm not sure it was obvious to anyone watching at the time."

"Go on." Susan lit a cigarette and waited for me to continue.

"I'm repeating myself, but we have the benefit of three decades, not the disadvantage. We're looking for a transcript of the trial, but the general public didn't give that a second thought back then. We don't understand additional items used to mutilate her body slipping through a trial unidentified, but in 1968, there was a strong respect for authority. The community didn't have cause to question the process. We question the failure to get Dick Boyer's dental impression, and again the community probably did not recall he stripped her of lighting the night before the crime because a year and a half passed between his actions and the dental testimony. We're looking at a big picture and it's not logical, and if one looks closer at that big picture Peggy's case is never meant to meet truth and her killer will never see justice."

"Are you suggesting there is a conspiracy? Do you think that everything is deliberate?" Susan was out on a limb, and I was not sure I wanted to join her or hold on tight so I could rescue her.

"I don't know what I'm suggesting, but I know something smells bad, really bad, and it's not just the slaughter of a fourteen year old kid. I'm reminded of my Dad's frantic reaction when I mentioned pulling up newspaper articles when I was fourteen. God, I was Peggy's age then. My Dad didn't mention Art Root Jr. when he cautioned me, and that is strange. His warning was about lawyers, suicide, money, power and secrets, but not Art Root Jr." I could still see my Dad's face when I closed my eyes and his expression was fearful. "I'm not saying my Dad was the smartest man in town, but his spirit was too calm to rattle, yet the mention of this upset him, and so many others get uncomfortable at the mention of her name. I thought it was the stigma attached to the murder, but I am starting to wonder. I don't think anyone is going to dispute the horror of the crime and it isn't the most pleasant topic of conversation. That alone would be one thing, but the cancer is growing."

"It's no longer the mere reaction at the mention of her name," Susan said. "Nothing about Peggy's life or death is normal. Peggy's killer stands out in a line-up of some of the most notorious killers even on today's standards. The trial, errors in the investigation, a lack of a court transcript, the file sitting sheltered from view even today because it's an unsolved case is a lot to buy in to." Susan waited for me to look at her. "I come from a small town too." She was sympathetic. "Nobody wants to believe that home isn't the sweet fantasy we recall on holidays, but one doesn't have to be a professional investigator to see something is amiss in good ol' Lebanon when it comes to Peggy Reber."

I didn't like what I was hearing and I really didn't like what I was thinking, but some things just didn't make sense.

That night I closed my eyes to sleep, and images of Peggy's assailant taunted me throughout the night. I couldn't see the evil man and I couldn't hear him, but I knew the shadow in my dreams was his evil presence. I woke myself up several times throughout the night to escape the nightmare, but every time I closed my eyes he was there, yet he wasn't. I struggled to wake from the torment repeatedly. Finally, I gave up and got up because sleep was not possible.

Susan saw signs of life at my house earlier than the norm and joined me for a cup of tea. "Hey Jude, don't bring me dowwwn!" She entered the door singing an aged tune.

"I give up," I growled. "You are doing oldies karaoke or something like that." I was not a morning person at all.

"Not quite." She was too damn happy, and it was too early in the day, so I didn't bother to respond to her. "You wanted to know about what music Peggy liked, so I did some homework." She continued singing the stale song. "I am serenading you with the number one song of 1968, my dear."

"How do you know Peggy liked that song?" I questioned her.

"She was fourteen-years-old, and it was the number one song of the year. Oh, and it was The Beatles. I emailed you the top 100 songs for that year, and I think it's safe to say the kid liked something on that list. After all, she was a teenager. I am not an authority on murder, but I know teenagers." The mother of four laughed at herself. Our interest in Peggy was not going to win us an award for normalcy amongst the other women on the block.

"I had hellacious nightmares last night," I said, staring into my teacup. "Sometimes I want to toss my hands up and chalk this up as ancient history, but after last night," I lifted my head, "Not a chance."

"Do you want to explain?"

"It's not that complicated. Some sorry bastard consumed with evil got away with murder. I don't know about a conspiracy theory, or any of the obvious things that slip through the cracks, but I do know a kid died, and the man that did it never paid for the crime. The press put Peggy's mother on trial due to her lifestyle, yet the real loser in the picture remains in the shadows. There was doubt if the killer entered the apartment intending to kill Peggy, but I don't have any doubts at all. He didn't go equipped with weapons, but he definitely had the intent. Donald Hall explained the difference of an organized killer and an unorganized killer to me. Peggy's killer lacked organization in his madness, but her death was not an accident. The dress belt and the bow were in the apartment when he got there, so he used what was readily available. The lunatic didn't value Peggy's life. He played out a sick fantasy of inflicting great pain and torture. I don't think his fantasies died with Peggy. I don't think one can engage in such a murderous frenzy and lead a normal life."

"What if he didn't intend to kill Peggy? What if he just wanted to get close to her and she rejected him? She was a beautiful girl and she was alone. The idiot didn't take weapons with him, so let's assume he entered the apartment and viewed Peggy's isolation as an opportunity, and the rejection made him snap."

"Call me crazy, but he took rejection to a new level if that's what took place, and I won't budge when I say there is no way in hell he went on to live a normal life."

"Do you think he killed other people, too?"

69

"I don't know." I shrugged my shoulders. "But to my untrained eye, he thought about killing before that day. Maybe not killing Peggy, but killing someone, and he enjoyed every damn minute of it. Think about everything you know about serial killers. They kill to achieve a sick satisfaction, and one kill doesn't pacify the desire, so they kill again."

"You're right Michelle, but serial killer means just that," she said as she raised her eyebrows. "We only have one corpse and I really think Lebanon would have noticed if some maniac kept ramming bows into teenage girls."

"I would hope!" I snickered. "But the bow is not the killer's signature, the bow was just handy at the time; anger and rage are the killer's identifiers. I wonder if Lebanon hosted other brutal murders and missed his signature because the bow attracted so much attention."

"What if the killer wasn't a resident, but a transient?" Susan offered.

"Nothing is impossible, but we know one thing for certain: the killer was not a stranger to the Reber apartment, and I personally think he is right there under everyone's nose the whole time. But how does he go unnoticed? There is so much to digest with the whole thing and the possibilities are endless, but one stupid nightmare tapped me on the shoulder." I let out a deep sigh. "Peggy's killer is made up of nothing but evil, and he can't conceal that evil forever."

"Why don't you ask that good-for-nothing cop about other murders in the area? He wouldn't be compromising any top secret information by answering that question, and I am anxious to see if he is capable of giving a straight answer."

"Touché my dear. There is no harm done in asking him."

Donald was impressed that my thinking was outside the box, and he commended my resistance to accept everything as it appeared. He didn't recall any violent murders after Peggy's death, but he shared a rumor that circulated around the area following the crime, and he cautioned me it was simply a rumor. One of the tenants in Peggy's building was a construction worker and he was a suspect along with every other male in town, but after questioning, detectives ruled him out. However, there was a tale of a murder committed in upstate New York involving a bow and that construction worker was working in New York at the time.

"Michelle, take the time to review the tenants in the building." Donald's words sounded simple, but three decades later with the building destroyed, the likelihood of success was limited. How in the hell was I going to find those tenants?

▪▪▪

"Mr. Root, I apologize for bothering you, and I know this phone call is going to be strange, but I am calling about your brother Arthur." My shaky voice exposed my nervousness.

"Who are you? And what do you know about Arthur?" His nervousness was obvious too.

"Mr. Root, my name is Michelle Gooden. You don't know me, and I realize the oddity of this call, but I am attempting to locate your brother. Do you know where I could find your brother Art right now?" I held my breath waiting for his answer.

"I haven't seen him in years. I'm sorry, but I can't help you," He replied shortly, implying his discomfort with the nature of the call.

"Listen, I am a native of Lebanon, Pennsylvania. I have been looking for your brother for months." I didn't want to mention Peggy's name. After all, Arthur Root Jr. was found not guilty in the crime. "Records in Lebanon indicate your brother is deceased, yet it doesn't appear that your family is aware of his passing."

"Is Arthur dead?" his voice lowered as he asked the sober question.

"I don't know, Mr. Root. That's what I am trying to find out and that is the purpose of this call."

"I told you I haven't seen or heard from him in years, so I can't help you." I could tell he was not going to allow the conversation to go on much longer.

"Mr. Root, when was the last time you talked to your brother and where was he living at that time?" I held my breath and waited for his reply.

"It's been a long, long time, but he used to call every now and then and tell us how his kids were doing in Oklahoma." I could sense nostalgia in his voice as he spoke.

"He would tell you how his daughters were doing. Are those the same daughters he fathered in the 60s?" I hesitated from bringing up the trial, but I remembered the pictures in the newspaper of Arthur Root Jr.'s beautiful wife and two small daughters.

"No, no, no," he quickly corrected me. "He got married again to some girl from Oklahoma."

"Look, I don't want to deceive you," I said, deciding to put my cards on the table. "I am looking into the murder of Peggy Reber, I wanted to know how your brother recovered after standing trial for the crime and that is what led me to you. Lebanon municipality has him listed as dead. However, as I researched reports of your family's obituaries, he is never listed as dead, so I had to wonder if the family considered him dead."

"No we were never told he's dead, but we haven't heard from him in years, so it could be." The man sounded resigned.

"Where in Oklahoma did he live?"

"It's been so long, I really couldn't tell you."

"What happened to his first wife?"

"Oh we lost touch years ago. After that, everything changed and we didn't keep up with them." I knew he was referring to the trial. "If I might ask, how did you find me?"

"I saw your name and state of residence listed in your father's obituary and then I looked through telephone listings. I do apologize, but I didn't want to call your mother, and yet I wanted to know if your family was ever informed of his passing."

"No, not at all," he said finally, and we both knew the phone call was complete. "Should you find him one way or the other," he cleared his throat, "I would really appreciate it if you would call me again and let me know what you learn."

Detective Donald Hall told me Art Root Jr. died out west somewhere, and there was some mention about a request for his fingerprints to identify the body. That was supposedly the inspiration for retiring Root's criminal file. For all intents and purposes, Art Root Jr. was dead in the eyes of Lebanon's police department, but no one bothered to notify his family.

I bolted to the computer to email Donald because two and two was not adding up to four. Donald's response was mechanical; Lebanon's police department was not responsible for notifying the deceased's mother, simply to provide the requesting law enforcement agency a copy of the fingerprints on file. Oh, I wasn't impressed with that answer at all and flames flew from my keyboard as I typed my reply.

Lebanon is growing, and its police department - much like every other police department across the nation - is overworked. But not one of the forty police officers could take the time to notify an aged resident that her son died, or that a request was made for his fingerprints on file.

Regulations did not require such effort, but basic courtesy and a sincere effort to protect and serve did. I no longer trusted the practices of Lebanon's police department and I certainly didn't believe Arthur Root Jr. was dead.

I returned to Lebanon in 1996 and I will never forget the front-page headlines. The police incorrectly identified a victim fatally struck by a train. Police told a mother her son was dead, and after reading his own obituary in the newspaper, the son called his mother on the phone to correct the misunderstanding. That was one hell of a mistake!

The incorrect identification of a corpse even in 1996 was inexcusable. I did not even think about that fiasco until the subject of Art Root Jr. found me. I was not on a mission to crucify the Lebanon police department, and equally, I was not going to accept their word without careful scrutiny for obvious reasons. Donald Hall was a part of that police department.

Donald never answered my inquiry about the green dress belt. He said he missed it, and he was certain the original investigators lost sight of it. I urged him to take the time to go to the evidence room and review it personally, and he failed to share his findings. Donald Hall finally provided a few answers: the current chief of police recently gave a foolish interview and stressed the actions of the female officer terminated for taking the Reber murder file home were justified because the file was all that remained of Peggy's case.

Donald reminded me that in 1972, Lebanon saw a flood that marked history and all the physical evidence pertaining to Peggy's murder was lost when the basement of the courthouse submerged in water. I remembered the flood vividly and Lebanon suffered catastrophic damage and losses. Donald Hall was telling me that the one of the losses Lebanon suffered during the natural disaster was the physical evidence in one of the county's worst homicides. He could not go to the evidence room to confirm the color of the belt used to strangle Peggy because it was gone along with everything else related to the case including the bow. He explained that he could not share that information before and the only reason he was revealing it was that the chief of police admitted as much to a newspaper reporter.

Donald vented his own frustrations because he didn't understand why a high-ranking law enforcement officer would expose such an important detail about an unsolved case. "Michelle he publicly told everyone and quite possibly the killer that all physical evidence is lost and that means the only way this case will be solved is with a confession." I slid back into my computer chair and read his letter a dozen times. Mother Nature and the chief of police joined the ranks of those that managed to step on the teenage girl once again.

"The chief of police did what?" Susan was stunned.

"He played the government's hand in a public forum. It was a crazy move for anyone, but for a man of his stature it was stupidity at its finest."

"No Michelle, that's not stupidity. That's politics. He didn't compromise Peggy's justice because he didn't care about Peggy's justice; he tried to nail that female cop to a wall and he's using Peggy to do it. The chief of police is attempting to hold that cop responsible for Peggy's case going unsolved, and again the general population does not share our benefit of a big picture perspective. Peggy is just a name from the past for him and she is not a factor in today's world, so he sold out any chance she had at justice to save a current lawsuit settlement."

"Maybe he didn't understand the mistake he was making."

"Well if he didn't understand the power of announcing that all physical evidence is lost in an unsolved murder, he sure as hell doesn't deserve to be chief of police. He would be lucky to issue parking tickets downtown if I were the mayor."

I rubbed my face with both hands in frustration. "I don't care about a loose-lipped chief of police, I don't care about some female cop that took this file home, but I can't help but care about the one thing that is constantly lost in this picture and that is Margaret Lynn Reber. Thirty years ago, the district attorney didn't talk about all the evidence in the case and now a top-ranking cop wants to admit everything is gone. Peggy's damned if they don't and she's damned if they do." I dropped my hands from my face. "Let's do it."

I got a pen and paper. "Since we don't have the testimony of the experts, I elect we find them. The oral pathologist had a very common name, so he will be the biggest challenge, but let's find those other jokers."

"And our goal would be?" Susan needed definition.

"What it has always been," I said resolutely. "Learning the truth about Peggy."

"Michelle, the evidence is lost. We're swimming upstream."

"Upstream, downstream," I playfully teased. "We're still swimming, and after watching the professionals do this, I've realized we can't hurt a damn thing. I wanted to write a book about Peggy and I longed to keep it tasteful, tactful and real."

I paused and collected my thoughts for a moment before continuing. "I may never write that book, but together we will uncover as much about Peggy Reber and the cast of characters in play that we can. I didn't want to push, offend, or violate anyone, but we are going into this with no holds barred. We are going to locate everyone and anyone that we can because after talking to Art Root's brother I know it's the right thing to do. The evidence is lost and the expert testimony was not recorded, but there is a slim chance those experts are still alive, so let's find them. I cannot defend the actions of the chief of police, but I can condemn the actions taken against Peggy and after his revealing interview, justice is a mere fantasy. So anything from this point on is truth learned."

"Wouldn't it be great if we had a criminal psychic?" Susan broke the mood. "It sounds crazy, but there are cases involving missing children where the authorities have used them."

"Listen woman, if you start talking about Ouija boards or performing a séance, I'm going to measure you for a straight jacket." I laughed, but I wasn't joking. I was willing to turn over any rock on the path to discovering the truth, but I was going to exercise prudence every step along the way. "Oh and strictly for your benefit I asked Donald about the autopsy report and he told me that he never saw that in the file."

"Why wouldn't the autopsy report be in that file?" Susan wondered aloud.

"I'm guessing the autopsy report is not included because it would sit in the D.A.'s file. Keep in mind police are responsible for investigating the crime and that would include collecting evidence, interviewing suspects and gathering facts, but the autopsy could fall under information used to prosecute the case. Now when I am elected king I will place a copy of autopsy reports in police files, prosecutor files, coroner files and I will even have a special vault for unsolved cases so floods or other natural disasters can't jeopardize evidence."

"What a great idea, Your Majesty." Susan pretended to bow down to my royal presence.

"I know I run the risk of opening an aged wound, but I am going to call Peggy's dad. I saw his name is listed in the phone book and Larry Kelly said he heard Mr. Reber will talk about the case, so it's worth a phone call."

"I still can't imagine the loss that man suffered."

"And it is because he suffered such a loss that I hesitate on calling him, but it's a chance I am willing to take. He lost his daughter and no one paid for taking her life. That has to compound the agony to some degree."

"He adopted Peggy, didn't he?"

"If the newspaper is correct, he married Mary Alice when she was pregnant with the twins, but the report was conflicting, so I'm not sure if the adoption finalized."

Herman Reber's Pennsylvania-Dutch accent brought a smile to my face because it was a dialect unique to the area. Herman was semi-retired and lived a quiet uneventful life on the fringe of Lebanon County and he did not take offense to the request to discuss his late daughter. Herman harbored bitterness about the collapse of his marriage to Peggy's mother, and he placed all blame on her. I listened carefully, but I knew enough from my own wedded union that every marriage has three sides to every story: his side, her side, and the truth.

He disapproved of Peggy's environment, and he offered Peggy refuge in his home. Unfortunately, she was fourteen and there were rules to follow in his home, and she didn't have rules at her mother's. I heard sadness in his voice and he explained that he couldn't force her to get out of there, but it was obvious he credited Peggy's vulnerability to the unstructured, undisciplined and unprotected environment on Maple Street. I smiled again because he talked about Peggy alive with typical teenage opinions and it was refreshing to hear about Peggy the person instead of Peggy the victim.

Herman talked to me the better part of two hours and while I didn't learn any earth shaking information, he shared his role in the nightmare and I gained great respect for a simple man. We agreed to meet for a bologna sandwich my next trip home, and I sincerely wanted to keep that date. I asked him if he had any pictures of Peggy and he told me he had Peggy's school picture, the same picture I originally saw on the evening news. I asked the kind stranger if I could borrow the picture, and I assured him it would be safely returned to him in a matter of hours. It had to be priceless to the man that bought the girl a headstone five years after her passing. My cousin Anne was stunned by my queer request but accommodating nonetheless; she agreed to retrieve the photo get it scanned on a computer disc immediately turn around and return the treasure to Peggy's dad in a matter of hours.

"Anne, I want you to have it scanned on two separate discs and mail them to me in two separate envelopes."

"Why? Is big brother watching us?" she asked sarcastically.

"Not quite. This is a one time opportunity and I don't want to risk losing it in the mail, so it's worth an extra two bucks to guarantee we don't lose the picture."

"Michelle, you have lived next to Fort Bragg too long because you're starting to sound like you're running a special operation." She laughed at her own humor.

"Hey!" I teased, "When I start wearing funny colored berets or jumping out of perfectly good airplanes you have my permission to slap me, but until then I am just trying to avoid any potential obstacle I foresee. If that means two envelopes and two discs, so be it." She thought I was being paranoid, but I knew I was being thorough.

After talking to Anne, I chuckled at the joke she made in reference to Fort Bragg, and I really thought about that for a minute. Fort Bragg, North Carolina is home of Special Operations and the infamous Green Beret and 82nd Airborne Division, they are some of the best-trained soldiers in the world, but in Fayetteville they are merely soldiers. Fayetteville, North Carolina residents don't worship the military warriors stationed at Fort Bragg, rather we share a community, and I thought of the many soldiers I have known over the years. I remembered a young military man dressed in civilian clothes tugging on his ball cap sporting the logo of his favorite baseball team. "Man, I hate leaving the country because I have to give up my cap!"

Soldiers are soldiers twenty-four hours a day, but they do get time off even on foreign soil, so I didn't understand his comment. "Michelle, the baseball cap screams 'American', and when your ass is sitting somewhere that you want to go unnoticed you have to give up the cap."

I never realized the ball cap was a staple of American fashion, but I did know that soldiers were drilled to blend into different cultures. I wanted to blend into Lebanon and I had an advantage unlike most soldiers because I grew up there, so I tried to remind myself of my roots. I paced around my dining room thinking about every detail from my childhood and I forced myself to remember annual city events, locations of importance, popular people, city transportation, the local hospitals, and the weather.

The city celebrated Memorial Day in a large way, so there was a parade and a ceremony just days following Peggy's death and the first Saturday in June hosts the annual hospital fund-raiser that everyone in the county attends. I remembered the weekend market that boasted fresh fruits, vegetables and meat. I remembered cutting up confetti for parades until the city banned it because of it collecting within the horns of local marching bands. I remembered the fresh smell of rain in the spring, the changing of the autumn leaves and winter snowfall. Oh yeah, I remembered winter because I shoveled a sidewalk or two. It was just a way of life.

"Tonight we are having steaks, salad, cheesecake and I am going to buy name brand soft drinks for a change. We are going to eat well, live large and party!" I called Susan oozing with excitement.

"Oh no! She's buying name brand soda!" Susan started to laugh.

"Girl!" I squealed. "I am so good, you should be happy I am in the neighborhood!" I giggled like a fool and clapped my hands in delight. "I found him, I found him, I found him!" I couldn't contain my joy.

"Okaaaaay . . ." Her voice dragged out and she was not impressed with my hysteria.

"I found Arthur M. Root Jr.! I found him. He's not dead, and I am slap damn happy!"

"What?" she was shocked.

"I just thought like anyone from my hometown when I was growing up there and it snowed," I excitedly explained. "Every winter it snows because that is just a part of life in central Pennsylvania and every time it snows, some poor guy says he wants to be in Florida."

"The Sunshine State," she murmured quietly, but I knew her West Virginia roots understood.

"Yes, the Sunshine State," I echoed. "Arthur Root Jr. retreated to the eclectic population surrounded by sand, sun and fun. Of course judging by the criminal record, I see he didn't fare too well."

"You just called and inquired about Art Root, and lights started flashing and the red carpet rolled out? I call every government office, church, school and cemetery in six states and you make one little phone call?" My friend was pleased and irritated with the success at hand.

"If it makes you feel any better I didn't hit gold with the name Arthur Root. I located his alias, and even that was weird because I was spelling it the way he spelled it in 1968 and the woman in Florida was spelling it differently, so I took a chance with the different spelling and I got lucky." I handed her the criminal record that I purchased on the internet courtesy of Florida's department of corrections.

"Michelle, he has over a dozen aliases!" Susan said, fascinated. "He's got more social security numbers than my entire household." I waited for her to finish reading the report. "What does all this mean?"

"It means he is not dead"

"That's obvious. So did you talk to him yet?" she was eager.

"Not quite."

"What do you mean, not quite? We finally found him and after all the time we devoted into locating him. I don't want to hear anything about stupid reservations, so don't even think about being polite or courteous."

"No proper manners in play." I defended myself. "Do you see the many identities the man has adopted?" I didn't wait for an answer "That is how many avenues there are to follow now because he is no longer in Florida. At least not using any of the names listed."

"Say what?" She threw her hands down, obviously frustrated. "You mean we found him, but we didn't, and now we have ten times the names to research?" She was not a happy camper.

I tried to sound encouraging. "We made progress today." I waited for her to show some sign of optimism.

"Michelle this is not progress. This is dissolving into chaos. We couldn't find him when we had two names to research and now the number is hitting astronomical proportions. I don't understand how you can view this as a victory."

"Think, Susan." I took a chance. "You're a nurse, and a nurse knows that a pulse means hope. Hope means you can't give up. We've got a pulse." I studied her face. "We don't have much, but we have something."

"Michelle I love you like a sister, and I believe in what we're trying to do, but look at this list of names this guy has manufactured for himself. We put a year of effort into two names he adopted and came up with nothing. It could take us five years to follow up on his multiple personalities."

"The victory is that we know he is alive," I pointed out. "We also know that he lived in Oklahoma at some point, so I am assuming that one of these names will show up in Oklahoma, but hell, that's just a guess on my part." I shrugged my shoulders. "Who knows?" Silence embraced the room. "I found him, I found him, I found him!" I broke the mood chanting with delight. I did not find Art Root Jr.'s body, but I did find a pulse and I was excited.

It took a few minutes, but she soon joined me "We found him, we found him, we found him!" And together we sang a new tune.

Arthur Root JR was not dead, but alive and living under assumed identities. He hosted a wide range of criminal charges in the Sunshine State, but nothing of a violent nature. He continued to be a petty con, but nothing to suggest he was a killer. He was alive everywhere except Lebanon, and one had to wonder why?

■■

Foolishly, I scanned telephone listings in Oklahoma looking for Arthur Root Jr. and his most recent and popular alias. I did not think in terms of a law enforcement officer because naturally, a cop would have checked his criminal record first, but I was not a professional, so I took the high road. The high road left me calling several people that found me to be very insane, but late one night I took a chance calling one of the last names listed. I ran through my usual introduction and caught a nerve on the other end.

"Who are you looking for?"

I explained to the young voice that I probably wanted to talk to her mother or father, and I knew I insulted her by my request because she was clearly of legal age to vote. I explained to the defensive young female that I was calling about an aged matter, and I was probably barking up a dead tree.

"What do you know about my father? You need to tell me what you know."

I heard desperation in the girl's tone and it made me uncomfortable. "I don't know that I am calling about your father."

She quoted the name I mentioned at the beginning of the call. "He doesn't live here, but he is my father, so why are you calling?" A matter of seconds passed. "Tell me what you know about him."

"I . . . I don't know anything about him," I stammered. "That's why I'm calling." I entered an emotional whirlpool, and I was at a loss for words. "I am actually looking for a man named Arthur Root Jr., and a string of accidents caught me dialing your phone number."

"But you asked for my dad," she said desperately. "So please tell me what you know about my dad."

"I was just asking about a name I have on a list," I tried to explain to the eager recipient. "The man I am looking for could be anyone. I'm not sure it's your dad at all." I repeated my request to talk to her mother.

"My mother is busy."

I doubted her because I heard an older female asking who was on the phone, and I could tell the young woman took the phone into another room to talk to me. "We haven't heard from my dad in years, and I need to know whatever you know about him."

I was definitely in over my head. "I am being very honest with you. I don't know anything about your dad. I am looking for a man that actually has a completely different name, and he is originally from Pennsylvania. I found the name that matches your father's listed on a criminal record in another state, so it's probably not your dad at all and just a big mistake on my part. I'm sorry for bothering you." I wanted to hang up.

"Well just tell me what you know because I think my dad did live in Pennsylvania a long time ago." She wasn't going to give up. "I need to know anything you can tell me about my father."

"Well, my name is Michelle, and I don't know the man I am looking for, but I did know his father, and I almost hate to tell you why I am looking for him." I struggled to find a tactful way to tell the girl about Peggy, and she sensed my discomfort.

"I'm Savannah." I heard her voice soften. "I am not going to be surprised at anything you tell me, but I want to hear what you have to say," she paused. "You knew my grandfather?"

"I don't know." I didn't like the situation. "I don't know if I knew your grandfather. I don't know if your dad and the man I am looking for are the same person, and I hate myself for even making this phone call. I got it in my head to research an old crime that took place in my hometown in Pennsylvania. I started looking for the man that was charged with the crime: Arthur Root Jr." Savannah's father's name was not Arthur Root Jr. "Well, I stumbled across a few other names that Arthur Root Jr. adopted and I know Root lived in Oklahoma, so that is why I called your number." I was rambling. "Please forgive the intrusion."

"You didn't do anything wrong, and I am really glad you called." I heard a rustling, and then a pause, and then she lowered her voice. "If there's a chance this Arthur Root could be my dad I need to know it. I haven't seen my dad in years and no one will really talk about him, so I want to hear whatever you have to say."

"Look, Savannah," I said cautiously. "It's not my place to tell you anything, because it might not have a damn thing to do with you, and ultimately it would do more harm than good." I knew the female stranger was not going to be satisfied with my reasoning. "But I will make you this offer because I want to be fair. Since you will not allow me to talk to your mother, I want you to talk to her and perhaps she can shed some light on this for you. I will give you my phone number and if there is a chance that the man I am looking for and your dad are the same person, feel free to call me, but until there is some reason to believe there is a connection I am not going to detail anything."

I felt bad for ever involving the girl longing for information about an absentee dad, and I was not going to compound her anguish. I hung up the phone and I was sorry I made that call. I reminded myself that Arthur Root Jr. could stand up, admit to Peggy's murder, and offer the finest of details in front of the Supreme Court and it wouldn't matter because of double jeopardy. The United States Constitution guarantees that an individual will not face judgment twice for the same crime, so Arthur Root Jr. was free and clear concerning Peggy no matter what. I respected the jury's verdict, and I questioned pursuing the man at all.

I called the clerk of court's office in the county where Savannah and her mother resided. I decided to check one thing before I walked away from pursuing Arthur Root Jr. any further and that was his criminal record in Oklahoma. I explained to the friendly man answering the phone that I was hoping to obtain a criminal record for Arthur Root's alias and the man immediately recognized the assumed name. I inquired about his familiarity with the name and he opened up as if I was a friend of years.

"Oh, he was a bad man," he said disapprovingly. "He put his wife through pure hell, and it was a terrible thing what he did to her daughter."

I still wasn't sure we were talking about Arthur Root, but the mention of a woman's daughter set off panic within me.

"He went to jail for a long time and he deserved every minute of that sentence. His wife went to work one day at the truck stop out on the interstate and he raped her little girl, but she never believed it and stood by his side through the whole thing."

I immediately envisioned a small child, and Savannah came to mind.

"She was only twelve years old, and it was a damn shame what he did."

I understood why Savannah's dad was a silent subject in their household. I asked the man if he was talking about Savannah and he said he couldn't identify the girl's name for legal reasons, but it was not Savannah. He said the rape victim was a stepdaughter of the man and Savannah was his biological daughter.

"You know it's just dumb luck that you talked to me because I am probably the only person in this office that remembers him," he said. He explained the process to obtain the criminal record and he provided his email address in case I had any further questions. I hung up with a ton of questions, but I needed the criminal record and confirmation that the individual was Arthur Root Jr. before I said anything else. I thought of the close proximity of the age of Peggy at the time of death and the victim in Oklahoma and found it too close for comfort, but I refused to read too much into anything until I did my homework.

I stared at the offenses listed on the report until my eyes hurt, and then I stared at the heavens shaking my head in disbelief. The report I obtained did not identify Arthur Root Jr., but I knew Arthur Root's birthday because he faced formal charges for Peggy's murder on his 26th birthday in 1968, and while the year of birth on the Oklahoma report sported a different year than Root's, the day was the same. I guess I knew that was not mere coincidence. The offenses against the Oklahoma man were too close for comfort, too. The convictions against the alias were first-degree rape and the one that sent me into a tailspin was forcible sodomy. Peggy's killer sodomized her with an archery bow. I was certain Savannah's dad and Arthur Root were the same and I started to doubt the Pennsylvania jury's verdict. The word sodomy echoed throughout my head until I could hardly stand it. I was starting to believe Arthur Root Jr. got away with murder.

I cursed the day I decided to look into the story, and I finally agreed with my dad's warning. I didn't need to know about a dead kid, small town drama, or the morbid details attached to the crime. I didn't want to learn anymore, and I knew I learned too much to rest well any time soon. I left the house several hours to escape the mountain of articles, information and files related to Peggy and to clear my thinking. I couldn't stop thinking about everything I learned, and new questions kept nagging me. I didn't possess the skills to understand the criminal mind, so I sought out a friend that was a police detective in Fayetteville in hopes he would enlighten me.

"Michelle, what does the word sodomy mean?" Chris Acre asked me a simple question, but I could tell by his facial expression that the answer was not going to be simple.

"It's anal penetration"

"You're cute, and I like you a lot, but you're wrong." He winked at me. "Sodomy is not solely anal penetration. Legally, its definition can possess many meanings. I am not going to be a sidewalk lawyer and I certainly cannot discuss laws beyond the state of North Carolina, but don't assume the assault was rectal because of the word sodomy in the charge because you could be wrong. I want you to go home and look the word up in a standard dictionary and then find out the legal definition used in Oklahoma, and you may gain a different perspective. You could be unable to see things objectively because of that crime in Pennsylvania." Chris had knowledge of my pursuits with the aged crime.

"Chris, I am a rape survivor and I did a tremendous amount of research on rape and rapists after I was assaulted and I am familiar with the understood habits of pedophiles; both are serial criminals."

"That's a safe bet in most cases, but the challenge is getting victims to come forward. Too often the bastards get away with crimes, and we never really know the extent of their rampage."

"Well, if this guy in Oklahoma is the same guy I'm looking for, then something bothers me. According to the age listed in Oklahoma, he is forty-eight years old. He was twenty-six years old when Peggy was killed and there is no proof of sexual assault in Peggy's crime beyond the murderous mutilation with the bow, and we can't overlook that he was found to be not guilty. He has a lengthy criminal record, but not one violent crime or sexual assault. I don't get it, did he wake up one day and just decide to rape his twelve year old daughter, or has he been an evil force all along?"

"I can't answer those questions for you." Chris was a gentleman in every sense of the word and a true professional. "I will tell you one mistake that trained law enforcement officers make all the time, and it is the one thing you have in your favor; cops want to solve cases using books and training. Michelle, you don't have the benefit of the books or training and you don't have the closed mind either, so don't rule anything out because every criminal is unique no matter what general profiles tell us. The truth is crashing in on you right now and, experience speaking, it happens to all of us. This isn't your professional calling, so you can walk away right now, but sleep on it a night or two. Listen, I gotta go. Oh, look up the word sodomy, sweetheart, because you will be surprised at what you find." He raised his hand in a playful salute and darted out the door.

Sodomy \ ***1*** *copulation with a member of the same sex or with an animal* ***2*** *anal or oral copulation with a member of the opposite sex*

Chris was right. I was surprised with the standard definition of sodomy, and I was an intelligent and well-read person, so I was feeling intellectually vulnerable. I immediately assumed sodomy meant rectal assault, but that was not the case at all, so my connection of the mutilation of Peggy and the victim in Oklahoma was not necessarily correct. I didn't know what to think and my brain was tired, so I did the only thing I knew to do. I prayed. And I cried a bit, too.

▪▪▪

The banging on the door rousted me out of bed.

"I come bearing wonderful news!" Susan had doughnuts on a plate and a coffee cup in her hand. "I am a research assistant deserving of a raise!" She was doing that perky morning thing again and I wasn't sharing her energy. I didn't bother to complain. I alerted my teapot it was time to go to work, and I headed to the bathroom. Susan knew the routine only too well so she fed my dogs and chattered away a while.

"This better be good or I am not authorizing that raise you want." I stumbled out of the bathroom cracking a wise remark.

"Not one, not two, but three phone numbers for you to call." She handed me a piece of paper. "A court reporter," she handed me another paper, "A state trooper," and there was a third paper, "A juror."

"I don't know if I am speechless because I am barely awake, or if I am amazed at your progress."

"It better be that you're still half asleep," she teased. "I worked damn hard to find pre-historic beings."

My tea kettle began to whistle, and I poured some of the steaming contents into my mug. I dipped a tea bag in, watching the brown color seep into the pure water. "Susan, I love you to bits and pieces, and I truly appreciate your efforts," I let out a deep sigh. "But I don't know if I can make another phone call after all this nonsense in Oklahoma."

"Michelle, we don't even know that they are the same man." The perpetual optimist in Susan was always at work. "And though I love you too, I am not going to sit here for three hours and talk you into taking the next step. We agreed to take it one step at a time and as long as information was available we would follow up, so dust yourself off and drive on."

I wasn't ready to do battle with anyone and certainly not my best friend. "I'm tired," I yawned. "I am absolutely exhausted."

"Read my lips." She waited for me to look at her. "I. Don't. Care. Have a cup of tea, have a doughnut, take a shower and then call these people. We made an agreement and I am holding my end, so it's up to you."

"Oh, the beauty of the buddy system." I was sincere, but not very appreciative as I yawned and stretched. I struggled to get motivated because I needed to follow through, but apprehension tugged at me. Researching Peggy's murder was intimidating from the onset, but the intimidation fell to the side, and I developed concern about discovering a truth that would ultimately escape justice.

I reminded myself that the intent was never to solve the crime, but simply to tell Peggy's story. I checked my email over my second cup of tea and engaged in an electronic conversation with a friend from Pennsylvania. I lightly explained the project surrounding Peggy, and my friend expressed amazement that I remembered the crime because I was so young at the time. The woman's fascination was evident, and she skirted around something to the point I finally told her to be blunt.

"Shelly, I don't want you to think I am crazy, but I had a stalker a few years ago and with the help of a person with special gifts, I figured out the stalker's identity."

"Are you referring to a psychic?" I asked.

She responded in the affirmative.

I tapped my desk with my fingertips and pondered the thought. "Would you ask your psychic to consider looking at Peggy's case?" I wasn't going off the deep end, but I wasn't going to shy away from any possibility to learn something either, and it wasn't going to hurt to give it a try. I ended the conversation and got a slight chill because I remembered Susan mentioned a desire to consult a criminal psychic and the thought did not deserve serious consideration, but suddenly out of nowhere, a psychic found us.

• •

There was an email from Donald Hall and he was ecstatic that Oklahoma presented new possibilities. He expressed a belief that it was possible that the criminal in Oklahoma was indeed Arthur Root JR and he encouraged me to research murders in that area. I didn't need a degree in psychology or crime to realize he thought it possible that Root went on to kill again, but that would force one to assume Root killed Peggy, and I wasn't ready to compromise my objectivity entirely.

I started calling the numbers Susan handed me; the state trooper was one of the investigating officers following the discovery of Peggy's body. He was direct and refused to discuss the case at all. I didn't take the rejection personally and I didn't even find his stoic nature queer three decades later.

The court reporter was the next phone call, and I was anxious to talk to him because potentially he could fill in so many blanks. There was a slim chance he kept a personal copy of his professional work and that could translate into a transcript of the trial. The news reported during the trial there was some buzzing about getting the court reporter to testify at the trial, and it crossed the line of strange that a court reporter would testify at a trial he was recording. But the reason never surfaced, so I hoped he could explain that, too. My disappointment was instantaneous when the woman that answered the phone explained he passed away years ago. I apologized for the unusual phone call, but managed to ask if he kept copies of the trials he covered, and naturally, he didn't.

A member of the jury that found Arthur Root Jr. not guilty offered the first sign of new information. I gave him the standard explanation, and I said it so much I felt robotic in my delivery, but he wasn't instantly repulsed at the topic. He inquired about how I located him and I detailed everything for him. I didn't have a great source of information I just accessed everything available on public record, and that was how I found him.

"Sir, I was told the testimony given concerning the hair and fiber evidence was overwhelming for the jury, is that correct?"

"No, no, no," he said, immediately rejecting that idea. "We understood everything they said, and there was nothing overwhelming about it."

I believed him. "So what inspired the vote to find Arthur Root Jr. not guilty?" I wanted to understand the course of deliberations because I remembered they returned a speedy verdict.

"He could very well be guilty, but there were just too many keys given out to that apartment, and that left everyone with reasonable doubt," he said articulately.

We talked a short while, and after I hung up I got the feeling that the trial had a personality of its own. Arthur Root Jr. was on trial for his life, but after listening to the juror, I understood Mary Alice's lifestyle was what actually stood trial. I was elated that the man talked to me, and I respected the jury's decision, but the fact that he didn't rule Root out as the killer spoke volumes. Arthur Root Jr. did not walk out of the courtroom because the jury was convinced of his innocence; rather they weren't convinced of his guilt. I thought of one particular city detective that walked Peggy's case through from beginning to end and I imagined his disappointment at the verdict. I also thought of Mary Alice Reber. The juror said there were too many keys given out to that apartment and I wrestled with that in my mind. In 1968 there were only three men identified as having keys to the Reber apartment; Art Root Jr, Ray Boyer and Richard Boyer. The jury was concerned about the amount of keys, yet it appeared they didn't debate facts, but instead they focused on rumors circulating about Peggy's mother.

Mary Alice was not going to win an award for maternal stability, and after the killer handed her a parent's greatest loss, the community flogged her. She divorced at a time divorce was the unthinkable for a mother with school age children and then she enjoyed the carefree lifestyle of the era. The Vietnam War was in full swing, the British invasion was dominating the musical charts and the sexual revolution on the horizon. Mary Alice enjoyed the buffet life offered her, and sadly, she took her daughters along for the ride. Mary Alice enjoyed a good time and the company of men, but I wasn't convinced she saw the harm her life style inflicted on her daughters before Peggy's death.

Mary Alice didn't act the role of responsible parent and I started to wonder if it was because she viewed her daughters as her friends, or an inconvenience to her. I repeatedly told my own teenage son we could never be friends because friends get drunk together, friends get loose together, friends break the rules together, and I would never do that with him.

I entertained the idea that Mary Alice embraced the pitfall of trying to be friends with her offspring. Peggy lived without electricity and parental instinct would be protective and corrective in nature, but Peggy and Mary Alice weathered the storm together much like two friends. I didn't know Mary Alice, and I didn't like all the choices she made, and equally I hated that her error in judgment with sharing keys to her home obstructed justice for Peggy. However, in many ways, her error in judgment cost Peggy not only justice, but also her life, and that wasn't cruel thinking, but realistic. The jury placed importance on the amount of men that had keys to the apartment. Art Root Jr. didn't stand alone on that list, and Mary Alice was to blame for that.

■■■

I decided to meet Susan's efforts and attempt to locate a few people on my own and while I didn't expect to be too successful I had to make every effort. I tackled the task of locating the F.B.I. experts and I knew I was battling the odds.

The dental expert's name was so common it wasn't worth considering, but the other two experts were not out of the question.

I amazed myself when I located the hair and fiber expert within an hour and learned he was living in the Carolinas. I carefully dialed the number and prayed I wouldn't find he was dead the way I did with the court reporter. The retired special agent that specialized in hair and fiber was alive, alert and he readily recalled the girl in Pennsylvania with the bow. "I have been waiting for years for someone to call about that girl. I will never forget her" I was amazed with his memory of Peggy because he handled high profile cases such as Captain Jeffrey MacDonald, and the assassination of JFK. He was easy to talk to and renewed my faith in my pursuit and he gave me a quick lesson on a citizen's right to request information from the F.B.I. known as the Freedom of Information Act. I couldn't thank the man enough for his time and the informative conversation. I was walking on air when I shared my wealth of information with Susan.

"I can't believe you found him!" She was stunned. "I don't know if it was skill, luck, or angels, but that's terrific!"

"It was all of the above," I said with delight, and I mapped out our pending strategy. "Though I am not thrilled about it I am going to take Donald Hall's advice and check one more thing in Oklahoma. I am going to call the clerk of courts again and see if he remembers any murders that could parallel the anger Peggy's killer hosted."

I was feeling so optimistic I reached for the cordless phone and after a brief conversation I hung up with a look of bewilderment that immediately sparked Susan's interest.

"I just talked to the clerk of court and *she* was very nice." I stressed the gender. "And she laughed at me when I gave her the man's name that I talked to earlier this week."

"You lost me. Why did she laugh at you?"

"In fact she told me he doesn't answer the phone." I played on the suspense. "Because he is not the clerk of court, but a Superior Court Judge. What did you say about angels? He told me I was lucky I talked to him because he was the only one in that office that would remember the name we were looking for, and now I learn he rarely answers the phone because he has a secretary to do that. What are the chances of placing a call to a clerk of court's office and a judge answering the phone?"

"It looks like we were meant to learn what he had to say" I wasn't going to question her theory because the phone call definitely had a strange twist. Peggy Reber's story came complete with its share of brick walls, but sometimes doors leading to information would open on their own and it always amazed me.

The Freedom of Information Act was not a top government secret, but one had to file a written request with the F.B.I., and the agency reserved the right to censor information released to the public. I didn't know if any information about Peggy was available because the case remained unsolved, so I drafted a written request without a clue as to its worth, and dropped it in the mail.

The Philadelphia medical examiner presented color slides at the trial of the bite mark Peggy suffered, and locating the man and the slides was the next goal. His picture appeared on the front page when he testified. He was middle-aged then, so the thirty years since the crime made the chances slim on finding him alive, but we started the search. Sure enough, the medical examiner died years earlier, and after a half dozen calls to the Philadelphia medical examiner's office there was no hope of finding the color slides of Peggy's injury. One more question we asked and though we didn't strike gold, we could check the block.

▪▪▪

My friend Alice sent me the contact information for the criminal psychic that she mentioned to me. I was skeptical, but I wasn't going to allow my personal opinion to restrict me. I made the initial contact with the psychic and intentionally refrained from telling her anything about Peggy. Claudia, the psychic, lived in Texas and our contact would be done through the internet and phone if I chose to do so, but I preferred the avenue of electronic communication over telephonic. Claudia requested a photograph of Peggy and she would contact me after seeing the photo, so I pulled out the computer disc my cousin secured for me and emailed the picture to the stranger at a distance.

"Donald Hall told you about some murder that took place in upstate New York involving a bow and for the life of me I can't find anything close and I have spent hours and hours searching" Susan was bird-dogging loose ends. "New York isn't the smallest state and this crime didn't exactly happen yesterday, but I pride myself on my patience. I have to wonder if there really was such a crime, or am I spinning my wheels in vain?"

"I'll see if he can shed any more light on the rumor, but I have to tell you I think whatever effort you put into it is plenty. I do not see the bow as a real factor because it was in the apartment before the killer got there. If the maniac took it inside with him, I think it would be a huge red flag, but he used things that were accessible in the apartment to kill Peggy. Let's face it: Peggy's crime hit legendary proportions, and I am sure there are a dozen tales being passed around at teenage slumber parties about a crazed man attacking teenage girls with bows. It's probably as popular as the infamous hook man."

"I lost my share of sleep due to that damn hook man!" Susan and I laughed at the childhood memory.

■ ■

"Michelle?" I answered the phone to a late night call and I didn't recognize the voice on the other end.

"Yes?"

"This is Savannah, and I'm sorry for calling you so late, but you told me if there was any connection between the man you're looking for and my dad I should call you" she paused a moment "Well I think they are the same man"

I forced myself to wake up "What makes you think so Savannah? Did you talk to your mother?" I was confident that Savannah's mother was the only one that could make a legitimate confirmation about the mismatched identities.

"No . . . Well . . . Yeah, I did," she stammered. "After you called the other night I went into my mother's papers and I found old tax forms from when my dad worked at the oil refinery. The name on his tax papers was Arthur Root Jr. Michelle, that means that he is the man you are looking for." I heard the confusion in her voice.

"Savannah did you talk to your mother about the papers you found?"

"Yeah I did, and she said that Arthur Root Jr. was the name his adoptive parents gave him, and when he grew up he went back to his real family name."

Savannah told me Arthur Root Jr. told his wife he was born to an unmarried Italian immigrant on a boat before it arrived in the United States, and the Root family adopted him.

"Michelle, please tell me whatever you know about my father," the young girl was begging for information.

"Savannah," I struggled for tact, "What was the reason that your dad left your family?"

"My sister lied on him."

"Your sister lied on him?" I was puzzled. "What do you mean your sister lied?"

"My sister accused my dad of raping her, but he didn't do it, and she even admits to that now," she said defensively. "My mom knew he didn't do it, but it didn't matter, and that was the end of my family the way I knew it."

I stumbled to the kitchen to get a pen and paper, so I could take notes. "Do I understand you to say that your sister retracted her claim?" I didn't accept Root's innocence as a motivator

84

for a retraction because youthful sexual assault victims commonly back down during the massive amount of questions during an investigation. The fact that the crime occurred within a family amplified the probability of a retraction.

"She lied." Savannah was bitter. "I don't know why she lied, but she lied on my dad, and now I haven't seen him in years."

The emotion Savannah was oozing was more than I could handle. "I will talk to you, but I want to talk to your mother first."

I wasn't prepared to deal with a distraught daughter, and I wasn't sure I was ready to talk to Art Root's wife, but I wasn't going to miss the opportunity. Savannah resisted my request, but I was firm on my conviction and refused to go any further until she put her mother on the phone.

Savannah's mother, Lana, was an extremely soft-spoken woman that didn't excite easily, and her mellow personality inspired a relaxed conversation. She told me she was married to Savannah's father almost eight years and they had two children together in addition to a daughter she had from a previous marriage. She reflected fondly on the life they shared together. He was a good man that worked long hours, raised his family and took her out once a week to keep the romance in their relationship. Lana's husband was not violent or abusive, and she never saw him engage in a bar room brawl. They rode from Oklahoma to Colorado on his motorcycle and actually lived in Colorado for a while.

I asked her about the assault against her daughter.

"I don't see where he would have had time to do that. I just left for work and I no sooner got in the door of the diner when my daughter came in saying he . . ." she stopped. "Well, saying he did things to her."

Lana was clearly not comfortable discussing the possible rape of her child. "I don't want to be a bad mother, but I just didn't see how that could happen." Again her denial was common for a family related sexual assault, so I just listened.

"When you called and Savannah asked me about his other name, I didn't remember it right away, but he didn't hide that from me. He told me he was born on a boat when his mother was coming to the United States from Italy, and the Root family adopted him. He told me he grew up in Pennsylvania, too."

"Mrs. Root," I caught myself as I said it because her name was not Root. She bore the name of his alias. "Lana," I said, my mind racing. "Tell me about the trial surrounding your daughter's assault."

"What trial?" She sounded strange. "He entered a guilty plea, and the court sentenced him to a minimum of five years."

"He pleaded guilty, but Savannah said your daughter retracted the accusation. I don't understand."

"He did enter a guilty plea, but several years later she admitted to all of us that she lied about the attack." Lana had obviously told the story enough over the years that she realized the level of unbelievable it tickled.

"Lana, please help to me understand." I was lost.

"I would love to, but I can't explain it myself." She adopted a flair of indifference. "I don't know what happened, but my daughter said he did it. He admitted as much when he agreed to being guilty, so I ignored his letters from jail and divorced him. But then after a couple years, my daughter said she lied. I don't know what happened, and it doesn't matter anymore."

"Lana, if he didn't do it, why did he plead guilty?"

"He told me that he didn't want to put us through a trial because that's hard on a family when you live in a small town." I heard understanding in her voice. He definitely knew about the drama surrounding small town trials.

"Lana, did he ever tell you that he stood trial for killing a teenage girl in Pennsylvania?" I had to know.

"No. . ." She took and released a deep breath. "He never told me anything like that, but he didn't talk about his past a lot. Did he kill her?" Savannah started ranting and raving in the background.

"He was found not guilty, so I don't want you to think the worst without cause, but the young girl that was killed was sodomized rectally, and I have to know if the assault on your daughter was rectal. I realize your daughter retracted her claim, but when your daughter first said he attacked her, did she mention a rectal assault?"

"That poor girl!" I knew she was referring to Peggy. "No, she never said anything like that, but I'm telling you he didn't have enough time to do anything like that, and he never hurt any of us. My daughter admitted she was angry because we punished her and wouldn't let her go to a school dance."

"Lana, I need to talk to Savannah because I promised her I would tell her what I know, but I would really like to talk to you again if you don't mind."

Lana's demeanor was so timid that I instinctively knew I needed to build a relationship with her to get her to open up. She agreed to talk to me again and gave the phone to Savannah. I empathized with Savannah and attempted to answer her questions honestly, but she was desperate for information from me, and I couldn't answer all her questions. I spent a good amount of time on the phone with Savannah because my heart broke for the young woman. The phone call was weird, and it was not going to be the last we would share. I went to back to bed and I slept like a baby for the first time in a long time.

The big picture showed a man cleared of murder charges going on to assume multiple identities, engage in petty criminal activity and settle down in Oklahoma to raise a family, only to reach his criminal peak with charges of raping his twelve-year-old stepdaughter. The smaller picture showed Arthur Root Jr. marrying a single mother and settling into domestic normalcy for over half a dozen years. It exploded when the adolescent female accused him of rape, and he entered a guilty plea. Years later, and without cause, the girl recanted her story.

I couldn't understand his plea if he didn't commit the crime. If the girl retracted the claim shortly after making the charge, I would tend to believe family pressure played into her recanting the story, but to deny the allegation years later puzzled me. The man admitted to the crime, served the time and lost his family, but I questioned the circumstances surrounding the girl's allegation and then her change of story.

"Michelle, do you believe the girl's story?" Susan couldn't read my mind, so she asked the obvious.

"I am a rape victim, so I never question the victim in a sexual assault. I adore children, and we started this inquiry because of a kid. I just don't know what to make of it." I was completely honest.

"Understood, but what if the child was a victim of molestation instead of a one- time rape? We know Root was a ladies' man."

"Well, doesn't that make everything better," I said sarcastically. "Instead of one bad day he did it on a long term basis"

"Well, we don't know that to be true, but it's not out of the question," she offered.

"I don't mean to be difficult, but I am getting tired of finding young female victims attached to his name and there are always questions surrounding the facts. It's not cut and dried that he killed Peggy and his guilty plea legally closes the case in Oklahoma, but not without some doubts. I know I am crazy to have any doubts, but I do. I know legal cases don't wrap themselves up like pretty little packages with ribbons and bows, and I know the average cop or judge is going to dismiss my doubts with a wave of the hand, but it just doesn't feel right."

I tried to explain my confusion. "Let's pretend I am a Lebanon native that believes Root is guilty. The girl in Oklahoma makes another young victim that encounters his wrath, but the girl in Oklahoma didn't meet the violent frenzy that Peggy did. I don't want to be rude, but Peggy died, and she didn't get the benefit of a quick kill. Peggy was tortured, and it was a time consuming process. Her killer didn't spend hours with her, but he wasn't satisfied with simply stopping her heartbeat because he expressed a need to inflict pain and vent his anger. The girl in Oklahoma reported a sexual assault and though that is violent in nature she was not brutalized. I know that appears to be a contradiction, but I trust you understand the point I'm trying to make."

I looked to my friend for feedback.

"You aren't crazy," Susan replied.

I continued, "I'm not going to take the foolish stand that crimes are identical, but criminals tend to leave a signature on every crime they commit, and I don't see the connection between Peggy and the girl in Oklahoma other than Root. I know an easy way out is to say he did both, but I'm the hard sell in the picture. Peggy went through pure hell and that isn't a minute factor. I foolishly believe the torture Peggy endured is the killer's personal criminal signature, but I have no sophisticated training in the world of crime, so I could be lost in my own ignorance. Let's assume Root raped the girl in Oklahoma and one has a rapist, and then run the same course with child molestation and one has a child molester, but we still don't have a personality consumed with uncontrollable rage, and Peggy's killer definitely had uncontrollable rage."

"I follow you." Susan didn't need detailing to understand my train of thought.

"Art Root Jr. is not my first choice for a next-door neighbor because he doesn't follow a path of integrity, but he doesn't display rage at any point either. I appreciate the importance that rape is a violent crime, but not necessarily a crime of rage, and Peggy encountered raw rage while the victim in Oklahoma did not, so I am the idiot in the crowd that says it is queer."

"I respect you being thorough, but be logical," Susan argued. "One man and two young girls is too much of a coincidence for anyone, and the multiple identities feed into the fact."

"Oh my God, Susan!" I sprung to my feet. "He adopted other identities before he even married that girl's mother."

"Why? Why did he adopt other identities?" she challenged me.

"I don't know. . ." I paced around my dining room table. "I don't know why he did anything, but he had an alias before he ever met Peggy. His identity issues had nothing to do with Peggy's murder"

"Exactly, he set the stage for a life of crime." Susan didn't give me a chance to offer an explanation.

I threw my hands up in the air and yelled, "So he's a criminal and his life is filled with crime!" I dropped my hands and sighed dramatically. "But is he a killer?" I wasn't convinced.

"I love your open mind, but I think you need to be realistic." Susan tried to comfort me. "Arthur Root Jr., under an assumed alias, admitted to raping a twelve-year-old girl, and that is a fact. If you can give me a good explanation for that admission to guilt I will shut up, but until then we have two young female victims, and he is involved in both cases."

"Susan," I said, pleading. "You have to see the difference between the two crimes." I was frustrated. "Peggy was brutalized, and we do not know that he was involved in the murder."

"I think you need to keep in mind how many men live their lives without ever being accused of a crime, and this one man ends up in a court room a couple times accused of harming young girls."

"Yeah, and how many other men questioned in 1968 went on to commit deviant crimes? We don't know that because Peggy's murder is a cold case file, a file that doesn't see the light of day, but I have to wonder about that, too. What happened to the other men attached to the investigation of Peggy's murder? We only followed up on Arthur Root Jr., but what would we find if we followed up on every man that was included in the circle of suspicion in 1968?" I challenged her logic. "It is easy to reconsider Root's guilt based on the information we obtained in Oklahoma, but let's assume we devote the same attention to one of the guys that provided a dental impression in the case. Don't forget Root's dental impression was ruled out as a possibility. If we would find that one of those jokers went on to be a wife-beater we would see rage where Root is still missing that single ingredient. I am convinced that violent rage is a factor in identifying Peggy's killer, and I still don't see violent rage and Arthur Root Jr.'s name in the same sentence."

"Michelle, he is a convicted rapist and rape is a violent crime!"

We were clearly at a standstill.

"On a different note," I said, changing the subject, "I asked Donald Hall if Peggy's killer was ever profiled. He said he did a profile of the killer, and he thought he was accurate, but he thinks it would be great if a professional in criminal psychology performed a profile."

"I think that's a wonderful idea, but Lebanon is going to have to give up the police file, crime scene photographs and the autopsy report for anyone to do it accurately," Susan replied.

"Well, we know that isn't going to happen." I hated the barrier around Peggy's file. "However, I have a good friend that is a clinical psychologist, and he works for a sheriff's department in South Carolina. I asked him if he would consider reviewing Peggy's murder. I know it's a primitive approach, and the accuracy is going to be limited because his access to the information is limited, but I want to give it a whirl."

"You know my theory is to leave no stone unturned." Susan was open to anything. "Did you ever ask the detective if Peggy was pregnant? It's never mentioned in the papers, but I wonder if that could be the reason she was killed."

"I did ask him, and he said she was not pregnant."

"I didn't think he saw the autopsy report." She was doubtful. "That information would be acquired posthumously."

"Factual information or an actual pregnancy test would be conducted posthumously, you're right. I wonder how they performed pregnancy tests in 1968, because goodness knows the home pregnancy test wasn't available."

"Your wish is my command!" Susan jumped at the chance to broaden her medical insight. "I have a few medical books at home that will answer that question, but if Donald Hall didn't see the autopsy report, how does he know she wasn't pregnant?"

I shrugged my shoulders.

"I'm sure the cops that investigated the crime asked that question, so maybe he's going on information in the file, but only the autopsy report is going to give an accurate answer to that question. I really want to see that autopsy report and the crime scene photos." Susan's passion for nursing and knowledge of the human body showed through. "Assuming they tested her for pregnancy, it would be in the autopsy report, but it's possible an examination of her cervix could confirm pregnancy too."

"I'm lucky to be able to apply a band-aid to my kid's knee when he falls, so the medical aspect of this is way beyond my understanding, but I have trouble believing her cervix would be in any shape to examine given the amounts of internal injuries she suffered."

■■

I knew Ron Frier the better part of fifteen years when I asked him to review what little information I knew concerning Peggy Reber's murder. He was a clinical psychologist and though profiling killers was not his forte, I welcomed any insight he could share from an abstract standpoint. Ron repeatedly cautioned me that without all the information, he was at a disadvantage and he reminded me that he was not a criminal profiler, but merely offering his opinion. Considering the physical evidence was lost and the case sits sheltered under the label *unsolved,* I welcomed any opinion he had to offer. I provided him with all the facts about Peggy's murder that I knew to be true and waited for his review.

"Michelle, the killer is definitely an adult male that was known to the family, and my first thought is that the killer could possibly be a jilted boyfriend, but the torture appears to be a displaced assault, perhaps with someone else in mind. I want to discuss this further with some of the homicide detectives in my office, but the girl does not appear to be the source of the rage, just the recipient."

Several days later Ron asked if Peggy suffered further mutilation with items other than the bow. I could not accurately answer those questions because that was protected information. I thanked my friend for his efforts, and I realized without the benefit of all the facts, I was wasting his time. I was deeply saddened at the thought that no one could really provide Peggy with justice except the Lebanon Police Department, and she was not a top priority even though her name decorated the newspapers three decades later.

Peggy Reber's murder file was stuck in the middle of a present day personnel issue within the Lebanon Police Department, and I seriously wondered if locating her killer would ever be a priority again. Donald Hall expressed a sincere interest in reviewing the case, and I didn't doubt there were other people in Lebanon that wanted a few answers concerning the aged homicide, but politics embraced the file. After holding a former officer responsible for compromising the case, the likelihood of Lebanon solving the case was limited. If the city managed to solve the case, their claim that the female officer that took the file home compromised its integrity would be a joke.

The chief of police and mayor defended the personnel actions against the former female police officer involved with Peggy's file, and I wondered if they ever really thought about Peggy during the course of their actions. I could hear the political banter in my mind.

Of course we care about Margaret Lynn Reber. That is why we found the actions of the former officer to be unacceptable.

But that officer received reprimands for infractions far beyond the Reber file. When the chief of police admitted that all physical evidence in the Reber case succumbed to the flood in 1972 in a news interview in 2001, he single-handedly did more damage to the case than any cop taking the file home. Admitting the physical evidence did not exist confirmed if the killer didn't actually confess, it would be almost impossible to identify him. That little bit of information was highly confidential because even if it was true that the evidence was lost, a good detective stood a chance of getting a confession if the suspect believed he was identified due to physical evidence.

Police officers are not required to be honest about such information when interviewing suspects and it was an obvious advantage for law enforcement to lead any suspect to believe the physical evidence existed. The release of the information that all was lost in the flood exposed the vulnerability of the case, and if the killer read the news, he knew he was home free thanks to none other than the chief of police. It was a very sad situation for anyone genuinely concerned about apprehending Peggy's killer.

■■

Claudia, the psychic in Texas, received a picture of Peggy, her date of birth and the date of her death, and Claudia's response took me by surprise. "It is important that you keep in mind I am not able to detail a lot of things with the limited information I have, and I would appreciate any confirmation you can provide in regards to my accuracy, but I will share what I have so far. There are brothers and sisters attached to Peggy, but they aren't all her siblings. There is definitely a connection between her and the female though a very strong bond. I think they are sisters, but closer than most sisters, it is a powerful connection. I see brothers, too. I think if you research the case, you will find two brothers are involved somehow. Now do not immediately assume that I am telling you brothers harmed Peggy. I am telling you that somewhere very near the time of her death or immediately following there were brothers close to her. Maybe the ambulance driver and one of the cops on the scene were brothers, or a neighbor and the coroner, but somewhere close to Peggy there are brothers attached to her somehow. I am also telling you that I feel a sister, and yet it is a closer relationship than most sisters.

Peggy's personality bordered shy and she was fearful, but I can't see exactly what she feared. She knew her killer, but he caught her by surprise. Peggy didn't expect the attack at all, but I don't think she stood a chance against the demon that day. Peggy's killer was a creature from the dark side. He was so evil that my spirit guide cringed when I looked at Peggy's picture, and it's hard to spook a spirit. There are people that know exactly what happened to her. I want to say there was a witness, but the witness is scared and longs to remain in the shadows. I keep seeing the person hiding behind a bush, but I think it is more symbolic than literal, but someone knows what happened that day. I could tell you a lot more if I could go to the scene of the crime, yet I almost feel that's impossible, but I can't explain why I have that feeling. There are people beyond the killer that run from the truth when she dies. Law enforcement worked hard to solve the case. I see a great deal of effort and fatigue attached to the young girl's death, but I see something else, too. I see an undercurrent during the investigation because not everyone wanted the truth uncovered. There were people fearful of the truth, fearful of exposure, but not because they killed the girl. I don't really understand it, but there are truths around the young girl before the murder that others don't want revealed, and it is not just one person, but several.

She could be the wrong victim, she died at the wrong place, or people knew her and they didn't want that known, but several people panic after her death and they want the truth covered up, but not necessarily the murder covered up. It's odd, but they were not helpless poor people; these people had some control at the time and they truly felt panic when the crime generated attention and questions. The brothers I mentioned are very different and you won't find them at

90

the same place for very long, but they are brothers nonetheless. There is conflict there, but they both know something about that day, something more than anyone realizes and it could be that no one asked the right questions. I feel the one brother wants to talk, but no one is listening. He doesn't have the answers, he has an obstructed view, but wants to discuss that day and no one really asks him, or listens to him. He is frustrated even today. The other brother doesn't want to talk at all. I don't know where these men fit into this but I firmly believe these brothers are real and they know the victim well. Maybe one was a schoolteacher and the other an investigating officer, but they both know Peggy somehow, and the information they possess matters. I strongly suggest locating them and asking the right questions. I, however, cannot provide you the right questions to ask.

The female presence that I believe is her sister is unique. Peggy and this girl are so close I cannot explain it, and they share every secret, dream and fear with each other, and it is quite natural for both. The sister could not imagine life without Peggy and I sense resentment or jealousy that Peggy managed to escape the realities of living even if it meant death to do so. This sister was not a serious consideration then and she is not a powerful being now, but she managed to escape questioning under the right conditions, so her true knowledge is sheltered, but she knows things that could help in the investigation. She didn't protect the killer and make no mistake she loved Peggy, but she is scared and her fear is not a wasted emotion because the evil knows her, too. That family knew the evil force then and he is still alive today.

Lastly, I know this is an aged homicide and the obvious question is how and why this is an issue presently, but in my line of work, it is not that difficult a question. Peggy is not a tormented soul, but like any victim of a horrible crime, she seeks the truth, and I don't know anything about you Michelle, but I am willing to bet you were a kid at the time. Peggy captured your attention in such a special way that it is beyond words. You aren't obligated to do a bunch of silly things and there is no similarity illustrated by Hollywood films, but you can tell her story. I think the answers are there, so consider taking the time to find them."

"Michelle, I know you don't believe in psychics, but she is so damn right I have chills running down my spine." Susan reviewed the psychic's assessment of Peggy Reber.

"Peggy had an identical twin sister and that ties into everything Claudia just said, but then you didn't give Claudia the benefit of telling her that, did you?" I shook my head to indicate that I did not tell the stranger that Peggy had a twin sister. "The girls were involved with brothers, and she didn't know that either, but she mentioned brothers being attached to Peggy." Susan was on a campaign. "She wanted to go to a crime scene that no longer exists, and I guess you will chalk that up to coincidence, too"

"Stop just for a minute." I was overwhelmed "My family is never going to be guilty of wearing out church steps, but this is crazy. I admit that I am impressed with everything Claudia said, but this isn't normal and I am not sure it is correct for a Christian to do this sort of thing." I suffered addiction to nicotine and enjoyed a beer or two, but I loved God, and I was fearful of what was transpiring.

"Michelle, keep an open mind." Susan picked up on my fears. "There are angels and miracles, so there are demons and those that can see the truth." I understood her point because every positive force has a negative force, but I refused to betray my faith and entertain the evil, and Susan shared my convictions.

"I realize that Claudia possessed so much accuracy that I am speechless, but I will not open myself or compromise my faith enough that evil will capture my attention." I was firm. "I have mixed feelings about psychics even in the world of criminal investigations, but I never doubt the force of evil and evil is what killed Peggy."

"You don't doubt the force of evil because you have a strong faith in God." Susan was correct. "Evil is not the temptation in this picture, but the opponent, and if Claudia is a tool provided to us, we would be fools not to use the information given."

'Christ is looking over her." I mumbled the words. "Christ is looking over her." I repeated the words, only I was louder and I tested my friend's memory because the words echoed in my mind.

"Yeah Michelle, Christ is looking over her just like the woman said at the cemetery when we looked for Peggy's grave." Susan knew exactly what I meant.

"I don't want to be difficult, but this is one more bizarre footnote, and I prefer we credit tangible facts when we tell Peggy's story. I appreciate any help we can get, but I don't want to cloud our effort in learning the truth by telling a tale involving the paranormal."

"We wanted to try everything we could to uncover the truth and this is a small part of the process. I don't think it's any different than anything else we tried. I am not going to lie, I am flabbergasted by what she said, but I think the bigger picture is the way a psychic found us and we didn't go looking for it. Come on, Michelle," she pushed her point. "I mentioned a psychic one time and then out of nowhere your friend Alice says she knows a psychic. That quick we're in business, don't you find that a little weird?"

"Oh, it's definitely weird to say the least," I agreed. "And it's nothing personal about Claudia or the reading, but it is all a little strange to me. Let's move forward with our research and see what we have when we're done because every day presents something new and interesting."

■■

My heart raced when I read the return address on the large yellow envelope because it was the information I requested from the F.B.I. I resisted the urge to rip the envelope open, and I rushed into the house to sit down and carefully read the documents in hand. The first few pages explained the agency's policy on providing information requested while protecting information that warranted confidential status or sheltering the identity of innocent individuals. I immediately understood the explanation when I looked at the first page that related to Peggy because there were blank blocks where a computer obviously deleted the contents in print, so the information remained protected. At first glance, I thought my efforts were a waste of time because the government censoring left me baffled, but I continued to read the gibberish page by page. The documents referred to specimen samples, hairs, fibers and various other items, and there was a code to the reports along with the many blank blocks censored out by the F.B.I.

I literally squealed with delight when I found the detailed list of evidence submitted to the bureau because it was the key to the coding in the reports. Item Q-3 was listed under the title "clothing of the victim". It was Peggy's dress. Item Q-77 fell under the category of "Items from Scene". It was the bow. The evidence list spanned over four pages in length and detailed almost 150 items submitted for the F.B.I.'s review. I was anxious to understand the new material I possessed, but it was not going to be an easy read, and it required a great deal of effort to decipher the reports using the codes. The translation was going to take days if not weeks, but I spotted one thing immediately. The original investigators realized the dress belt used to strangle Peggy did not match the dress she was wearing. I wondered what other truths rested between the pages in my hand.

The report identified three suspects and their personal items confiscated by law enforcement and of course, Arthur Root Jr. was included in the trio. Eight men submitted to dental impressions, and that didn't include all the male key holders to the apartment. But only three men fell under the scrutiny of their personal belongings undergoing F.B.I. analysis. The report I received from the federal agency did not mention dental impressions or anything relating to that aspect of the investigation, so that continued to nag at me with no explanation in sight.

After many months, I viewed the report like classic literature not because it was excellent reading, but because every time I looked at it I found something new that I overlooked the first dozen times I read it. I didn't sport the professionally trained eye that would allow me rapid understanding, so I worked long and hard to comprehend the contents of the material. I was determined to understand everything I could.

Susan's research into pregnancy tests available at that time produced a cute reminder of yesteryear for both of us.

"Don't you remember your mother whispering about the rabbit that died?" she quizzed me.

"Not really, because my rabbit was pretty damn healthy." I was commenting on a family pet, and Susan didn't get the joke.

"No you dumb bunny," she laughed at her pun. "The most common pregnancy test in 1968 involved taking blood from a woman and injecting it into a rabbit because the hormone HcG indicates pregnancy in humans and kills rabbits, so if the rabbit died it confirmed pregnancy."

"Damn, that was a tough job for the rabbit. I hope it offered great survivor's benefits." I was feeling the need for some comic relief. "I don't mean to crack jokes at your hard work, but I haven't read one thing about a dead rabbit, so on a serious note, explain it to me."

'That's what friends are for," she said, delighted to educate me. "The medical examiner needed a vial of Peggy's blood to inject in the bunny to test the HcG level, and the alternate method of indicating pregnancy required an examination of the cervix because the medical community discovered the cervix took on a blue color in pregnant patients."

"I hate to be the bearer of ill tidings, but we don't know what they did in the autopsy room, and please don't forget there is still a cloud covering everything the killer did to Peggy. We may want to know everything, but government gatekeepers block the truth, and sadly there isn't a damn thing we can do about it because we'll be told it is an active investigation."

"Yeah well, I watched a movie last week about something like this in New England, and a former cop pointed out to that police chief that their active file remained unsolved after twenty five years, so they weren't exactly productive and he couldn't hurt anything by trying. I guess I don't have to tell you he solved the case. We're trying too, Michelle, and I am not saying that Lebanon's Police Department isn't trying, but after thirty some years, they need to can the professional arrogance and accept help from anyone that can provide it."

"I am not going to debate or defend my hometown police department, but you can't forget that we aren't exactly legitimate help either, so we can't expect them to listen to a damn thing we have to say." I knew our limitations.

"What if we hired a private investigator, or we contacted that same cop that went to New England?" Susan rambled. "What if Peggy was our daughter or better yet, what if Herman Reber wanted someone objective and qualified to look into Peggy's case? What would the local law enforcement say? 'Oh gee nice thought, but it's an open and active case, and in another decade or two we'll catch the bastard.'" she scoffed. "That is insanity at its finest because if they can't close a case in thirty years, they have no right to stop someone else from trying to identify the sick mind responsible for Peggy's death."

"You're right, I agree 100%, and we can stand here and bitch for days, but that doesn't change the status quo."

"I want to change the status quo." Susan was sincere.

"We're definitely going to try, my friend, so don't lose that passion. We can't rewrite history, and we aren't going to be law enforcement certified anytime soon, so we simply need to be thorough and then tell the story."

"What if we tell the story and no one cares?" she was softening.

"I said it before, and I will say it again: This whole story is not an accurate representation of my home town, and even if the powers that rule are suffering from overprotective egos the public won't embrace the injustice. We don't need to identify a killer. I really think we need to educate the community on the events surrounding Peggy and remind them of the forensic technology available today."

"My turn to shed doom, but there isn't anything left to put under a microscope since the great flood."

"Not buying all that, sorry." I was cocky. "If modern science can identify an entire body using only one tooth, there has to be something in this case that can make sense on a forensic level."

"Donald Hall said all of it was lost," she reminded me. "Or at least the chief of police said that during that newspaper interview."

"Yeah, well, I'm starting to think that the local police file on Peggy's case is weak, and I think that all the information is scattered, so I have doubts." I jumped to my feet. "Call the media! Michelle Gooden is questioning authority!" I clapped my hands. "I don't believe everything I read or hear, and I think there is something somewhere that can tell the story better than we can. We are going to press forward, we are going to tell the story and though there is no reason to believe it right now, I think there is something, maybe just a little something, but something that can seal the deal. I know I sound crazy, but I embraced crazy for lesser things, so I am not giving up hope until the fat lady sings. We don't know what happened in the autopsy room, we don't know the other items or means of Peggy's mutilation, we don't know a lot, but we do know that the crime remains unsolved, and since a jury didn't find Arthur Root Jr. guilty, we won't either."

"I won't argue any of that, but what do you think about a dead rabbit?"

"Well we don't have a dead rabbit, but we definitely have a dead teenager, so we will move on with what we know to be true."

∎∎∎

"I think it's time to return to Pennsylvania. I can't articulate why, but it's the logical thing to do." I didn't really have a plan to support my suggestion. "It's time to research any available documents at the courthouse, meet Donald Hall, talk to the legal counsel that conducted Root's trial, and locate Peggy's twin sister and mother - if she is still alive. It's okay to sit at a five hundred mile distance and read articles, but it's time to get down in the trenches, and the trenches are in Pennsylvania, so let's plan a trip."

"I will never refuse an invitation to escape dust bunnies or the mountains of dirty laundry my family produces on a daily basis, so count me in."

Susan was ready to travel, and in a matter of days we were on the road. The plan was vague, and we didn't hold ourselves to a militant schedule, so we took a relaxed approach to exploring Lebanon, Pennsylvania.

The Prothonotaries Office was our first priority because any public record relating to Peggy and the trial sat in their files. We didn't have a thimble-full of knowledge between us concerning researching public records, but we were about to learn. We decided the local newspaper deserved a visit too because even though their video viewer was inoperable, the better part of six months of relentless reading had made our articles reporting Peggy's death worn and torn. The original photographs taken by the staff photographer captured our interest.

The district attorney that prosecuted the case continued to practice law in the picturesque community, and Donald Hall was little more than an email address to us, so there were options to explore. The one place we knew we wouldn't visit was the cemetery because we didn't earn the knowledge we deemed necessary to make a return visit to the young girl's grave.

We checked into a local hotel in the wee hours of the morning and entered a rather comfortable room. I unloaded a filing cabinet that housed all the information we obtained regarding Peggy and I set up my laptop computer on a desk before we considered calling it a night.

We relaxed on a small patio readying ourselves for the day ahead, and I looked at the tranquil beauty of the town I called home. The row houses were randomly showing light because it was the middle of the night, but I could see children's toys in yards, bicycles, and porch swings. I looked up at the many stars in the sky and I smiled because no place could ever be as peaceful to me. I loved everything about the place I called home and viewing the community while it slept confirmed my belief. Lebanon was a beautiful place to grow up, live and call home, but then I thought of Peggy.

Lebanon was Peggy's home, too, and she didn't fare quite as well. I looked at the all-American neighborhood again, and I wondered about the secrets that the small town kept tucked away under layers of years and lies. I didn't believe that Peggy met such a violent death and an entire apartment building didn't hear or notice anything out of the ordinary. The questions surrounding Ray Boyer's apprehension by the constable nagged at me for many, many reasons. There was doubt presented at the trial about the last person that saw Peggy alive, and I pondered that thought for a while.

Arthur Root Jr. admitted to seeing Peggy around 6 p.m. when he made yet another visit to the apartment looking for Peggy's mother in hopes of securing money Mary Alice stored for him. Two women that worked at the city's comfort station testified that they complimented Peggy's beautiful dark hair at 8 p.m. the evening of the crime. Two hours of Peggy's timeline of life was critically important that fateful day, and I desperately wanted to understand any discrepancies.

Dental impressions of eight men warranted comparison to the bite mark, yet there were obvious oversights when officials composed the list of suspects, and I wondered why. The report from the F.B.I. revealed that local police submitted clothing from three different men for hair and fiber analysis, and I didn't grasp the small number of men under review. I still didn't comprehend why two men questioned after the crime committed suicide within weeks of their police interviews, and the F.B.I lab results cleared both of suspicion after their deaths. The trial escaped a full transcript, and I reminded myself that my perspective at a range thirty years down the road could be unreasonable. 1970 didn't know the legal litigation that I accepted as the norm, and perhaps it was not out of the ordinary to skip the process of a full detailed and documented court recording. The old saying about hindsight being so accurate lent itself to my ignorance. I didn't understand a verdict against the state going unrecorded because it left the case unsolved. I resisted thinking the worst. Peggy Reber's killer evaded conviction and the injustice screamed out from her grave, yet the lack of a transcript preserving all the original testimony almost confirmed prosecutors had no intention of ever pursuing justice any further.

We found a parking lot that provided access to The Lebanon Daily News and the government municipal building, so we flipped a coin to decide our first destination. I introduced myself to the librarian at the local newspaper because I talked to her on the phone several times during my quest. Upon our meeting, I was surprised to see that she was old enough to remember the crime making the front-page news, but when I first called her about the case, she didn't immediately recall it. It continued to puzzle me that anyone could really forget the murder of Peggy Reber, especially considering I couldn't read at the time of the crime and I couldn't forget the young girl's picture on the evening news.

Boxes of newspapers, random articles, and a variety of related materials cluttered the librarian's work area. The librarian's workspace did not qualify to be a modern day cubicle because of its size, but it resembled a cubicle setting because it was in a large room that others worked in as well. We talked at a normal tone and immediately realized we sparked the interest of her coworkers with the mention of Peggy's name, and though it appeared, others wanted to hear our conversation no one really wanted to get close enough to be obvious. Susan and I exchanged a smile because the reaction to Peggy's name produced the same result almost everywhere we went in the conservative town.

The equipment to view newspaper archives still needed repair and the kind woman repeated the claim that the Reber films suffered due to heavy use. I cracked a cheap joke about the broken equipment because it needed repair almost a year prior, too.

We inquired about seeing the actual newspapers and the photographs taken at the time of the crime. Lebanon's police department did not employ a trained technician to photograph crime scenes in 1968, so the photographer for the daily news assisted the police force at the crime scene. I did not believe for a minute that the crime scene photographs sat in a file at the newspaper office, but I didn't doubt that photographs used in news articles would be available.

The librarian requested the assistance of a young man to go to the storage location used for such archives, and after a lengthy wait, we hit one of those infamous brick walls; the photographs that appeared in the news articles relating to Peggy's death were gone. They didn't fall victim to a flood, they just vanished. Somehow Susan and I didn't blink an eye at the strange disappearance because it wasn't the least bit surprising. The librarian couldn't explain the disappearance of the pictures and she appeared baffled, but she didn't have the benefit of our insight of the fact that few things pertaining to Peggy remained intact.

The impressive architectural structure that accommodated the local legal proceedings was the second stop on our agenda, and we decided to split up upon entering the building in pursuit of different information. Susan headed toward the Prothonotaries office to research any legal records on file and I entered the office of county sheriff, Michael Deleo. I only lightly remembered hearing his name while I was growing up, but Donald Hall thought it was worth the effort to chat with the man. Luckily, he graciously welcomed me into his office to sit down and talk with him. I felt my face flush due to my nervousness, and the uniformed officer noticed my discomfort and eased the moment with idle chatter. I looked at his tanned skin and the lines that represented years of smiling and I thought of my own dad because they were close in age, and I started to relax.

He was in his mid-seventies and was still an attractive man, and he possessed a silent charm. I explained my memory surrounding Peggy. Naturally, he commented on the tragedy of her fate and the shock it spread across the community at the time. I explained that of course, I was at a disadvantage of first-hand knowledge in light of my age at the time of the crime, but I certainly understood the horror attached to the crime. I listened to the man recant the amount of police work the investigation into Peggy's murder warranted, and through his words, I gained confidence because it reminded me of why I made the trip to Pennsylvania.

"Peggy's boyfriend was jailed on an outstanding warrant for failure to pay child support the day she was murdered," I said. I knew I wasn't telling him anything he didn't already know; rather I chose to refresh his memory. "The man that apprehended him was a North Lebanon Township Police officer, and I thought that was kind of strange at first because he issued the warrant within the city limits. That would place him out of his jurisdiction. Then I learned he was a constable. I almost hate to admit this, but I didn't have a real understanding of the office of constable, so I had to detour my research on Peggy to educate myself on the authority of a constable." I giggled a bit at my own ignorance. "Anyhow, I have to wonder how and why it was decided that Ray Boyer was deserving of being jailed that weekend above a few others that had outstanding criminal charges."

"Well," he leaned over his desk, "perhaps the constable wasn't aware of the other people you have uncovered."

"That's a definite possibility, but I just thought for a man that was on top of his game so much that he could locate Peggy's boyfriend at her apartment instead of the boyfriend's place of employment or his legal address, he would be a little sharper. My memory does serve me well enough that back then employed men that failed to pay child support normally met up with the authorities at their place of employment during their workweek. One has to wonder if we reviewed the records for 1968, how many men got the special attention Ray Boyer received that day."

"Well I am sure the constable probably worked for the sheriff's department and was looking to pick up a little extra money that weekend." He had a quick answer.

"That certainly makes sense, sir," I answered respectfully. "But I really would like to review the policies in place at the time for apprehending anyone guilty of such a violation because Ray Boyer definitely received individual attention that day. I hate to repeat myself but it was a Saturday, and he didn't legally reside at Peggy's address, so there was some effort involved in jailing him. Once Ray Boyer hit a jail cell he was out of the net so-to-speak for almost three days, and he really was Peggy's protector, so it was all too convenient for the killer if you ask me."

"You present an interesting point."

"The coroner testified that there were other items used in the mutilation, yet they were never identified, and I find that very odd. I can't imagine a crime of such magnitude and a trial that didn't reveal every aspect of the torture inflicted on the victim. I realize it is easy to look back and question the past, but surely, the community demanded a conviction in regards to this crime, and yet the details of the murder went untold. I don't understand."

"I can't explain that to you, but it *is* a little strange, isn't it?" he appeared sincere. "I hope you keep in mind that I was not a detective on the force at the time, so I wasn't in the loop of real knowledge."

"Oh, I don't expect anyone to have answers to my silly questions," I lied. "I just question a little here and a little there."

"According to Peggy's mother, Peggy's brother-in-law had access to a key to the apartment, but when officials took dental impressions from potential suspects he didn't make the list. I don't know his alibi and I trust the police knew what they were doing, but I find that strange, too. Oh, please make no mistake, I am not a qualified law enforcement officer, but it just makes good common sense to take dental impressions from any male that had access to a key to the scene of the crime especially considering the killer didn't break into the apartment. The lawyer landlord was not included in dental impressions either, yet we know he had a key as well." I slowed down a bit. "I apologize for my ignorant ramblings, but I desperately want to understand what happened." I didn't give him a chance to respond before I continued. "I don't know if Lebanon realizes even today the magnitude of Peggy Reber's killer, because he was way ahead of the world as they knew it at the time."

"What do you mean?" he was perplexed.

"If you think about it, he was a killer before his time." I let a moment pass before I continued. "In 1968, criminal profiling was a mere fantasy and Charles Manson didn't yet hit the headlines, but right here in good ol' Lebanon, Pennsylvania raw evil went into action. Peggy's killer didn't rape her and kill her. No, he was far more complicated than that and he escaped detection. God forbid he still lives in this town."

"I guess you are aware that a man stood trial for the murder." He knew the answer to his inquiry before he said it.

"Arthur Root Jr." I met his volley. "If I read the papers correctly you accompanied a couple other officers to Illinois to question his first wife during the original investigation." He nodded in agreement. "I won't say every jury throughout time rendered an accurate verdict, but I won't question the verdict in that case." I chuckled. "Odd thing about Arthur Root Jr." I sat upright in my seat." Several years ago, I placed a call to Lebanon's Municipal Building in search of his criminal record and I learned it was retired. I got a quick lesson that the status of Art Root Jr.'s file resulted due to his death, but I happen to know he is alive and well, so it's more than weird that his local file is retired."

"To say the least." I knew the charismatic senior citizen was in over his head, and I wasn't on a mission to strip him of dignity or self respect, but I needed to mention one more thing.

"My spirits really took a dive when I attempted to get a copy of the court transcript only to learn there was no such thing."

"What do you mean?" I had his attention.

"There is no real court transcript of the trial," I repeated myself.

"I can't answer all your questions about Peggy Reber, but I can tell you that anything that is testified to in a court of law is public record, and a transcript is mandatory, so everything you want to know should be recorded in the Prothonotaries office."

"Sir," I slid to the edge of my chair. "From a business standpoint you and your department cannot afford to pay one individual a salary to do what I have done with the Reber case. No reasonable businessperson could justify the cost of labor, research and silly other things I pay for without a second thought regarding Peggy. I am an ignorant private citizen that has too much free time and a few extra bucks to spare, so I can give Peggy Reber my undivided attention, and it is only because of that that I can have this conversation with you."

"You're right about that." He was back in his comfort zone. "I could never devote one person to any cold case much less just one case and still keep my job. You clearly understand the limitations on manpower and the politics involved."

I got up from my seat and extended my hand to the man seated behind his desk. "Sir, I got an idea to write a book about a kid I just couldn't forget, and I simply wanted to come home and talk to the experts before I started writing."

"Michelle, I would say you are the expert." He shook my hand. "You did your homework and you aren't silly, so I have to say you are the expert on the Peggy Reber murder case."

I winked at him. "I appreciate your kind words, but until the case is closed complete with a conviction, we are all just amateurs. There is no real expert in the Reber case or justice would be served."

It wasn't until weeks later that I learned the constable that apprehended Ray Boyer worked for Sheriff Michael Deleo right up until his death a few years before I met with the county sheriff.

::

I sought Susan out in the Prothonotaries office immediately following my meeting with the senior law enforcement officer.

"I don't know about you, but I think I could stand a little bit of sunshine."

"You know how to lure a girl away from a day's labor!" Susan laughed and grabbed her purse before following me outside. Once we were outside Susan began to talk "Please tell me you didn't mention the name Peggy Reber and encounter that doe-caught-in-the-headlights stare."

I laughed at her and said,"No, I didn't encounter the robotic stupidity that normally finds Peggy's name, but I didn't really learn anything either."

"Michelle, I can't even explain to you the reception I received when I requested help in locating information about Peggy Reber. The military has names for the chief butthead in charge, and I don't want to use those vulgarities, but if not for the assistant in the Prothonotaries office, I would still be standing there looking stupid."

"And I am hoping someone eventually assisted you in finding the information requested?" I could only hope she broke through the barriers.

"I didn't push and I didn't pull, but I wanted to smack somebody up-side the head."

Susan possessed such a passive personality, and it never ceased to amaze me how issues involving Peggy sparked her protective passion almost on a maternal level. "You obviously met the challenge head on"

"Damn right I met the challenge! I wasn't asking to see anything that compromises national security; I just want to look at papers about a crime that took place thirty years ago." She definitely needed a break from the research.

I didn't say another word because I respected her frustration at the response she met in the Prothonotaries office, so I enjoyed the pretty view in silence. "Would you please explain the oddity to me?" she continued, fuming. "A teenage girl died at the hands of a total bastard, but every time we mention her name we hit a forbidden subject. Damn, Michelle, Peggy's name isn't dirty! The asshole that killed her is the guilty party, and why does this town refuse to see that?"

"Oh I can actually answer that question!" I jumped up and down. "I know the answer to that question because it's too damn simple," I giggled. "Peggy's name is suspicious because no one really knows the killer's name." I stopped my charade of jumping up and down and stood still "Think about it for a minute and it will make sense to you, too. There are only three names that one can associate with the case: Peggy, Arthur Root Jr., and Peggy's mother, Mary Alice. Root walked out of the court room a free man. That leaves only two names, and that explains the stigma surrounding Peggy and Mary Alice, doesn't it?"

"You make it sound simple, but I think instead of running from the kid's name, someone needs to hunt down her killer because the more I look at the documents relating to her murder the more enraged I become."

I started to get the picture "I guess you hit the jackpot in terms of public records, and you aren't happy with your findings."

"Well the best way I can explain it is that I found the court transcript. Yep, I found all ten pages of it."

"I see." I didn't have the benefit of seeing the transcript, so I was in the dark, but ten pages didn't offer much hope in terms of learning anything new. We returned to the pile of books Susan spread out on a table in the records room to continue the search for any information available.

We worked diligently throughout the afternoon locating everything from fees paid to jurors to witness subpoenaed by both sides. I scanned aged criminal records for many of the names mentioned throughout the case and struggled to read the handwritten recordings entered into huge books.

"Look at this!" Susan called me over to inspect a yellowed piece of paper. "They filed a motion to allow Arthur Root Jr. to attend the memorial services for his little brother when he drowned, and I don't mean to be disrespectful of the dead, but that's a rather kind gesture toward a man they believed guilty of killing Peggy Reber."

"Isn't that amazing?" I laughed bitterly at the legal document in my hand. "A year after Peggy's vicious murder and six months after formally charging him with one of the worst crimes in local history, he is allowed to pay his last respects when his family suffers a tragic loss. That is almost a slap in the face where Peggy is concerned because if the state thought they had enough evidence against him to charge him with killing a teenager, he sure as hell didn't deserve the right to mourn a dead teenager."

"He was charged with the crime, but not convicted, so don't go off the deep end."

"Hey I support innocent until proven guilty, and I am certain that the death of his kid brother saddened the community, but don't lose sight of that murder charge hanging over his head or the first dead teenager in the picture."

"It was a kind a compassionate gesture on the part of the court."

"Yeah, well I want the courts to start being kind and compassionate to Peggy."

I didn't resent Arthur Root Jr.'s release to join his family in burying their loved one, but I wondered about the passion to secure justice for Peggy because twelve months prior the community wanted Peggy's killer off the streets, and yet the man accused of the crime received a favor from the court. It was a different time and I repeatedly reminded myself of that fact, but it was an interesting call considering the severity of the charges against him.

Later in the day, I met Donald Hall on a street corner, and I was excited at the prospect of meeting the man that acted as my sounding board throughout my journey of research. I approached his patrol car and introduced myself, and I could feel his visual head-to-toe inspection even though his sunglasses prevented me from actually seeing his eyes. Donald was a man of average height sporting a few extra pounds, and he appeared to be in his mid-40s.

"That's an interesting license plate you've got there." He motioned toward my North Carolina tags on my vehicle. "80's mom?"

"My son's name is Bo, so Bo's Mom just made sense when I decided to get personalized plates." I didn't give it too much thought before, but my North Carolina vanity plate stuck out like a sore thumb in the central Pennsylvania town. I wasn't on a top-secret mission, but I was also asking questions about a murder and the killer wasn't in a jail cell. I wasn't fearful of my safety, but I wasn't going to take too many chances either. I also wondered about a detective that couldn't even read my license plate correctly.

"How is your research coming along? Are you making any progress, or is this just a social visit?"

"Oh I take two steps forward and three steps back. I never really get the feeling that I am making any progress, and to be quite honest it pisses me off at times, but I'm not one to walk away from a challenge."

"What you are doing is good old-fashioned police work and you are making great progress." He offered a few words of encouragement.

"I appreciate that, but I want nothing more than a legitimate investigation of Peggy's murder instead of the stage that's set."

"Well you know the deal as much as anyone, and I can't say too much right now because it is an open case and the brass insist they're giving it their best shot." He hesitated. "The investigation definitely leaves a lot to be desired and it is less than the best the department has to offer, but it's the only game in town."

"Gee, coach," I said with a smile. "If the home team isn't careful we could catch up with them and run them off the court, and you know that wouldn't go over too well with the local government."

"I'm glad you said that because even though I can't assist you directly, I will gladly coach you where ever possible. I don't think you see the value of your ignorance regarding police investigations, and it is the key to your success because you aren't taking anything for granted. I will anchor you when you need it and I will offer guidance, but the real story is someone without any police training tearing into this story and making a difference."

"Donald I can't really make a difference because I am not a law enforcement officer."

"You can't arrest anyone and you can't access the police file on the murder, but you can make a difference in the case if you apply yourself and your knowledge effectively."

I walked away from the cop feeling optimistic about my capabilities and I felt rejuvenated in my efforts.

Lebanon's Public Library is a pretty building tucked behind the main thoroughfare. It offers all the conveniences of any big city facility, but I wasn't interested in the modern technology it offered, rather the dusty old books in the reference section.

"We want to know Peggy's neighbors and friends, and I know exactly where we can find them."

"I am going to pretend I understand what you're saying, but the truth is you lost me." Susan followed my lead.

"When I get all emotional and I want to take a trip down memory lane reminiscing about high school, what is the first thing I pull out?" I quizzed her. "High school memories are recorded annually in none other than a year book, and the library houses copies of local yearbooks."

"Oh you're good. You are very good!" She stroked my ego, and we both started laughing.

"If you think that's impressive wait until I tell you about the second part of my plan," I said, baiting her curiosity. "It's a long shot, but on the chance that Lebanon published city directories back then, we would have a gold mine in terms of locating Peggy's neighbors. One of the several features in current city directories is the ability to look up a specific address. The directory lists the name of the resident at that address, so if that information is available in 1968 we would know the residents of the building."

"You stayed awake all last night thinking of this, didn't you?"

"We both stayed awake a whole lot of nights thinking of everything possible, and this happens to be one thing we missed until this point, so let's hope it's worth the time and effort."

I felt butterflies in my stomach when I spotted decades of city directories on a lower shelf, and I dropped to my knees to review their contents. We walked out of the library on a natural high. "This was an absolutely awesome day and I think we need to celebrate."

"Amen, sister!" Susan shared my delight in all the information we obtained throughout the day. "I just love how we can get so frustrated and tickle the fringe of giving up, and then something always pops out of left field and keeps us in the game a little while longer."

"That, my dear, is part of the beauty of Peggy Reber. I don't think she is ready to be put on a shelf forever, and we could be her last hope, so every now and then we get lucky."

We returned to the hotel to refresh ourselves and make a few calls home to check on our children before we set out to celebrate over dinner.

"I have one more thing I want to do." I picked up the telephone to make one more call. I grabbed a pen and paper and tapped the pen against the tablet while waiting for the party to answer the phone. "Kathryn, I apologize for bothering you and I regret that I am calling about such a sad topic, but my name is Michelle Gooden, and I am reviewing the death of your sister."

Susan had no idea who I was calling, and she slid down in a chair with a look of total disbelief.

"I just want to ask you a few questions and I really hope I haven't called at a bad time." I prayed that the woman wouldn't terminate the phone call, and I was pleasantly surprised when she assured me it wasn't an inconvenient time to talk to her.

"I know this is a painful subject for you and I can't tell you enough how sorry I am up for poking at old wounds."

"It's okay, really, and it's not a great subject, but it's been a long time so it's not as hard to talk about it." Kathryn was extremely soft spoken.

"It's definitely been a long time," I agreed. "But I still respect the loss you suffered, so I want to make this quick and painless. I know you were just a kid yourself at the time of the crime, but you were married and had a newborn and then you lost Peggy, so I know that was a very eventful year in your life. I guess I will start at the top. I saw that you testified at the trial on behalf of the defense and I must ask if you think Arthur Root Jr. killed your sister?"

"No, I never believed he killed her." She didn't hesitate for a moment in her response. "He was a nice man, and I still don't believe he killed her."

"Kathryn, what was Peggy like as a person? By that I mean what did she enjoy?" I wanted to know about the person instead of the victim, and I did not want Kathryn to feel trapped by a bunch of questions about the crime.

"Peggy was shy, but she loved to laugh, and we laughed together a lot."

I almost knew she was smiling on the other end of the phone just by the tone of her voice and the recollection of her sister's laughter. "We were teenagers so of course we loved listening to the radio, but the one thing I really remember is that Peggy loved to read books."

"So Peggy was a reader." I nodded my head more for Susan's benefit than anything else. "What kind of books did Peggy like to read?"

"Oh my, it's been so long."

I hated asking the question because I didn't want Kathryn to feel the thirty plus years that passed.

"I remember she liked the romance novels. I just can't remember what they're called."

"Kathryn, keeping in mind that you and Peggy were twins I trust you shared secrets. I have to wonder if there was anyone Peggy was genuinely scared of." I struggled to deliver my question tactfully.

"I don't know how much you know, but there was a high traffic of people that went through the apartment." I could tell she was weighing her words carefully.

"I realize that the two of you didn't enjoy a traditional lifestyle," I said, trying to ease her discomfort. "And I am familiar with the fact that your mother entertained quite a few people in that apartment."

I literally heard her sigh in relief. "Yes that's right, so it wasn't a dangerous place but it wasn't the safest either, and I think Peggy and I both sensed that."

"It was never mentioned in any of the reports that I read so I have no real reason for bringing this subject up, but I have to ask you if Peggy was pregnant." I was taking a chance by violating Peggy's image after death, but I had to run the risk.

"I think she thought she was."

Oddly I could sense again that the woman was probably smiling at the memory of her slain sister because it was an intimacy shared between them.

I went out on a limb trying to get a certain answer about the potential that Peggy was sure about a pregnancy. "Goodness knows we didn't have the luxury of home pregnancy tests back then so I am going to foolishly ask if she knew for certain that she was pregnant."

"No, she didn't know for sure, but I think she thought that she was and just didn't tell anyone." I wondered if anyone bothered to mention that to the investigators at the time of the crime. "She told me she wanted to tell me something, but we never got the chance to have that conversation"

"Again, I apologize for stirring up any difficult memories, and I sincerely appreciate you taking this time with me. If I violate your privacy please just give the word and I will stop. The news reported that your husband beat you a few days before the crime and police had to be called."

She confirmed the event.

"Kathryn, the newspaper reported you were wearing the orange dress Peggy made in home ec the day of that assault."

She admitted to that, too.

"The news said the dress was torn in the altercation. Is it possible that Peggy could mend that tear?"

Kathryn told me the orange dress Peggy made in her high school home economics course was torn beyond repair the day her husband and she had the altercation. I knew she didn't like the direction the conversation took, so I offered a different approach.

"There was a man charged with attempting to ravish Peggy in 1967 and according to the newspaper it went before the courts in February of 1968, yet the man was never identified in the newspaper."

"Oh," she went cold. "Well, I don't know what that's all about. I don't remember anything like that." I was losing her at a rapid pace. In April of 1967 she and Peggy were two thirteen-year-old identical twins and it was really had to believe she didn't know about the violation of her sister.

"I talked to your stepfather a few months ago and I have to tell you he was the sweetest man. I truly enjoyed talking to him, and I remember reading that shortly after the crime you moved in with him."

"Yes I did."

This time I knew she was remembering the past and not necessarily smiling.

"He was always very nice to us, and I think he is a good man."

"I never met the man but he spoke freely with me and I guess he captured my undying respect when I learned five years after the crime, and after going on to start another family, he bought Peggy a tombstone. I listened to the man speak, and I could hear the love in his voice when he talked about her and you, too."

"He was always very good to us, and I haven't talked to him in a couple years, but it's not because he did anything wrong. When we lived with him our lives were. . ." she couldn't find the right word to finish her sentence.

I didn't want to plant thoughts in her head, but her actions spoke volumes when she moved in with him after the murder of her twin sister, so I threw out a word.

"Safe?"

"Yes." She embraced the word. "We were always safe when we lived with him and our lives were normal. Oh, he didn't hesitate to scold us and spank us at times, but we weren't in any danger when we lived with him"

"Kathryn, was there anyone that you can think of that would want to take Peggy's life?"

Her answer left me stunned. I listened to Kathryn recant her memories of May 25, 1968 and I stood dumbfounded. "Kathryn, did you tell detectives what you just told me?" The information she shared with me during that phone call was meant for the ears of detectives, prosecutors and jurors.

"I told detectives exactly what I was instructed to tell them. I was very young and I had to protect my baby, so I did what I was told"

I was not going to pursue the issue any further.

"How is your mother?" I tried to change the subject and hopefully learn something, too.

"She's getting older."

I could sense she was protective of her mother.

"It's been a long time and she is not the same person today that she was back then."

I knew our conversation was approaching its end "I want to thank you again for talking to me, and I should probably go because I need to grab some supper before everything in town closes, but I would love to buy you a cup of coffee. There is one more thing. . ." I took another gamble. "I was looking over some public records today and I noticed that your husband fathered a child by another woman a few months before you gave birth to your daughter." I waited for her response.

"Yes. That's true." She sounded defeated, and I wanted to reach out and hug her because it was too obvious her life was never easy. The call closed on a quality note and I didn't trust she would open up again, but she didn't close any doors to communication.

"There is nothing quite like going for the gold." Susan sat amazed at the conversation she listened to second-hand. "I can't believe you just picked up the phone and called that woman." She bounced to her feet "And how did you get your hands on her phone number?"

"There will never be secrets between us, and I love you to no end, but sometimes one has to be a native of Lebanon to get the inside scoop. A little bird helped me out with a couple names and a couple phone numbers."

"Well, the minute we are done having the best meal of our lives, I think we should stop by a feed store and buy some bird seed because that little bird earned a quality meal, too."

Dinner was not near the celebration we played it out to be, mostly because we wanted to read the material we obtained at the courthouse and plan our strategy for the following day. But our spirits were high nonetheless.

■■

The following day I waited until my house was empty to call Ray Boyer. I didn't want any distractions during our conversation, and I was pleased when he answered the phone.

"Mr. Boyer this is Michelle Gooden. I apologize for taking so long to get back with you, and I missed you during my time in Pennsylvania."

"It's really funny you should call! I was just telling my son the other day that you must be full of it because you just called that one time, and then I didn't hear from you again." Ray Boyer was a straightforward man and I didn't get the impression that he sugarcoated too much of anything for anyone. I liked that part of his personality.

"I regret the delay, and no, I'm not full of it. I'm still digging my way through bits and pieces of Peggy's story, but information doesn't come easy."

"You ain't telling me nothin' new. Right after the crime, I went a little crazy and got it in my head to play detective." He made a weak attempt to laugh at himself, and he didn't elaborate on the story.

"I'm far from a detective, so I am battling the odds. With the new investigation into Peggy's case, I spend a lot of time questioning myself."

"Boy, that's a joke, isn't it?" He let out a hearty laugh. "They hype this new investigation and plaster that shit across the newspapers, but not one person has bothered to talk to me, so they don't want to know too much, do they?"

"No one has contacted you about the review of Peggy's case?"

"Lady, no one ever wanted to hear what I had to say. Not then and not now. You are the first person in over thirty years that has taken the time to listen to anything I have to say on the subject, and we ain't covered half of what I know."

I could tell he wanted to talk, and I certainly wanted to listen.

"Mr. Boyer, I would love to hear anything you have to say on the subject."

"Oh, call me Ray. My dad is Mr. Boyer. Ever since they threw me in that cell they have been telling me what happened that day instead of listening to a damn thing anybody has to say."

"Could you give me an example of something you tried to tell them and they wouldn't listen to?"

"Gladly. Let's start with that damn dress they say Peggy was wearing that day. That's the first thing I wanted them to explain to me, and nobody has got it right yet. I was with Peggy that day until that bastard picked me up and threw me in jail. The dress on her body was not what she was wearing that day. They left me in a room with pictures of her body, an open window and a gun. Oh, they questioned me about the murder, and I kept trying to tell them about that dress, but they just wouldn't listen to me."

"But the paper reported and the testimony at the trial clearly stated that Peggy was wearing a burnt-orange dress that she made in a home economics class."

"Lady, I know what the paper said, and I know what she had on in those crime scene photos because they are carved in my memory forever, but I'm telling you that when I left her that day, that is *not* what she was wearing." He went on to describe the outfit the young girl was donning the last time he saw her alive.

"Ray, maybe she changed clothes after you were taken away, and she put that dress on later." I didn't really see the significance on the issue of the dress Peggy was wearing.

"I remember the last time I saw her alive just like I remember those damn photos of her body. She was standing outside that building with her little purse in her hand when I was hauled off." He was indicating that she left the apartment building at the same time.

"Tell me about the bite mark." I wanted to hear the details surrounding one of the most interesting aspects of the crime and the trial.

I had to wait for him to stop laughing. "I want to tell somebody about that damn bite mark they tried to tag on me. One of those experts said Peggy suffered a bite to her breast something like a five or ten minutes before she died, and I was sitting in a jail cell at that time, mind you. They took a bunch of dental impressions from some guys that hung out at that apartment, and wouldn't you know I would be the match."

He started laughing again, only Ray Boyer wasn't laughing at the situation, rather the authorities that failed Peggy.

"They got me up on the witness stand and tried to make it that I inflicted that bite when we were making love. I told them straight out. A hickey was one thing, but I didn't bite her. I did everything I could to protect that girl. I sure as hell didn't hurt her. And what happened to the bite being inflicted so close to her death? I am telling you I didn't bite her"

"Ray, your brother didn't have to give a dental impression, and yet he had a key to the apartment, so I am forced to wonder if your teeth shared the same dental imperfections the way siblings sometimes do."

"I'm no dentist and I don't know about all that, but I think every man that had a key and entered that apartment that week deserved consideration." He didn't resent being a suspect, but he clearly resented obvious candidates escaping the basics in identifying Peggy's killer.

"I don't know if you realize it," I started, "but the bow and its splinter fell victim to the flood. Speaking of a bow, I stopped by your house, and my heart stopped when I saw a toy archery set on your front porch."

"Oh, that must be my grandson's. Damn right you're going to see bows here, and anything else associated with hunting." He didn't shy away from the subject.

"Did you say a splinter of the bow? Because if you did, that's another one I would like someone to explain to me. That was a fiberglass bow in Peggy's room, and it's not going to splinter." He went on to explain various types of bows to me.

"I saw something just the other day in the old news reports that captured my attention, and I am anxious to hear what you have to say because it threw me back a few steps."

The same constable that apprehended Ray Boyer on the afternoon that Peggy Reber lost her life jailed him illegally when he returned to Lebanon to testify at the murder trial almost two years later. A judge literally had to intervene on Ray Boyer's behalf.

"After I read that account, I didn't have too many doubts that you were not necessarily a random pick, but maybe that guy just didn't like you very much. I was shocked. After what happened to Peggy, he put you in jail again and illegally at that!"

The constable apparently didn't view Ray Boyer's apprehension as a factor that led to Peggy's vulnerability. I could hear the official dialogue in my mind how the constable possessed a professional standard and attempted to rid Lebanon's streets of lawbreakers. While Constable William Kimmel spared Lebanon the threat of Ray Boyer, a killer cut loose on a teenage girl. Never to be deterred, Kimmel jailed Boyer the next chance he got, even thought the jailing itself was illegal. Kimmel appeared to have his own agenda where Ray Boyer was concerned.

"Why did Kathryn and your brother move out of the apartment building that weekend?" I asked.

"It didn't have anything to do with Peggy or me. They moved into my parents' basement," he replied.

"I wonder if your parents would consider talking to me." I bounced the idea off him.

"Hell, I don't know, but they moved away years ago. They live in Oklahoma now."

"Your parents live in Oklahoma now?" I wanted to make sure I heard him correctly.

"They moved out there years and years ago. I can't even remember when, it's been that long."

I wondered what the chances were of so many people from Lebanon, Pennsylvania finding their way to the great state of Oklahoma. I explained to Ray how I located Arthur Root Jr. in Oklahoma, and I asked if he was aware of any connection. He didn't know of any link between the moves, yet he agreed that it was an interesting coincidence.

"Ray, did Peggy tell you by any chance that she thought she was pregnant?"

"No, she never said anything like that, and I know she would have told me if she was."

I didn't trust the accuracy of his words because his ego was in full force.

"I don't want to be disrespectful, but you were married to a woman that was pregnant with your second child, and you had a small child." I didn't want to offend or anger the man. "The last thing you needed to hear was that your teenage girlfriend was pregnant, too. Is it possible Peggy didn't tell you for that reason?"

"Peggy didn't keep any secrets from me," he said adamantly. I didn't want to excite him too much over mere speculation.

"My friend presented an interesting scenario to me just yesterday." I shared Susan's theory about a man violating Peggy and possibly impregnating her and that being the source of the killer's rage.

"No one got near Peggy once I saw how vulnerable she was. I protected her and she knew that." I could hear his voice oozing testosterone. "I ran my brother off when he beat Kathy, I put that landlord in his place when he crossed the line and I wasn't going to let anyone hurt Peggy. That's why they waited until I was in a cage to go after her." I never really appreciated macho men, but I respected his protective instincts and I knew he wasn't lying to me. I also knew Ray didn't know Peggy for a long period of time. He only met Peggy after his brother married Peggy's twin. Richard Boyer and Kathryn Reber exchanged vows February 21, 1968 in Hagerstown, Maryland. Realistically, Ray Boyer barely knew Peggy three months before her death, if that, so he wasn't exactly aware of everything going on around Peggy, or the Reber home.

"You mentioned you tried to play detective" I didn't get to finish my sentence.

"Damn right I did. I knew good and well she only ended up dead because I got picked up that day. I went over it in my mind a million times. Hell I shacked up with Kathy for awhile trying to learn everything I could about what went on while I was sitting in that cell"

"You lived with Kathy and Richard after Peggy was killed?"

"Oh hell no lady!" he laughed at me. "I lived with Kathy. Yeah, isn't that something?" he almost marveled at the absurdity of his words. "If you think that's strange we all went on a double date the summer Peg was killed" I was beyond confused. "Yeah, Linda and me and Kathy and Dick we went to the Key Drive-In for one of those weekend all-nighters like they used to have back then"

"Let me see if I understand you correctly…after Peggy was killed you went to an all night drive-in with your brother, his wife Kathy and Linda the mother of his other newborn baby?"

"That's what I am telling you"

"Then sometime after Peggy's death you and Kathy lived together? Well, forgive me for asking, but what happened to Richard?"

"Lady, that marriage didn't last too long after Peg was murdered and that was a crazy time for me. I couldn't get over what was done to Peg. Kathy and I shacked up because I needed to learn anything she knew about Peggy and she needed somebody to protect her. I don't expect it to make sense to you or anybody else and quite frankly I don't give a damn what anybody thinks. I was the one living it and you just can't explain it to make sense. I knew one thing to be a fact and that was that son-of-a-bitch waited until I was out of the way and then he went after her. I could barely live with the feeling of guilt for not being there to protect her. It still tears me up inside. If I had been there that day Peggy would still be alive. I might be dead or that bastard might be dead, but Peggy would have been safe because there would have been a fight-to-the-death before I let anything happen to her. Lady, I don't expect you to understand this either, but I would give up all my tomorrows for one more hour with Peggy" Ray Boyer was only eighteen years old when Peggy was brutally killed that day.

After talking to Ray I had two more calls to make, and I knew they would be two of the most important calls I would place regarding Peggy.

■■

"Anne, it is your ever-loving cousin requesting yet another favor!" I hated to bother her again, but I needed her assistance. "Would you please call Ruth and ask her a really simple question for me?"

I called Kathryn next. "This is Michelle Gooden again, and of course I am sorry for bothering you, but I would like to know one thing if you don't mind me asking."

Kathryn was agreeable.

"The papers reported awhile back that the police were going to review Peggy's case again, and I was wondering if anyone from the police force has talked to you regarding your sister's death."

She told me no one bothered to talk to her about Peggy's murder since the time of the trial until I called her. Any claims of an investigation into the Reber case were clearly a joke. It was thirty-one years after Root's trial and no one from law enforcement bothered to talk to Ray or Kathy, yet officials were taking claim to a new investigation?

Quietly, I researched the murder of Peggy Reber throughout the time Lebanon's Police Department was investigating it. I didn't have the benefit of the compromised file, and I had no clue what to do with evidence even if it existed. But I knew enough to locate every living being that I could to ask every question I could think of, yet a trained detective failed to talk to Peggy's twin sister and her closest companion at the time of the crime. I traveled five hundred miles to talk to people that were right under the police department's nose. I struggled to learn the identities of people listed in the police file readily available to the detective assigned to the case. I doubted the legitimacy of the new investigation and I questioned the integrity of the politicians that used Peggy's name in vain. I knew without any doubt the claim of an investigation into the murder of Peggy Reber was definitely a farce.

The chief of police fired the female police officer claiming she compromised the file and the case. She, in turn, filed a wrongful termination suit against the city of Lebanon. Well, the last thing the city wanted, or needed, was to have their investigation solve the murder of Peggy Reber confirming the female officer was not at fault with the file. They would look like complete idiots.

Meanwhile, the people of Lebanon were told there was a new investigation into the Reber case, and they took officials at their word. Average citizens had no way of knowing that investigation failed to include talking to the family and friends of the victim, or witnesses from the trial. Oh, once Lebanon realized Art Root Jr. wasn't really dead, they flew a detective to Arizona to interview him. It was almost funny to watch from a distance. The administration was willing to pay the expense of airfare and lodging to send a detective to Arizona to interview a man that was found not guilty, and could never be charged with the crime again, but that same detective couldn't manage to interview witnesses right there in good ol' Lebanon.

Ultimately, the female police officer had the last laugh. She actually had the permission of her supervisor to remove the Reber file, and Lebanon's police department did not have a written policy prohibiting officers from taking such files home. She did not return to the police force, but she did receive a settlement.

I no sooner hung up the phone after talking to Kathryn, and the phone rang. Anne asked Ruth what Peggy was wearing the last time Ruth saw Peggy alive a little after 8 p.m. the night she died, and Ruth described the same outfit that Ray mentioned. Ray didn't know anything about Ruth, so it was interesting that they both said the same thing without ever discussing it prior to that. Peggy was NOT wearing an orange dress.

■■

My heart raced the day I actually talked to Art Root Jr. because it was the climax to years of searching, and I was overwhelmed with emotions. He was in Lana's house when he and I talked, and after a very nerve-racking conversation with him, I talked to Lana.

"I told you that you didn't see the last of him," I teased the woman that shared her most intimate secrets with me.

"He is just here to see the children, Michelle, but what did he say to you?"

"He said he didn't kill Peggy Reber, and he told me that he explained that to the cop that talked to him just a few weeks ago." Lana didn't appreciate that point, but I knew it was the detective from Lebanon. I had to wonder if his criminal file in Lebanon, Pennsylvania continued to sport the status of retired after the detective's trip to Arizona.

"Lana, he was upset that I bothered his family. That makes perfect sense to me because he went to a lot of effort to hide his identity and spare you any exposure to this part of his life."

"Michelle, you don't think he killed that girl, do you?"

"He can never be tried for that crime again, so Peggy is a closed chapter in his life, but if I had been on that jury…" I stopped on that note and wished the woman the best before I hung up the phone.

I studied the F.B.I. reports until my eyes hurt and while I don't have formal training in the field of forensics or law enforcement, I think I see things the authorities overlooked. Arthur Root Jr.'s clothing and Peggy Reber's dress exchanged fibers at some point in time. That is a fact. Days before the crime against Peggy, her sister was wearing that same dress when her husband beat her, according to court testimony. Arthur Root Jr. was there at the time of that domestic dispute, and he was wearing that same green suit. A battered woman and a murder victim wearing the same dress without the benefit of being laundered would definitely complicate hair and fiber issues associated with the dress. The F.B.I. stated the dress was torn since it was last laundered.

Did Kathryn wash the dress before she returned it to her sister? No. The dress was torn too badly during the altercation between Kathryn and her husband, Dick Boyer, a few days before the murder to be worn at all.

"Susan, how could people testify to seeing Peggy wearing that orange dress that day if it didn't survive a domestic dispute earlier in the week? I don't get it. Oh, and then there is the little matter that Ray Boyer and Ruth Winters, two people we know for a fact saw Peggy that day, have her wearing something completely different than the orange dress."

"My first thought is suggestive thinking," she responded immediately. "I don't doubt for a minute that those people actually saw Peggy that day, but I am willing to bet they really had no idea what she was wearing until they read it in the paper, or learned it in some other manner." She waited for me to say something. "Michelle, what was I wearing yesterday?"

"I barely remember what I had for breakfast, and you want me to remember what you were wearing yesterday?"

"That's my point exactly. We see people all the time and we don't pay attention to all the details. People saw Peggy that day and it was nothing out of the ordinary, or of great importance, until they realized she was murdered."

"Damn Susan, there was a whole lot of emphasis on that dress. The whole case against Root hinges on the fibers at the scene, many of which came from the dress. I don't get it."

"Michelle, we are never going to have all the answers, but let's think reasonably for a minute. The cops had to be called because Dick Boyer assaulted Kathryn while she was wearing that dress a few days before the murder. She was 14-years-old and just gave birth to his baby in the weeks prior. My daughters aren't twins, but they are still sisters. Can't you see Kathryn seeking refuge in her mother's apartment and changing clothes in her sister's bedroom?"

"What's your point?"

"There is a huge part of your dress fibers found in Peggy's room" she was convinced. "Well, we know one thing for sure and that is there is something strange about the dress, and someone is wrong in their testimony somewhere down the line."

The state tried Root based on hair and fiber, but a neighbor covered Peggy's body with a blanket that Peggy's mother admitted to having sex on with several men. Arthur Root Jr. was one of the several men Mary Alice engaged in sex with on that blanket, so that complicated everything in the world of hairs found on Peggy's body. The F.B.I. report lists many hairs and fibers found at the crime scene that remain unidentified even to this day. Art Root Jr. aroused suspicion because he admitted to seeing Peggy in the apartment that day, so he received special attention during testing.

The ugly truth is that they based a case against Root because they had a match in hair and fibers, while the dental impressions didn't match at all. Of course Art Root Jr.'s hair and fibers were going to be present because he was a frequent visitor to the apartment, and engaged in sex on the blanket that was used to cover Peggy's body. Officials got a match with him and were satisfied with that, but they failed to identify the source of many, many hairs and fibers. Other men with keys to the apartment were not included in the pool of testing for hair, fibers and dental impressions. Perhaps if investigators tested all the men with keys to the apartment, a different suspect would emerge due to a process of elimination, or the population of evidence. Detectives did not test all possible suspects, but settled on Root once they had a match.

If only they had applied themselves to being thorough in the process, Peggy's murder could be solved. There was no effort to identify and eliminate the hair of Ray Boyer, yet we knew he was in the apartment. There was no effort to identify and eliminate the hair of Dick Boyer and he, too, was a frequent visitor of the apartment. Constable William Kimmel was in the apartment that day and modern science is teaching us he probably left hair behind as well. The landlord had a key to the apartment, so he was not above forensic testing either. Mary Alice lived in the apartment and there was no effort to identify and separate her hair in the process. Kathryn was not included in comparison testing.

The case against Root sounds so impressive from a forensic stand point until one realizes investigators settled for a match with Root. They failed to test all obvious members of the family's inner circle and the forensic possibilities they presented. A hell of a lot hair and fibers went unidentified.

Mr. Killer likely left more hair and fiber at the scene than anyone else, but once detectives had a match in Root, the investigation came to a halt. We are told Root's forensics were present at the crime scene, but he wasn't alone. We don't know for a fact he dominated the scene. We know Root's forensics are all detectives bothered to identify. It's rather amusing because the community stood up in arms about the amount of men Mary Alice dated, and detectives failed to accurately include the family circle in their investigation, so Mary Alice's male companions completely escaped consideration, and identification. Oh, a killer missed out on consideration, and identification, too.

■■■

Reviewing the evidence obtained from the crime scene presented a few questions because at one point someone shared with me off the record that police officers frequented the apartment socially before the crime. Sure enough, one of the items taken into custody after the crime was a pair of handcuffs. Possessing handcuffs in the modern world is quite simple because one can buy them at a variety of stores, but in 1968, one couldn't obtain such devices with ease, yet a pair of handcuffs found its place on the list of evidence obtained from the crime scene.

Oh, the explanations danced on my mind, but the real wonder didn't escape me, and the queer item taken into custody never warranted serious scrutiny in public records or on an investigative level. The apartment didn't always embrace the traditional norm, but handcuffs crossed the line, and they went unmentioned in the hectic investigation except for the evidence report.

Keeping in mind that handcuffs were far from an easily obtained item at the time and assuming the cuffs belonged to a member of law enforcement on some capacity, I longed to review forms recording equipment issued to law enforcement officers at the time. I was willing to bet the farm that someone within local law enforcement received new cuffs within a matter of weeks of the slaying. Not because he killed Peggy, but because he played a little too much at her home on a social level, and his original cuffs fell into evidence secured at the crime scene. Even I laughed at my theory until I bounced it off a modern day C.I.A. agent with Pennsylvania roots.

"Michelle, you're probably right when you mention that cuffs were not readily available to the public back then. You have a good point when you hit on the fact handcuffs obtained from the crime scene are on the list of evidence obtained from the crime scene, and it warrants exploration."

Even with the confirmation of a professional in the field of intelligence on an international level I was still swimming upstream, and I knew local officials wouldn't give it the benefit of the doubt. Handcuffs were not an everyday item, but they hit the list of things secured from the Reber apartment when Peggy died, and though it was odd, it never hit the status of a hot topic in the investigation.

There was a half bottle of beer at the crime scene, and it sported 22 fingerprints. After all the testing of fingerprints on the bottle, thirteen fingerprints remained unidentified on that one item. The killer himself couldn't manage to place thirteen different prints on that one bottle. It's no surprise the local police force met challenges in handling all the evidence at the crime scene, especially during the hours following the discovery of Peggy's body. No one had experienced a crime of such magnitude before, so naturally, a few errors enveloped the collection of evidence. Thirteen fingerprints on that one bottle of beer remain unidentified, and a killer remains unidentified, too.

Evidence collected at the crime scene included a container of Humphreys #11. Humphreys #11 was an over the counter product credited with assisting in irregular or delayed menstrual cycles. In 1968, when a young woman had concerns about being pregnant, she would take Humphreys #11 in hopes of inducing the menstrual cycle. No one can attach ownership of the pills to Peggy, but their mere presence had to beg a few questions about a possible pregnancy, and the fact they joined the evidence taken into custody can't go ignored. I wrestled with the fact that pregnancy testing never hit the spotlight, yet the papers mentioned a man charged with corrupting and ravishing minors a few months prior, so I pondered that possibility more than most, and I took it to a new degree.

Two tubes of lipstick underwent testing because a pair of panties taken from the apartment hosted foreign smears of an identified substance, but there wasn't enough adequate substance on the panties to make the match conclusively. The mere suggestion of lipstick on her panties sent my imagination into a spiral. I wondered if Peggy's panties silenced her throughout the assault, thus resulting in her lipstick smearing the intimate apparel.

A Caucasian head hair dyed black while not matching any of the hair samples taken from the victim or Root, Reyes, or Rivera found its place on the list of evidence when investigators removed it from Peggy's left thigh. One single hair doesn't give the appearance of importance, but the report only identified one hair from Peggy's head on Art Root's coat, and he was charged with the crime. The origin of one unidentified hair on her thigh deserved consideration, yet it was little more than a notation on an aged report. No, that single hair on Root's coat didn't make a murder case, rather it was a stepping-stone, but if one hair on her thigh remained unidentified, it took on the form of a stepping-stone, too.

The more I looked at the report the more I realized that numerous hairs found at the scene never reached the point of identification. I empathized with the original investigating officers and the frustration that they battled on a daily basis, and I realized that every unidentified hair represented an unidentified killer, and quite possibly the key to revealing his identity.

Arthur Root Jr. didn't escape my suspicion, but I could support his guilt more if not for all the unidentified hairs, fibers, his alibi, and the dental impressions. Also, when considering all the overlooked candidates, Art Root Jr. almost faded from view. Did the evidence point at Arthur Root Jr., or did his arrest stem from the fact his hair and fibers actually met identification, while so much remained a mystery?

The F.B.I. report listed so much in technical form that it challenged my ignorance in forensics, but I understood enough to know that the report didn't provide a smoking gun in regards to Peggy's death. Lebanon, Pennsylvania endured the great flood of 1972 and all the physical evidence remaining from the case supposedly washed away, but I fantasized that the F.B.I. still possessed something of worth concerning Peggy's case file. Sadly, information in relation to the F.B.I.'s actual evidence remaining proved to be the first real brick wall in my review of Peggy's case. The information I could obtain from the F.B.I. hit certain limitations because I was not a member of a law enforcement agency, but I submitted a written inquiry just the same. I also wrote to the Armed Forces Institute of Pathology in hopes of locating the dental pathologist that testified at the trial along with the dental impressions used in comparison to the bite mark on Peggy's breast.

Three decades passed and the chances were slim, but technologies offered Peggy's murder so many possibilities for justice that I had to make every effort from a nonprofessional's perspective. I longed for law enforcement to embrace the case if only for a brief period to give it one last chance at resolution before it faded from view forever, but chances of that were slim to none. Lebanon's police department sat at the helm of Peggy's ship and unless they took the case seriously one more time, everything stood still, but local officials answered to a force stronger than their own standards: the people of Lebanon that voted them in office.

■■

"What do we do now?" Susan stared at the laboratory reports spread across my dining room table.

"We keep going until we run out of places to go and we eventually tell the story. The plan doesn't change; knowledge of the crime is simply taking on a different perspective."

"Do you really think we can make a difference?"

"A philosopher once said that evil lives because good men do nothing. Well, let's test that theory. We can list a dozen things we can't do, or we can take the approach of what we can do, and I think I speak for both of us when I say we need to do everything we possibly can."

"I'm not abandoning my post, but I guess I am losing sight of what we hope to accomplish."

"We wanted to know what happened to Peggy, and we have a better understanding of that today than we did a year ago, so we are making progress. We can't force anyone to apply professional investigative skills to this case, but I am hoping that if we continue to learn and tell the facts the way we found them, the voters of Lebanon will demand a review of Peggy's murder because we both know it all has to start with Lebanon."

"What if we wrote to the attorney general of Pennsylvania or the governor?" Susan was shooting high.

"I would skip up the steps of the capital building in Harrisburg if we had something concrete, but right now we would be looking at matching straightjackets when we approach the governor's office." I laughed at the thought. "I really think it's pretty simple if you think about it and then present it in the correct light."

I gathered my thoughts for a moment. "The Commonwealth never identified Peggy's killer and that means there is a good chance that he walks among the residents of the community even today. If that doesn't spark public interest in the case nothing ever will."

"Gee, that's enough to make you look at your neighbors a little more closely, isn't it?"

"Only your male neighbors over the age of fifty-five." I shrugged my shoulders. "There is no reason to believe the killer was not a native and there sure as hell isn't any reason to believe he left the area after the crime. There is a chance the killer sat right there under their noses the whole time and he could remain there today. If that is the case, don't forget that public statement about the loss of all the physical evidence was music to his ears."

"Michelle, do you think he still looks over his shoulder in fear of being exposed?"

"Susan, something deep inside of me tells me that man never looked over his shoulder a day in his life. I don't think he looked back at Peggy, and I don't think he feared too much because my gut tells me he is the epitome of arrogance."

"Do you think he even thinks about Peggy after all these years?"

"No, I don't. I don't think he values human life enough to think about her or anyone else for that matter."

"So he's not going to be the leader of a neighborhood community watch program, then."

"Hardly!" I snickered at her sarcasm. "It's more like he'll be the grumpy old man on the block."

"Don't forget the bastard could be dead by now because after all it's been over thirty years."

"Just remember that saying: *only the good die young*. If that holds true, that son of a bitch is going to live a long, long time. I rarely wish harm on anyone and Peggy's killer is no exception, but I must admit I wish him a long, long life."

"Long enough to be identified in his golden years?" Susan caught my drift.

"I couldn't have said it better myself."

■■

I called the judge that sat on the bench during Arthur Root Jr.'s trial for Peggy's murder, and unfortunately, he was in the Pittsburgh area on business matters when I placed that call. I talked with his wife a little while and she invited me to call back later in the week when her husband was due home. I called a few other lawyers that participated in the legal proceedings during the 1970 trial.

I stood stunned when one asked, "Is this call being recorded?" I assured the man that I was not using any recording devices, and I scratched my head at his concerns because my initial questions were quite harmless in matter. Peggy Reber's name continued to spark the strangest responses from all ends of the social scale.

Peggy's autopsy report was not going to be easy to locate, but there were avenues that I needed to travel. The local hospital told me they only kept autopsy reports twenty-five years, so I was too late to obtain the last medical report on Peggy by that means.

I called the county coroner and that eventually mounted to a series of calls only to hear that they did not know the location of that file, so again I stood empty handed. The district attorney got a copy of the autopsy report and if it still existed, it sat obstructed under the cloud of an unsolved homicide. The little bit that really did remain relating to the teenage girl's murder stood sheltered by the very people that were responsible for securing her justice, and it angered me every time I came face to face with that fact.

The newspaper mentioned at the time of Peggy's death that child protective services knew of the hardships within Peggy's home, and that was my next target. The Nixon tapes warrant release, the Watergate files hit public view; John F. Kennedy's executive orders joined the ranks of public record, but a file in child protective services relating to a teen that died over three decades earlier is a different story. I respected the professionalism associated with the principle, but I literally laughed at the oxymoron. Child protective services did not protect Peggy when she was alive, but a third of a century later her file was safe with them.

"Call me a bitch, but I wish the evidence and autopsy report were placed in the care of child protective services because that's the most secure spot in Lebanon, Pennsylvania," I griped.

Susan looked up at me over the top rim of her reading glasses. "You aren't being a bitch, but you know that they work under pretty strict guidelines, so don't take it too personally."

"Susan, work with me for a moment," I said, highly irritated. "Let's just think about the name of the agency because it speaks volumes child protective services. At Peggy's ripe old age of fourteen, she still qualified as a child and she didn't receive any protection back then, but today that file is safe as it can be."

"You're confusing apples and oranges because it was a different time back then. What we call child abuse today was discipline back then, so think about what you're saying."

"Yeah, well I am going to hold on the thought that if documents on a national level can be released to the public, a file on a dead kid is not any more important than that. Who and what are they protecting now?"

"Peggy is dead, but there are still people alive that deserve the benefit of privacy in such matters, so it's a little bit more complicated than you want to admit."

I could feel anger welling up inside of me, hot and overwhelming. I knew Susan was right, but the injustice of the situation seemed absurd to me. "I can't support privacy rights under these conditions, and if that makes me unreasonable then so be it, but I think the time to protect, defend and shelter died when Peggy took her last breath."

"You are talking from your heart, not your head. If you calm down enough to be realistic you will see that."

"Yeah, well, realistically speaking, Peggy manages to slip through a hell of a lot of cracks in the system, and I'm not just referring to child protective services. You name one thing from the beginning until the end that is close to normal in the life and times of Margaret Lynn Reber. Peggy's home life, her brutal death, her killer, the stigma attached to the mere mention of her name. It is all bizarre, and my patience is growing thin with the nonsense. There was no conspiracy to kill Peggy, and I don't think there was a massive effort to shield her killer, but a whole lot of factors failed to protect her in life and secure her justice after death."

The mounting frustration from working toward finding answers about Peggy was taking a toll on me. I decided to go out on the back porch, enjoy the weather and clear my mind.

Though Arthur Root Jr.'s guilt did not jump out at me, I secured criminal records reports on him from a variety of locations even after talking to him. Arthur Root Jr.'s criminal record labeled him a serial criminal, and I guess I looked for a history of violence. Beyond the very questionable circumstances surrounding his stepdaughter in Oklahoma, Arthur Root Jr.'s criminal records did not represent him as a violent offender.

I didn't know what I expected to gain by contacting the attorney that represented Root in 1970, but it was one more person that remained from the original saga, so I dismissed my doubts and called the retired lawyer. His raspy voice gave hint to his age, but he was sharp and witty as I asked a few general questions about the trial. He captured my attention with one simple statement, "The Pepe Theory said it all."

Peggy Reber died May 25, 1968 in an apartment building that didn't afford its tenants any privacy due to its paper-thin walls. Peggy's murder was one of the most brutal crimes to ever take place in beautiful Lebanon, Pennsylvania, and the community stood stunned at the evil that stole the young girl's life. The police department shared the public's shock, but quickly recovered and worked around the clock using all resources available to locate the lunatic that walked their streets. The district attorney made repeated requests to the public for any information that would aid authorities in identifying anyone seen in or around the building that day. In a desperate attempt, the district attorney mailed letters to each apartment in the building requesting anyone with information to come forward on an anonymous level, but the efforts failed to get a response. It was highly unlikely that Peggy's killer entered the building, killed her and left the building without at least one tenant in the building seeing or hearing something, but no one came forward.

A local merchant sitting on her front porch a couple hundred yards away claimed she saw Arthur Root Jr. on the building's fire escape that day. She owned a Laundromat Root had recently burglarized, so her objectivity left room for doubt. A man came forward offering a description, but he went on to be charged for providing a false statement to police. The insurance salesman, Marlin Jones, took his life shortly after the crime, and he also assisted police with a composite sketch of a man he saw in the area the night of the crime, but the tenants in the building did not claim to see anything out of the ordinary during the massive manhunt for Peggy's killer.

Well, true to form, the tenants did not come forward to assist police with securing justice for Peggy, but at the midnight hour of the trial, literally, a tenant came forward with enough information to cast doubt on the entire trial. The defendant on trial for his life deserved any testimony that could ultimately save his life, and the victim deserved the benefit of anyone with information to give it to police during the search for Peggy's killer, yet once again, someone failed Peggy.

A female tenant testified for the defense that on the night of the crime shortly after midnight, she returned home after a date with her boyfriend. She said that as she approached her door, Chico Reyes attempted to block her entry to her apartment. She testified in a court of law that police questioned her after Peggy's death, but she didn't tell them about the incident. A teenage kid died in the same building, the man she allegedly encountered at her door sat in jail after questioning about Peggy's murder. There was an outstanding warrant for Reyes' arrest prior to the murder, so he was no real threat to anyone, and yet the tenant remained silent throughout the investigation.

I donned my imaginary police badge and fantasized about charging the woman with obstruction of justice in regards to a murder investigation. Her boyfriend at the time testified as well, and he echoed her accounts of the event, but he witnessed the exchange from his car parked in front of the building. He, however, said he gave the story to investigators, but no one questioned him.

The couple went on to get married after Peggy's murder and the Lebanon Daily News printed a picture of the happy couple when they testified at the trial. I pulled out the article with their photograph and I stood utterly disgusted when I saw their huge smiles during their fifteen minutes of fame. I respected their civic duty to testify to the truth on behalf of Root. Chico Reyes endured just as much scrutiny as Arthur Root Jr. if not more and more than likely, he was not the killer either. But the couple's actions left a bitter taste in my mouth.

The female blatantly testified in a court of law that she failed to tell investigators about an odd occurrence the night of the crime. I could not understand for a minute how anyone could do anything but help the investigators that dedicated themselves to solving Peggy's crime. A teenage girl died at the hands of a maniac, the whole town stood fearful, and yet at least one person stood within a courtroom and admitted to holding back information. I weighed out all the possibilities for her silence and nothing made sense to me. The couple didn't testify about an unknown intruder that could return to cause them bodily harm. Their personal safety stood no threat because he was a tenant in the building that they knew by name, and he sat behind bars immediately following the crime. I had no right to act as anyone's judge or jury, and I didn't think anyone had the right to hold back any information that could lead to the arrest of Peggy's killer.

The female tenant didn't put forth the effort to give police a clear view of the happenings in the apartment building that night, but she could step up to the plate almost two years later. I didn't have a desire to hear any explanation from the woman or her husband thirty years after the fact. Their testimony went down in local history as The Pepe Theory and while it assisted Root's defense (and rightfully so, if it was true testimony), it never assisted the men that searched for a killer.

I wondered how many other local residents knew something, or saw something that day and looked the other way for whatever reasons. No one could ever say that Peggy Reber deserved the fate that found her, and her killer certainly didn't deserve to walk away from the crime scene only to remain a nameless and faceless executioner. The Pepe Theory did not identify Peggy's assailant, and it did little more than assist the defendant to gain the jury's favor, but it represented so much more to me. People in the community knew things about Peggy's murder that could assist the authorities and they failed to come forward, but why? Peggy Reber was not a disposable being, and her killer was not larger than life, so why did anyone protect him?

I considered my own thoughts for a moment and I wondered if the inspiration for the silence included protecting the killer at all, or was it simply raw fear on behalf of anyone that knew anything about that day, or anyone that knew her killer and what he did that fateful day in May of 1968? If anyone knew for sure who killed Peggy Reber, of course there was a deep fear that he could kill again, and that fear would breed silence. I thought for a moment about anyone that could possess such knowledge for such a long time. I thought of how one would live throughout those years, and my heart broke for that person. Peggy Reber met evil in its rawest form and it stripped her of her life in a brutal manner, but Peggy was only his victim for a brief period, and anyone that carried the secret of her killer's identity was his prisoner forever. I sympathized with the unknown face that held the real knowledge of Peggy's crime because I didn't believe for a minute that the killer walked away totally undetected. Somewhere someone knew who killed Peggy Reber, and that person is the one that received a life sentence in the case.

Deep in my heart, I knew there was one person that endured the loss of Peggy even today, and I knew in my heart that she did not hold the answers to solving the crime. Peggy's mother lived a simple life not far from the apartment that she shared with Peggy at the time of the crime when I first talked to her. I couldn't escape the thoughts of all that the woman endured over the years and I respected her age and her fragility.

Peggy's mother marched to her own drum during a time of national unrest and I trusted she never envisioned the events of May 25, 1968 of ever being a possibility. It was easy for the public to condemn her in her hindsight of Peggy's death, and so few people must face their personal mistakes and tragic heartbreak in public view, so she became a public spectacle. Mary Alice was an easy target for criticism and folks stared at her on the streets of the small town, but not always in disgust. Rather, they looked at her in fascination because she didn't conform to the normal imaginary standards of the era, and sadly, her defiance to society's norm cost the ultimate price.

Granted, Mary Alice was different, and her parental judgment left room for desire, but I found her to be so naive in many ways when I talked to her that I couldn't imagine the woman intending to cause harm to anyone, much less her children. Mary Alice came from an era that taught young women to grow up and be homemakers and she broke ranks from that standard.

The community held Mary Alice's life style responsible for Peggy's death, but the truth be told, I don't think Mary Alice ever saw the danger signs along the way. I tend to believe Mary Alice wanted to be a non-restrictive parent and she wanted her children to live beyond the limitations that she knew growing up as a young woman in the community.

I refused to embrace the public's snobby attitude that Mary Alice lived her life and dragged her children behind her; I don't think anything could be further from the truth. Mary Alice didn't abandon her twin daughters, and their stepfather made it clear they always had a home with him. She took her children with her on her journey through life, and though that wasn't a wise choice under the circumstances, her intent fell short of evil. I can't defend Mary Alice in the spectrum of being an irresponsible parent, but even then, I don't think she truly understood that responsibility rested solely on her shoulders. She and her daughters walked side by side and she just missed the mark that it was *her* responsibility to take the lead, protect them, defend them, nurture them and make sacrifices in their best interests. The living arrangements shared suggested a mood of roommates more than parent and child. Personally, I think that during a time that the word 'freedom' found itself everywhere in the news, music and the mood at the time, Mary Alice gave her children freedom. Unfortunately, freedom comes complete with responsibilities, and that's where the trouble began.

"Do you think Art Root Jr. killed your daughter?" I tried to be gentle with Peggy's mother.

"No, I never thought he did that because he was a really nice guy, and I never understood why they thought it was him." She had a soft voice and kind nature.

"Was Peggy pregnant?"

"She told me she thought she was, but I don't know for sure."

"What stands out the most in your mind about the time before the crime?"

"The landlord. He was a dreadful man. He approached me about settling the overdue rent I owed him. If. . . " She stammered for quite awhile, trying to find tactful words. "Well, if my daughter and I would. . . " Her voice trailed off, leaving room for my imagination to fill in the rest. "I told him no way in hell."

I got her point loud and clear even without her saying another word.

"Do you think the landlord is responsible for Peggy's death?"

"I don't know. It's hard to imagine actually knowing anybody that could do those horrible things to Peg. I just know he was a sick man"

"Tell me about the investigation after you discovered Peggy's body." I didn't expect too much because the shock the woman suffered at the time was so tremendous.

"I took a lie detector test and that was fine with me, but I was shocked when they had the nerve to ask me if I had sex with my daughter," she said, her voice cracking. "I couldn't believe that question, and it just made me sick to even think like that. The police were rude and almost cruel at times. I tried to answer their questions and help them as much as I could, but it was like they already had all the answers and they didn't want to listen to what I had to say. It wasn't an easy time. It's hard to believe, but it got worse when it was time for the trial. I will never forget this one county detective taking me to the municipal building to question me right before the trial. He picked me up on the sidewalk near where I lived and he drove me there. It felt like I was in there for hours answering all kinds of questions. When we got in the car for him to take me back home he got really rough with me. He grabbed me by the hair and tried to push my head under the steering wheel. I did everything I could to fight him off, but he was a big man"

"What did you do?" I was terrified by the woman's recollection.

"What could I do, Michelle? Call the police?"

"Who did that to you? Why didn't you go to his superiors?"

"Oh, I will never forget him because no woman can forget such a horrible thing. His name was John. It's easy to say now that I should have gone to his superiors, but you just don't understand how it was back then. Those cops stuck together and no one was going to believe me. I don't think you realize how they treated me or how they treated my girls. I couldn't go anywhere without being called the most horrible names. I couldn't walk down the street without getting things thrown at me. Oh, at first I tried calling the police, but they weren't much better. My daughter was dead, my family was ripped apart and the world wasn't a very nice place" I could hear her voice crack.

"Your former husband bought Peggy's headstone." I changed the subject. "I could hear in his voice that he loved her, and he loves Kathryn, too."

"We had our problems in our marriage, but that was really nice of him. He was always good to the girls, and I have nothing against that man," she said in a child-like voice.

"You moved around a lot after Peggy died." I let the comment stir a reaction.

"Like I said, it wasn't a good time for me. I guess I was a gypsy for awhile, but I couldn't find peace anywhere."

"You had a new tattoo on your left hand at the trial, and if I recall it was something about walking alone and the year's date. I looked up song lyrics, book titles and all kinds of things trying to understand, so could you explain it to me?"

"It had no meaning other than that." Her voice got stronger. "Walk alone, and that's what I did." There was no doubt in my mind that the aged woman truly walked through life as a lonely soul, but not always alone.

"I read in the newspaper that the police are looking into Peggy's death and staging a new investigation."

"Yes, I saw that in the newspaper, too." She sounded hopeful.

"Did they come to talk to you about the new investigation?"

"No." She sounded surprised at the suggestion that someone would actually want to talk to her about the crime. "I haven't talked to anybody about this for years." I almost felt like I was on sacred ground, but I continued my conversation with her. I knew I had to ask the hardest question before I ended my final call.

"Who do you think killed your daughter?"

"I really don't know, oh I have a suspicion or two, and I have heard the rumors, but like I said it is hard to imagine knowing anyone so evil. Peg was just a kid and it's still hard for me to think of the terrible things done to her. My girls weren't bad girls. I know I made some mistakes as a mother, but I love my kids. I know there are people that still judge me and I know there are still a lot of people that don't understand a lot of things. Goodness knows nobody understands why Peg had to die. But you know, I am getting older and my health isn't the best, and I keep hoping before I leave this earth that someone will be able to tell me what happened to my daughter and who did it. Peggy deserves the truth. There are so many things they can do these days to catch people like that, and I just want to know who killed Peggy, so I keep hoping before I die, they'll figure it out. Somebody out there knows what really happened that night and I just keep waiting for them to tell the truth. I think Peggy is waiting for the truth, too. After all these years she sure deserves it, doesn't she?" I hung up and wiped the tears from my eyes.

Sadly, more years passed and Mary Alice Reber died without ever seeing her daughter get the truth and justice she deserved.

▪▪▪

"Detective Snavely." A deep voice answered the phone number I dialed, and I recognized the name from a newspaper report about the detective reviewing the cold case murder of fourteen-year-old Peggy Reber.

"Good afternoon Detective Snavely, my name is Michelle Gooden, and I am going to win the award for being your weirdest phone call today. I understand you are investigating the murder of Peggy Reber." I paused a moment.

"Yes, that was Michelle, right?" He verified my name. "I am investigating the Reber file, and why are you going to be my weird call of the day? Do you know anything about the murder of Peggy Reber?"

"Well detective I will never say I know anything worth a damn, but I know too much to ignore anyone that is sincerely going to look into the case. The last time a police officer was plastered on the front pages with claims of investigating the case it was a farce, so assuming this is a legitimate effort on your part I decided to give you a call."

"Michelle, I am not aware of the details surrounding previous investigations into the case, but I assure you my efforts are very legitimate. If you don't mind me repeating myself do you know anything about the Reber case?"

"Well detective, and I say this with the utmost respect, the one thing we do know is that police knowledge of the case is inadequate because the murder remains unsolved, so if I know anything that can help you I am willing to provide it to you. I don't have a lot of time to talk to you right now because I have a meeting in a few minutes, so allow me to ramble for a minute, and you can chalk me up as weird. I trust you can see by your caller identification I am calling you from North Carolina, but I am a native of Lebanon. I will spare you a lot of the details, but

120

after graduating from Lebanon High School I married a soldier stationed here at Fort Bragg, and that is when I left Lebanon. I never knew Peggy, I didn't know her family and I have no connection to her or the case what so ever, but I never forgot Peggy."

I waited for him to interrupt me at that point, but he didn't. "Look I know it sounds crazy, but I remembered her so much that several years ago I went home to learn about her. I wanted to answer my own questions. I was amazed by some of the things I discovered."

He didn't hesitate to interrupt on that note. "What did you discover Michelle?"

"Tell me Detective Snavely, did you look over the transcript of the trial yet?"

"You have a transcript of the trial?" I could hear the surprise in his voice.

"My point exactly, Detective Snavely." I paused merely for effect. "Detective I was just a little kid when Peggy was killed. Hell, I don't think I could even write my name at the time of the crime. I returned to Lebanon about five years ago to pull up some newspaper articles, buy a copy of the transcript of the trial and answer the questions that haunted me for decades." I tried to laugh. "The joke was on me. Oh, I can quote the news reports at the time, and it blew my mind when I realized the assault with the bow was not vaginal, but rectal because I trust you realize that puts a whole new complexion on her killer. I possess news reports, FBI reports, state and county records, but I stood dumbfounded the day I learned the trial was not transcribed. I am going to assume you realize that is a sad fact at this point in your investigation. Like I said detective, I don't have a lot of time because I have a meeting in a few minutes." I was juggling a cell phone to my ear while attempting to carry my lunch up a flight of stairs. "I guess I have to ask you a few questions before I waste your time or mine."

"Shoot" he was quick on the draw.

"Do you want to figure out who did this, or do you want to know who did this?"

"Both."

I loved the speed of his response because he didn't miss a beat.

"I suggest you start by talking to Peggy's twin sister and Peggy's boyfriend, Ray Boyer. Look, I apologize for being the weird call of the day, I also apologize for my limited time to talk, and if you will forgive me I am going to ask a really dumb question of you. Are you from Lebanon?"

"No." He answered the question, but sounded puzzled by the inquiry. "No, I am not from Lebanon."

"Detective Snavely, that is going to be your biggest strength in your investigation of Peggy's murder, and it will be your biggest weakness in your investigation. I love Lebanon, and I am Lebanon born and raised, but it's a funny little town at times. Peggy is the forbidden topic of conversation, so you have your work cut out for you. The people of Lebanon are not quick to talk amongst themselves, and they rarely talk to anything less than a native. Your roots will give you objectivity, but your lack of roots could prevent you from learning the truth. I really have to run, but I am going to ask you to do something for me and your investigation."

I waited for the cop to tell me I was a complete lunatic.

"What's that Michelle?" Good. He didn't scare easily.

"Peggy is buried in Grand View Memorial Park. I am not telling you anything new, and it isn't anything you don't know. I don't mean to insult your intelligence, but do yourself a favor and look at her file at Grand View."

"Her file?" he was puzzled.

"I warned you I was the weird call of the day." I dropped my phone in the midst of my juggling act. "Detective, I know it sounds stupid, but look at the file. I trust you have my number. I will understand if you think I am a basket case, but I thought it was worth a phone call to you."

Several days later I was on the receiving end of a phone call from Detective Kevin Snavely.

"Michelle, I took your advice and made that trip to the cemetery."

"Good deal." I was impressed with his effort. "Then you got to see it first-hand."

"I saw it."

"I sounded strange when I suggested you go and see it for yourself, but it's the only way one is really going to believe it. A child was savagely murdered, the defendant in the case was found not guilty, so the crime is unsolved with a killer on the loose, yet it was Peggy's mother that was asked to leave town. I loved the part where a county detective drove her to the Harrisburg Airport. He should really be proud of himself. Forgive my sarcasm, but I am not very pleased with the way my hometown treated Mary Alice Reber. I realize there were issues with the way she was raising her daughters, but she did not kill her daughter, and she deserved a little more compassion than she received at the time. If you read the news reports from 1968, the townsfolk complained because police provided her lodging in a local hotel immediately following the crime. The good Christian tax payers in Lebanon begrudged her a safe place to rest her head while her home was a crime scene due to her daughter's murder."

"It does seem a bit callous, but there are also a lot of questions that need to be answered about what went on in that apartment in the weeks and months prior to the crime. My investigation is still in its infancy but more than one person suggested there is a possibility Peggy's mother arranged a date for her that night."

"Bull!" I stopped him in his tracks. "Anyone that would make such an assumption does not have a clear understanding of the last few hours of Peggy's life."

"And *you* have an understanding of those hours?" It was his turn to be sarcastic.

"Detective I was five-years-old on the other side of town trying to figure out how to tie my shoes, so if you're asking if I was personally in attendance the answer is no. I also wasn't present for the signing of the Declaration of Independence, but I can tell you a little about that, too. Peggy's mother went out on a Friday night, met up with a couple guys and made an unplanned trip to New Jersey. Her mother's absence is the first factor in her vulnerability that day. Peggy's constant companion and very protective boyfriend, Ray Boyer, was picked up on an outstanding warrant for delinquent child support that afternoon. Ray's apprehension was the second factor in her vulnerability. Her twin sister Kathryn, and her husband Dick Boyer, moved out of the apartment next door to Peggy's the days prior to the crime, and that would be the third factor in her vulnerability. Individually none of these factors jump out at anyone, but collectively they were the recipe for disaster. Allow me to say it now: I am not a detective, and you are allowed to call me crazy at any point in time. There's one factor folks always overlook when they toss out a date-gone-wrong theory, and that is the human element. Peggy didn't enter that apartment to meet anyone. Detective, she wanted her girlfriend to return to the apartment with her and spend the night because Ray was in jail and she didn't want to be alone."

"How do you know that?"

"Long story, and Peggy's girlfriend could detail the events much better than me. Peggy wasn't on her way to a date, and if there was a surprise date scheduled for her, well that doesn't make good common sense either. What was the guarantee Peggy was going to return to the apartment? She could have just as easily spent the night at that girlfriend's house."

"You make a valid point. I guess you are referring to her friend, Pinky"

"Oh goodness no, detective! That wasn't the last person with Peggy that day."

"It wasn't? Why would you say that Michelle? Who do you think was the last person with Peggy that day?"

I broke the mood with some bad humor, "The killer was the last person with Peggy that day, but just before she entered that apartment she was with Ruth Winters."

"Ruth Winters? I don't recall that name off the top of my head, but that's why I take so many notes. Is that a married name?"

"That's funny, detective, because the last time Lebanon's Police Department picked up this case I provided her name then, too, but no one took the time to talk to her. No detective, that is not her married name, and if you would like I can give that to you, too."

"Michelle, by some strange chance do you know when was the last time someone questioned her about this case?"

"If I understand things correctly, police NEVER talked to her."

"Am I hearing you correctly? The last girlfriend with Peggy on the day of her murder was never identified, or questioned by police, and you managed to learn this information. How?" He wasn't shopping for a bridge in Brooklyn, and I wasn't in the business of selling bridges.

"I always credit the bits of knowledge I have about the case to angels, but I don't think that explanation is going to impress you, so here goes nothing. I've been studying this case for years, and one day I got a call from a relative that told me about Ruth. I won't call Ruth my friend, but our families knew each other since the beginning of time. I don't talk to her, but I asked enough questions on the fringe to know police didn't talk to her at the time. My understanding is police talked to her Dad and that's all she wrote. I certainly wasn't going to call her because like I said earlier, I am not a detective, so I left it to the professionals. Unfortunately, when I told police a few years ago they didn't seem to take me seriously, or care."

"Michelle, if this is true you could go from being a weird call as you said, to a very helpful call."

"It seems it's as simple as talking to Ruth Winters. No disrespect intended, but some of the issues with this case appear to be that simple."

"How so?"

"I am sure you heard the suggestion it was a case of mistaken identity. Common sense shatters that idea because there isn't enough beer in Milwaukee to fool anyone into thinking fourteen-year-old Peggy was her thirty-five-year-old mother, no matter how dark the room was at the time. Common sense also differentiates the identical twins. Kathryn's hair was shorter than Peggy's and Kathryn gave birth to a child three weeks earlier, so it wasn't a matter of identical twins appearing to be identical. I guess I am guilty of making things too simple, but some practical thinking sorts through a lot."

"You definitely put some thought into this, and I respect your insight, but I don't think there is too much that is simple about this case, and the fact it was such a long time ago doesn't help things. Tell me a little bit more about Ruth Winters."

"Like I said, I didn't talk to her because I held on to hope that Peggy's file would receive serious police attention at some point in time. If I understand correctly she was with Peggy until 8:15 that evening, and they parted company a couple blocks away from Peggy's apartment building. I don't have to tell you, but the trial against Art Root Jr. hinged on Peggy being killed sometime around 6 p.m., yet she was with Ruth a couple hours after that time. If you recall, the attendants at the comfort station also testified to seeing Peggy alive at 8 that evening. The one silly question I threw in Ruth's direction was what was Peggy wearing that day? I talked to Peggy's boyfriend a few years ago and he told me Peggy wasn't wearing the orange dress she was found in that day, but considering he was picked up and jailed early that afternoon his knowledge of that evening is nil. Oddly enough, Ruth said the same thing and she recalled vividly what Peggy was wearing that evening. I don't know if it matters, but the news reported the orange dress was torn a few days earlier when Peggy's twin was wearing it during a domestic dispute between her and her husband Dick Boyer. It really jumped out at me that she was strangled with a green dress belt while wearing an orange dress because the two don't go together. It sounds so silly, but I remember the 70s and all the earth tone colors, but that wasn't the case in 1968."

"What are you suggesting?"

"I don't know that I'm suggesting anything, but there's something weird about the dress. Peggy was not going to put a torn dress on. Again, the case against Root was sporting a hell of a lot of testimony about hair and fibers, but the dress was torn days earlier, yet that little issue went ignored. The belt didn't match the dress, so it's one more thing the killer utilized from the apartment. It really doesn't look like he entered the apartment with a plan of any sorts."

"So you don't think the murder was premeditated?"

"No, I don't think the madman entered the apartment with the intention of killing Peggy, but he definitely snapped, and it is horrible to think he is still free. He is one angry individual."

"That's an understatement."

"Well, it was one of those things I had to really struggle to understand because the headlines at the time were about a sex-maniac, and that's not an accurate description of the killer. The crime is sexual in nature, but the fact that the attack was rectal supports a crime of rage. There was a brief period I entertained the thought of a female killer, but the strength required to penetrate her body ten times with an archery bow is a bit more than a woman could muster."

"A female killer?" the detective posed the question, but I could tell he was thinking aloud. "Is there any female in particular you considered as a suspect?"

"Detective, there was more than one jealous wife that hated the activities that went on in that apartment. Please don't forget that Peggy herself was involved with a married man. I realize he was only four years older than Peggy, but he was a married man nonetheless."

"True." The detective's voice trailed off.

"Look I am not speaking ill of the dead, and I mean no disrespect, but if one hopes to arrive at the true identity of a killer one must take an honest approach to the truth."

I felt guilty for saying Peggy was involved with a married man. "Peggy's mother entertained quite a few men in that dwelling, and I should tell you now unlike most people in Lebanon, I will not call her a prostitute because I don't recall her ever being charged with prostitution. Again, if one wants to stick with truth and facts it is a fact Peggy's mother enjoyed the company of men, but there is no proof she was soliciting herself. Personally, I think the self-righteous community at the time was too busy judging her in 1968, and they lost focus on the true villain in the picture."

"So you don't believe she sold herself and her daughters?" He obviously heard the rumors, too.

"Unless you know something I don't. There isn't anything of a factual nature to support such vicious claims. Detective, I am not defending her parenting at all. Again, if we look at the facts, her fourteen-year-old daughter is a mother and married without completing ninth grade, and the other daughter is left in the company of her married boyfriend while mom skipped off to New Jersey without a care. Mary Alice Reber was not winning any awards for mother of the year. She entertained a lot of men in the home she shared with her teenage daughter and sadly, Peggy ended up dead. By the way, did you notice the local paper's overkill about the large number of men Mary Alice welcomed through her door, but the failure to identify any of those men with the exception of Art Root Jr.? Mary Alice was scorned for being a tramp, and the men that crawled in her bed were sheltered from public identity and scrutiny. It's definitely a man's world, isn't it, detective?"

"Do you think Peggy knew her killer?"

"Sure looks that way, doesn't it? We know there wasn't forced entry, but we also know the locks were flimsy. One of the tenants told me a butter knife could open the doors in that building. I don't think a stranger broke in and killed Peggy. I think he knew Peggy and he was comfortable there. He didn't seem to be concerned about Ray showing up and interrupting him, yet Ray was Peggy's constant companion, so it almost suggests the killer knew Ray was incarcerated. Don't you find the apprehension of Ray to be an eyebrow-raiser?"

"You think there's something wrong with jailing a man that's behind in child support?" Spoken like a true member of law enforcement. I understood his stand.

"I think there's something very wrong with a man that fails to support his children, and he deserved to be jailed, but the apprehension itself baffles me. Why did the constable decide to go after Ray that day? How did the constable know where to find him? 770 Maple Street was not Ray Boyer's legal address. Art Root Jr. shacked up in that apartment for weeks, there was a criminal warrant hanging over his head, and the constable didn't go after him. Detective, how many men were jailed on outstanding criminal warrants when police started questioning people after the murder? I think the answer is just shy of a half dozen, yet Ray Boyer and delinquent child support was the top priority for Constable William Kimmel on May 25, 1968. How did Ray win that lottery that day?"

"Perhaps someone tipped him off to Ray's whereabouts, Michelle."

"That would put a whole new complexion on things, wouldn't it? The answer to that one question would confirm if Peggy was alone by chance, or if someone had a hand in her being vulnerable that day. I guess it's safe to say the constable took that information to the grave with him. Hey, did you catch the part where the same constable threw Ray Boyer in jail *again* when he went back to Lebanon in 1970 to testify at the trial? Yeah, the beauty of that apprehension rests in the fact that it was an illegal jailing. Ray Boyer sat in jail five days illegally, and it was the same over-zealous constable that put him there."

"Michelle, you weren't kidding when you said you studied this case, were you? I don't think I've talked to anyone yet that covered so many bases. You realize I am professionally limited and I can't comment on a lot, but I appreciate you sharing this information with me."

"Detective Snavely, I appreciate you giving this case your attention. I don't expect you to say anything, or tell me anything, but I will do anything and everything I can to give this kid the justice she deserves. I considered writing a book about this crime. A book doesn't require a conviction, and we know that to be true because Jack the Ripper has yet to be identified, and there are plenty of books detailing his crimes. I kept waiting and hoping for someone such as you to take this child under his or her wing. A book would generate some attention to the horrible crime, but it won't convict a killer. You have the ability to collect facts and put this bastard behind bars."

"That's the goal."

I didn't doubt him for a minute, and I didn't know why, but something told me the man on the other end of the phone was going to fight the good fight on Peggy's behalf.

"Michelle, what about the killer? You are detailed in your delivery about Peggy, and the events surrounding her, but you skip over the killer. Is there a reason for that?"

"But detective, it is an unsolved crime, so no one knows the identity of the killer."

We both chuckled a little bit at my dry wit.

"Rather than zero in on the possibilities, let's rule out a few people. The mayor of Lebanon did not kill Peggy Reber. The District Attorney did not kill Peggy Reber. Ray Boyer did not kill Peggy Reber. Scaramuzzino did not kill Peggy --"

Detective Snavely interrupted me. "Scaramuzzino?"

"Yes, the only convicted murderer hanging out in Lebanon at the time. He was convicted of first-degree in 1979. Scary stuff. But we know it wasn't him, I was just being facetious. Anyway, as I was saying, ignorance breeds and feeds gossip and drama, and that combination also assisted the killer in escaping identification. Two men committed suicide shortly after the crime, and while it was a peculiar to say the least, F.B.I. forensic testing cleared both men as suspects. Some insist the F.B.I. forensic testing proves Art Root Jr. was involved in the murder of Peggy Reber, and then they reject the F.B.I. findings that the suicides weren't involved. If the F.B.I. testing was right about Root then it was right about the suicides. We can't pick and choose which F.B.I. tests are accurate. We either accept the forensic testing at the time, or we don't. Forensic evidence points at Root all day long, but poor forensic testing was one of the biggest problems with the original investigation. There is a case against Root, and a hell of a lot of hair and fiber evidence that remains *unidentified* even today. Investigators did not identify a source of hair and fiber and *eliminate* a suspect; instead they got a match with Root, and built a case around that fact. Detective, it's not rocket science for one to realize Art Root Jr.'s forensics were going to be in that apartment in abundance because he lived there almost two months. Guess what? Ray Boyer was laying his head in that same damn apartment for almost two months and there is not one - not *one,* detective - identification of his hair, or any fiber attached to him."

"How do you know that?"

"Look at your evidence reports, look at your crime lab reports, and when you're done reviewing what those documents," I paused, "humor me and look at what they *don't* report."

"No, Michelle, what I am asking is how did you see those reports?"

"Detective Snavely, I worked with what's available to any citizen. I located the public records available in Lebanon County, I researched aged news articles, and I utilized the Freedom of Information Act available through the F.B.I. It's not an easy read, but it isn't impossible, and it's available to anyone at no charge if they request it. I threw all those papers out on my living room floor many nights and struggled to understand what I was reading."

"Michelle, I sincerely respect your efforts."

I got the impression he thought he offended me.

"I just wanted to know how you knew about lab reports and evidence."

I stopped him quickly. "Detective Snavely, I would be disappointed if you *didn't* question my methods and means. I don't expect you to hang on my every word and accept the things I say as the truth. I am at peace being nothing more than a weird phone call for you, but I am a weird phone call that devoted a lot of effort to obtaining an understanding of the murder of Peggy Reber."

"It's definitely fair to say you devoted effort in expAnneng this case. I am impressed by your effort, and your knowledge. I received more than a few calls that were weird, and you are nowhere close to that, but I must always be thorough and objective in my approach to this investigation."

I liked the honesty and integrity in his words.

"Detective, do you have a list of the tenants in the building at the time of the crime? Oh, don't insult your intelligence or mine by answering that question. I have a list of tenants, too. You picked up the file and there it was at your fingertips. I sat on the floor of the Lebanon County library with an ancient city directory on my lap composing mine. Naturally, I didn't just utilize the 1968 city directory, but the 1967 edition as well as the 1969 edition. I traveled 500 miles to compose that list. Your list is 100% accurate, and mine might have a few errors, but my list is coming from someone that was 5-years-old at the time of the crime. Do you see the power of that at all? I don't have an explanation for my determination beyond the fact I remembered Peggy from the evening news. We can dismiss angels, but the truth won't change no matter how many times I tell it. I remembered this kid from the evening news, and I returned to Lebanon three decades later to answer my own questions about her. I didn't settle for the accounts of the Lebanon Daily News at the time. Mind you, I learned a great deal from the news reports and the reporter was a skilled craftsman in his delivery of the events, but that is only part of the story. My friend and I stayed in a local hotel and we spent many hours in the Municipal Building pulling up documents related to Peggy, the trial and facts surrounding those close to her at the time of the crime. My God detective, I was speechless when I realized Peggy's brother-in-law didn't just father Peggy's niece born a few weeks before her death, but he fathered another child with another woman a few months earlier. The facts sitting in public records confirm he impregnated two teenage girls in the same time frame, and one of them was Peggy's fourteen-year-old identical twin. Does it matter in regards to the murder of Peggy Reber? I don't know about that, but I do know it illustrates the caliber of people in Peggy's intimate circle at the time. My research of the case did not answer my questions; rather it inspired a whole new list of questions. I invite you to question me, my motives, my methods, my means, and I want you to do the same damn thing with everyone else you talk, too."

"You know about the other baby?" His voice was bland.

"Yeah, I know about the other baby." I hesitated before I said anything else. "I know Peggy's fourteen-year-old twin got pregnant and married a man while another teenage mother was changing diapers for his newborn baby at the same time. I am not seeing a case of accidental conception between two love-struck teens for either girl. He was a busy man. I assume there's no need to tell you how the story goes from there."

"The story?"

I just knew he was playing dumb to see how much I really knew.

"Detective, Dick Boyer had a pregnant girlfriend at the same time Kathryn Reber conceived his child. He married Kathryn Reber in February of 1968, and their baby was born in May 1968. Please never forget Kathryn was fourteen-years-old at the time. Public records host a court order for him to pay child support for a child born in January of 1968 to the other woman. If we utilize the theory of common sense we will see he impregnated one teenage girl around April of 1967, and the other teenage girl in August of 1967. Like I said, he was a busy guy. Yeah, yeah, yeah he actually married Kathryn, and if we really do our homework we get a different picture, don't we? He fathered several children with the other young woman before he finally divorced Kathryn, and ultimately married the other woman. They are together even today.

Again, none of that identifies a killer, but it is a snapshot of the people closest to Peggy. I have no doubts that you know Kathryn didn't raise the child she birthed with Dick Boyer. His parents adopted the little girl, and I believe they moved her to Oklahoma for a good part of her childhood. I always thought that was fascinating."

"What was fascinating? Some guy could make kids easier than he could support them?" Detective Snavely clearly respected parenthood beyond the ability to impregnate women at a rapid rate.

"No, no, no I thought it was fascinating when I finally located Art Root Jr., he was in Oklahoma, and coincidentally another family attached to Peggy's murder was also in Oklahoma. What are the chances of that? Root settled in Oklahoma, and Boyer's family members moved to Oklahoma. They raised the child Kathryn conceived in Oklahoma. I just thought it was all kind of cozy."

"Do you think they were friends?"

"No, Detective Snavely, they weren't in the same town, and I don't know if they were in contact at all, but doesn't it strike you odd that two major names attached to the Peggy Reber murder in Lebanon, Pennsylvania end up in Oklahoma a few years after the crime? Am I being stupid? Because I think that is pretty strange. When did Oklahoma become the great escape for Pennsylvanians? Let's just take it for what it's worth at face value."

"I guess it's possible." The man with the badge was treading softly.

"Detective Snavely, when I first set out on this journey, the city of Lebanon classified Art Root Jr. as dead. He is far from dead, and he stopped being Art Root Jr. years ago. Hell, he had an alias at the time of the crime, and the trial. His wife and daughters did not carry the name Root then, and he uses a different name now."

"Michelle, have you talked to Art Root Jr.?"

"Yes sir, I talked to Art Root Jr.," I answered honestly.

"I hope to have that same benefit some day."

"I hope you get that benefit, too." I knew his efforts were only going to be as good as the investigation and interviews he conducted. A thorough investigation would demand he get the opportunity to talk to the defendant in the murder trial of Peggy Reber, and that would mean talking to Arthur M. Root Jr.

"Detective, we must always respect the fact a jury found Art Root Jr. not guilty, and the laws pertaining to double-jeopardy prevent him from ever being put on trial again for the murder of Peggy Reber.'

"That does not prevent him from being charged as an accessory, Michelle."

The cop knew the law far better than me. "Using your own words about facts there is substantial evidence to suggest if he didn't actually kill Peggy, he was present at the time."

"Well forgive me, but that goes back to the ever-popular multiple killer theory."

"You don't think that's possible?"

"Detective, *anything* is possible, and nobody knows anything for sure because the crime remains unsolved, but the possibility of multiple killers angers me for a completely different reason. The Commonwealth has only ever charged one man with the murder of Peggy Reber, and the district attorney did not preserve the testimony of witnesses and the experts that testified at the trial. A simple little thing like a transcript of the original trial could be very useful in prosecuting someone else for the child's murder. Not to mention if there was more than one killer, why did the investigators at the time of the crime settle for one arrest? It's hard enough to believe one person could commit a crime of such magnitude and go undetected, but for a couple people to enter the apartment, commit the crime, exit the apartment and actually get away with it? It's unbelievable! Detective, just the thought of two or more individuals entering the building and exiting the building without being seen is impossible. I grew up in Lebanon, and I couldn't walk to the store for a soda without one of my neighbors seeing me. Then there's the little issue of no one hearing anything unusual coming out of the Reber apartment that day. Oh I read the reports how the entire apartment building was drinking beer at Shay's Tavern that day. Let's keep our wits about us and accept that not everyone that lived in that building was sitting in a bar that day. Some-damn-body saw something, heard something and knew something. So these criminal masterminds entered the building undetected, *quietly* committed one of the most brutal murders in Pennsylvania history, and then exited the building without drawing any attention? We are to assume they went unnoticed, didn't have any blood on their clothes, and that's not even tickling the thought of the adrenalin that such an act would generate in the perpetrators? Then the criminal geniuses engage in a vow of silence and mutually protect their secret for years, and years, and years. No one can say it's impossible because of the many years the crime sits in the pile of unsolved homicides, but isn't that a far stretch of reasonable thinking?"

"I want to try and find the answers to those questions and more. We know mistakes were made in 1968 because Peggy's killer wasn't convicted; yet I respect the efforts of the original investigators. I am approaching this with the hope that a fresh set of eyes could provide the difference this case needs. Hey, with a little luck maybe a witness or two that was scared to talk at the time will come forward now. I am more than willing to start from scratch and try my best to find the missing pieces of the puzzle. We have technology available today that people couldn't even dream of in 1968, so there are a few rays of hope even after all these years. Please don't forget there are many challenges, too. I know going into it locating the original witnesses alone is going to require time and effort. After all these years some of them are dead, or moved away, or married and changed names, or they simply forgot things over time. It is imperative to locate everyone because every piece of information matters. Did you ever talk to any of the witnesses?"

"I talked to several people that testified at the trial, a couple jurors, neighbors, her relatives, the DA, assistant DA, the defense attorney, the F.B.I. expert, several of the original investigators."

"Stop" he interrupted me. "You can stop right there; I get the picture." He didn't really laugh at me, but sounded a little amused just the same. "You spent some time on this, didn't you?"

"Remember the words 'weird phone call'?" It was my turn to chuckle.

"Did you keep any of the contact information for the people you talked to? I have a list a mile long of people I want to talk to, and I located some of them, but for the most part I work this case on my down time, so I am still bringing it all together."

"And that is exactly why I called you, detective. I have names, addresses, phone numbers, and notes of the conversations. I want to offer everything and anything I can to help give Peggy justice."

"Somehow, Michelle, I just know you do." He paused for a moment. "I don't know how to say this, and I don't want you to take this the wrong way. . ." He hesitated.

"Detective, play it off the cuff. I am an adult."

"I won't say you are a weird phone call in a negative manner just yet, and I get a lot of weird calls, but you are certainly a different phone call. I won't say you are right, and I won't say you are wrong, but you clearly put some time into learning about Peggy Reber. I will say I want to learn everything I can about Peggy Reber, too."

"Listen, I understand exactly what you are saying, and I respect your professionalism. I would give you the shirt off my back and you wouldn't owe me a damn thing, but please arrest the bastard that killed that poor girl. Sometimes I credit angels because I was so young when I saw her on the evening news, and sometimes I think I relate to her because I was a poor girl in the same town, but I realized awhile back my efforts aren't about me. It's all about Peggy. My personal belief is Peggy didn't want to be forgotten, and the logic behind that spiritual thought is a killer needs to be held accountable. I can't arrest a killer, but you can, and if I can assist you in any way it is a beautiful day."

"I just wanted to make sure we both understand each other." I liked his diplomacy. "Is it possible for you to email that information to me?"

"Email, fax, or I can deliver it to you?" I gave him an option.

"I don't expect you to drive five hundred miles to give me a list of names I probably already have."

"Oh Detective I am a weird phone call, but not completely insane." I giggled. "I will be in Lebanon next week for a family celebration, and I thought I could drop it off while I am in town."

"You're coming to Lebanon next week?"

"Yes sir. I am so excited about this trip I can't stand it!" I got caught up in the thought of a family gathering to rejoice.

"Michelle, since you are already planning the trip, and it would be nice to meet you, just bring the papers with you. If you can find the time to get together for a few minutes during your visit, that would be great."

"Consider it done." I pressed the button to disconnect the call and stared at the phone receiver in my hand. I thought of Peggy's smiling face and I wondered if my efforts were starting to serve a purpose. I jumped when the phone in my hand started to ring because it startled me.

"Hey Mom, would you bring my blue shorts to the field when you come to the game?" The game? Uh-oh! I grabbed a few things and bolted out the door for a little league baseball game scheduled to start in ten minutes. I juggled a couple kids, a few dogs, a career, a house, and quality friendships as a single mom. Peggy always managed to find her way in the mix, but I definitely had a full plate.

■■

A week later I met Detective Snavely for lunch on a hot summer's day. I was a little surprised by his youthful appearance, but it dawned on me Peggy was dead several years before he was born. "Thanks for taking the time to meet me. I know this is your family vacation."

"Oh, it's not a problem." I smiled. "Our meeting saved me from allowing my family to see how scared I am of roller coasters."

"I'm guessing your family is enjoying Hershey Park."

"Yes Detective, my family *is* enjoying Chocolate Town's amusement park, and my children don't know about my fear of the old wooden roller coaster there, so this is a much welcomed distraction." I laughed a little. "Maybe I should be thanking *you* for this meeting." I removed a few sheets of paper from my purse. "Here are the names and contact information I collected along the way, and remember some of this information is close to five years old."

"I understand, and I will cross reference everything, but every little bit of information helps." He lowered his eyes to the sheets I presented him. "You talked to Peggy's mother?"

"A long time ago."

"You know she passed away a couple years ago?"

I nodded my head in response to his question.

"She was a soft spoken and kind natured woman that almost came across as being very fragile. We talked several times and I am really glad I had the opportunity to get to know her a little bit."

"What did she share with you about the case?"

"Well I must be honest with you; I didn't push her very hard at all. I was very respectful of the fact she lost her daughter. The questions you would ask of her and the questions I asked of her are worlds apart. I wanted to know Peggy's hobbies, favorite meal, and silly details mothers cherish. I did ask her if she thought Art Root Jr. did it, and she didn't hesitate to tell me no. I asked her why she had to go the neighbors for a flashlight that night if the apartment didn't have power, and the answer would surprise many. She didn't leave Peggy in an apartment deprived of power that day because the power was on when she left that afternoon. Walter Graeff, the landlord, kept an office in the apartment building where he collected rent from the tenants on Friday afternoons. He disconnected the power source to their apartment that Friday before he left, and that was *after* Mary Alice left that day, so she wasn't aware of it until she entered the dark apartment the night she found Peggy. Now it's bad enough Peggy was in the dark for one night, but the reports at the time lead one to believe she was living in the dark, and that's not completely accurate."

"I read the reports, Michelle, and I don't think it's reported that she went a long period without power, but it's definitely not reported that Walter Graeff turned the power off the day before the crime." He was correct.

"I guess it was so much easier to point out the faults of Mary Alice than a heartless act by a local attorney that was owed a few weeks rent."

"That was a standard practice back then if someone was behind in rent." He was right again. "Did she mention anything else?"

"I asked her if anything was missing from the apartment and she told me a set of rings and some meat she had in the refrigerator."

"Meat in the refrigerator?" He made a funny face and looked puzzled.

"Detective, your guess is as good as mine, but I swear to you that is what the woman told me. We discussed her marriage to Herman Reber, and having been through divorce myself, I thought she was respectful." I filled him in on the other things Mary Alice Reber and I discussed several years prior. "I am convinced the whispering and gossip about her really did a number on justice. The self-righteous hypocrites at the time were so busy passing judgment on her, they let a child's killer escape identification."

"Michelle, they arrested Art Root Jr., and a lot of people still think he got away with murder."

"Allow me to point out it took almost six months before he was arrested for the murder of Peggy Reber. Granted, he was incarcerated during that time on other charges, but six months doesn't support a smoking gun. I talked to his mother, too, and my heart broke for the woman. Her son's trial resulted in a verdict of not guilty, but her family carried the stigma of the charges against him until her dying day."

"Like I said," he raised his brows with a look of doubt, "A lot of people think he got away with murder. There was a strong case against him, Michelle."

131

"Yeah, they obviously thought their case was strong because the prosecutor failed to tell the jury everything that was done to Peggy. Tell me, detective, was that arrogance, ignorance, or stupidity?"

"Excuse me?"

"Detective, I respect the sensitive nature of the murder at the time. Goodness knows the television networks refused to show a woman's navel in a popular comedy show at the time. News reporters *today* aren't comfortable reporting the facts about the assault. A man was put on trial for this murder. Peggy lost her life at the hands of a madman's rage; the district attorney presented a case against Art Root Jr., portraying him to be that monster. Oddly, the DA *failed* to tell the jury the true details of the murder. If the DA really *wanted* a conviction, why didn't he tell the jury the whole story?" I threw my hands up in disgust.

"How do you know he didn't tell the jury the whole story?" Detective Snavely held a strong poker face.

"Well Detective, since there is no detailed transcript of the trial, my understanding is as good as yours. The limited court testimony we *do* know comes courtesy of the local newspaper, and the paper reported the weapons used in the murder were a cloth dress belt and a 5-foot archer's bow, but that is not completely correct. I spent some time with the evidence documents, and all is not as it appears. Public records and evidence reports suggested there were other items used to violate Peggy, but that's not worth a hill of beans, so I asked one of the original detectives about my suspicions."

"Oh, you did?"

"Look, I am not Sherlock Holmes, and reading the evidence reports isn't exactly a walk in the park, but there was blood on a dust mop, and it really bothered me, so I twisted it around in my mind every way imaginable. Did the killer have blood on his hands and try to clean up after himself? Did someone discover Peggy's body before Mary Alice, and again, try to cover their tracks? Did the assault against Peggy extend beyond the use of a cloth dress belt used to strangle her, and a 5-foot bow used to mutilate her? I didn't have the answers, but I definitely had my share of questions, so I contacted an original investigator from the time of the crime. He confirmed for me the mop was also used in the assault against Peggy, and the list of foreign objects used in the murder didn't stop there. I still have his email if you would like to see it." I extended an offer to the cop seated before me.

"Yes, Michelle, I would like to see that email, and anything else you might have that I haven't seen."

"I brought some of my files with me, and you are welcome to look at whatever I have, but I feel obligated to throw out the disclaimer that I am not a detective. I just took each piece of information on an individual basis and looked at it from various angles. It is why I don't understand how anyone can take the trial against Root seriously when the prosecutor didn't take the details of the murder seriously. How can one expect a guilty verdict for murder, yet fail to tell the *true* nature of the murder? It was once suggested to me that such details were sheltered to keep from enraging the jury. That's ridiculous! If Peggy had to endure it, and Root had to defend himself against such charges, the jury needed to know *all* the facts. One shining star on Lebanon's police department suggested a few details of the crime were sheltered until they captured the *real* killer. If they were holding out for the real killer, then why put Art Root Jr. on trial, and yet fail to transcribe the testimony? I don't need a badge or a degree in law to tell you it just doesn't make good damn sense." I was exasperated by the facts.

"If life made sense, Peggy would still be alive, and if the case made sense her killer would be sitting behind bars." He shook his head and rubbed his hand across his mouth. "You have the right idea though. Each piece of information, each piece of evidence, and every person available needs to be reviewed individually, and from every angle. The truth about Peggy's murder is somewhere in the mix, and I won't put this file down until her killer meets justice."

"I hope you are a man of your word because that's the kind of determination Peggy deserved all along." I meant no disrespect, but I didn't really know the man seated across from me. "The bow pierced her heart five times, and the bastard responsible for that needs to be taken off the streets." If the young detective and I agreed on nothing else it was the fact Peggy Reber's killer did not deserve the benefit of freedom.

∎∎

Months passed, and Detective Kevin Snavely and I didn't exchange Christmas cards or meet for coffee, but we did share emails and phone calls. He investigated Peggy's case from a legal perspective, and I continued my own pursuit of understanding the life and death of Peggy Reber on my own. In April of 2007 I received a brief email from Officer Snavely, and I called him to obtain a better understanding of its meaning.

"What's the deal, chief?" I entered the call on a light note.

"Well," he hesitated. "I hope you won't be mad at me, and you aren't obligated to anything, but I mentioned your name to a local newspaper reporter."

"Okay?" I wasn't sure what I was hearing.

"I don't have to tell you, but the anniversary of Peggy's death is approaching. I saw the reporter on the street and suggested he do something to mark the event." He paused. "Michelle, he's a good guy, and he's a kind heart when it comes to kids, but he's also a news reporter." Kevin was hesitating. "He didn't shoot the idea down, but he asked if I had anything new on the case because it's been the same story for decades. Michelle, I understand his point because it *has* been the same story for decades, but I can't reveal anything new without compromising my investigation."

I loved his dedication to justice for Peggy.

"Anyhow," he continued. "He asked if I had anything new to add to the story, and I thought about it for awhile before I mentioned your name." He took a deep breath. "You don't have to talk to him, and I was probably wrong, but you are something new to the story of Peggy Reber, yet completely separate from my investigation."

I could tell he was uncomfortable, so I rescued him. "It's alright."

He kept talking for a little bit, so I repeated myself. "Kevin, it is okay."

"Did he call you yet?" He got to the point.

"No, but I've been out of town" My life was more than a little hectic.

"I don't think it's any big deal, but he wanted something new, and Michelle," Kevin laughed. "You are definitely a new twist to the story. You might not be a member of law enforcement, but you definitely put some real effort into this case, and if it gets Peggy's name out there. . ." His voice trailed off. Then, he said finally, "Well, it's up to you, and I apologize if I was out of line, but I wanted to give you a head's up."

The call ended on a positive note, and I wasn't mad at Detective Snavely because I knew his heart was in the right place. I went about my day and the conversation danced on my mind. What did I *possibly* have to offer the story of Peggy Reber? Oh, I studied the case, I researched the dumbest things to understand the times, but I wasn't a professional. I possessed a strong belief that only a court of law could deliver justice to her.

▪▪

"Michelle, that's wonderful!" Susan was ecstatic. "This is where all our efforts will actually break the sound of silence."

We were wandering through a grocery store when I told her about the phone call with Detective Snavely. "Michelle, this *could* be the difference in this case!"

"What are you talking about?" I was slightly embarrassed by my friend's enthusiasm in a public place.

"Michelle," Susan stopped pushing her shopping cart for a minute. "You were just a baby when this happened, yet you didn't forget it. You grew up, became a woman, got married, moved 500 miles away, and it traveled with you." Her face was beaming. "You didn't even let it go then." She stopped long enough to remove a box of cereal from a display. "You were *supposed* to do this." We turned into another aisle in the grocery store. "Peggy needs you to tell her story." Susan was on top of the world.

"If I could tell her story, her killer would be behind bars." I didn't follow my friend's train of thought.

"You're wrong," she snapped at me. "There is a difference between telling her story and convicting her killer."

"Why bother to tell anything if a killer doesn't see justice?" I was confused.

"The *truth* is what matters, Michelle. You are in a position to tell the truth you discovered and hopefully others will step up and give that child the truth she deserves."

That night, I thought about the words of my friend. The truth? A 14-year-old kid was brutally murdered, her killer escaped justice, and *that* was the truth. I couldn't convict her killer, or change the status of her file, and *that* was the truth. I felt powerless, but that was nothing new. I kept tossing around the word the truth, and I knew in my heart it was the one thing lacking from every story about Peggy Reber. I thought about the news reports of how Peggy's mother left her in an apartment deprived of electricity, yet I knew that wasn't the total truth. I thought of the trial against Root that claimed Peggy lost her life around 6 p.m., and I knew that wasn't the truth either. I recalled the last known girls to be with Peggy that night, and that wasn't correct. I thought of the men that legitimately held keys to the apartment, yet a couple managed to escape forensic testing. I thought of Peggy being discovered in an orange dress she made in her high school home economics class. The dress was torn days before while her sister Kathryn Boyer was wearing it and her husband assaulted her, yet Peggy's corpse was found in that same dress. I thought about a constable apprehending Peggy's boyfriend, Ray Boyer, for delinquent child support on May 25, 1968, and I thought of all the outstanding criminal warrants that same constable overlooked in his pursuit of one dead beat dad in 1968. I started to think about a trial that left a kid's murder unsolved; yet there was no transcript of the trial. I thought about a district attorney that didn't tell a jury every detail of the crime, yet supposedly expected a verdict of guilty. Oh, I thought about the truth, and the truth haunted me for the first time ever.

▪▪

"Mr. Latimer?" I was nervous.

"Yes, can I help you?" A deep, yet compassionate voice answered my call.

"This is Michelle Gooden." I was unsure of myself. "I believe Officer Snavely mentioned my name to you."

"He did." I could sense the reporter on the other end of the phone was gathering a pen and paper for notes. "I was going to call you, but it got crazy around here."

"I didn't miss your call?" I voiced my doubts aloud.

"No, no, no," he assured me. "It's been a zoo around here, and I didn't get a chance to call you, but it is on my list of things to do."

"You aren't alone," I said, giving a sigh of relief. "I have been busy doing a lot of things, and Kevin mentioned talking to you, so I decided to give you a ring."

"Yeah, yeah, he did." I could tell there was organizational effort on the other end of the phone. "He didn't get into all of it, but he told me you are looking into the Reber case."

"That's fair." I was at a loss for words. I honestly didn't know what to say to the voice on the other end of the phone.

"So," he began in a relaxed tone. "Kevin told me you are originally from Lebanon?"

"Born and raised," I said, trying not to sound nervous.

"When did you leave the beautiful city of Lebanon?"

"Oh, years ago," I lightened up. "I married an army paratrooper stationed at Fort Bragg, and this became home. My dad died years ago, so I moved my mother here, too. My mother passed away awhile back, and North Carolina is pretty much home to me now."

"North Carolina is your home, yet you pursue information about the murder of Peggy Reber. Why is that?"

"I wish I could explain it, but I don't have a concrete explanation for you, or anyone else. Goodness knows it drives my son wild." I was at a loss for words.

"It drives your son wild?" The reporter laughed a little.

"Yes sir, it does." I didn't back down from the odd humor. "I don't know why I remembered Peggy, or why I felt compelled to answer my own questions about her, but I did it just the same, and yes, sometimes my family is baffled by my efforts."

"Has this been a hardship for your family?"

"Not at all." I understood his point. "My family is confused, yet always supportive." It was time to put the cards on the table. "I have a good life, great kids, a career, home, pets, hobbies, and all the bells and whistles one could ask for in life. I just remembered this kid's face from the evening news, and it wasn't going away. So I went back to answer my own questions."

"Did you find the answers you were looking for?" He was soft in his approach.

"No, I just kept finding more questions." I was honest. "Have you *really* looked at Peggy's case? I don't mean to be rude, but you are a reporter." I trusted he was going to do some homework on the case.

"I have looked at the reports." He wasn't a stupid man. "The community is aware of this case."

"Are they?" I was sneaking up on the truth. "Is the community *really* aware of this case?" I started rambling a few silly facts, the reporter offered great rebuttals, and we agreed to disagree. The sad reality of an unsolved crime is nobody is right, or wrong, and that's why the crime is unsolved.

"So, I take it you don't think Art Root Jr. killed Peggy?"

"No, I don't, and a jury of his peers didn't think he was guilty either."

"Michelle, there are many people in this town that would beg to differ with you, and the jury."

"Well, that's the beauty of being an American, and without a conviction we are all free to believe what we choose, but I don't see Art Root Jr. yielding that bow. I could be wrong, but it seems to me Art Root Jr. is the only name and face people have to attach to this evil, and perhaps if folks knew a few more facts about the case, perceptions would change."

"How so?"

I suddenly felt I had Mr. Latimer's attention.

"The investigation left a few too many holes to be conclusive in any direction, and that is why the crime is unsolved. Oh, and I should tell you I absolutely love the prosecutor's theory the forensic evidence presented at the trial was too complex for jurors to understand. Talk about some arrogant nonsense! It says a lot about the opinion of the intelligence of Lebanon residents, doesn't it? The jury understood the evidence, but they didn't see guilt beyond a reasonable doubt."

"How do you know the jury understood the evidence at the trial?" He quickly interjected.

"I talked with several members of the jury, and there wasn't any confusion about the testimony about hair and fibers. They weren't stupid people."

"How did they dismiss the evidence linking Root to the crime?"

"John, sad as it might be, in many ways, I don't think the trial was about Root at all. The person that was really on trial was Mary Alice Reber. She was a divorced mother living an unconventional life style, and her fourteen-year-old daughter fell victim to her poor choices. Look at the news reports at the time and it is evident the community blamed *her* for Peggy's death. While fingers were pointing at a grieving mother, the true killer walked away. My God, women stood in line for a seat in the courtroom, the local newspaper gave daily reports on her wardrobe and hair!"

My disgust was evident. "There is one edition of the local paper where a sidewalk reporter asks a random question on the street, and in response to a question about Peggy five out of the six people asked wanted her mother charged with the crime. The woman was out of town, a monster murdered her daughter, and the residents wanted *her* arrested?"

"Do you think those opinions influenced the jury's decision?"

"If ever a trial deserved a change in venue it was the trial of Arthur M. Root Jr."

"Interesting point."

I could tell he was thinking about my words. "I remember that was mentioned in one of the articles I looked over."

"Yes sir." I was glad to see he did his homework.

"Do you think a change in venue would change the outcome of the trial? Are you saying Root *could* be guilty, but the public's opinion about Mary Reber was stronger than the evidence against him? "

"We'll never really know, will we? I am not being difficult, but I think every effort should have been made to convict the person responsible for murdering a child, and that is not the case."

"Michelle, that was the most expensive trial in Lebanon's history at the time, and there was a tremendous amount of manpower devoted to investigating that case. I recall some of the experts that testified at the trial were some of the best in the nation."

"You're correct, and it's at this point I am always amazed that the expert testimony wasn't preserved in a transcript of the trial. There's always some joker that will tell the tale of how the defense transcribes a trial for an appeal, but in this case the lawyer representing Peggy, and the people of the Commonwealth, lost the case, so that responsibility was his. Nowhere is it written that only defense attorneys request trial transcripts. The murder is unsolved, and it would be damn nice to have the detailed testimony of the F.B.I. forensic expert, the medical examiner, or even an eyewitness that passed away over the course of the last three decades. Is it just me, or does the failure to preserve such important testimony suggest this case was never going to see the inside of a courtroom again?"

"I try hard not to judge such things without knowing all the facts." He was obviously an objective man. "You mentioned holes in the investigation?"

"Peggy endured at least one bite mark. That is documented fact. A dental expert from the Naval Institute of Pathology testified about it at the trial, as did a few others. There was a great debate about when the bite was actually inflicted, and testimony ranged from within a half hour of her death to twenty-four hours prior. Nine men gave dental impressions to be used in comparison to the bite mark on her breast. Naturally, Art Root Jr. submitted dental impressions along with Peggy's boyfriend, Ray Boyer, and over a half dozen other men. Art Root Jr. was ruled out as a match along with the other seven men, and while not an *exact* match, Ray Boyer was the closest comparison in the pool."

"Okay," he said, prompting me to continue.

"I am certain at the time the community was impressed with such efforts, but looking back on the facts, there are a few people missing from consideration. The apartment had no signs of forced entry, and while that's not a huge factor, one would hope investigators would at least test every man *known* to have a key to the apartment, and that is not the case. Investigators took the time to test Ray Boyer even though he was sitting in a jail cell at the time of the crime, yet they overlooked his brother Dick, and it was reported he had a key to the apartment. Let's not forget the landlord had a key to every apartment in the building, and he didn't submit dental impressions either. If we broaden the scope to men that knew Peggy was alone that day the constable shouldn't be excluded either because he is the one that jailed Ray Boyer earlier that afternoon. It sounds pretty stupid, but if there really was such a manhunt for this kid's killer, how did they overlook anyone with access to the apartment?"

"I think I remember reading Ray testified he inflicted the mark on Peggy the night before the crime, while they were having sex, but I would need to look at that again to be certain."

"You're right about testimony suggesting Ray inflicted the mark, but that is a gray area. Ray testified to giving Peggy a *hickey*, and experts testified about a legitimate *bite* mark. Oh, it makes for juicy storytelling to credit the young girl's lover with the mark, but is that accurate? Ray was the closest match out of the nine dental impressions used in the comparison, and one has to wonder if his biological *brother* would be an equal or better match if compared? I have two nieces wearing the steps out to an orthodontist because they both have the same genetic dental imperfections. Hey, I am not saying they should test his brother just *because* he has a brother, but because that brother was not sitting in jail at the time of the crime, and he had a key to the apartment."

"I'm sure he had an alibi at the time."

"Forgive my sarcasm, but who had a better alibi than Ray Boyer? He wasn't excused from submitting dental impressions, so I don't understand how any man outside a jail cell could be excused."

"You mentioned testing the constable, isn't that a bit of a stretch? He was, after all, a member of law enforcement." John Latimer was a reasonable man.

"He was a member of law enforcement, the landlord was a lawyer, and that wasn't an excuse to exclude either one of them from testing. What kind of manhunt was it if they were excluding possible suspects due to their occupations? Are we to assume officers of the court are above breaking the law?" I laughed at my own joke. "When I spotted a pair of handcuffs on the evidence list with the F.B.I. it sparked my curiosity. It wasn't impossible to obtain handcuffs in 1968, but it wasn't as easy as it is today. It was a different time back then. Now we have adult toys stores and the Internet, but in 1968 the average citizen wasn't walking into a super discount store buying handcuffs. We know the constable had handcuffs, don't we? More than that I always wonder if a member of law enforcement was missing their standard issue of handcuffs at the time? That little piece of evidence never made print in the news, and it wasn't mentioned during the trial, so most people don't even realize it's on the table."

"Perhaps it was of no importance, Michelle."

"Perhaps it wasn't, and I simply think too much, but I found a few other things to be a bit queer, too. The inventory list of evidence includes clothing from Root, and a couple of Hispanic males. While we know for a fact Ray Boyer was staying at the apartment, his clothing wasn't included for testing, but his teeth impressions were of concern for dental comparisons? Surely I am not alone in seeing the tunnel vision oozing out of this investigation. Not everyone with a key had to give dental impressions, and not all men frequenting the apartment gave hair samples, clothing was tested, but not the clothing of a man that actually lived there. Oh, the case against Root was strong, and one can only wonder what a thorough examination of all evidence and all possible suspects would have indicated? Far too much went overlooked and unidentified."

"Do you think that was deliberate?"

"Are you asking me if I think there was a conspiracy?" I didn't wait for him to answer my question. "No! I don't think for a minute there was a collective effort to kill Peggy, or to contaminate the investigation of her murder. I will also tell you I don't think county detectives, or city police, were surprised when they got the call there was a murder in that home. I do, however, think they were floored when they learned the identity of the victim, and the nature of the crime. They never expected Peggy to be the one to die there."

"I'm not sure I follow you."

"Local police were aware of the things that took place in that apartment building and the lifestyle of Mary Alice Reber. The constable's actions that day speak volumes. He clearly knew where to find Ray Boyer, so it is safe to say he knew Ray was involved with fourteen-year-old Peggy as well. The cops at the time knew a whole lot of what was going on in that apartment *before* the crime, far more than they ever admitted publicly. It still makes me wonder about a dumb pair of handcuffs."

"Back to the handcuffs." He kind of chuckled.

"John, I don't doubt for a minute those handcuffs belonged to a cop that stopped by that apartment for, oh, let's say a cup of coffee, but investigators failed to let the public know about that possibility. I guess self-preservation truly is everything. When that call hit the police radio on the morning of May 26th, 1968, I am certain every cop responding expected to find a middle-aged Mary Alice Reber dead on the floor. No, there definitely wasn't a conspiracy to kill Peggy Reber, and there was no preventative measure taken to protect her either. That same community that stood in judgment of her mother failed to do anything for the living child. The self-righteous community so quick to cast stones, yet it was that community that truly failed Peggy in life."

"So, what do you think happened to restrict the investigation?"

"I debate that question quite a bit, and it appears it was either a lack of competence, indifference, or arrogance with a hell of a lot of self-preservation."

"Those are powerful words." I could tell my conviction set him back a bit.

"Well, in keeping with the spirit of the times, the arrogance suggested this crime only happened because Mary Alice Reber was not the perfect mother, and that almost gave the madman a permission slip to unleash his fury on a young girl. The ignorance in motion not only blamed Mary Alice Reber, but overlooked several men that warranted serious consideration as suspects. The stamp of incompetence is present when the simplest of suspects escaped forensic testing. The indifference of the prosecution comes to light by the failure to tell the jury all the details of the crime, and then an additional failure to transcribe the trial after the case was lost. Self-preservation is in the wings, too." I laughed. "Mary Alice Reber was such a compromised woman, but the men compromising her sure as hell weren't being identified, were they? It was definitely a man's world."

"Michelle, I believe Art Root Jr. was identified as one of Mary Alice Reber's lovers."

"You're right again, but for a woman that was supposedly so loose, can you name two other men identified at the time also known to be bedding her? I will answer that for you, and the answer is, no."

"Would you say you are defensive of Mary Alice Reber?" His question was within reason.

"I wouldn't say I am defensive of her, but I will not join the masses that judged her without a conviction. I don't have blinders on, and I am not stupid, but one can never lose sight of the truly evil person in this picture, and it is not Mary Alice Reber. I don't mind telling you I don't care if she hosted an orgy and entertained a dozen men within an hour; the fact is nothing issued a permission slip for any man to commit such a crime against Peggy. Hell, sexual promiscuity on the part of Mary Alice Reber didn't give her lovers the right to do such a thing to *her*. In my opinion, far too much attention was given to Mary Alice Reber's dance card, instead of the identification of her child's killer."

"Isn't it safe to say the community simply thought if Mary Alice had been home taking care of Peggy this tragedy wouldn't have happened?" I understood his thoughts.

"If the judgment of Mary Alice stopped there I could accept it, but it didn't stop with such a simple thought. The community at the time was blatantly cruel to her. I compare it to a story in the Bible where the self-righteous approached Jesus about stoning a woman guilty of adultery, and Christ welcomed the person free of sin to cast the first stone. Judging the actions of the people at the time, I must come from the land of saints, huh?"

"So, what are your thoughts on the killer today?"

I didn't have to think too much before I answered his question. "He needs silence, arrogance, ignorance, incompetence and indifference to survive."

"Do you think he's still alive?"

"I think it's quite possible he's alive and well, and enjoying all the benefits of life in Lebanon, Pennsylvania."

▪▪▪

May 27, 2007 the headlines of The Lebanon Daily News read: "A Killer Walks Among You." There was a picture of me holding a picture of Peggy. In the interest of print space, the article ran two days after the 39th anniversary of Peggy's murder. The editor of the paper was quite generous with giving Peggy's story the most exposure it received in years. John Latimer reported on the aged homicide and my unique contribution to the story.

I set up an email address for information about Peggy, and I converted my home office phone line into a toll free tip line for any information about the case. The conscientious journalist interviewed Lebanon's chief of police, and the county district attorney to give the report a good sense of balance. I didn't get to see the article in its entirety by the time it hit the newsstands, and I wasn't even sure what time the paper hit the streets, so the early morning call on the toll free line caught me by surprise.

■■■

"Hi, this is Michelle." I didn't have a scripted dialogue, so I played it off the cuff.

"Is this the Peggy Reber line?" The caller asked.

"This is Michelle Gooden, and yes, I welcome any information you have about Peggy Reber."

"I remember when that happened and it was awful, oh it was just awful." The caller sounded like an older woman with a raspy voice.

"Did you know Peggy?" I slid into my desk chair and reached for a pen to take notes.

"No, I didn't know Peggy, but I remember watching that mother of hers walking the streets. She should have been ashamed of herself."

"I think it's safe to say Peggy's mother made a few poor choices, but don't we all?" I was almost disappointed that the first call on the toll free number started off with the same old song. "Did you live near the Rebers at the time?"

"I lived a few blocks away, but I could still see that woman at all hours of the night and day. I heard she sold those poor girls, too. Oh, the whole town knew exactly what she was, and what she was doing."

I listened to the woman a few minutes until call waiting alerted me to another incoming call. I excused myself from the first call to pick up the next call.

■■■

"This is Michelle."

"Yeah, are you that lady in today's newspaper? It says in the paper you think the killer is still here, so I guess you know it was a lawyer that killed that poor kid." The caller was an outspoken man.

"Do you know the name of the lawyer you're talking about?" I had to ask.

"I don't know the exact name, but everybody knows it was a lawyer, and that's why everything got covered up."

"Why do you think there was a cover up?"

"Lady, *everybody* knows it was covered up, and if you looked into this as much as the paper says you did, you should know that, too."

"Okay, I appreciate your call, and is that everything you wanted to say?"

"No lady, I didn't call to *tell* you anything." He laughed at me. "I called to find out which one of those bastards did it?"

■■■

"Is this Michelle?" I could barely hear the soft voice on the other end of the line.

"Yes, this is Michelle, can I help you?"

"You don't know me and I don't want to give you my name because I don't want anyone to know I called you." She was clearly concerned.

140

"You don't have to tell me your name." I assured the nervous woman. "Did you want to tell me something?"

"I just don't want *him* to ever know I called you. He is still a very powerful man around here, and I am too old to move."

"Forgive me, but who is the powerful man you are concerned about?" I was at a loss. "The Sheriff."

"You are concerned about the sheriff?" I wanted to make sure I heard her correctly.

"He must never know I made this call." She sounded fearful.

"Ma'am, I only ever talked to your sheriff one time in my life and I promise you whatever you have to share with me will never hit his ears."

"I was a hairdresser in my younger years and back then the saying was only my hairdresser knows. Women didn't go to counseling then like they do now. If a woman was upset, or having a crisis, she went to see her hairdresser." There was a lot of truth to the point she was making.

"I recall that with my own family members."

"Well, I worked in a really nice shop and one of my regulars was married to a lawyer involved with this case, the landlord of the building where that girl was killed. I will never forget how that poor girl looked spread out on that floor." Her voice started to crack.

"Excuse me?"

"She brought the pictures into the shop and showed them to everybody." She struggled to clear her throat.

"What pictures?"

"The pictures the police took the night they found that child."

"Are you telling me this woman brought the crime scene photographs into the beauty parlor?" I wanted to make sure I was hearing her correctly.

"Yes, she showed us the terrible things done to that girl, and I couldn't get those pictures out of my mind for years after that."

"Do you remember *when* she brought those pictures into the salon?"

"I most certainly do remember because you just can't forget something like that. She brought the pictures into the shop when that man was on trial. I know you were kind of young then, but everybody was talking about the trial."

"Ma'am, I don't want to question your memory, but if the trial was in session, the pictures would remain in the courtroom." I was having trouble wrapping my thoughts around the woman's words.

"Well, then her husband got them out of the courtroom because she brought those pictures into the shop when that guy was on trial." She sounded confident.

"I have no cause to doubt you, and I really appreciate your call, but I don't think anyone removed the original crime scene pictures during the trial."

"I don't know about any of that, but I know what I saw, and when I saw it. It just didn't seem right that she would bring those pictures into the beauty parlor." I could hear the disgust in her voice.

"No, it doesn't seem right, I agree with you. In fact it would be highly unethical for the wife of any attorney to even see such photographs, much less have them in her possession." I started thinking the worst. "I pray to God in heaven this doesn't mean the officers of the court made copies of those photos for their own entertainment."

I was sickened by the thought of pictures of Peggy's body being passed around at cocktail parties for the amusement of the shallow people trusted to guard such things in the name of justice.

■■

"Hello? Is this the number for Peggy? I was so happy to see this in today's paper. It's been far too long and somebody needs to do something about this tragedy. God bless you for being brave enough to stand up and say something." Another female caller greeted me on the phone.

"Thank you, but I wouldn't call myself brave. Did you know Peggy?"

"No, I didn't know Peggy, or her mother, but I was a witness at Art Root Jr.'s trial. I testified for the defense." I was pleasantly surprised by her words.

"Did you know Art Root Jr.?" I presented a logical question given the facts.

"No, not at all!" She sounded insulted by the mere suggestion. "I worked for a local merchant, and Art Root Jr. made a purchase that day. I had to testify about what time I waited on him the day of the murder. I was never so insulted as when one of the county detectives looked at me and made a comment about me being one of Root's girlfriends, too. I was no such thing, and I resented his remark. Those cops were so full of themselves back then. I remember when I worked at a diner out on Route 72, and they would come in there and make royal fools of themselves. I didn't call you to get into all that, but there is something that's bothered me all these years. I never said anything because I have to live here, but I am old now, and I am not long for this earth because I have cancer. There was talk back then about a fraternal organization that a lot of the high and mighty belonged to." She paused.

"What does a popular fraternal organization have to do with the murder of Peggy Reber?" I didn't know what to expect.

"That organization wasn't just popular. It was an elite men's group, and the community really respected them. Anyhow, every September those men would take their funny little hats and big gold rings and attend a convention in Atlantic City."

"Okay." I waited for her to fill in the blanks because I was lost.

"Well, not that it was ever mentioned publicly, but everyone knew that group of men took Mary Alice Reber along with them during their last convention before Peggy was murdered." She didn't express an ounce of doubt. "When her little girl was killed those same men dragged Mary Alice Reber through the mud. Isn't it funny how they forgot about that little weekend get-away?"

"I'm still not sure I understand. What does the convention in Atlantic City have to do with the murder?"

"Don't you see? When that poor child was killed those hypocrites plastered it all over the papers about the amount of men Mary Alice Reber dated, but none of them ever took claim to being with her! They sure didn't want anybody to find out about their little rendezvous with her in Atlantic City. I always wondered if one of those coat and ties had something to do with Peggy's murder."

■■

"Lady, I don't know what you're trying to pull, but you were too damn young to know anything about Peggy Reber." A gruff voice barked at me.

142

"I'm sorry you feel that way. I wasn't present for the signing of the Declaration of Independence either, but I can discuss that, too." I matched his attitude with one of my favorite expressions.

"You think you're funny, don't you? Well, I was there and you have a lot to learn." He was almost abrasive.

"You were there?" I wondered if the killer got brave enough to call me.

"Oh, I wasn't in the apartment if that's what you're thinking, but my buddies and I were in front of that building that night. We stole a couple quarts of soda from the beer distributor across the street and we were just hanging out. We saw that sleazy landlord with his overcoat and hat sitting in his car that night. That guy was a real work of art, and everybody knew it."

"So, you think the landlord was involved in the murder because you saw him sitting in his car in front of a building he owned?" I wasn't impressed with his revelation.

"Lady, everybody knew he had peepholes and two-way mirrors throughout that building. Why do you think they tore it down before the case ever hit a courtroom? They couldn't let a jury actually *see* his house of horrors. Like I said, you have a lot to learn!"

■■■

"Hello, Michelle Gooden speaking."

"Take the time to talk to the brick masons in town and they will tell you what happened to that girl."

Then the line went dead.

■■■

"I might be the last person that saw Peggy alive that day" my heart sunk as I listened to an older man with a Pennsylvania Dutch accent on the tip line. "I saw her on the pay phone in the William Penn restaurant that afternoon. Yeah, it was the middle of the afternoon and I just got out of the afternoon matinee at The Academy Movie Theater. I stopped in there for a piece of their home-made pie. They made the best pie. Did you ever have a piece of their pie? I lived the apple the best. I moved out here to Missouri to be closer to my kids and they sure don't make pie like that here. Yep, I can still see her standing there with her long blonde hair running clear down to her hips"

"Sir, Peggy did not have long blonde hair extending to her hips"

"Oh" the phone went dead.

■■■

"Yeah, hey, is this Miss Gooden?"

"Yes sir, this is Michelle Gooden. How can I help you?"

"Yeah, well, I am calling about that article about Peggy Reber. I don't know if you know this, but two guys killed themselves right after that happened, and I think they did it." The caller reminded me of the recent suicides following Peggy's murder.

"Sir, the F.B.I. performed testing on both those men, and excluded both of them from consideration based on their test results."

"Oh."

■■■

"I don't want to give my name, but I always heard Peggy's boyfriend, Ray Boyer, slipped some money to one of the guards at the jail, and he killed her."

"Thanks for calling, but beyond the fact I believe in my heart Ray actually loved Peggy, I have some issues with that theory." I rapidly rejected such an idea. "We would have to believe Ray bought off a guard, walked to the apartment without being seen, killed the girl he loved and tried to protect without getting a drop of blood on his prison clothes, exited the apartment, walked back to the jail, and entered his cell without a single person seeing a thing. I don't want to be rude, but I grew up in Lebanon, and I couldn't check the mail without someone seeing me."

■■■

"Yeah look, I'm gonna tell you like I told that cop. The secret is in the drowning."

Drowning? I thought, as I doodled on my notepad.

"What about the drowning?" I didn't understand his point.

"You don't know about the drowning, but when you learn the truth behind that you will know about the killer." He was being cryptic.

"What would you like to know about the drowning, sir?"

"What do *I* want to know? You are the one that has a little bit to learn, and I will give you twenty-four hours to come up with a date for the drowning before I tell you anything else." He was being coy.

"The date was May 25, 1969 and the location was Stoever's Dam." I knew exactly what he was talking about. "What does that have to do with the murder of Peggy Reber?"

"Very good!" He was impressed with my knowledge. "You *do* know what you're talking about after all." My knowledge pertaining to his riddle caught him by surprise.

"Arthur Root Jr.'s sixteen-year-old brother drowned in a local dam almost a year to the day after Peggy's death. Yes, I know about that, but I don't understand what that has to do with Peggy."

"If you identify the last person with him at the dam I think you will find Peggy's killer. That kid didn't just drown. No buddy, that was a calling card for Root to keep his mouth shut and take the fall for the real killer."

"Sir, I think if you do *your* home work you will find that poor kid was swimming with his Converse All Star sneakers on, and they weighted him down a bit. He yelled to his friends for help, and they thought he was joking. It was a senseless loss of life, but it had nothing to do with the murder of Peggy Reber. I will give you this much though." I had to hand it to the guy. "I thought it pretty strange that officials allowed Art Root Jr. to attend his brother's memorial services. He was, after all, up on charges for the most heinous crime in Pennsylvania history. He stood accused of murdering a teen, yet was allowed to honor the passing of a teen."

"Yeah, well I know more than that about the case." He didn't sound quite so cocky. "I was behind the apartment building that night. My buddies and I stole a couple quarts of beer from a nearby beer distributor and we were behind that apartment building drinking."

I thought of the call from the man claiming to drink stolen soda in front of the building, and now there were kids drinking stolen beer behind the building. How did that beer distributor manage to make a profit with such frequent theft?

"Did you see anything out of the ordinary that night?" I had to ask.

"What if I did?" He was back to being cocky.

"Well, in the interest of justice for Peggy, police could benefit from anything you saw." The time for tight lips had long since passed.

"I've got a few more things I need to look in to, a few more people to talk to, and we'll see." I didn't appreciate his game.

"If you know something, I beg of you to please contact Officer Snavely. He is doing everything in his power to give this kid the justice she deserves, but if people with information refuse to tell him what they know, he doesn't stand a chance of success."

"I talked to him, and *you* know more about the drowning than him." He was hung up on the death of Art Root Jr.'s kid brother.

"Why would Officer Snavely have to know about that drowning, or even care? It had absolutely nothing to do with the murder of Peggy Reber, and he is investigating her murder."

"He's not from around here, so he doesn't know shit about this case," he snapped angrily.

"So because Officer Snavely is not a native of Lebanon you are withholding information? I hate to break it to you, but I am from Lebanon, and I knew exactly what you were talking about, so what's the problem?" He was trying my patience, but in the event he really knew anything about Peggy I maintained a civil tone. "Did you see anything out of the ordinary that night?"

"Oh, I saw plenty, and when I'm done looking into a few things I might call you back." He was impossible.

"No offense, but please just talk to the professionals, and do the right thing."

▪▪▪

"The brother-in-law did it." I was greeted by one more aged voice on the toll-free line.

"Hi, this is Michelle." I tried to remain perky.

"Her brother-in-law killed her." The voice repeated itself.

"You think Peggy's brother-in-law committed this crime?" I turned the statement into a question.

"Of course he did, and you know it." The caller gave no hint of emotion.

"He raped her sister and when she ended up pregnant he married her to escape prison. Her mother knew it, and she didn't want to be tied down with a pregnant teenage daughter, so she signed for her to get married. He was a dog."

"Where does Peggy's murder fit into that fairy tale?"

"Well, if he could rape one teenage girl he wasn't above raping both." The voice on the phone remained monotone.

"I think there's a big difference between rape and the horrific murder that robbed Peggy of her life." I silently wished the madman had settled for raping Peggy.

"Oh, he raped both of those girls, but he could only marry one, and he didn't want to face the mother, or his brother, so he killed her. The Bible told us about the first real fight between brothers, and he didn't want to die."

"How do you know he didn't fall in love with Peggy's sister and celebrate the conception of their child?"

"Yeah, I guess he was celebrating the kid he had with another woman at the same time, too." The caller wasn't budging. "He was a bad seed. If he was in love, borrowing your words, why did two women have his kids in the same year? If you see some kind of love story around the marriage of Peggy's sister you need to go back to the drawing board. Her brother-in-law killed her." The caller was adamant.

"How do we know he didn't fall in love with Peggy's sister and have every intention of making a life with her? What does this have to do with Peggy's murder?"

"If he loved Peggy's sister, and their child was such a loved child, can you tell me where he is today? Where is that child today?" The caller wasn't backing down.

"If I am correct he is married to the mother of the other child born that same year, but that doesn't make him a killer." I knew the brother-in-law's history.

"You're right, it doesn't make him a killer, but it kills any thoughts you had about a great romance with Peggy's sister, doesn't it? He wasn't Casanova, but a devil in disguise, and he killed Peggy Reber. Take a really good look at his alibi. Didn't Peggy's sister attempt suicide within hours of the discovery of her sister's body? Is that a coincidence or fear? "

"I can't imagine being a teenager in her shoes." My heart broke for Peggy's identical twin.

"He used their mother to his own advantage, he used both those girls, and he stuck it to his brother when he used his brother's bow to kill her."

"Wow!" I wasn't quite sure what to say at that point. "Why do you think he would do such a thing? Why did he get away with it all these years? Why don't you tell authorities such things?"

"I told you why he did it. He got off easy when he raped the first girl and married her to avoid jail time, but he couldn't marry both girls. His brother was already married, so that left Peggy in the wings, and Mary Alice Reber didn't want any parts of a pregnant teenager."

"Are you saying Peggy was pregnant at the time?"

"Are you saying she wasn't?" The voice volleyed back.

■■

"Hi, hey, I don't know if you realize this because you were pretty young, but we were at war back then. We were fighting in Nam. I think one of those son-of-a-bitches got over here on our soil and killed that girl. They were baby killers. Nobody wants to talk about it anymore, but they'd strap bombs to their own babies in strollers, so they could kill our G.I.s when they walked up to talk to the babies. I really think you should be looking for a slant-eyed-enemy on our soil"

■■

"He bragged about it." A voice whispered into the phone.

"Who bragged about what?" I replied with a whisper.

"Her brother-in-law." I struggled to hear the caller. "He told people he rammed a bow up Peggy Reber's butt, and he wasn't above doing it again."

"Who did he threaten?" I had to know if there was a name to attach to the claim.

"Ask around and you'll know what I'm talking about."

■■

"Hey, did you check out that mayor we used to have? Everybody said he was gay and maybe he had something to do with the crime."

■■

"I was thinking about this crime and suddenly I know exactly how it was committed. I kept thinking about the bite mark, and then I started thinking about the original Dracula. Ivan the Impaler took a great stand on the Carpathian mountainside when 20,000 warriors were impaled on their spears. I just know one individual held the bow still as Peggy's body was pushed up and down on it and inflicting the five holes in her heart."

■■

"I used to wait tables at The Elks Lodge. I waited on all those big-shots back then. Oh, they would come in for lunch and sit around drinking and talking about Peggy Reber"

"Local officials were drinking during their lunch hour?" I wanted the woman to confirm what I thought I heard her say. I was beyond shocked by the thought of Peggy's investigators drinking during the investigation of her murder. D.U.I. could take on a whole new meaning and that could translate into detectives under the influence. I fought the urge to scream! Today's standards would never allow a member of law enforcement to have an alcoholic beverage during lunch without the risk of professional self-destruction. A smart lawyer, judge, detective or layman would never engage in the consumption of alcohol in the midst of a work day. I had to remind myself Peggy was killed in 1968. No, the effect of alcohol was not any different in 1968, but society's acceptance of it was different. Drunk driving was a crime, but there wasn't blood alcohol limits, breathalyzers as we know them today, or campaigns for designated drivers. Cops decided who was drunk during public disturbances and traffic stops. Cops decided a lot back then. The years since then taught us as a society the consumption of alcohol does indeed impair one's thought process. Was it even possible those responsible with delivering Peggy's justice were drinking during the process? I wasn't even sure I wanted to hear the woman's answer to my question.

"Oh yes they were drinking during lunch! Some drank more than others, but they were drinking. Judges, the lawyers, the prosecutors, the detectives, patrol cops all ate there back then. It was nothing for people to drink cocktails or have a couple beers during lunch. It wasn't like it is today. I had to smile while I waited on them and I smiled like a fool because I had kids to feed, but they were a miserable lot. I had to put a county detective in his place one day because he decided to pat my butt when I leaned over the table to empty the ashtray. I was just a waitress and my husband was just a bartender at another private club, but I wasn't going to put up with that kind of crap from anybody. He was a pig not because he was a cop, but because he was a pig. They walked around this town like they owned the place. You should have seen it. It was like they were untouchable. I had a daughter the same age as Peggy and I was scared for her. I think the whole town was scared. We didn't know what really happened or what was really going on and it was just a frightening time. We all gave a sigh of relief when they finally made an arrest in the case. I remember that was the one day I actually gave in to the temptation and talked to them about Peggy. I felt a little bit safer after they arrested Art Root Jr. I think the whole town felt safer. I can't explain it, and you probably won't either, but I wanted to throw up when they started joking about how they had to arrest somebody and Root was willing to play the game"

"Did you just say Root was willing to play the game?"

"That's what they said and they were laughing about it. I thought I misunderstood them. I thought maybe they were being cocky and just referring to the investigation as a game. God knows Peggy's murder wasn't a game and there wasn't anything funny about it. I thought they meant Art Root Jr agreed to play the game when he killed her, yet it was weird for me. It was really weird. They just kept laughing about Root being willing to play some kind of game. It was all pretty weird, but then I looked at the picture in the paper of Art Root when he was taken before the magistrate. He was smiling. Did you ever get the chance to see that picture? He wasn't scared or evil or defensive. Art Root was charged with killing Peggy and he was smiling while it was happening. I didn't know what it meant. I just knew it wasn't right. Did you see the picture of him after the trial? He was smiling again. Yeah, I know you're gonna tell me he was smiling because he just got away with murder, but I am telling you he agreed to play the game – whatever that mean"

"What are you saying?" I was overwhelmed.

"Don't you see it?"

I didn't see the point being made.

"Root just had to agree to be some kind of fall guy. I am convinced he agreed to play whatever game it was those bastards offered him. They weren't stupid and they knew they needed to arrest somebody, so they arrested him to shut everybody up. Root didn't kill her and he knew he wasn't going to be convicted. He wasn't convicted, was he? I don't know what deal they cut with him, but nothing was as it appeared. I didn't keep the newspapers from back then, but just go back and look at the pictures. I know that doesn't let you see or hear what I did, but Root was never scared. He knew. He knew he was just being charged with the crime, but he knew he would walk, too"

"Why would Root agree to such a thing? Why would officials do such a thing? I am trying to understand what you're saying, but help me" I was being honest.

"This community was scared when Peggy was killed. I just don't think you realize how much her murder touched every citizen here. We were locking our doors, looking over our shoulders and watching our neighbors like we never did before. Peggy Reber's murder changed life in Lebanon because we were all scared of her killer. Yeah, the rumors kept pointing at her mother's boyfriends, but we didn't know that for sure, so we were scared. We stopped our lives, locked our doors and prayed. Honestly, I don't know how we made it six months without somebody being arrested for her murder. You do realize nobody was arrested for six months? That was a long summer"

"So, you think they simply needed to arrest someone and Art Root agreed to be that man?"

"I am almost forty years older today and I will tell you I have no doubt they had to arrest somebody. We couldn't live with that fear forever. We all felt better when they made an arrest. We didn't bounce back to normal, but we started to relax. We started to trust cops and our environment again. Peggy Reber's killer was behind bars, so we thought. We didn't forget Peggy, but we almost understood Peggy died because her mom got involved with Art Root Jr. We knew it didn't have anything to do with us normal people, yet I still watched those guys laugh about Root agreeing to play the game"

"Normal people? Help me understand what defines normal people"

"Peggy's mom didn't live her life or raise her kids like normal people. I don't want to get into all that, but she wasn't taking care of those kids. I don't need to paint you a picture. Her daughter ended up dead and her married boyfriend was charged with the crime. It just wasn't normal. Her other daughter was close to the same age as Peggy and I heard she was already married and had a baby. I don't know what was going on over there, but normal people weren't living like that"

I gave up on the definition of normal.

"Why would Art Root Jr agree to be charged with such a brutal crime? Why would he agree to play such a sick game?"

"He walked, didn't he? He didn't lose a damn thing. We trusted them"

"I think I am closer to this case than I want to be." A voice expressing obvious nervousness uttered a few words.

"What makes you think so?" I replied.

The details of that phone call are excluded in the interest of justice for Peggy.

∎∎∎

"Yeah, hey, like I saw that thing about Peggy Reber, and I think I know who did it."

"Oh really?" I was more than ready to learn the identity of the killer.

"I used to date Ray's son when I was in junior high school, and I always thought he was a little weird, and he had something to do with it."

"You think Ray did it?' I asked.

"No, his son," the caller clarified.

"Is that even possible considering he was in diapers at the time of the crime?"

∎∎∎

"Is this Michelle?"

"This is Michelle." I was starting to feel like a broken record.

"You know you don't have to go too far if you want to know about all of this because the district attorney knows the Boyer family."

"Are you talking about Lebanon's current district attorney?"

"That's the one. His wife was engaged to Dick Boyer's son, and I think she was the maid of honor in one of his other kid's weddings. Yeah, he knows the Boyer family up close and personal."

"The district attorney has personal involvement with the Boyer family?" I guess stranger things were known to happen.

"He damn sure does." The caller was almost proud to make such an announcement. "If he starts looking into this case it will be nothing but one big family reunion."

"You're telling me the district attorney's wife was engaged to the son of Peggy's brother-in-law, and she was also in a Boyer family wedding?"

"That's what I said."

"How long ago was that? I don't mean to be rude, but she obviously ended up marrying the DA."

"Let's see." The caller hesitated for a moment. "They split up right after that little domestic dispute."

"A domestic dispute?" I tried to keep up with the dialogue, but it was difficult.

"The word on the grapevine is their little dispute happened because she was still playing around with Boyer's son even after they got married."

"Are you saying the district attorney's wife was spending time with Dick Boyer's son after she married the district attorney?"

"If the walls could talk, that's what they'd tell you." The caller almost snickered. "I don't remember the exact year, but he supposedly caught her fooling around and that's when the cops were called out to his house. Oh, they talked about it during the elections, but he did his best to cover it up like a cat in a litter box. They had a pretty ugly divorce, too. He ended up filing for bankruptcy and blamed everything on her."

"Are you a friend of hers?" I didn't understand the caller's motives.

"No, and I am not a friend of his either. If somebody is going to prosecute this case I'm not sure he's the man for the job. It's going to be hard enough to nail this guy after all these years, and we don't need a DA dragging his own soap opera into the court room."

∎∎∎

"I used to work at the steel plant and I remember hearing how two guys did this, and they laughed like hell about it. The sick sons-of-bitches"

"Do you know who the two guys were?" I knew we needed more than rumor for the call to be worth the time.

"That was a long time ago, but I think the one guy's name was Ronnie, or Donnie. It could have been Lonnie, but it was something like that, and I don't remember the other guy's name. I know I'm not much help, but I wanted to call just in case it helps."

"Thank you, I appreciate you taking the time." I hung up frustrated.

∎∎∎

"I remember you. I remember your mom and dad, too. She was fat and he was skinny. They used to sit outside at their picnic table drinking quarts of beer. You got a lot of nerve bringing this stuff up"

"Well you're only half way right, buddy. My parents did sit at their picnic table and drink beer, but they drank it from a can. Oh, and let's get one thing perfectly clear my parents didn't kill Peggy Reber"

****

"My friend worked night shift at the hospital. He was a janitor. He was there the night they brought Peggy in and he said it was really bad. He said she had bite marks everywhere and he said something about the bow and the arrows"

"Do I understand you to say your friend the janitor saw Peggy's body?"

"Yeah and he said the whole hospital was just in total shock"

"I don't doubt the hospital, along with the rest of the city, stood in horror. However, Peggy did not have bite marks all over her body, but she did suffer one horrific bite to her breast"

The caller interrupted me "Listen I am telling you what he told me and he saw her that night, so he should know what happened to her"

"Sir" I dug deep for diplomacy. "I have no desire to upset you or insult your friend"

The caller interrupted me again "My friend died years ago, so you can't insult him, but I still know what he told me"

"I am sorry about the loss of your friend. Sir, the county coroner testified Peggy endured one bite to her body. Prosecutors removed her breast to make a mold in an effort to identify her killer through dental impressions. I know there have been many rumors about the use of arrows in the assault, but that is not the case. Peggy was assaulted with the five-foot bow not the arrows. There weren't any arrows present at the crime scene"

"You aren't listening to me. He was there that night and he saw it with his own eyes" the caller was getting angry with me.

"Forgive me, but I find it very upsetting that your friend, the janitor, was permitted to view Peggy's body. It's disrespectful, unethical and a good lawyer could point out it compromised any evidence removed from the body"

"I said he saw her. I didn't say he touched her"

"No sir you didn't say he touched her, but I really have to wonder what police were thinking. Her body should have been closely guarded. Oh, by the way" I braced myself for his fury. "Peggy Reber was not taken to the Good Samaritan Hospital the night she died. Peggy was found dead a little after three in the morning, her body remained at the crime scene until shortly after ten that morning and that would not be consistent with her arrival during a janitor's night shift"

"I don't know about all that, but I still know what he told me" the caller hung up on me.

▪▪▪

"Did anybody check into the boys she went to school with? Maybe one of those guys really liked her and got mad because she didn't like them back?"

"I don't have an answer for you, but I will pass your thoughts on to the police. The crime remains unsolved, so we really don't know who killed her, do we?"

▪▪▪

"Is this Michelle? I think it's great what you're doing, Peggy used to babysit me and she was a really nice girl. She would walk me home from school so I would be safe and to think this happened to her is just awful. I remember crying my eyes out when she died. I just didn't understand it"

"Oh, I am so sorry. I am certain that was a terrible thing to deal with as a child. I am also grateful you shared the nice memory about Peggy walking you home from school. Do you recall Peggy being scared of anyone?"

"I don't know any names if that's what you're asking, but I know she had a knife in her purse. I wasn't very old back then, but I knew enough that she didn't trust people. I really wish I could tell you more, but I was pretty young at the time. I just wanted to thank you"

▪▪▪

"Yeah, hey, why don't you just leave well enough alone? Everybody knows Art Root got away with it and we don't need you stirring this up again"

▪▪▪

"I work in a local office and we have a few senior citizens come in and help a few days each week. Well, a few months ago one of our seniors was visited by a couple detectives and it was pretty weird. She is exceptionally bright and sharp, but the minute those police officers arrived she changed her whole personality. It was the weirdest thing.
She went from being a dynamo to being almost confused and fragile. Naturally, we asked her what it was all about and she said it was about Peggy. None of us in the office had heard of Peggy before because we aren't that old, but this lady's son was dating Peggy when she died. We asked around a little bit and found out her other son was married to Peggy's sister. I don't know what it's worth to you, but it was really weird for us to watch"

▪▪▪

"My mom and I had to stay in that building for awhile after she and my dad got divorced. The place wasn't the best, but it wasn't like people say. There were good decent people living there. It makes me mad when people put the place down because most of them never even stepped foot in the building. We did alright there, but the creepiest part about living there was the guy that owned the building. It was like he knew the women that didn't have husbands and he'd show up and pound on their doors at all hours of the night. He did it to us one time, but my mom made us stay real quiet and pretend like we weren't home"

■■

"I got a question for you. Why didn't the cops just follow the trail of blood? There ain't no way in hell that guy wasn't covered in blood after he did that to that kid. I just don't get it. There had to be footprints and somebody had to see him. He would have been a big bloody mess. It just doesn't make good common sense. It had to be easier than tracking deer in the snow"

"Sir, I know it's hard to imagine, but it wasn't the blood bath we immediately think of when we first learn about the crime. Peggy was struck pretty hard in the face and chances are the blow knocked her unconscious. The killer then strangled her with a cloth dress belt to the point she suffered not only brain damage, but a deep laceration to her throat. The coroner actually listed that as her cause of death in the autopsy report. Peggy was pretty much gone by the time he assaulted her with the bow and the lack of her blood pressure would limit the splatter one imagines. Peggy endured the blow to her face, the bite on her breast and the gash from being strangled, but Peggy suffered massive internal injuries due to the bow"

"I just don't get it. I still think that twisted freak was covered in blood and I think somebody saw something"

■■

"My brother went to that house one time. I remember my mom throwing a dish at him and it hit the wall when she found out about it, too. She kept yelling at him and saying things like that was nothing but a whore house and my brother couldn't live under her roof and run with whores. I never saw my mom so mad"

"Do you think your brother would talk to me about his visit to that house?"

"I wish he could talk to you. My brother got drafted later that year and he never made it back from Viet Nam"

■■

"You know why this murder ain't solved? I will tell you why. Those city cops were too busy skinny-dipping out at the apartments by the plaza when they were supposed to be on duty"

■■

"Hey, is this the place you're supposed to call with questions about Peggy Reber?" I was learning quickly the tip line designated to receive information about Peggy was also serving as a question line, too. "Yeah, well, I thought I heard something about that Root guy and one of that girl's neighbors taking a stereo or a television out of her apartment that day" The caller was referring to Art Root Jr removing Mary Alice Reber's stereo in lieu of the money he allegedly robbed from Wenzler's Laundromat and it was reported one of Peggy's neighbors did assist him. "Yeah, well, what about that guy that helped him move that stuff? Maybe he helped him knock Peggy off, too"

"Sir, Art Root Jr was not convicted of killing Peggy Reber"

"Yeah, well, what about that other guy? I mean I am just trying to help you out, but that right there tells you that Root guy wasn't the only guy in that place that day. Did anybody bother to look into that other guy?"

"Sir, you make a good point and I will pass it on to Officer Snavely"

"Yeah, well, I am not always the sharpest tool in the shed, but shouldn't one of those cops thought of that already?"

"Sir, I can only tell you what I know and that is Mr. Wida supposedly assisted Art Root with removing Mary Alice's stereo. If I understand correctly Mr. Wida then accompanied his girlfriend to buy eggs"

"He took his girlfriend to buy eggs, huh? Yeah, well, maybe she lied for him. How does anybody really know that's what he was doing? Women will do that, ya know. I remember one time the truant officer came to the house because my brother skipped school and my mom told that truant officer she knew my brother didn't go to school. Yeah, well, she didn't know until the truant officer showed up on the doorstep. My brother got his ass beat, but I still remember how my mom lied to that truant officer. I ain't saying all women lie, and my mom was a good woman, but somebody should check into that. Hey, didn't I hear somewhere that that Root guy with his old lady that night? How can everybody be with their old lady that night and yet that girl ended up dead? Somebody wasn't where they said they were and somebody's old lady is lying.

∎∎∎

"Lady somebody needs to take a good long look at that judge, but you ain't gonna find a cop in Lebanon with enough back bone to do it. Hell, they were all too busy picking his drunk-ass up at The Bluebird Inn. He didn't have to call yellow cab when he was sloppy drunk because he could just dial-a-cop and they'd pick his fat ass up. He was the biggest drunk in this town and everybody knew it. He'd screw a hole in a fence if he could and nobody said a damn thing. Lebanon was just a playground for him. What about that girl he knocked up? Yeah, those lawyers don't think we know about that little fiasco, but everybody knows the story"

"Sir, are you suggesting a judge had something to do with Peggy's murder?"

"I am not suggesting anything. I am telling you what everybody knew back then. He drank like a fish and screwed anything he could get his hands on and I do mean anything. Are you hearing what I am telling you? That bastard broke all the rules and got away with it because he was a judge"

"I am trying to understand. Are you referring to the judge that presided over Peggy's murder trial?"

"Lady if you gotta ask that question you have a lot to learn"

∎∎∎

"Hi, yeah is this Michelle?" a soft-spoken female was on the other end of the phone. "I hope you can hear me, but I don't want to talk too loud. I don't want my grandchildren to hear me. I watch them for my daughter when she has to work. Her husband died in a car accident and she is really having a rough time, so I try to help her out with babysitting, so she can save some money. Anyhow..." the woman was clearly struggling to get to the purpose of her call. "When I was a kid my dad was not the best person. He worked second shift at the steel plant and he didn't always come home after work. My mom would get upset, but it never made a difference to my dad. Anyhow, one night my mom decided to follow him after he got off work. She packed us kids up. There were three of us. We waited for him to clock out and we followed him, but he didn't know we were following him. I guess today they would call that stalking, but back then I don't know what they called it. My mom and us kids followed my dad to an apartment building on Maple Street. Are you there? Can you hear me?" I assured the woman I was listening to her. "My mom pulled up next to a car lot. I think it was called Sholly's, but I might be wrong. We were in my grandpa's car and my mom had trouble finding the parking brake. Oh geez, I mean the emergency brake, but back then I think they called it the parking brake. She struggled to park the car, but managed and we followed my dad into that building. My little brother started to cry, but my mom grabbed his arm and almost dragged him. It was like he knew not to make a sound. Anyhow, we followed my dad to an apartment on the third floor. I will never forget it. Are you still there? Anyhow, by the time we got to the third floor my dad was nowhere in sight, yet my mom just knew where she was going. My mom knocked on an apartment door and I could hear music playing from the apartment. My mom no sooner knocked on the door and it opened. I will never forget this as long as I live because the woman that opened the door was smiling, laughing and naked. She was holding a beer and a cigarette in her hand. She had no shame. My mother started screaming, my little brother started crying and I just couldn't take my eyes off the naked woman. My dad came out of the apartment yelling at my mom, but all I could hear was my mom screaming "Mary Reber you are a whore! You are a home wrecking whore! " The naked woman closed the apartment door after my dad came out into the hall, but my folks, and my little brother were screaming at the top of their lungs. I will never forget that as long as I live"

"I am not sure what to say?" I was at a loss.

"I didn't call you for you to say anything. I just thought you should know what was really going on there. My dad followed us home that night and though he was mad as hell I guess they worked it out. He and my mom celebrated forty-three years of marriage before he died. I will never forget Mary Reber answering her door naked as a jaybird. I would like to talk to you more, but my grandson is starting to get hungry" I sat numb by the call.

■■

"You seem to know so much, so I guess you know Art Root's old man was charged with statutory rape. How do you know they didn't charge the wrong Root?"

■■

"Peggy used to scare me" a woman caught me completely off guard.

"Peggy scared you?' I was floored.

"I was eight or nine years old and I had to walk past the Maple Leaf Apartment Building to go to school. Peggy would stand outside smoking cigarettes with her friends and they would make fun of me. They scared me. I don't know if you remember, but fishnet stockings were popular for kids back then. Peggy and her friends would always make fun of my stockings. I hated walking past that building, but it all changed after she died. It was horrible. I am older now and I understand it's almost a right-of-passage for teenagers to make fun of little kids. I don't hold any ill feelings toward Peggy. Hell, it is probably the complete opposite. My neighbor was a waitress at a nearby nightclub…the Sho-Bar and I remember some guy staying with her for awhile. I was just a kid, but I remember adults around me saying he was staying there because he killed a girl. My neighbor's name was Jackie. Has anybody talked to her?

■■

154

"Is this Shelly Gooden? Are you the daughter of Mike and Minnie? You grew up on Scull Street, didn't you? Honey, I knew you and your parents from the Speedwell Fire Company. Man, it is great to know you're alive. I always wondered what happened to you. Hey, I knew Peggy Reber, too. Hell, she lived in West Lebanon, too. It's a small world" I recognized the name, voice and our history. "Shelly, I used to work at The Gap and I remember one of my buddies talking about some guy that bragged about killing Peggy. Hey, if you give me a couple hours I can have him call you, but you're gonna have to be patient because I think he works late today. So tell me how have you been?"

I was thrilled to hear from an old friend, but I was more excited by the fact he could possibly hold a key to Peggy's justice. "You know someone that bragged about killing Peggy?"

"I can't recite everything first-hand, but if you sit tight I will make a few calls and see what I can do for you. I don't remember all the details, but there was some guy working at The Gap and he pretty much said he killed her. I guess he thought he was going to look cool in front of the other guys, but there ain't nothing cool about the guy that killed Peggy Reber. That was a sick mother fucker"

I immediately relayed that information to Kevin Snavely.

"Kevin, if you give this man a few hours he just might have a break in the case" I was beyond pleased. "We just have to be patient and after forty years I don't think a few hours is going to make a difference" I was content with the progress of the tip line.

Two hours later the man-from-my-past called and he wasn't happy "Shelly, what in the hell did you do? I told you to give me a couple hours and I would call you back. I no sooner hung up with you and this cat Snavely started calling and calling and calling. Man, he was burning that phone up! He didn't just call me, he called the dude I told you about and our women. There ain't no way in hell that dude is going to say anything now. Shelly, I told you to give me a couple hours. I wouldn't have said anything if I knew this was gonna happen" I looked toward the heavens and I felt betrayed.

●●

I called Kevin and confronted him about his actions. He was arrogant and filled with conviction. He took some claim-to-fame about being the actual law enforcement officer handling the case. I sat amazed. "I set up a tip line, received a tip, delivered the tip and you simply had to wait a few hours for some feedback, but you decided to push the envelope? You just ignored me, ignored the lead and called these people a half dozen times in the matter of an hour?" I was irritated, embarrassed and saddened. The tip line was only going to be effective if the leads were handled with the utmost of care and professionalism. Kevin dropped the ball. Needless to say, that particular pocket of information ran dry quickly because suddenly nobody remembered a damn thing.

"I could have handled that better" I listened to Kevin apologize to me, yet I wasn't sure he truly realized a 40-year-old crime didn't leave too much room for error. He was the cop and I was the nobody, yet he failed to grasp the fragility of the situation. His badge was not going to push anybody into talking. If he thought for a minute the world was going to cave in because he was a cop he was sadly mistaken. I knew I had to continue to share all leads with him, but I no longer trusted his approach.

●●

I spent 18 hours on the phone before I even got a chance to read the news report online. I was exhausted, but I needed to see what the callers were responding to.

Of course there was the background information about the hours leading up to the murder and then the details of the crime itself. My efforts of researching the crime offered the new twist to the story, but the focus was on assisting Officer Snavely's investigation and capturing Peggy's killer.

Police Chief William Harvey, a stocky, silver-haired man with Southern roots was not overly familiar with the details of the case, but confirmed Lebanon's police department continued to actively pursue information about the murder of Peggy Reber. He acted as the spokesperson for the Lebanon City Police Department.

Lebanon County District Attorney David J. Arnold Jr. didn't take his first breath until three years after Peggy lost her life, and he echoed the sentiment that Peggy's murder was an open and active investigation. He went on to say he reviewed the Reber file, and while he saw a suspect he did not view that person as a threat.

My heart stopped.

The district attorney admitted to looking at Peggy's file, and while he *saw* a suspect in that file, he didn't view him as a threat? I was stunned. How in the hell could any district attorney *see* a suspect in a child's murder file, and not pursue justice? It was late, I was tired, and I convinced myself it would make more sense in the morning.

I woke up to the phone ringing, and the day followed the same course as the previous day. It didn't take long to realize Lebanon never forgot about Peggy, and they were none too happy that her murder remained unsolved. I weeded through the calls of concern, legitimate information, crackpots and the curious. I was grateful for each and every person that made an effort to make a difference. After a full day on the phone I sat down at the computer and my jaw dropped when I saw dozens of emails about Peggy. There weren't enough hours in the day, yet each call and each email held the possibility of being that one piece of information that could make all the difference with the case. I burned the midnight oil as I responded to each individual letter.

Within a week of the news feature the first letter to the editor appeared in the Lebanon Daily News, and that was just the beginning. Letters poured in from all over the country screaming for justice in the name of Peggy Reber. Assuming timing is everything it was definitely the time to pull the tragic injustice of Peggy's murder out from the shadows. The frustrated public didn't just want to remember the youthful victim, or talk about her; rather they wanted her killer behind bars. The Lebanon Daily News ran an editorial appealing to the district attorney to take the case before a grand jury.

I placed a call to the district attorney and I found him to be quite pleasant. I thanked him for taking Peggy's case into consideration and he told me he would love to deliver justice to Peggy Reber. The district attorney told me he needed the police department to give him the file before he could truly pursue the case. I knew Officer Snavely was going over the case with a fine-tooth comb, so I hung up confident Peggy would get her day in court.

The next call I made was to the Chief of Police. I politely introduced myself and thanked him for taking my call as well. He wasn't quite as pleasant as the district attorney. Through his thick Southern accent he attempted to patronize me, and I didn't find it amusing at all. After a few snide comments about my position as an aspiring author, he stressed the preponderance of evidence law enforcement required in such an aged homicide. I got the impression he liked to hear his own voice. He went off on a tangent about not wanting to repeat the errors of his former police department.

The good Chief had the benefit of serving twenty years on a Georgia police department that gained fame for botching a homicide investigation. The faulty murder investigation resulted in a best-selling book and a popular motion picture. The Chief had nothing to do with the case, but it obviously left him gun-shy.

The more I listened to his misplaced accent, the more I wondered why a Georgia murder should even be compared to Peggy. It occurred to me the Chief didn't have a vested interest in Lebanon because he wasn't from Lebanon, and he wasn't going to retire in Lebanon. The more he discussed the need for evidence, the more I got the impression he lost sight of his role as a member of law enforcement. He seemed to forget his job was to investigate, gather facts, and present files to the district attorney to prosecute. Listening to him, one would have thought he was the lawyer doing the prosecuting. It was apparent if Peggy was going to receive justice it sure as hell wasn't going to be due to him. He had the file, and it needed to leave his hands before the DA could pursue Peggy's killer. Peggy Reber deserved the efforts of the DA, a grand jury, and the Chief had no right to stand in the way of that.

Several weeks later, I placed a call to the mayor. It was late on a Friday afternoon, and the mayor was gone for the weekend, so I sent him an email. I then called the police department, and the Chief was also gone. I talked with a senior police officer and said, "Peggy should be celebrating her 54th birthday this weekend."

"Miss Gooden, what can I do for you?" He was curt.

"A grand jury would be nice." I tried to be playful.

"I don't have that authority, and you know we are pursuing this investigation. Officer Snavely is following up on the leads you are providing him. Is there anything else I can assist you with?"

"Get your Police Chief to give Peggy's file to the DA, so he can take the case before a grand jury." I didn't want much. I just wanted the wheels of justice to start turning.

"Miss Gooden, the Chief doesn't have to give the DA anything. The district attorney is the *ultimate* law enforcement officer in Lebanon County."

I thought about the officer's words throughout the weekend, and I knew he was right. I thought about the pleasant conversation I had with the district attorney, and I realized I wasn't talking to a man of the law, but a politician. I wanted to kick myself in the ass for being so trusting.

Monday morning I felt my heart race as I read an obnoxious email I received from Lebanon's mayor. He was about as polished as his Chief of Police. He suggested I was receiving leads about the case and not providing them to the police department, but his door was open if I wanted to deal with him. He informed me he copied the Chief of Police and the district attorney on his correspondence to me. I could sense he was rather proud of himself, but the joke was going to be on him before the day was over.

I emailed the district attorney and copied the mayor. I refused to include the Chief of Police in the correspondence because he was little more than the second notch in the belt. I didn't pull too many punches when I told the district attorney I would not tolerate being slandered by the mayor of the city of Lebanon. He was accusing me of withholding information and that could almost be construed as obstruction of justice. I set up a toll-free tip line for Peggy at my own expense because the city of Lebanon didn't provide such a tool. I pointed out each and every call I placed to Lebanon, Pennsylvania was a long distance call and was detailed on my phone bill, so

I could prove my conversations with law enforcement in black and white. I suggested the DA have the mayor listen to the recorded conversation I had with one of his senior officers the previous Friday. He would hear his own employee saying the police department was following up on the leads I was providing Officer Snavely. Clearly, the mayor didn't have a clue as to what was going on within the police department. No, I wasn't impressed with the Chief of Police, or his boss, the mayor.

The district attorney responded that he was by no means accusing me of withholding information. I took that for what it was worth, but I think the boys at the courthouse knew I was not going to accept being lied about. It was bad enough I was being lied to.

■■

Local radio talk show host Laura LeBeau filled the a.m. airwaves throughout the Lebanon Valley each weekday with a wide variety of subjects. Her listening audience would burn up her phone lines to offer their opinions on the wide range of topics Laura discussed on air. Laura and her listeners didn't hesitate to take Peggy under their wing. I called into her show on several occasions to better educate her audience about details surrounding the crime, and the obstacles on the path to justice. Laura's listening audience quickly shifted gears from listening to talking once they realized the unacceptable way Peggy Reber's murder was put on a shelf for such a long time. It was always refreshing to hear her callers speak out on behalf of Peggy.

The Pandora's Box containing the story of Peggy Reber was open, and it was long overdue. It was a new day, a new generation, and the community not only wanted justice for the murdered child, but they didn't want a child killer living in their midst. The four decades that lapsed since the crime taught average people they could make a difference, and the people of Lebanon wanted their voices to be heard.

Six months after the 39th anniversary of Peggy's death and the article announcing my efforts with the case, I sat baffled by the lack of action from the district attorney's office. I certainly didn't expect the DA to march to my drum, but it was growing increasingly obvious that without further action of some sort he wasn't going to budge on the Reber case. The local paper and Laura LeBeau were great sources of exposure, but Peggy needed more.

I looked at the computer sitting on my desk, and I knew the answer was in technology, but I was computer illiterate. Hell, I wanted to write a book, and I didn't even know how to type. I didn't stand a chance of giving Peggy the computer exposure she needed. I paced around the house and thought of every person I knew with computer knowledge. I quickly realized most of those people were my son's friends and they were all away at college. I thought about those kids and a light bulb went on overhead.

I didn't have a clue how to set up a MySpace page, but I knew that was exactly what the situation needed. I didn't need all the graphics and frills, but I did need a place where I could bring the facts together collectively and educate the public about Peggy. The plight of Peggy Reber was generating the support of so many people that weren't even alive when she lost her life, and I stood convinced if they really knew the facts they would demand justice.

I carefully navigated my way through the process of designing a page in honor of Peggy. I highlighted the events of her last day alive, the discovery of her body, and a couple dozen points of concern with the investigation. I included her photograph and I knew the perfect song was, *The Sound of Silence*. After all, every effort being made was designed to break the silence surrounding Peggy. Upon its completion, I wrote a letter to the editor of the Lebanon Daily News and unveiled the web address in the paper's public forum.

The response to the MySpace page was overwhelming! I sat speechless when I saw the hundreds and hundreds of hits the page received on a daily basis. The page gave people not only the opportunity to read about Peggy, but people could comment on the injustice as well, and comment they did!

■■■

Once again the district attorney had to address the murder of Peggy Reber, and once again he expressed a desire to pursue justice in the case. He claimed he just didn't have enough evidence to convene a grand jury. The young politician already taught me I couldn't believe everything he said, so I rolled up my sleeves to learn about a grand jury in the Commonwealth of Pennsylvania.

I learned once a Pennsylvania district attorney impanels a grand jury it is good for well over a year and can be used for multiple cases in that time frame. Just a few months earlier the district attorney utilized a grand jury in another homicide case, so he had a grand jury impaneled. Why wouldn't he take Peggy's case before that grand jury also? I recalled how he admitted to seeing a suspect when he looked at Peggy's file, and if the grand jury saw that suspect they could render an indictment.

There were whispers that the local government didn't want the huge expense the aged homicide would tote, and that enraged many taxpayers. Naturally, no sane politician was going to admit to that publicly. The public wanted Peggy's killer indicted, cuffed and put on trial. The DA's resistance raised more than a few brows and many wondered why he refused to walk into a courtroom with Peggy's unsolved murder. If the district attorney had a personal, or professional, conflict with the Reber case he always had the option to request the assistance of the State Attorney General's office, and that would relieve Lebanon County of the expense of the trial, so he had options.

Local officials were dragging their feet and it was queer to say the least. Unlike 1968, today's community was not going to sit by silently while a child's murder went unsolved. The toll-free tip line in my home office continued to ring:

Caller #1: "Lady, let it rest. Everybody knows Art Root Jr. got away with murder."

Caller #2: "Hey, if you really want to understand Lebanon back then, just find out about the baby they rescued at the dump. Yeah, that will show you exactly what was going on back then. Let's call it 'fishy'."

Caller #3: "Mary Reber SOLD those girls, and this is what happens when you don't take care of your children!!!"

Caller #4: "Scaramuzzino did it."

Caller #5: "Did Judge Gates ever take a polygraph?"

Caller #6: "Just look at the facts: two men committed suicide right after the crime and the truth died with them. Why else would they kill themselves?"

Caller #7: "Somebody told me the guy that strangled all those women in Boston did this, and I was wondering if you looked at him? Boston isn't really that far from Pennsylvania."

Caller #8: "I'll bet Ray Boyer's wife was pretty pissed when he left her for Peggy. Are you sure a man did this to Peggy?"

Caller #9: "Check out the gay guy in an apartment on the second floor. He was jealous of Peggy getting all the men's attention. His boyfriends were liking Peggy better."

Caller #10: "The killer didn't want to kill Peggy. He confused her with her mother. It was mistaken identity."

Caller #11: "What cops were on duty that night? She opened the door for somebody she trusted. I'll bet they didn't even look at the cops, did they?"

Caller #12: "That girl was killed by a guy from the Gap, and he is long gone."

Caller #13: "Are you sure Ray Boyer was in jail that night? Maybe he got out and caught her cheating on him?"

Caller #14: "Talk to the forest because if rumor has it right, her Mom was entertaining the trees."

Caller #15: "The constable that picked her boyfriend up that day knew she was alone and he liked young girls, too. Everybody knows he married a girl young enough to be his granddaughter."

Caller #16: "Could someone have followed her from the comfort station and saw she was by herself?"

Caller #17: "If I tell you my ex-husband did this will you put him in jail? He really deserves to be in jail."

Caller #18: "I didn't say anything back then because my mother told me to mind my own business, but I saw Peggy open the door that night….the next thing I knew Peggy was dead. My mom didn't want us to get involved, and I was just a kid, so I listened to my mom."

Caller #19: "Peggy had a boyfriend in the army and everybody knew it except Ray. I'll bet that army guy did it."

Caller #20: "I don't know if it's worth anything, but I went to a picnic awhile back and a cop and Dick Boyer were both there. The cop kept saying to Dick, 'Come on Bowflex you know you want to confess to me!' And we all knew they were talking about the murder of Peggy Reber. It was like a big joke to them."

Caller #21: "What about that Puerto Rican that lady saw running out of the apartment building that night? Did anybody every check him out?"

Caller #22: "My old man is a mechanic, and if I can help you get DNA from anybody I will. I am a nurse, so I know how to handle such sensitive specimens." (This particular caller followed up with an email and an almost unhealthy zest to bag cigarette butts from unsuspecting individuals attached to the case)

Caller #23: "I got a new roof a few years ago and one of the guys told me I should just stay in the house because one of the crew is the guy that killed Peggy Reber."

Caller #24: "You need to leave this alone. You need to let police solve this case."

Caller #25: "I went to school with those girls, and I lived across the street from Monument Park back then. I remember looking out my window late at night and seeing them slide down the rain spout and run to the park like they were hiding from something, or someone."

Caller #26: "I can't believe I am making this call, and I know he didn't do it, but my brother…My brother was not a good person back then. Anyhow, I was just a kid myself and I heard my brother bragging about busting into Mary Reber's house and sticking it to her, her boyfriend and her kid, and then taking her stuff. I don't really remember how old I was, but I remember the night I heard him talking about it because it was the night MLK was on the news. MLK got shot that night. Anyhow…I just wanted you to know that."

Caller #27: "I really hope you get to the bottom of this because I am tired of people always blaming Peggy's mother. I lived near them when I was a kid and she was a wonderful mother. I remember wanting the twins to spend the night at my house and Mrs. Reber wouldn't allow it until she met my parents. I went swimming with them one time and the woman made me eat peanut butter crackers to keep me from having stomach cramps. She was a good mother and she didn't have anything to do with this nightmare. She adored her kids."

Caller #28: "I don't know anything, but I have a question. We know two guys killed themselves after Peggy was killed, but I think I remember reading Peggy's twin tried to kill herself, too? What's up with that?"

The phone continued to ring at all hours. Oh, the callers offered extreme insight, and it was more attention than Peggy's unsolved murder received in decades.
I passed each message on to Lebanon law enforcement at rapid speed.
I listened to each tip, suggestion and question and almost studied them for a new perspective on the complexion of Peggy's life and death.

Caller #1: DID Art Root Jr. get away with murder? Arthur Root Jr. was put on trial for murdering Peggy Reber in February 1970, the jury did not find him guilty of the crime, and in fact, delivered a verdict at rapid speed. Prosecutors argued at his trial that he killed Peggy during his 6 p.m. visit to the Reber apartment, yet witnesses testified at his trial to seeing Peggy alive well after 8 p.m. that night. His dental impressions did not match a severe bite mark on Peggy's body.

Root was jailed on an outstanding warrant for other charges when he was questioned about Peggy's crime in May of 1968, but he was not actually charged with Peggy's murder until November 1968, almost six months later. Root was also in violation in neighboring Lancaster County because he walked away from a work release program while serving time there in 1965.

Caller #2: Oh, the talk about a live baby rescued at a county dump was nothing new. Folks still ramble about a married judge and his pregnant teenage secretary. Supposedly, the popular unwed teen gave birth to the married judge's child. Afterward, panic set in, and she placed the live baby at a local dump. The child was almost immediately discovered. The story goes on to tell how upon discovery of the baby, the same teen left town to marry a young Lebanon lawyer to put the issue of the married judge and the illegitimate baby "at rest".

Caller #3: Obviously, Mary Reber was not providing her children a safe, healthy or stable environment, but Mary Reber did not sell her child's life to anyone.

Caller #4: Lebanon likes to blame a notorious convict in Lebanon for everything short of the crack in the Liberty Bell.

Caller #5: No, I don't think the judge took a polygraph.

Caller #6: Two men did take their lives during the course of this investigation and both were subjected to forensic testing. The F.B.I. investigation cleared both from the list of possible killers.

Caller #7: It is a safe bet The Boston Strangler did not kill Peggy Reber.

Caller #8: There is no indication by the facts of the crime that a man killed Peggy Reber beyond the brute force of the sadistic attack. The killer remains unidentified. The attack against Peggy was brutal, but did not host signs of a sexual assault, or semen. Headlines at the time demanded the apprehension of the sex maniac that killed Peggy, but time has taught us the nature of the attack epitomizes raw rage, and rage is not gender exclusive.

Caller #9: Mary Reber was always faulted for her scandalous behavior, yet was it possible the activities of a gay man on the second floor of The Maple Leaf Apartment Building might truly hold the secrets to this crime? The gay man on the second floor entertained a large volume of men just like Mary Reber did, and while all the men frequenting these apartments wanted to remain anonymous, his male visitors *needed* discretion. In 1968, the slightest hint of homosexual indiscretions could destroy families, careers and social acceptance. Oh, the gay man wasn't killing anybody, and of course he wasn't subjected to forensics by detectives, but his list of visitors might solve this murder more than Mary Reber's visitors. Perhaps the bigger question is the identity of the men that frequented both apartments. Did Peggy see a man enter his apartment that she wasn't supposed to see?

Caller #10: It is a reasonable thought to think Peggy's murder was a case of mistaken identity, yet keep in mind her mother was a generation older than Peggy and Peggy's identical twin had just given birth to a child three weeks prior to the crime. These three females hosted very obvious differences in their body types.

Caller #11: How many LPD officers were included on the list of suspects during the investigation? The constable definitely deserved consideration because by apprehending Ray Boyer that afternoon he knew Peggy was alone and vulnerable. He was not included in forensic testing.

Caller #12: Perhaps a guy from the Gap did kill Peggy and then disappeared. The fact this crime is classified as unsolved makes it impossible to rule out such a possibility.

Caller #13: All indicators suggest Ray Boyer was in jail that night and did not escape at any point in time. He remained in jail throughout the weekend.

Caller #14: Some suggested Peggy's mother entertained a well-respected fraternity.

Caller # 15: The constable will always inspire a multitude of questions.

Caller #16: Of course Peggy was vulnerable to any freak on the street, yet it is hard to imagine her opening the door for a stranger when she was so fearful of being alone that night, and it's extreme to think a stranger could enter the apartment without any detection.

Caller #17: More than one disgruntled wife made claims that it had to be her evil ex-husband, yet the claims lacked proof.

Caller #18: Bingo! A witness stepped forward after almost 40 years, and that made every bit of effort and expense all worthwhile.

Caller #19: There was indeed a young man in the army that told detectives he spent some time with Peggy during the same time Ray was seeing Peggy. Ray Boyer continues to claim he knew all the activities in the Reber apartment, yet it appears he missed things right in front of his nose. Ray was employed full-time at a local steel mill, so he was not present at the apartment around the clock.

Caller #20: The thought of any member of law enforcement making a joke about the brutal unsolved murder of a child is sickening. While it was confirmed the police officer named was definitely known to socialize in the social circle mentioned, I sat rather puzzled because early in my research efforts that same cop approached me by means of email. The law enforcement officer wrote to me about a police call he responded to in the late 1990s for a domestic disturbance, and in his email he told me how he had never encountered such a temper in over sixteen years of being a cop. He went back to the station and was telling his colleague about it when it was pointed out to him the individual he was referring to was Peggy Reber's brother-in-law, Dick Boyer. He was told I was researching the life and death of Peggy Reber, so he initiated contact with me to share his experience.

Caller #21: Arthur Root Jr.'s defense presented "The Pepe Theory" in part of their defense for their client. Strangely, right before the trial, a female tenant of the apartment building recalled a Puerto Rican male rushing past her as she returned from a date with her beau that fateful night. Considering investigators interviewed everyone in the apartment building and the district attorney sent letters to the tenants pleading for any information they had to offer about events that night it was a bit queer the young woman waited so long to come forward. However, the Puerto Rican male in question had been identified and he was cleared of suspicion due to forensic testing of his hair, clothing and dental impressions. He was also 30 miles away at the time of the crime. What took the female so long to speak up?

Caller #22: The caller approached the subject wanting to get involved and make a difference. Her medical knowledge was to be respected, and her understanding of DNA was not in question, but solving Peggy's murder was not that simple.

Caller #23: Clearly somebody killed Peggy, but limiting the identification of alleged suspects to "some guy" or "that guy" does not assist in cuffing THE GUY.

Caller #24: Peggy Reber's unsolved murder file sat ignored by officials and collecting dust for years upon years. The Lebanon Police Department failed to pursue or revisit this child's unsolved murder for almost 40 years. Public attention is not the obstacle to Peggy's justice, rather public attention is the true inspiration for any administrative action taken with this case the last few years.

Caller #25: Kathryn and Peggy lived within walking distance of one of Lebanon's public parks, Monument Park, for the last couple months of Peggy's life. The girls did not have a curfew and their home was not always a safe haven.

Caller #26: Martin Luther King Jr. was killed seven weeks before Peggy was murdered. There is no police report on record of a home invasion involving Mary Reber, her children, her guests or the theft of her belongings, so it is not fact or fiction.

Caller #27: There is no denying Mary Reber was a dedicated, doting and loving mother for years after the birth of her twin girls, and son. Mary Reber kept a nice home, tended to her children with a protective eye and put dinner on the table like clockwork. Mary Reber was the epitome of a nurturing mother striving for domestic bliss. However, her husband, Herman Reber divorced her and the divorce was final in April 1967. Herman Reber remarried eight months later in December of the same year. There is an old saying that there are three sides to a divorce: his side, her side, and the truth. I had the benefit of discussing the topic with both Mary Reber and Herman Reber before their deaths and both accused the other of cheating. Meanwhile, Lester White was charged with violating Peggy in April 1967. There is no disputing Mary Reber's life, and the lives of her children, were drastically changed by divorce.

Caller #28: Peggy Reber's identical twin attempted suicide within hours of learning of Peggy's death. She had a three-week old daughter. Kathryn Reber-Boyer was taken to the local hospital, had her stomach pumped and instead of being sent to a nearby mental health facility (the standard procedure) for further treatment she was released to the custody of her husband within hours of treatment.

■■■

The calls and letters continued to dominate my home office. I wasn't sure if a floodgate just opened or if people had been trying to talk to officials for years, but there certainly wasn't any hesitation in discussing Peggy Reber now. Oh, some of the questions and tips were bizarre, yet the murder of Peggy Reber was far from normal, so every bit of effort mattered. It was equally amazing the amount of people born after Peggy died and it was obvious they were disgusted by the status quo of an unsolved murder of a child. Granted, Peggy was living in a scandalous environment and undeniably involved with a married man, yet the fact remained she was only 14-years-old. It was refreshing to see time exposed her youthful vulnerability to a community that was once so focused on her mother alone.

The public outcry for justice reached beyond me. People from around the country were aware of the resurrection of Peggy's case and they wanted answers. Suddenly, folks were turning toward the Lebanon City Police Department and they wanted answers. I definitely stood among their ranks. I respected Officer Snavely and his dedication toward Peggy's case, yet I never lost sight of the fact he wasn't even born when she died. I guess I also realized Officer Snavely could throw himself into the fire in a pursuit of delivering Peggy's justice, yet without the support of his superiors it was never going to happen. My concerns were confirmed during a phone call with Snavely:

"Michelle, I don't know about all of this anymore. I believe in my heart Peggy deserves justice and I worked damn hard for it, but sometimes it is just too much. Last year I guess I didn't think too much of it when the Chief told me I could interview suspects, but I couldn't video tape the interviews. It's standard procedure almost anywhere in the country to video tape interviews with suspects, and it just made sense to do it with such an aged case. It's not always admissible in court, but when you are talking to some guy for the first time in thirty years about a kid's unsolved murder it is worth capturing on tape. My chief didn't allow it, so I did the interviews anyhow, but I didn't use video recordings. He never supported my efforts with Peggy's case, he never assisted with Peggy's case and sometimes he was a brick wall with my investigation, but I kept trying. Now that you have gone public he is a bastard. I can't leave a shift meeting without him making a remark about my 'girlfriend in North Carolina' and it's a big joke. I don't know what his problem is, but you would think a chief of police would help me in solving a kid's murder, yet that's not the case. All I do know is this is making my life and my career miserable. Suddenly, it's like I am the cancer of the force and you are my partner. It's not about Peggy or identifying a killer. I really want to give Peggy the justice she deserves, but I wish you could see the way I am being treated. I am not going to walk away from the case because of this bullshit, but I just don't understand why the chief and the department aren't supporting this cause. Damn, all I am trying to do is identify a child killer and put him behind bars" I felt my stomach turn as Kevin talked to me. I knew then Peggy still, after 40 years, was not embraced by the administration. Why? "Michelle I interviewed a suspect and he lost his cookies. I watched him melt right before my eyes. He was floored by the fact anyone was even talking to him after all these years. He said things that would just blow your mind. Damn, the following day his wife was losing her cookies, too. The chief doesn't even want to hear anything

165

about the case. Doubt me? How much help have I been given? When I picked up the file it was pretty much me, when you contacted me, it was pretty much me and now all these leads come in and it is still me. There is no extra effort, no support, no task force, but a lot of insults and snide remarks by my boss"

Dear God in heaven what was Lebanon doing AGAIN?

Herman Reber called me in the midst of Peggy's injustice generating public attention. "Michelle, this is such a wonderful thing you're doing. They are finally going to get that guy that killed my daughter. She deserved better than this and if it wasn't for you and Officer Snavely it wouldn't happen." My heart broke for the father of a murdered child. He clearly had the utmost respect for the law enforcement officer that dusted off his daughter's unsolved murder file. "I just know this is going to do it. I can tell we are going to be able to give Peggy peace" I made small talk with Peggy's daddy before I asked how the rest of the family was handling all the attention to the case.

"Michelle, they got what they wanted. Kathryn finally got her daughter back and I guess that's all my kids wanted. It kind of pissed me off when one of them said it was okay to stop now. They just think since they made contact with Kathryn's daughter and her kids that Peggy doesn't matter. I got news for them. It's a damn shame Kathryn didn't know her daughter; it's a damn shame Dick's parents took her away all those years and raised her as their own, but it's even worse what was done to my daughter. I know they ain't seen each other in over 35 years, and I am happy for Kathryn, but I sure as hell ain't forgetting about Peggy. I know she doesn't want to get into all that nonsense about her mother anymore, but it still ain't right what was done to Peggy, and I ain't just gonna shut up about it because Kathryn has her daughter back. I've been marching into that police station a lot of years trying to get answers about my daughter's death and I ain't about to stop now. I would do the same thing for any one of my kids. I love each one of them and I know they'd do it for their kids, too. I ain't a rich man, Michelle and I always knew if I had more money this would have never happened. I still went in there every week and asked them what they were doing with my daughter's case. Finally, it's like you and Officer Snavely are an answer to this old man's prayers. People are listening to the two of you and maybe now we will get some answers"

"Well, I think it is wonderful if Kathryn and her baby were reunited"

"Damn right it is wonderful. It took a lot of years and you being in the newspaper for that to happen. This family was ripped apart so much you just don't know. I know all the stuff that happened, but to take that girl's baby from her was just wrong. Kathryn was young, but that was still her baby, and she never got to know her. I am grateful to Ray Boyer for finally telling the truth, but it still doesn't help Peggy"

Kathryn was a very new mother when Peggy died. She was also fourteen-years-old, too. She had the same scandalous mother. Kathryn's life was not easy. After Peggy's death and Kathryn and her husband divorced. Her husband's parents took custody of her baby. Kathryn did not have contact with her child for decades. Suddenly, almost magically, Ray Boyer decided to approach his niece and tell her the truth surrounding her roots after the public interest attached to Peggy's murder. It was queer, it was twisted, yet it was the truth. He revealed to her that while his parents raised her as their child, as his sister…that was not the truth. She was in fact his brother's child.

I will never detail anything relating to Peggy's niece because she was a mere three weeks old when Peggy was tragically assaulted. I will confirm she was raised by the parents of Peggy's brother-in-law and she did not have contact with her biological mother for decades. I will always celebrate the fact there was a mother and child reunion. One can only imagine the heart break of a young teen that buried her murdered sister and did not have contact with her baby throughout the years. Herman echoed the celebration of their union, yet he was deeply concerned about indifference toward Peggy's justice. Surely, Peggy's twin was not content to settle with her sister's lost justice in exchange of the reunion with her child. Yes, many years passed and it was a new relationship for both of them.

I did not stop delivering tips and leads to Officer Snavely. Equally, he did not stop pursuing justice for Peggy Reber. We both knew we were swimming upstream, yet much like a true salmon we kept swimming. We also stood baffled as to why the administration was not jumping on board with identifying a child's killer. We simply had to trust the public would demand some answers and Peggy's justice was still within reach.

"Oh Susan, look at that!"

I fought the urge to cry as I looked at the big beautiful neon sign displaying Peggy's name in bold letters. "Isn't that beautiful?"

I was overcome with emotion by the display of support the sign represented.

"Well, my friend, it's a far cry from the first time we came to this town in search of answers about Peggy Reber."

I nodded my head in agreement and fought the lump in my throat. "I want to stop and thank that area business and shake hands with everyone that works there, but right now we have a few other matters to tend to."

Thoughts of the illuminated sign danced in the back of my mind as I drove down the road to a popular Lebanon eatery. I pulled into the restaurant parking lot and we were both grateful for the opportunity to stretch our legs. In a matter of a few hours we traveled over 500 miles by car and plane to pay our respects to a murdered child that neither of us ever knew.

We exited the rental car and marveled at the mild January weather Pennsylvania was providing us.

"Father Winter must be in support of this memorial service," Susan said happily.

I grabbed my purse and purchased a local paper before entering the country diner. We took our seats at a booth by the window shortly before a waitress greeted us at our table. I looked down at the front page of the newspaper.

"*A memorial service is scheduled tomorrow for a 14-year-old Peggy Reber,*" I read the headline aloud.

The waitress patiently waited for our beverage order as I glanced at the paper in front of me. The waitress appeared to be a bit nervous when she quietly asked, "Are you here for the memorial service?"

I looked into the woman's eyes and I could see signs of several decades of waiting tables. I extended my hand to shake hers.

"Allow me to introduce myself. I am Michelle Gooden, and yes I am here to attend Peggy's memorial service." I studied the woman's face for a reaction, but she merely excused herself to prepare our order. I didn't pay it too much mind as I excitedly looked over the menu hosting the many Pennsylvania Dutch entrées I missed so very much.

The woman returned to the table to take our order and almost whispered, "That was such a shame."

Susan and I just looked at each other because we knew only too well local residents were never comfortable discussing the fate of Peggy Reber. We enjoyed our early dinner and couldn't help but notice our presence in the restaurant was generating attention.

"That must be her."

I fixed my gaze on the parking lot outside the window. My friend and I were scheduled to meet a complete stranger. The very attractive thirty-year-old redhead entered the dining room, and I stood up to let my presence be known. She approached the table with a jubilant smile.

"Michelle, it is so nice to finally meet you in person!"

I shared her sentiments.

"Susan, allow me to introduce you to Jennifer*."

The women shared in a handshake.

"Jennifer called me several weeks ago with some interesting information, and while she was initially nervous about placing that call, we quickly became comfortable talking to each other. Jennifer was kind enough to agree to meet us today to share with me some documentation that could prove useful in the future."

Susan smirked and said, "Well, we can never have too many friends around here."

The three of us engaged in some light social banter, oblivious to the other patrons whispering and pointing at us. Daylight was escaping us so I knew it was a time to embark on the next step out of our journey. I excused myself to visit the restroom before paying the check and getting back on the road. Upon exiting the restroom the waitress went out of her way to privately approach me.

"Are you on the computer?" She expressed an obvious interest in Peggy and my efforts in regards to Peggy.

"Yes ma'am, I am." I was a little surprised by her question because so much of my efforts were focused on a MySpace page I set up on the internet.

"Would you mind writing that down for me? My daughter has a computer and I am sure she would look this up for me."

I took the pen and paper the waitress offered me, and I wrote down the website address, so she could better learn about the injustice surrounding Peggy.

"Will you be attending the memorial service tomorrow?" I asked.

She lowered her eyes and said, "I wish I could, but I will be working a twelve-hour shift tomorrow. I will keep you in my thoughts though."

I smiled at the small- framed woman with just a hint of gray in her hair, and I returned to the table to pick up my purse. We made our way to the foyer of the restaurant and the waitress approached me once again with tear filled eyes, and I could see her hesitation, but it was obvious she wanted to embrace me. I eased her discomfort and opened my arms and she immediately responded, "Thank you so very much."

I continued to hug the frail woman, and asked "Did you know Peggy?"

She stepped back, "Oh goodness no, but thank you for standing up for her and thank you for standing up to them."

I wiped a tear from my own eye because I knew how hard it was for her to reach out to a complete stranger, and I truly understood her words.

"I just have to do this." I didn't even turn the car off.

I entered the local business that hosted the purple neon sign sporting Peggy's name to extend my heartfelt appreciation for supporting the memory of a murdered child. I barely made it inside the door before I was overcome with emotion. I looked around the storefront and knew I was looking odd, and I struggled to regain my composure. I stepped up to the counter and asked to see the store manager, and my tears were flowing quite freely. A bespectacled man in his early 40s walked out to greet me and I struggled to speak clearly

"My name is Michelle Gooden, and. . ." My voice trailed off and my tears began to flow.

"Michelle! What a pleasure to meet you!" The kindness in his voice and sparkle in his eyes made it apparent I was on friendly ground. John Gingrich Jr walked around the counter and took my hands in his because he knew I was overcome with emotion and I could tell he understood why.

"I can't begin to thank you enough." I found a few words after all. "I am so deeply touched by your support and the fact that Peggy's name has such visibility. There aren't words for everything that I am feeling at this moment, and a mere thank you is nowhere near enough."

"Oh Michelle, there is no need to thank me because it was the right thing to do. I am somewhat embarrassed because I lived here all these years and it is only because of you and your voice that I even know about this tragedy. Michelle, I ran for mayor, and I didn't know this dirty secret was in the closet all these years."

I accepted a tissue from a woman standing nearby. "It's just amazing, isn't it? A child suffered one of the most brutal attacks in the history of the state of Pennsylvania right here in Lebanon, and for over three decades she was always a forbidden topic."

I shook my head in disbelief. "Sir, I want to thank you because with your support and things such as that beautiful sign we are about to change all of that."

I could feel myself stand a little taller and believe in the strength of my own words. "As average citizens none of us can guarantee Peggy Reber will receive justice in a courtroom, but individually, and as a community we can guarantee that the injustice against her is never forgotten."

I extended my hand one last time and we shared a firm handshake, "Please forgive me, but I have several stops to make before meeting with the organizers of the memorial service later this evening. I simply had to take the time to meet with you face-to-face and personally thank you."

I headed toward the door. "May I ask you a personal question before I leave?"

The gentleman was willing to grant my request.

"Do you believe in angels?"

He didn't even blink an eye with his response, "Why yes, Michelle, as a matter of fact I do. Why do you ask?"

I made a gesture toward the large neon sign outside the establishment, and sm iled "I know it's going to sound crazy, but I always wanted a billboard in the middle of this city for Peggy. Isn't it kind of funny how with your help my wish came true? I look forward to seeing you tomorrow and thank you again."

The manager frowned. "Michelle, I am unable to attend tomorrow's services. I have to work. But my wife, my sister and my mother will be there, and I will say a prayer."

I turned my back and walked away with a restored faith in mankind.

"How did that go?" Susan was still waiting in the car.

169

"If it is any indication of the next twenty-four hours, I think we should invest in a tissue company," I said, sniffing my reddened nose.

I fastened my seatbelt and started to merge onto the highway looking up at the sign one last time. I looked up to the heavens and thought, *It's all about you Peggy, and it is long overdue.*

Darkness was rapidly approaching, and I wanted to visit the cemetery privately before the memorial service scheduled for the following day. We didn't waste time sightseeing as we drove through the quiet little town, yet it was hard to resist sharing memories from a different time. My friend and I pulled into the cemetery shortly before sunset and we crept along the winding road just like we did several years before.

"Susan I almost feel guilty because we made a vow the next time we would come back here it would be with the truth. I really wanted to wait until tomorrow, but I'm just not sure how well I will hold up emotionally."

We both got out of the car and started to walk up the hill toward Peggy Reber's final resting place.

"Michelle, I don't think Peggy, or anyone else, will mind that we took this little bit of time to finish this exactly the way we started. After all, all those years ago when we stood here just the two of us, we never imagined a memorial service was ever a possibility, and we really don't know what to expect tomorrow." We offered a moment of silent respect as we stood at the head of Peggy's grave and I reached out and hugged my good friend.

"Thank you for everything that you have done to help me answer my questions and show my respect to this child I never knew."

I looked over my friends shoulder and said, "Christ is looking over her."

She turned to join me in looking at the statue. "How very appropriate! Is it me or does it appear that statue is glowing?"

The faint light that remained from the sunset gave the stone statue of Christ an illuminated effect. I said a brief prayer and got down on my knees and ran my fingers across the letters of Peggy's name.

"I promised you I would be back one day, and tomorrow I will bring others with me."

I rose to my feet, returned to the car and the radio was playing an old song, "Knocking on Heaven's Door".

I turned and looked at my friend. "Of all the songs in the world that could be playing on the radio right now. . ."

I started to cry.

■ ■

I set out to meet the human angels that assisted in planning a memorial service for a child that died 39 years prior. It was going to be our first face-to-face meeting, yet I knew I was about to join ranks with some of the most loving individuals I would ever know in my lifetime. I was nervous at the prospect of walking into a room where I didn't know anyone, but oddly enough, I knew I would be with friends.

"What time is Max* going to arrive?"

I had to laugh at my friend's question. "Oh you know Max, he'll get here when he gets here."

I pulled into the parking lot of a social organization of which my Daddy had proudly been a life member. I noticed an expensive SUV entered the parking lot at the same time.

"Don't tell me that's Max, right on time!" Susan said, teasing me.

"Your guess is as good as mine," I replied.

Sure enough my friend Max emerged from the vehicle.

"Hey cutie! It's the first time in over twenty years we got our timing right."

He was always quick with a joke and never allowed me to forget the fact I was usually tardy. "What's the plan? This is one time in our life that you will call all the shots." He winked at me and said, "Within reason of course."

I hugged the large man that towered over me, and he smiled as his eyes sparkled.

"Well sir, we have a meeting scheduled in this restaurant and you are more than welcome to join us, but if I know you as well as I think I do you will probably want to wait for us in that private club."

No one needed to convince him that he had little desire to meet with a dozen or so women in a small restaurant, so we agreed to reconnect after the meeting.

Susan and I walked up a small ramp and entered the lobby of a small well-lit restaurant, and we could hear the voices of several women engaging in conversation and laughter. I slowly entered the room and saw several tables pushed together to accommodate over a dozen people in attendance.

Nervously, I said, "I guess this is where I belong. My name is Michelle Gooden." The conversation and laughter came to a halt, and in a matter of seconds the smiles returned. Everyone started to talk and we began to exchange names. One by one I shook hands, and embraced, the loving hearts joined together by a true respect of the life and death of fourteen-year-old Margaret Reber. We enjoyed some light-hearted socializing before sitting down and coordinating the details of the memorial service for the following day.

"Shelly Belly!" I heard a squeal from across the room. My heart started to melt as I saw the first familiar face from my childhood. I fought back tears as I greeted a woman that loved me my entire life.

"Oh Shelly it is so good to see you!"

I wrapped my arms around the woman that was easily a foot shorter than myself.

"You know, when I was a kid you were a whole lot taller." I teased the woman that was once my babysitter, yet so much more than that in reality.

"Very funny young lady," she said in mock sternness.

I had to giggle because at my ripe old age of forty-four years, I didn't get called young lady too often anymore.

"Shelly, this is just an amazing thing that you're doing. I can't begin to tell you how proud I am of you."

I stepped back from the short dark-haired woman that had her arm around me and I signaled for the attention of everyone present.

"Ladies allow me to introduce you to my loved one, Allecia. We go back more years then some could even imagine, and I count that among my life blessings. Allecia just said something to me, and I would like to clarify it. Allecia said what I am doing is amazing, and that is not completely correct because it is what we, together, are doing that is absolutely amazing. No one person is to credit for bringing attention to the horrible injustice given the crime against

Peggy. It might be my big mouth that was the first to speak out and sometimes the loudest, but I don't speak out alone anymore. The strength and the beauty in all of this is the fact that we have joined together to show respect to a young life lost and her grieving family. I appreciate the fact that anyone would think I did anything amazing, but the truly amazing thing taking place is a community standing united, and the beautiful people in this room that assisted in making tomorrow a reality."

We all smiled and nodded in agreement because we were bound by respect for a young girl few present ever knew.

"Mr. Mike," I said, extending my hand. "Allow me to say thank you. I sincerely appreciate everything you have done."

I introduced myself to the owner of the restaurant that allowed us to meet in his dining room. He was also a very vocal supporter on the local a.m. radio talk show that assisted greatly with promoting Peggy's memorial service. He was one of the first local business owners to welcome a petition in his establishment requesting the County district Attorney to take Peggy's case before a grand jury.

"If you don't mind, I am a weary traveler and I would enjoy indulging in one of the fine delicacies on your menu." Granted, Susan and I weren't exactly starving, but good manners dictated sampling one of the homemade dishes available. Mr. Mike was a man in his early thirties with an athletic build, closely cropped dark hair and a radiant smile. He would proudly tell anyone willing to listen that his faith in God was his number one priority in this life and beyond.

While standing at the counter making my selection, a stack of papers next to the cash register caught my eye. A picture of Peggy's smiling face with the flowers in front of her seemed to look back at me and it was on a flyer promoting free self-defense classes. Once again, I was fighting the urge to cry as I read the small paragraph underneath her picture.

I would like to offer free self-defense classes next month in remembrance of Peggy Reber. Maybe if she would have known a few things to do to protect herself, she might have lived. Take a stand now and find out what you can do to protect yourself in dangerous situations. There are different things to do according to your age and size but there is something to do for everyone. Don't be bullied.

I picked a copy of the flyer up, folded it and placed it in my pocket. Vicki Spike made such a huge gesture of kindness not only in honor of Peggy, but in the interest of educating and protecting people today. Peggy made a friend thirty eight years after her passing. Vicki's kind heart confirmed for me people understood Peggy died unnecessarily, and it still mattered thirty-eight years later.

Black and white bumper stickers with Peggy's picture were scattered across the tables "Justice for Peggy – Peggy Sent Us".

I picked one up and said, "Ladies, I want all of you to know the story behind these stickers." I waited until I knew I had the group's attention. "The man that designed these stickers and paid for their printing is merely a kind heart in a crowd, but he has my undying gratitude and respect. He didn't know Peggy and he doesn't know me, yet when he learned about this tragedy he was moved to action, and this is the fruit of his efforts. I can't wait to meet this man, shake his hand and thank him for caring about justice for a murdered child because it is with the support of people like him we might be able to make a difference with this case. It is a wonderful thing when a total stranger reaches out with such a loving act. I don't mind telling you I was moved to tears because he had one unique sticker made for me. Throughout the years of my effort when folks would ask me why I was so determined I would simply smile and say 'Peggy sent me' so my bumper sticker reads just that"

We were an eclectic group, yet we stood in agreement that the bumper stickers and their creator were blessings from above.

We took our seats at a long table and got to the business at hand when a young woman entered the room carrying a bundle of pink in a baby carrier. Naturally, I had no idea the identity of this new addition to our group, and I seemed to be in the minority with my ignorance. It didn't take long to realize I was in the presence of a local radio personality, Laura LeBeau.

Laura was one of our biggest supporters in not only making the memorial service a reality, but petitioning for the attention of the district attorney to put this case before a grand jury.

I stood up to introduce myself. "I am so honored to make your acquaintance." Radio Laura earned my undying respect.

"I am so sorry I am late!" she started to gush. "I had a production dead line, and I had to pick the baby up at the babysitter."

Collectively we made an effort to put her at ease and almost instantly all eyes were on her beautiful baby. Laura was very new to the world of motherhood and she was juggling the challenges of career, romance and successful parenting of an infant. One could see she was still growing accustomed to all the necessary accessories that accompany transporting an infant, and equally, we knew she was handling it all with great finesse.

Laura joined us at the table with a baby on her knee and her auburn hair framing her smiling face. I thought of the first time I heard her name. Days following a local newspaper article that featured the injustice of a murdered child and my efforts to research the crime, I received several calls from strangers as well as friends in Lebanon telling me how I was the subject of criticism on a local radio talk show. I didn't know the talk show host and I wasn't sure what her beef was with me, but surely she didn't support lost justice for a murdered child. I believed in my heart if folks were aware of the tragic events surrounding Peggy's death, and the lost justice, they would stand up on Peggy's behalf.

"Michelle, you need to call her and explain it to her." The advice was the same from everyone calling me.

I had no desire to call into a radio talk show, yet if Peggy was going to be a topic of discussion, I wanted the truth to be the focus rather than rumor and folklore. I asked only one question: "Is Laura from Lebanon?" The answer was negative. I trusted Laura's only knowledge about Peggy rested with the recent news article, and that was a broad-brush account of a huge blemish on Lebanon's history.

Convinced Laura simply didn't understand the true tragedy surrounding Peggy, I sat down and wrote her a letter. Oh, I couldn't detail everything in one letter, but there was so much more to the story than any newspaper article could ever report in one edition of any paper. I probably started the letter a half dozen times before I was satisfied with my own words. I addressed the envelope to her in care of the radio station where she worked, and placed it on my desk in the pile of outgoing mail. I busied myself throughout the weekend, but I kept thinking of

Peggy being discussed on the radio show. If the years of research taught me anything at all, the one thing I learned was that Peggy Reber was almost a forbidden topic in Lebanon. I looked at the pile of outgoing mail on my desk and I removed the letter to Radio Laura. If the people of Lebanon were starting to open up about Peggy, and they were doing it on the Laura LeBeau Show, I didn't want my letter to get lost in a pile of junk mail delivered to the radio station.

A couple of angels in the wings assisted me with having the letter delivered to the radio station attached to a bouquet of flowers. I wanted to make sure Laura received the letter detailing information about the young life lost before Peggy lost the attention of Laura's listening audience.

Laura was surprised by the floral delivery, and after reading the letter attached to the flowers, realized the subject of Peggy Reber ran much deeper than recent news reports. Shortly after the floral delivery, I unexpectedly called into her show.

"Hello caller!" she answered in a perky voice.

"Hello, how are you?" I was beyond uncomfortable.

"I'm fine, and your reason for calling?" She was the typical radio talk show host in that every minute mattered.

"Well," I stammered. "I am Michelle Gooden and I understand my name hit your airwaves recently." I stopped at that point.

"Michelle Gooden?" for a moment she sounded confused. "Oh yes, Michelle Gooden." Her voice picked up energy as she recognized the name. "Yes, Michelle I don't recall exactly what was said, but your name hit a nerve with some of my listeners."

I waited for her to finish her sentence. "It wasn't my name that struck a nerve with your audience. It was Peggy's name."

She didn't hesitate with a response. "Michelle, I think you're right. I read your letter, oh, and thank you for the flowers. Michelle, I would love to discuss this with you, and I know my listeners expressed a lot of interest on this subject, but I have to break now for the news. Could you possibly call back?"

Laura and I talked a bit off the air while the news broadcast, and I was pleasantly surprised by her kind nature off the air.

"Did we get all the petitions collected?" Laura had her business face on, and the volunteers responded to her affirmatively. Two of Peggy's former classmates counted the amount of signatures on the petition. Meanwhile, we finalized the details surrounding flowers, candles, the music scheduled for play at the memorial service, and the program format for the following day.

I excused myself from the table to step outside for a few minutes. I wasn't alone.

"It is nice to finally meet the person I talked to on the phone every day."

I fought a chill because it was a crisp January night in Pennsylvania. "Carol, my friend, you are worth your weight in gold to me. I remember the first time you called me like it was yesterday. You read the article about Peggy's murder, and my research, and it touched your heart. What you don't know is that I was so very impressed by the fact that you weren't even alive when Peggy lost her life. It is a powerful thing when one can be so moved so many years later. I know that part of your motivation is derived from the fact that you are the mother of two little girls, yet it is actually your own loving heart that embraces the memory of this child, and that says a lot about your character. You epitomize the reason I spoke out publicly. I believe in my heart that if people truly understood that evil that Peggy faced that fateful day, they would be enraged to the point they would demand justice for this murdered child."

Laura's show had such a wide range of listeners and it was a great format to teach people about the injustice surrounding Peggy. I remembered an unidentified caller during one show explaining that she just didn't understand how Peggy's challenges at home were even legal. She was almost hostile as she told how she was a retired school teacher with thirty years teaching experience and she was required by law to report suspicion of child abuse. Sadly, what the retired teacher did not realize is Peggy Reber was dead almost five years before that standard was put in place for educators in Pennsylvania. It was only a year before Peggy's death that doctors were required to report suspicion of sexual abuse of a child and according to public records Peggy was one of the first documented cases in the state. Legislation didn't move fast enough to save the child's life and Lady Justice didn't run fast enough to catch her killer, but Father Time was not going to allow her to be forgotten.

I returned to the restaurant, but not before I overheard a country-western song coming from a car radio on the parking lot. It was a song about a child losing her life in the middle of the night, neighbors looking the other way, and the concrete angel that marked her grave. It almost described Peggy perfectly.

"There you are!" My absence did not go unnoticed. "Tell us again what music you selected for tomorrow."

Laura immediately responded. "I thought we agreed to stick with music that was popular at the time of Peggy's death." Such decisions had already been made; rather it was a confirmation of our understanding. Peggy's close childhood friends continued to count the signatures on the bright pink paper, and the rest of us anxiously waited for the total number. The funeral home that handled Peggy's services in 1968 generously agreed to print pamphlets identical to those offered at her original service.

"Michelle, you're going to absolutely love this!"

I was handed two pictures of elementary school class pictures.

"The twins are on each side of the teachers, aren't they precious?"

I held the pictures in my hand and looked down at the beautiful little girls with beaming smiles on their faces. Never before had I seen a picture of Peggy's so young, and I started to dwell on all the potential life had to offer the small child in the photograph.

"Has anyone talked to Kathy?"

I wasn't certain who asked the question, but I arrested the conversation quickly. "Ray is in touch with Kathy, and he is encouraging her to attend tomorrow's service, but we must all respect the fact if she chooses not to do so. We must never forget Peggy was her identical twin and her loss is beyond anyone's comprehension. I cannot stress enough that it is a very important to me that we make every effort to show the utmost respect to the Reber family, especially Kathy. Of course we hope she would join us, but we must respect that she must do what is in her best interest".

We were all in agreement that we respected the loss and feelings of the surviving twin. I looked at my watch and signaled my traveling companion that it was time for us to take the next step on our journey.

We walked to the end of the parking lot in silence because the many miles covered in the course of the day were starting to take their toll on us. We joined the gentleman that patiently waited for us to attend the final meeting before the memorial service. I took a seat at the bar next to him and ordered a bottle of beer, while Susan went in search of the restroom.

"Well how did you make out, kiddo? Was it everything you had hoped it to be?"

"Ask me that same question tomorrow and I might have an answer for you." I honestly did not know what the following day had in store for me, or the supporters, or the Reber family, and I was scared. "Max, what have I done?"

He rubbed his hands across my shoulder blades and said, "You followed your heart. Michelle, how many years has it been since we met in the same town so you could research this crime? Don't tell me you forgot," he said, testing my memory. "It's been several years."

I knew exactly what he was referring to. "But I never expected any of this to happen".

He tossed his head back and laughed a little. "That's the beauty of this, Michelle. You didn't set out for this to happen, you never expected this to happen, but it's happening nonetheless. It's one of the beautiful things in life. Nothing is ever really predictable."

I sat silently digesting his words.

"Relax. I don't think any possible harm can come from people gathering to show their respects to a child. Sure, you got a little bit more than you bargained for, but the wheels are in motion, and you've come too far to turn back now."

I looked at the man sitting next to me and while he always warranted my respect I found myself questioning his insight. "Max, what if I made a terrible mistake? What if I do more harm than good? What if no one shows up tomorrow and I assisted in making a mockery of this tragedy once again? This town didn't get it right in 1968, and what if they don't get it right tomorrow?"

He winked at me and smiled. "We shall see."

His words weren't comforting, but they were truthful.

Susan took a seat next to me and ordered a beverage before asking, "So buddy, where are we going to sleep tonight?" Susan knew only too well I requested Max to accompany us in the best interest of our personal security. "Do we get a safe house, tree house, or tent in someone's backyard?" Oh, she definitely had her second wind.

"Actually, I made reservations at a rather nice hotel in Harrisburg," Max said. *Like we would expect any less from you*, I thought to myself.

Instead, I said, "Harrisburg? What happened to the nice hotel a mile from here?"

I was not looking forward to driving another twenty-five miles before I could kick my shoes off.

"My job is to keep you in one piece, and that is exactly what I intend to do. You're the one that got the brainstorm to allow yourself to be on the front page of the newspaper claiming a killer walks the streets of Lebanon, correct?"

I nodded my head.

"Do you really think it's wise for you to stay in the same town that you made such a declaration? Not to mention I made reservations in a hotel with an indoor pool and a Jacuzzi. Now it really doesn't matter to me if you use those facilities, but they are available to you, and you will be safe while you are there."

I wasn't excited about a drive to Pennsylvania's state capital, yet I knew he had my best interest at heart. One hour and thirty-five miles later Susan and I were celebrating the comfort of sweat pants and T-shirts.

I ventured to the lobby and took a seat at one of the computers available to those staying in the hotel. I nervously checked my e-mail looking for the slightest hint that something was going to go wrong. I no sooner pulled up the screen showing my new e-mails and the voice behind me said, "Boy, you're popular." Max was looking at the computer monitor that announced I received over three dozen e-mails that afternoon alone.

"Correction." I offered a volley. "Peggy is popular."

I put my feet up on the upholstered chair in front of me. "How did you know I would be here?" I instinctively knew he came looking for me.

"Don't flatter yourself. I needed some ice," he said innocently.

"Didn't you forget your ice bucket?"

He started to stretch, showing his own signs of fatigue. "Technicalities."

I always enjoyed his witty responses.

"Look you're a grown woman, and I'm not here to be your father, but if he was here he would tell you to forget those e-mails and get some rest because you have a busy day ahead of you tomorrow. I am not going to stand over your shoulder and tell you what to do because I trust the person that you are, and I think it's time you trust yourself. On that note, I will see you in the morning for coffee."

I dropped my feet to the floor and called after him, "Hey, I'm not old enough to drink coffee, remember?"

He walked away chuckling at my silliness.

I sat there for a while and tried to concentrate on the e-mails I received in the course of the day, but his words echoed in my mind. The wheels were in motion and there was little I could do to change or alter what was unfolding. I returned to my room and while Susan was sound asleep, I prayed.

■■

"Leave it to secret agent man to put us in a no-smoking room," Susan griped.

I opened my eyes and blinked at the bright morning sun beaming against the white walls and ceiling of the hotel room.

"No, let me correct myself." She threw both her hands up in the air in a display of defeat. "He put us in a no-smoking *hotel*. According to this little table tent there is a $300 fine for smoking in this room."

I had to laugh a little bit. She really wasn't upset about the no smoking policy and we both knew that wasn't an issue. It was her jovial way of greeting the day and addressing all the fears only my closest friends knew I sported.

I knew it was time to get up and greet the day. I sat up, yawned, and looked at the clock. I felt butterflies fill my stomach, as I knew it was a matter of hours until we would see exactly what all this effort and commotion birthed.

I wandered down to the lobby in search of a cup of hot tea and I went out to the rental car for a few minutes of solitude. A tap at the window interrupted my deepest thoughts.

"Good morning!" Max stood next to the car with a cup of coffee in one hand and his pipe in the other. "You're up bright and early. Open up." He motioned for me to unlock the passenger's door.

"This is beautiful weather for Pennsylvania in January," he remarked. As a native of the Pocono mountain region, he was very familiar with Pennsylvania winters. I also knew him well enough that he was trying to present a high point in the day before it even started.

My cell phone started to ring, and I just looked at the number on the display without answering the call.

"You know you can't hide." He put his cup of coffee to his lips. "I know you pretty well and I know you are scared, but I also know everything is going to be fine."

I took a sip from my own cup of tea and it was my turn to wink at my friend and smile. "Damn right everything is going to be fine because today is all about Peggy."

I ran my fingers through my hair and tossed my head back "I don't know a lot right now, but I do know I was compelled to remember this child from the evening news, I was compelled to educate myself on her life and her death, and that journey brought me to this point, so I am going to carry this torch."

Max raised his Styrofoam cup of coffee in a toast. "It's going to be a good day."

▪▪

"Are you sure this sweater looks good?" It was so unlike Susan to be so fashion conscious.

"You look great." My friend and I were sharing those silly compliments that schoolgirls share in a high school bathroom. "Look, I think the biggest thing that matters is that we both wear the colors black and red. Carol was nice enough to research the colors that represent a murdered child and she educated me on the fact those colors are black and red. I told everyone via e-mail I would be the woman in a red blazer, so these black pants and this black sweater along with the blazer will just have to do."

Time quickly determined we were ready whether we liked it or not. Our personal security guard didn't even allow time to debate driving arrangements.

"I will be doing all the driving today." His tone told me it was nonnegotiable. "I know I had to point it out to you that you declared a killer walks the streets of Lebanon, and I am guessing you probably missed that little part where you pissed off every law in enforcement officer along with the County DA." He made a good point. "I just don't think it is in your best interests to be operating a motor vehicle in the state of Pennsylvania right now. So ladies, enjoy the ride."

Our first stop was the Lebanon Municipal Building. Peggy Reber's boyfriend at the time of the crime agreed to meet me on the steps of the Municipal Building, so we could meet with a state senator. I spotted the large man with obvious dyed hair dropping down to the middle of his back looking a bit uncomfortable in his Sunday attire, but with a look of determination on his face, and I knew I was meeting Ray Boyer for the first time.

We had little time for small talk because we had a scheduled appointment with a state senator. I gave it little thought as I walked away from my friends to join Ray.

When we entered the senator's office, we were definitely out of our comfort zone, but we shared a common determination to make our point, and our point was it still possible a child killer walked the streets of Lebanon, Pennsylvania.

We were ushered into a meeting room and the female attendants were quite cordial, but the politician was running late. It was almost insulting that a public servant could be tardy for a meeting scheduled weeks in advance. It grew increasingly amusing as his female assistants gave us a motorcade update. One would have thought we were meeting the president of the United States.

Eventually, the politician entered the meeting room and he busied himself with offering beverages he obviously expected his female assistants to prepare. Ray and I were not impressed. It didn't take long for this public figure to start discussing the questionable reputation of Peggy's mother to which Ray and I both questioned the importance. A child died a brutal death thirty-nine years prior and politicians still wanted to discuss the questionable conduct of the victim's mother? It was hard to believe the year was 2008 and not 1968!

He reached in to the breast pocket of his sport coat waving the Pennsylvania state constitution in the air claiming he could be of no help whatsoever in regards to a murdered child according to the state's constitution. Ray excused himself from the situation because it was obviously pointless, and he was scheduled to pick up Mr. Reber for his daughter's memorial service.

A knock at the door alerted us to other activity. The media was looking to talk with me. I remained seated and respected the company present. Before long I gave in to the importance of scheduled events, and I excused myself with a few words.

"I trust I will see you at two o'clock this afternoon."

Of course one of the female assistants present said,"Oh, it's in his day planner!"

Well! That just made me feel so much better about our elected officials, or did it? Perhaps I walked away with a bad taste in my mouth. Personally, he could have the state constitution tattooed on his forehead and it mattered not to me. Having been a manager for many years I absolutely hated the phrase "It's not my job" and that is exactly what that senator was saying to us. When a child is a murdered it is the responsibility and duty of every one to stand up and make a difference, to include elected officials. It was very sad to watch a Pennsylvania state senator hide behind the state constitution in an effort to avoid addressing such an injustice. It did, however, explain a great deal about the political complexion of Lebanon, Pennsylvania. True to his word, and his day planner, the senator was present for the memorial service for a murdered child later that afternoon.

I returned to the lobby of Lebanon's municipal building, and I was uncomfortable by the amount of media present. I stood firm in my convictions as I addressed the issues and how I wanted to know how this crime could remain ignored for all most forty years.

Why did a community have to petition a DA to address the aged murder of a child? I chuckled a bit as several television reporters interviewed me and repeatedly referred to the district attorney on a first name basis. I was definitely the visiting team playing on the home field.

■■■

"Michelle" A mild-mannered gentleman with dark hair appearing to be close to my age approached me with his hand extended outwardly. I didn't recognize the face, but I immediately knew his voice.

"John! What a pleasure to meet you!" The man in front of me assisted in giving Peggy public attention that was long overdue, and I didn't hesitate to extend both my hands to meet his.

John Latimer was the local reporter for The Lebanon Daily News, and with the support of his editor, Paul Baker, they bravely gave the aged murder of a child the benefit of being featured in their publication. John and I spent many hours on the phone while I recounted my vague childhood memories about Peggy on the evening news, and the nagging questions that lead me to return to Lebanon as an adult to answer my own questions. It was sometimes difficult to articulate my ignorance and the necessary research that gave me a better understanding of a crime that took place when I was only five years old.

I knew the sharp reporter wasn't taking anything at face value when he asked me about Peggy's neighbors. He was gently probing to see how far my journey reached in educating myself about the young girl. Peggy was killed in a building that was leveled within two years of the crime making me all of seven years old by the time the tenants scattered. Naturally, the police had a list of the tenants at the time of the crime, but a five-year-old child almost forty years later?

Of course I composed a list of the tenants, and John knew only too well such information was on public record in Lebanon's public library, but the real question was if I knew where to access such information and if I'd taken the time to do so. Oh, our conversations weren't limited to one area, or means by which I studied the case, and after time he got the picture of the amount of effort I devoted to trying to learn facts from a different time.

■■■

I looked at my watch and knew it was time to depart for the church. Covenant United Methodist Church was truly an answer to a prayer when they agreed to host Peggy's memorial service. Scores of area churches rejected the request to welcome Peggy's service. Almost forty years after the young girl was brutally murdered and local churches still weren't willing to embrace her. We were denied permission to gather in the parking lot of a local social club. The many rejections were frustrating and sad at the same time. An area woman contacted me by email and told me she talked to her pastor, and he was willing to open his church's doors to Peggy because it was the Christian thing to do. The kind woman, the loving pastor, and Covenant United Methodist Church were an answer to a prayer.

"Michelle, you should eat something," Susan chided me gently.

We stopped at a fast food restaurant for me to collect my thoughts and visit a restroom before going to the church.

"That sounds nice." I was a bundle of nerves. My cell phone started to ring.

"Build it, my friend, and they will come!" Allecia said excitedly.

"What are you talking about?" I replied.

She barely slowed down long enough to take a breath. "Shelly, it is wonderful. There are so many people here!"

I took a deep breath and ended the phone call quickly. "Well, Allecia said we will not be walking in to an empty room." I rubbed my fingers across my forehead. "Of course we will not be walking into an empty room."

Susan was the perpetual optimist. "We are going to honor Peggy Reber today, and we are not going to be alone as we do that."

I wasn't quite as trusting. Max pulled up to the curb in front of the church and I had a cigarette in hand. I made a smart remark about my dad telling me a lady should never walk the street with a cigarette in her hand.

"Your dad was a wise man and you're a lady. Lose it," Max ordered.

Before I had a chance to argue, there was a camera in my face. I stepped back, took a deep breath and looked at my surroundings. I wasn't exactly sure what I was walking into, and there was no turning back. Max nodded in my direction and I knew he had things covered from there, so Susan and I entered the church. We climbed the handful of concrete steps leading into the church before crossing the threshold hosting large wooden doors.

I walked past several people asking questions and taking pictures, not really sure if they were media or not. The time for questions, photographs and interviews was not at hand. I entered that church with every intention of paying my utmost respect to Peggy Reber, her life, her death and her family. I was barely in the door when I looked to my left and I saw a small group of people. I wasn't completely certain, but I almost knew, I was in the presence of Peggy's identical twin.

Susan and I climbed the steps up into the church quietly, separately, yet together. We didn't exchange a word. We arrived at the top of the stairs at the same time, and I know we both experienced a whirlwind of emotions by the amount of people joined together to honor Peggy's life. I stood still momentarily in utter disbelief. There was an open book on a podium for those in attendance to sign much like any funeral or wake any of us ever attended. The petition appealing for a grand jury was also available for signatures of those in attendance. Organ music grew louder as I moved forward at a snail's pace.

"Hello, I'm Laverne."

I immediately embraced the silver haired woman wearing black- framed glasses with her hand extended to me.

"No ma'am, you are not Laverne, you will always be Ms. Longenecker to me." I wrapped my arms around my fifth grade teacher.

I fondly recalled talking to the pastor a few weeks prior when he said, "One of my parishioners approached me and said, 'I didn't know Peggy Reber, but I do know Michelle Gooden and anything I can do to help her I will do.'" His words at the time caught me quite off guard, and when he told me the source of that prose I simply cried. I didn't have to take too many steps deeper into the church to realize the crowd was nearing standing room only. I fought a lump in my throat that just wouldn't go away, yet I knew I needed to move forward.

I slowly walked down the aisle looking at the mass of people that gathered to honor Peggy Reber's life and her family when a man stood up to look me in the eye. I stopped in my tracks, extended my hand, "You're a good man. You are a very good man, and I am honored to know you."

That exchange did not receive special recognition nor should it, but that memorial service would have never happened if not for that man, I shook the hand of Officer Kevin Snavely. We looked at each other and smiled because Peggy was no longer the forbidden topic of yesteryear. A few steps further I spotted the last friend to see Peggy alive that fateful day. I nodded in her direction without saying a word. She wasn't identified at the time of the crime, and her identity and account of her last few hours with Peggy needed to be guarded in the interest of justice.

I continued to move toward the front of the church, and I could see Peggy's family gathered in a small group. I grew increasingly uncomfortable because I had never met Peggy's family members. I approached what was obviously her daddy, and I fought back tears as I tried to introduce myself. It was at that point another family member said to me, "We welcome you to join us and sit with the family."

I took a deep breath, took my seat and fought tears. I looked around the beautiful church and saw people from wall to wall, and then I looked up on the second level and I saw even more people. I was speechless. It was a Friday afternoon in January, and people filled the room in the middle of the day to show Peggy Reber respect almost forty years after she lost her life at the hands of evil. Every fear I had, every concern I had and every doubt I had faded away.

I quietly gave a prayer of thanks for the many people there to pay tribute to a beautiful soul that was never allowed to mature. I looked up on the second level and saw one of my own family members, and I voiced the words "I love you" because I knew she took off from work to support and pray for justice for Peggy. I looked at the many floral arrangements and I struggled to maintain my composure. Someone was kind enough to hand me a candle. I looked down at my hands holding the slim white candle and I looked up at the altar and I knew everything was going to be fine.

To everything there is a season, and a time to every purpose under the heaven:
A time to be born, and a time to die: a time to plant, and a time to pluck up that which is planted.
A time to kill, and a time to heal: a time to break down, and a time to build up.
A time to weep, and a time to laugh: a time to mourn, and a time to dance;
A time to cast away stones, and a time to gather stones together; a time to embrace, and a time to refrain from embracing;
A time to get, and a time to lose; a time to keep, and a time to cast away;
A time to rend, and a time to sew; a time to keep silence, and a time to speak;
A time to love, and a time to hate; a time of war, and a time of peace
The message of Ecclesiastes Chapter 3:1-8

The tears rolled down my face as we stood up and sang "Jesus Loves Me". Peggy's treasured childhood friend nervously approached the lectern to share childhood memories filled with girlish laughter and hopes for the future. Her voice oozed with emotion and she shared her precious memories about the sweet personality behind the name Peggy Reber. Her beautiful tribute single-handedly captured the true purpose of the memorial service, and her delivery was flawless. The emotion in the room was thick, and no one was spared its power. We prayed together, sang together, cried together, and we honored the memory of Peggy Reber.

The church service came to a close and it was amazing to watch strangers embracing strangers. The room was truly filled with love, respect and a sense of loss. The group lingered awhile, but the congregation made its way to the door, so we could gather at Peggy's grave to pay our respects. A volunteer arranged limousine service for Peggy's loved ones, and it was nice to see the family treated with such respect because they didn't have that benefit throughout the years.

While driving to the cemetery Max made the most profound statement "It's rather obvious Peggy mattered, but someone else's agenda mattered more"

People were assembling under the white canopy when we entered Grand View Memorial Park. "I thought the shelter would be a nice touch, and it reflects my own security measures. I just didn't like the thought of us standing in the middle of a green field like targets for a madman, and while today is about Peggy the monster that killed her isn't exactly behind bars. I know I sound crazy, don't I?" Max reached over and patted me on the top of my head like a puppy dog. "I'm proud of you, and I am relieved to know you are aware of the element of danger in speaking out about an unsolved murder."

I wasn't scared of the coward that brutally killed a teenage girl. The crime against Peggy confirmed her killer was far from mentally stable and four decades was not a cure for his mental illness, yet it was prudent to take a few precautions.

I held Susan's hand as we walked toward the growing crowd.

"Thank you, Susan." I didn't need to say anymore than that because Susan knew I appreciated her assistance, support and presence.

"I love you, kiddo." She squeezed my hand.

"I love you, too, Susan." We took our place on the fringe of those joining around Peggy's grave, and cars were still entering the cemetery.

Peggy's daddy and her sister were seated on two of the dozen or so folding chairs available for those unable to stand for the service.

We stood together for several minutes when I cleared my throat. "Eight years ago my friend and I stood over Peggy's grave, and we made a promise to return one day with flowers and the truth. We never imagined we would have the company of a hundred or so new-found friends." My voice was shaking, and I cleared my throat, "This is so very wrong." I lowered my eyes to Peggy's headstone. "Oh, joining together to honor the memory of Peggy Reber, and her family, is the right thing to do, but we should never have to be here at all. We should be celebrating her children, and grandchildren, but she was never allowed to know such pleasures. No child should die at fourteen years of age, and while we can't undo this wrong, we must vow never to forget her."

Unexpectedly, Peggy's twin stood up and moved in my direction. "How do we ever thank you?" She opened her arms to embrace me.

"You don't owe me a thank you, but there is one thing you can do for me." I looked into her tear-filled eyes, and softly said, "Don't be afraid." I opened my arms toward her and raised the volume of my voice so others could hear me, "Don't be afraid anymore. You and your family suffered long enough, and now it's time for the monster that did this to be afraid. It's his turn to live in fear."

Kathy squeezed my forearms and with a hint of conviction said, "I won't be afraid anymore, I won't."

Kathy and I shared a loose embrace, and I turned my attention to Peggy's daddy. "It's a good day, Mr. Reber." I could hear Kathy whisper in agreement. "These beautiful people respect the loss your family suffered not only in 1968, but every day since then. We can't fix your yesterdays, or take away your pain, but we will never turn our backs on this tragedy again."

Reverend Daniel Herner from Covenant United Methodist Church took his place in the center of the large crowd. "I think Michelle is correct because while we should not be standing over the grave of a fourteen year old child, it is indeed a good day when a community joins together to celebrate a child's short life, mourn the loss of her life, and respect her family's loss."

Kathy took her seat next to her aged, silver-haired adoptive father and they held hands while they listened to the honorable clergyman deliver words of comfort.

I looked at the bespectacled man of God and his loose curls being tossed about by the January wind. I said my own prayer of thanks. *Dear God, please bless this man and his parishioners for taking Peggy, and all of us, us under their loving wing.*

It was a good day, but a day that would not have happened if not for one pastor and his loving church. He sang only a few words alone before everyone joined him in singing Amazing Grace. I stood in awe by the power of love when people join together with kind hearts. Equally, I stood in amazement because for such a long time the mere mention of Peggy's name sparked the strangest reactions throughout the community, but at last Peggy was embraced by the world she never really got to know.

The crowd started to talk amongst themselves, and I stood still in deep thought.

"Michelle, I think today delivered honor and respect to this tragedy." Pastor Herner was standing next to me.

"Oh, thank you for everything," I said as I put my hand to his shoulder. He looked at me with a bit of puzzlement. I hesitated, but I knew he could see through me.

"I lied to my dad," I said, fighting tears. "Today is wonderful, but I lied to my dad. My dad made me promise I would never even read the news reports about the murder of Peggy Reber, and look where we are, and why."

My dad had passed almost twenty years prior, and I was suffering from guilt for having broken a promise to a man I adored.

"Michelle," Reverend Herner lifted my chin with his kind hands. "I think he would forgive you, and not only understand, but he would be pleased by your efforts"

I smiled and appreciated his words, but I was tormented by the fact such a beautiful service came at the expense of lying to my own daddy.

Tearfully, people placed carnations on Peggy's grave. I stood to the side and watched her family hug strangers and friends misplaced along the path of life. I turned toward my own friend and said, "It is a beautiful day in Lebanon, Pennsylvania!" And with that she raised the palm of her hand to meet my own.

Someone handed me a balloon and I stepped out from the canopy and released it against the powder blue sky. Fourteen purple balloons released for a fourteen-year-old girl that only had fourteen years of life, and purple was her favorite color. I smiled and cried at the same time.

News media lingered while the crowd started to thin. John Latimer looked to me for an on the record response for the daily news, and I gushed, "This is just an amazing day. I love my home town."

I hated the crime, wanted a killer brought to justice, yet I loved every individual that stepped up on behalf of a murdered teen, and her family, almost four decades after the fact.

"Can someone help me? I need some help." The request for assistance caught my attention.

"What do you need?" I instinctively placed my hand on the woman's elbow.

"I can't really see. My sight is impaired, and I need to get to the road." I offered a firmer grip on the woman's arm. She was older than me with short-cropped blonde hair resting on the top of her tinted eyeglasses. "I can't see so good, and I got to get up to the road."

I paused for a moment, then said, "I have no problem helping you to the road. In fact, there is nothing I would rather do right now. I just want to thank you for taking time out of your life to attend the service today."

It was her time to stop walking. "I am Kathy's friend." Her words displayed the loyalty only true friendship inspires. "Kathy was scared and nervous about attending the service, and she was a wreck on the drive from the church to here, but this was a good thing for her and her family. I don't know you, and I don't know why you did this, but it was a good thing not just for Peggy, but Kathy, too."

We reached the road and I stood with the woman for a moment, I wanted her to understand.

"I didn't do this." It was easy to blame me if things went wrong, or credit me if things went right, but the truth ran deeper than credit or blame. "A community did this. Today, a community joined together to honor Peggy, Kathy, and all those that suffered silently for so long."

January 25, 2008 was one day in time where Peggy's life, her family's loss, her friends' grief and an emotional community mattered more than anything else on Lebanon's calendar. I entered the day with fear and doubts, but I walked away from Peggy's grave that afternoon with a sense of peace, and a sweet taste of the roots of my hometown.

When everything settled and it was time to leave the cemetery, there was no sign of Susan or Max. I instinctively walked toward the road knowing my friends would find me. I glanced to my right only to discover Kathy was exiting next to me.

"I don't get nervous too often, and I am rarely at a loss of words, but I hope today was a good day for you." I prayed she was not upset with me, or the events of the day. I had not seen or talked to Kathryn since the day I appeared unexpectedly on her doorstep years prior.

She didn't miss a step, yet paused for a moment. "Michelle, today was a wonderful day. I almost missed it by refusing to attend, and I am so glad I was here to join in this celebration of my sister's life. The last forty years have been filled with fear, and today was amazing. I never thought anything like this could ever happen." She stopped for a minute before continuing. "I don't know how to thank you, and I don't know if you are an angel sent to help us, but today reached beyond my wildest dreams."

I dismissed any theory about being an angel and repeated, "Don't be afraid anymore." Kathy and I smiled and parted company when Max pulled up in front of us. I got into the vehicle and gave into a heavy sigh.

"We need a gas station."

I don't know if Max really needed gas, or if he was quick with a distraction of thoughts. I uttered some vague directions to the nearest convenience store.

"Michelle it was a beautiful memorial service," Susan said from the back seat. I just stared out the window. "Michelle, if you had not come back here and busted through the brick walls this would not have happened." Susan knew me too well.

I broke my silence by saying, "My Dad's words keep dancing in the back of my mind and I really feel I lied to him. Susan, we both know Peggy deserved the respect she received today when she died. I am thrilled she, and her family, finally got respect, but I can't let go of the words of my own dad so many years ago, and his obvious fear for me. He was convinced bad things would happen to me if I ever even explored Peggy's case. Oh, today was remarkable, but my dad was not a stupid man. I just have to wonder if this is the calm before a storm."

Max fueled the vehicle and asked, "What's our next destination?" It was so out of character for him to be asking direction, instead of giving it, and I chuckled a bit.

"I am going to have the best hot dog in my life, care to join me?"

It was an ongoing innocent joke between Peggy's daddy and me that we would someday enjoy a hot dog together. The day of Peggy's memorial service was an ideal time for such a meeting. I invited several people to join us, but upon arrival we realized it was apparently viewed as a private moment for Peggy's dad and a select few. I took a seat in a booth with a Formica tabletop, ordered the feature menu item, and allowed my mind to wander back to another time. I could almost see Peggy's mother at the end of the counter just like I did decades before. I was a kid back then, but I sat in the presence of Peggy's daddy after a memorial service for his daughter a few decades later, and it was pleasantly strange.

A patron motioned for me to approach the lunch counter. When I walked up, he asked, "Aren't you that lady that's been talking about Peggy Reber?"

I nodded my head, and before I could say anything, he asked gruffly, "Who did it? Why don't they arrest the sick bastard?"

I definitely shared the sentiments, but it was a conversation I wasn't going to have.

"Those are questions for the District Attorney, and I encourage you to call him, and ask those questions. In fact, don't just call him, send him an email, write him a letter, and write a letter to the editor"

The elderly man in a plaid flannel shirt gave into a hearty laugh, "Lady, you know damn good well that isn't worth the quarter to make the phone call or a stamp to send a letter"

I didn't hesitate to voice my disagreement. "It is worth the quarter, and it is also worth the effort. I traveled a lot of miles to be here today because I believe there is strength in numbers, and the more people that voice their concern the better. It is easy to ignore a voice or two, but it's impossible to ignore a community that stands united, and this community is standing up on behalf of justice for a child."

He shifted on his stool and adopted a sense of seriousness. "You believe that don't you? Lady, I have lived here over sixty years and some things are just never going to change."

It was my turn to laugh a little bit. "Life is all about change, and today was a great start. If you don't mind me asking, did you sign the petition requesting the DA to take this case before a grand jury?"

He corrected his poor posture and sat up straight with a sense of pride, "Damn right I did, the first chance I got."

I winked at the older gentleman, "See, you do believe in change after all."

(Photo-M.Gooden)

186

(photo-M.Gooden)
The Little Girl That Couldn't Forget…..
Michelle Gooden May 15, 1968 – ten days before Peggy's tragic murder.

(photo-M. Gooden)
An area business promoting the DA's tip line for information leading to…
JUSTICE 4 PEGGY

(Photo- Lebanon Daily News)
January 25, 2008

(photo- Lebanon Daily News)
Peggy's twin Kathryn and Michelle Gooden January 25, 2008

(photo-Lebanon Daily News)
"Don't be afraid anymore"

(photo-Lebanon Daily News)
Kathryn and Peggy

(photo-Lebanon Daily News)
Peggy's final resting place

(photo- Lebanon Daily News)
Margaret "Peggy" Lynn Reber

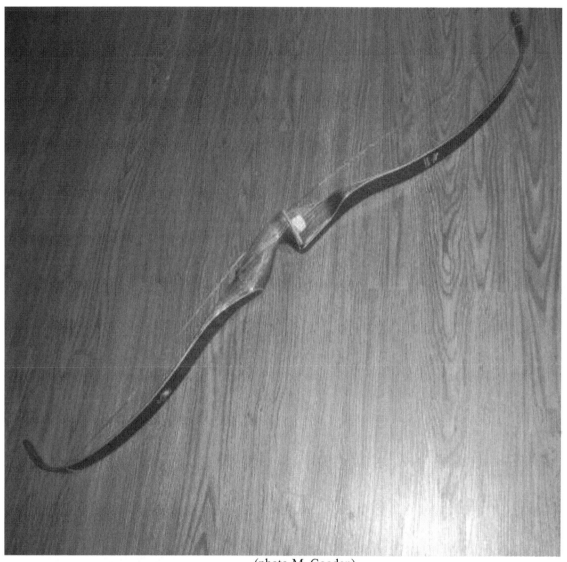

(photo-M. Gooden)

After 14-year-old Peggy was beaten and strangled to death…

Peggy's killer then thrust a five-foot recurve hunting bow in the teenage girl's rectum sixteen (16) times. Peggy had eleven (11) perforations of the lungs and respiratory tract, ten (10) perforations of the diaphragm, nine (9) perforations of the cardio vascular system. Her heart suffered five (5) punctures from the bow.

The bow pictured above is not the actual bow used in the assault. It is included simply to offer a better understanding of the attack staged against the defenseless child.

Peggy was slightly taller than five-foot at the time of her death. The bow used to kill her was five-foot. Upon the discovery of her body less than twenty inches of the bow could be seen from her lower body because the remainder of the bow was still lodged deep inside the young girl … the bow was protruding from her chest almost piercing the skin just above her breasts.

(photo-M.Gooden)

"Peggy is not forgotten" supporters erected a cross at the site of the place where Peggy died.

(Photo-Lebanon Daily News)

Almost forty years later hundreds of people gathered to pay their respect to the murdered child.

Detectives Cliff Roland and James Smith inspecting Peggy's bedroom floor.

Lebanon Daily News   The invitation to Peggy's Memorial

••

Following Peggy's January 25, 2008 memorial service her twin finally spoke out publicly by writing a letter to the editor of The Lebanon Daily News:

February 15, 2008
Section: Opinion

Letters to Editor

Sister's memorial only the beginning

Editor: I, along with my family, would like to extend the deepest gratitude to everyone who was physically and spiritually involved with the Memorial Service for **Peggy Reber** *on January 25th. I truly don't know how to thank everyone as much as they deserve. If I died tomorrow I would know peace knowing that she, my beloved sister, has finally gotten the respect, honor, and love that she deserves. I know she has gotten some peace now.*

Unfortunately, none of my siblings could make it because of work commitments. But I know they were there in spirit. Just as all of her other supporters who couldn't make it were spiritually sending their love

and support, and it was just as heartfelt as from the ones who were physically present. To all of those I send out a spiritual hug and deep gratitude.

Abounding love and thanks to the Covenant United Methodist Church for their true Christian love and charity in holding the service there. Christman's Funeral Home for the limo, pamphlets, etc.

Everyone, including my great old school chums Doris Schaeffer and Libby Mease, has been a welcome blessing, joining the fight for justice. From helping with the pamphlets, ribbons, magnets, bumper stickers, ribbons, to flowers and basically everything. Along with my new friends Alecia and Joni who have been a great support. I was extremely moved by the beautiful words Doris and Michelle had to say, along with the clergy. I also hope that everyone takes up Spike's Karate offer for the free 'self defense' classes. I intend to.

I'm still amazed and astounded at everything that came from everyone. The amazing support of all of the business services in and out of the county. I burst into tears the first time I went past Eyeland and saw this giant Marquee shouting for Justice for Peggy. I could never name them all, for fear I would accidentally forget a few. But hey, we all know who they are, and they've been amazing!

What a great supporter Laura from WLBR has been. My work often precludes me from listening in, but some friends usually fill me in on some of her shows. I heard she thought of the petitions. What an amazing idea that was. I heard there was actually someone who called in on her show and gave the idea for the Memorial Service. Bless you!!

I originally declined an invitation to go to the Memorial. Mostly out of fear for my loved ones. (ex: them being recognized by the wrong people). After all, there are still ALL kinds of monsters out there. But thankfully, I was convinced otherwise. I found out that they, the loved ones I was worried about, had already joined an army in the fight for justice. This being worlds away from that nightmarish decade, there are a lot more 'good soldiers' around for protection. My brother-in-law, Ray Boyer, and his army for instance. He has been my rock and I will love him forever. He knows he has my eternal gratitude for everything he has done for me! So no, I won't need to worry about myself or my loved ones anymore.

I was so impressed by the blogs on www.myspace.com/justice4peggyreber, I started communicating with some of the wonderful people there. (Of course my granddaughter Kaylan had to show me everything and actually help me to set up my 'own' page on the website. But I'm learning). After all it was here where I completely realized who one of my sister's biggest, true heroes was. Michelle Gooden.

I believe my Angel sister has visited Michelle and convinced her to recruit an army of warriors in this 'fight for right.' She has an astounding amount of knowledge that any P.I. would be proud of. And her relentless fight for right, paired with her unwavering faith in God and mankind has made me wonder if she were a descendant of Joan of Arc? (No joke!)

I'm sorry to say that I ignored things for quite awhile though. Partly because I had thought that nothing would come of all this hoopla. No one really cared. Right? Well, I was never so happy to be proven wrong! Along with Michelle, Officer Snavely finally did give me a glimmer of hope, and I will always be grateful for his part in all this.

Another part of my hesitation had to do with being hounded for months by some 'slimy snake' that has the nerve to call himself a reporter. And then let his sicko sister hang onto his rattle so she can also get her 15 minutes of fame. Those two are only one of the types of monsters I've had to deal with. Hopefully they've crawled back under the rock they came from. (I doubt it, but I can always hope) But at least I'm sure you can see my frame of mind was not the best. Which reminds me to thank you John Latimer! Through your tact, your sensitivity and tasteful interviews, you've proven how to be a great reporter, without trying to destroy someone.

Yet another part that made me drag my feet in all of this, was the fact that I was a bit jealous of Michelle's ability to form an army of people who believe in the fight. Not that I ever thought she was as bad as the ones I just mentioned, I just haven't learned to trust a lot of people. I was actually just admitting this to Laura last week before her show. I told her of so many times when I wanted to find something out so we could give my sister some justice. But back in those days, with the mindset of that society, I truly think that if my mother or I would have tried to protest anything, or fight for justice, we would have been strung up in the town square and/or burned at the stake. And nothing could keep me from believing anything different. Just simply 'surviving' was like hiding from sharks in a feeding frenzy. All in the name of righteous Christianity! The self-proclaimed Christians of Lebanon, that is. Hah!

Excuse me you self-proclaimed b-------!

I have met many true Christians! And I am proud to know them!! And you should be ashamed of yourselves!

Do you know that I was actually spit on and called names by adult women? Yes, spit on, and more than once. I won't even go into the horrors I had to endure from some men. Even from some men in authority, who I was actually stupid enough to go to for help! Hah! Yet again, the joke was on me. I was a 14-year-old abused child, trying to protect her child. What kind of threat was I to anyone? Those self-proclaimed Christians should have been the ones strung up. Not only for their actions, but for calling themselves Christians.

Please don't think that I'm judging everyone for the actions of half of the people I've met from that generation.. After a lifetime of being unfairly judged, I would never do that. But it was quite a scary world for me.

So, I do apologize for my bit of jealousy Michelle. Believe me, I thank God for you everyday! And I thank my Angel sister for sending you. I guess I am rambling on a bit, but I've finally come to the most important part of this letter. First of all, there will be another warrior in this 'fight for right.' So let the battle begin. Or with a more popular phrase for our younger warriors: Bring it on!

A message to the killer:

I know you. I know you well. And at last you know that I'm not the only one who knows you did it. And you weren't alone. I've gotten reports that you're already tortured by all of this. good! I know that there will be a time some day, and sooner than you think, I'll hear a whisper from an Angel that knows something more. And more warriors will join our army. Maybe even the one who will talk when he decides he's not afraid of you anymore. Or finally racked with enough guilt they can't live with themselves anymore.

Listen! Listen! Can you hear me coming? I'm holding on tight to the "Hounds of Hell" that are nipping at your heels. And when you slip and fall, I'll be waiting. After all, since you've already put me through hell and back for 40 years. I'm not afraid of monsters anymore! I'm not that terrified abused child anymore. I have an army of warriors beside me! Pegs' Memorial was only the start. We've only just begun.

Earnestly waiting,

The Other Twin

Kathy Meador Lebanon

Her "Message to a killer" was powerful beyond words. Obviously, a grand jury needed to hear whatever truth she had to offer her twin sister's unsolved murder.

Susan and I threw our carry-on bags in the overhead storage compartment of the plane and we slid into our seats to make the flight from Philadelphia to Raleigh, North Carolina. "What a wonderful trip!" Susan patted my knee. I smiled at my friend and nodded in agreement. "It was an absolutely beautiful service and Peggy is no longer the forbidden topic of conversation. Mr. Reber was so happy with the support he received from everyone and he seemed pretty excited about delivering the petition to the district attorney next week." My friend was correct. "You don't look very happy for someone that assisted in making such a monumental change in Peggy's favor"

I reached into my purse, pulled out an envelope and ran my fingers around the edges. "There is no doubt in my mind the memorial service was one of the most loving and sober ceremonies I will ever attend in my life. I stand amazed at the love, respect and fellowship I just got to witness in Peggy's honor. I am so grateful for each flower, balloon, candle, prayer and person that took the time and made the effort to right the wrong. The subject of Peggy should have never been a forbidden topic and her unsolved murder should not have gone ignored for so many years. Susan, next month it will be thirty-eight years since Art Root JR's trial and the powers that rule didn't conduct one honest, thorough and department-supported investigation into that child's murder since then. Yeah, a few years ago a detective flew out to Arizona to talk to Art Root JR, yet that same detective didn't bother to interview Kathryn, Ray or Mary Alice, so it sure as hell wasn't a thorough investigation. I talked to the former district attorney that approved the trip to Arizona and she told me the case presented its challenges because the evidence was lost in the flood of 1972. I almost laughed at her and I probably should not have said it, but I told her that was a lie because Kevin Snavely located the physical evidence in a police storage facility. She was speechless. Yeah buddy, so much for the investigation conducted under her administration. I got nothing against the woman, but her office could pay for a detective's plane ticket to Arizona in the name of Peggy, yet her office couldn't manage to interview Peggy's relatives living right there in Lebanon or, and I love this one, or make a visit to a police evidence storage facility. She didn't do it personally, but she trusted investigators to do their jobs when they failed to do the basics of an investigation. She clearly had no idea what her detectives were doing. It's a damn shame"

"Well, thank God Kevin Snavely is handling the case now. He's not trying to solve the case from behind a desk, Michelle. He's going the extra mile. He really cares about this case and anyone can see that fact. Mr. Reber sure respects him"

"You won't get an argument here, my friend. Kevin Snavely isn't getting airline tickets handed to him and he sure as hell isn't getting any support from his superiors, but he's fighting the good fight. He got up off his ass and made the effort to see for himself what was in the evidence storage area and contrary to all the nonsense-on-the-street he found the evidence from Peggy's murder. It wasn't lost in the flood of 1972. He took his efforts a step further when he was told the autopsy photos were lost and he managed to locate the negatives of the photos and had them developed. I respect Kevin Snavely greatly and I know he wants to do everything he can to give Peggy the justice she deserves, but he can't do it alone, and that's what worries me. We just attended a memorial service for a murdered child and the event was dedicated to honoring the victim of an unsolved crime. Did you see the district attorney? Did you see the Chief of Police? How about the mayor? Susan, the service was held in a church the mayor attends regularly. Folks traveled from states away to honor Peggy, yet senior public servants and high-ranking law enforcement snubbed the event? I can accept one of them having a prior commitment, maybe even two, but not one of them could attend a service honoring a child murdered within their jurisdiction? We both watched the same news reports the day of the memorial service and the district attorney wasn't camera-shy while he was in his office. He gave the media interviews. I doubt he was going to court considering he was wearing a sweatshirt. I heard the mayor was out-of-town on a previously scheduled trip. I guess the Chief of Police was planting seeds for a garden of good, or maybe evil, and the senior police officers were all lounging downtown. I can theorize, crack jokes and be cynical, but the truth remains the big-wigs responsible for enforcing the law in Lebanon did not attend Peggy's memorial service. Oh, I already know it's going to be dismissed as their noble effort at trying to keep politics out of the gathering. I wish it was that simple" I handed my friend the envelope in my hand.

"We were pretty busy during our 48-hour visit to Lebanon and we didn't slow down for much of anything. I looked at those papers lightly, but I didn't truly digest their impact until we made the drive from Lebanon to the airport in Philadelphia" Susan looked at the papers in the envelope. "The district attorney is married, it is his second marriage and I wish him much wedded bliss, but his first marriage offers a new complexion to Peggy's case. No one knows if Richard Boyer is the monster that killed Peggy Reber, but it's obvious he should have been included in the pool of suspects. Richard Boyer had a key to the apartment, he argued about electricity being supplied to her apartment the night before the crime and he did not provide dental impressions or even testify at Art Root JR's trial though he saw Peggy within the last 24-hours of her life. He was married to Peggy's identical twin at the time of the crime, assaulted his bride days before Peggy's death and he lived next door to the crime scene up until days before Peggy's murder. Richard Boyer is at the very minimum a witness to Peggy's life. He is Ray Boyer's brother. Ray Boyer was Peggy's boyfriend when she was killed"

"I see" Susan stared at the papers in her hands.

"How do you like the wedding invitation which clearly states the first Mrs. David J. Arnold JR was the maid of honor in a wedding for one of Richard Boyer's sons" I repeated myself. "The DA's ex wife was so close to the Boyer family she was a maid-of-honor for a family wedding"

"It's a small town, Michelle. I don't think that has anything to do with Peggy, or her justice"

"Keep reading"

"I see it. You have a police report showing the DA had a domestic squabble with his wife. Care to clue me in? I know there is more to the story"

"It appears before the DA was the DA he met a woman, fell in love and got married. She just happened to know the Boyer family up close and personal back then. She dated Richard Boyer's son."

"She was allowed to have a life before him Michelle" Susan was reasonable. "I don't think that has anything to do with Peggy Reber"

"Okay, skip over the fact the DA had the police called to his house years ago for a domestic dispute with his wife. The DA and his wife were approaching divorce and divorce is ugly for everyone, but that particular night the DA was upset" I stopped and waited until I had her undivided attention. "He was upset with her because she was with the Boyer family, and her former boyfriend, Richard Boyer's son was present at the gathering. I don't care if she was simply eating shoe-fly-pie on a friendly note because the bigger point is the DA has a personal connection to the family of Richard Boyer. You are looking at documents that prove that fact. It doesn't matter anymore that he was born three years after Peggy died, or that he is a respected county official now. The district attorney's personal baggage suggests a conflict of interest"

"You got a point" she put the documents on her lap.

"It just makes sense for the DA to hand this case over to the state attorney general" I talked about it before, but it was truly starting to make sense.
We returned to North Carolina and resumed our lives.

I knew in my heart the DA could never prosecute the Reber case. The identity of a defendant in the case was not an issue because it was a two-edged sword for the DA, and Peggy Reber. On the chance Richard Boyer SR was ever a defendant in the case of Peggy Reber's murder a skilled defense attorney could accuse the DA of being a jealous jilted husband seeking revenge against a romantic rival. Of course the senior Boyer was not the actual rival, but the soap-opera would be played out in a court of law and it would muddy Peggy's justice. Equally, if the DA attempted to prosecute any other suspect a slick defense lawyer would point all fingers at Richard Boyer SR and accuse the DA of sheltering his own past by overlooking Boyer. The DA simply could not prosecute the case of Peggy Reber on any level without having his own personal history come into light. I remembered how the DA admitted to seeing a suspect when he looked at Peggy's file, yet he didn't view him as a threat. Surely the DA knew at that point in time he, personally, could never prosecute the Reber case without compromising any chance of justice.

I debated long and hard, and I told no one of my efforts, but I appealed to the legal powers that govern lawyers within Pennsylvania to remove him from overseeing Peggy Reber's murder file.

Meanwhile, Peggy's twin Kathryn was building a backbone unlike ever before and she was embracing the popularity generated by her sister's cause. I was still busy fighting city hall to get a grand jury for Peggy, but Kathryn had a different plan. She wanted to create a non-profit foundation to assist children in Peggy's honor. It was an honorable goal and I loved the compassion and spirit supporting it. I particularly loved Kathryn's desire to give Peggy her public support.

It was a very respectful gesture when she wanted not only me, but talk-show host Laura LeBeau to be board members of her new venture. It was more than either of us could take on in addition to our already full-loads personally and professionally. I declined the offer not out of a lack of support for her project, but because I was still very busy pursuing justice for Peggy. I also did not see how I could be on the board of any non-profit in its infancy stages given it was 500 miles from my residence. Kathryn was insulted "How can you not support this? After all it's for Peggy?"

Naturally, I supported it, yet I did not want to commit myself to a project so far from my home. I was already battling a District Attorney trying to get Peggy a grand jury. I tried to explain my goals were really exclusive toward Peggy's justice. My limitations and desires angered her and she made a huge point of dividing her non-profit goals from my efforts to seek justice for her sister, but not until she asked for a copy of the petition signed by two thousand county residents requesting the DA to convene a grand jury for Peggy. Kathryn wanted the list of names so she could solicit them for support of her new venture. I was saddened by her request and unable to honor it because her Daddy was given the only copy of the petition to present to District Attorney Dave Arnold Jr three days after Peggy's memorial. I was glad I couldn't provide her with a copy of the petition. The people that signed the petition were making an appeal for Peggy's justice and they did not volunteer to be on a mailing list requesting donations.

Kathryn was not only insulted and angry by my failure to participate in her quest, but she was vindictive, too. Meetings for her budding foundation hosted a "swear-jar" only unlike traditional curse words hosting a penalty; the swear word during foundation meetings was my name. She made and nurtured a deliberate divide between myself and Peggy's justice, and her humanitarian enterprise. She repeatedly said "But this is about Peggy and YOU support Peggy. People listen to YOU about Peggy" We both knew I was the only voice the public heard regarding Peggy until that point and my dedication was strong toward securing Peggy another day in court. I was not going to shift gears just yet.

I don't know if she got lost in-the-mix, but simply attaching Peggy's name to a cause was not going to change my focus. I wanted justice for 14-year-old Peggy Reber. Her determination to make it clear her efforts were one thing and mine were another was almost sad. She spoke with a forked-tongue when she would say "I want justice for my sister, but I want this, too" The non-profit foundation was admirable-in-theory and a true possibility, yet she was almost prepared to continue the status-quo of her sister's case in an effort to build an empire like we see on nightly news.

I quickly became the enemy. Oh, it hurt my feelings, but I kept moving forward with Peggy's justice as my goal. Kathryn had a new voice, an audience and a purpose. It wasn't the ideal scenario for securing a grand jury for Peggy, yet it was a "God bless America" scenario for Peggy's twin.

The kind woman that offered free self-defense classes in honor of Peggy called me. "Michelle I supported this foundation-thing because I read about Peggy in the paper and I listened to you on the radio. I wanted to help make a difference and at first I thought you were part of this non-profit stuff, but clearly you're not. I thought I was helping you with your efforts to get Peggy justice" I had to explain the divide created by Peggy's twin and her efforts with a non-profit and my continued efforts toward securing justice for Peggy.

Other individuals contacted me and accused Peggy's twin of trying to make money off the murder of her 14-year-old sister. Suddenly, I found myself devoting a great portion of my time explaining to supporters of Peggy's justice the difference between my efforts, and the efforts of Peggy's twin. It was too much, too soon and hopefully not at the expense of Peggy's support.

■■

"There are going to fire me!" I answered an unexpected call from Kevin Snavely. "They think I told you everything, gave you everything and they are pissed" I could hear panic in his voice.

"What are you talking about?" I was confused.

"I just got called into my boss's office and I thought they were finally going to take the Reber investigation seriously, but instead they ripped me a new ass. I am getting accused of telling you everything you know, sharing reports, shaming the department by attending Peggy's memorial service. The chief is pissed, the DA is pissed, and the mayor is pissed. I am screwed and I know it. They kept accusing me of lying and I offered to take a polygraph, but they just kept on hounding me. They took the Reber file, all my notes and pulled me off the case. I walked out of the office with a job, but I am not stupid"

Kevin Snavely was indeed fired the last week of March in 2008 – two months after Peggy's memorial service. He was fired for an alleged infraction committed in 2005 almost a year before he ever touched the Reber file, or talked to me. Kevin was devastated. He was stripped of his career, his income and his reputation was dragged through the mud. The community was outraged! Folks throughout the small town were suspicious of the administration that fired the young detective who investigated a child's unsolved murder on his own time. More than one person uttered the words "He knows too much" or "He got too close to the truth" Oh, Kevin's firing was highly suspicious to say the least. The fact it was a personnel matter forced not only the administration to be silent, but Kevin as well.

Kevin Snavely was the only member of law enforcement that knew the Reber file like he knew the palm of his hand. He devoted countless hours to locating evidence, locating witnesses and conducting interviews on his own time. Kevin worked diligently in hopes of one day uncovering enough truth to deliver an arrest or a grand jury investigation into Peggy's murder. Officials knew when they fired Kevin Snavely all his efforts with the Reber case were destroyed. Did his alleged infraction justify not only his firing, but the investigation of a child's murder being sacrificed? Officials did not opt for alternate means of reprimand against the law enforcement officer. Kevin Snavely was not suspended pending an investigation or suspended at all, instead his superiors elected to terminate him and compromise every case the young officer ever touched, not simply the Reber case. Kevin Snavely's termination had the potential of a far-reaching impact on pending trials within Lebanon. He was deemed to be unworthy of being a cop, thus any defense attorney defending any individual Snavely arrested could argue Kevin's credibility when making such an arrest, or conducting an investigation. On the slim chance Peggy's case ever got the benefit of a grand jury it would be a tainted process. Kevin Snavely and Peggy Reber both took one hell of a blow at the hands of the administration trusted to handle justice within the city of Lebanon, Pennsylvania.

Granted, the city and county could assign other officers to Peggy's case as well as the other cases Snavely handled, but the damage was done. Kevin Snavely loosened the lid of the jar on many investigations and any other detective could follow behind him and then take claim to opening the jar. Hell, after Snavely did all the leg work it would almost be cake walk for detectives following in his footsteps, yet there was no justice in sight. If there was a conviction with Snavely's prior arrests it was credited to the skills of the second-string detectives assigned to his cases and if justice was lost it was blamed on Snavely's investigative skills. The investigation of Peggy Reber's murder, and possible justice, got lost in that abyss.

Investigative Grand Jury proceedings within the Commonwealth of Pennsylvania are legally sheltered. Grand jury investigations are based on the theory of ideal justice at its finest because it is an anonymous decision delivered "by the people". A panel of jurors is selected without bias, they remain unidentified and they are legally bound to silence regarding the proceedings. A judge oversees the proceedings, yet not from within the court room. There are no dramatic decisions of "over ruled" or "sustained" like one would see on television shows capturing justice within an hour of viewing time. A grand jury court room is a sacred place of witness testimony presented by the prosecuting office seeking the opinion of the jury. The prosecuting office selects not only the jurors, but the witnesses that provide testimony before the grand jurors based on the efforts of police detectives. It is intended to be an unbiased review of facts in pursuit of truth, yet it is vulnerable to the skills and opinions of the investigative detectives and the decisions of the prosecuting office. Ideally, the officers of the court are objective and they present thorough and objective information and testimony for the jury's review. The jury also has the right to select witnesses and ask questions based on the information they are provided by witness testimony and prosecutors. The process is supported by the Constitution and if it is delivered by competent and ethical investigators and prosecutors it will deliver the true voice of the people. The only individuals present for all witness testimony are the jurors, the court attendants, the prosecutors and the investigating officers.

Kevin Snavely worked countless hours to earn the right to be the investigative officer present for any grand jury convened for Peggy Reber's murder. Kevin Snavely dusted off the aged, unsolved murder file and pursued its truth. Kevin Snavely located evidence, located witnesses, and interviewed those witnesses. Kevin Snavely knew exactly what those witnesses said to him about the events surrounding the murder of Peggy Reber. Any investigator can attest to the challenge of getting witnesses to come forward on current cases, yet Kevin managed to talk to witnesses from decades prior. He showed up on many doorsteps unannounced decades after the crime and witnesses responded to him. He knew exactly what witnesses said to him without any warning, or chance to rehearse a statement. Oh, there were witnesses that gave accounts from years ago, but Kevin managed to locate new witnesses and several aged witnesses offered different accounts of the events surrounding Peggy's death. He had the true benefit of raw, unplanned and unscripted interviews with witnesses. He looked them in the eye, studied each witness individually and took notes. Kevin Snavely just knew the day would come that a jury would hear all the revelations he heard and he was hopeful it would solve the murder of Peggy Reber.

The firing of Kevin Snavely removed him from the prosecuting team. The firing of Kevin Snavely guaranteed he would never see the witnesses of Peggy Reber's murder testify before a grand jury. Chances were the witnesses that talked to the young detective would never talk to him again. They would never sit on the witness stand and tell the facts with him sitting in the court room. Kevin Snavely had been discarded by the world of law enforcement and Peggy's justice, at a minimum, was discarded, too. The termination of Kevin Snavely's employment shifted the names on Peggy's case like a finely maneuvered move in a game of chess. Kevin Snavely was no longer the lead detective handling the Reber investigation.

Kevin Snavely was allegedly fired for issues involving a piece of evidence that was not really destroyed. Kevin Snavely was the officer in charge of evidence-in-custody and allegedly a court order was issued to destroy a piece of evidence and it was not destroyed. The events involving the evidence in question took place before he ever talked to me, or picked up the Reber file. Public documents suggest it was the norm for "expired" evidence in police custody to be retrieved by various members of law enforcement throughout the department's ranks.

The issue was not simply about evidence that served its legal purpose, but more the integrity of the signature of the officer assigned to destroy such evidence. If Kevin Snavely received a court order for the destruction of evidence and he failed to destroy it? Such actions would be in violation of a court order. It matters not if other officers or senior law enforcement officers engaged in the practice because it is still a violation of a court order for the destruction of certain evidence, yet it appeared the department made a random determination to arrest its faulty practices by terminating Officer Snavely's employment.

Four weeks after Officer Kevin Snavely was fired, the community was suspicious of the motives behind his firing and the public's trust in their local government was at a critical low. The general public didn't need the official findings of a union arbitrator to know Officer Snavely was fired because of the Reber case. It was ninety-one days since Herman Reber presented the district attorney with a petition hosting 2,000 signatures from county residents appealing to him to convene a grand jury to investigate the murder of his daughter, Peggy. April 29, 2008 I answered my phone to the sober news the district attorney exhumed Peggy Reber's body. I said a prayer and cried. My phone rang off the wall throughout the day and the general consensus was the district attorney was finally addressing Peggy's case. It appeared to be a victory on the path to justice for Peggy, yet it certainly wasn't the type of victory worthy of celebration. Logically, I understood the necessity of the exhumation for the benefit of forensic testing, yet emotionally I was pained that even in death Peggy did not to get to rest in peace.

It was one month shy of the 40th anniversary of Peggy's funeral and disrupting her final resting place just felt like such a violation of everything that was sacred. I truly had to wonder what they hoped to find after so many years. Contrary to the ramblings of an ignorant chief of police years earlier the evidence from Peggy's murder was not a victim of the Flood of 1972, but there was no denying Peggy's body was vulnerable to the flood waters. Oh, Grand View Memorial Park is located on a hill, but Peggy's grave was not on an incline and the flooding was so severe it was unfathomable to think the dearly departed weren't affected by the strange act of nature. It wasn't necessary to exhume Peggy to obtain her DNA because her identical twin could provide the same DNA.

Television dramas offer 60-minute scenarios of a crime, an investigation, a last-minute break in a case which is commonly overlooked forensics and ultimately a courtroom verdict, but it isn't like that in real life or actual murder investigations. Many failed to realize exhuming Peggy's body was not the equivalent of studying her body at the crime scene. It was not the threshold to finding a hair, a fiber or the magic clue that would identify the killer. The burial process itself eliminated any likelihood of finding anything on Peggy's body remaining from her murder. Few of us think of the details involved in being a funeral director, but bathing the deceased is a rarely-mentioned part of their responsibilities. Forty years after being robbed of her life, the cross-contamination of being covered with a lavender blanket by a well-meaning neighbor, the transporting of her body to various locations, an autopsy, bathing for burial and a flood offered little hope of the exhumation being beneficial from a prosecuting standpoint. The question of pregnancy, if it could be answered, was not going to identify a killer either because it would not prove a child was conceived during anything less than consensual sex, and she certainly did not conceive on the night of her murder. The exhumation seemed to pacify the skeptical residents of Lebanon County, yet they were not convinced Peggy would get the justice she deserved.

It was late on a Friday afternoon when a press release was issued offering a reward for information relating to the murder of Peggy Reber. It was the first time in 40 years any reward was offered for the unsolved murder of 14-year-old Margaret "Peggy" Lynn Reber. Crime Stoppers offered a $1,000 reward. I laughed and cried at the noble gesture. I laughed at the nominal amount because it broke down to about $2.09 a week for every week Peggy was dead. I cried tears of joy because it was still more than Peggy ever had before in the form of a reward. In defense of Crime Stoppers they have my undying respect because they are not government funded and it was a truly compassionate offer. The press release also announced a local tip line and an email address as a means for individuals to provide information about Peggy. The rusty wheels of justice were starting to turn.

May 25, 2008, the 40th anniversary of Peggy's death Peggy's twin decided to plan an additional memorial in honor of Peggy. She promoted it using a My Space page she created for Peggy, the local newspaper and Laura's radio show. Few realized I was not invited. Kathryn and a select few took lawn chairs and a battery operated radio on to Peggy's grave. They prayed, reminisced, laughed and tossed glitter in the air. Members of law enforcement as well as the media attended the small gathering. I simply heard the scattered details from miles away.

My heart almost stopped when I heard the eyewitness account of how one of the kindest supporters of Peggy's justice was greeted at the May 25 service. The man that created and personally paid for bumper stickers promoting justice for Peggy was asked "What are you doing here?" He was insulted and confused. He was there for the same reason he created the bumper stickers months prior. He cared about Peggy. He didn't know about any efforts geared toward a non-profit organization or a problem between Peggy's twin and Michelle Gooden. He simply cared about a murdered child and her lost justice.

He took the insult and walked away.

It was a sad thing for Peggy Reber. She waited a long time for folks just like him to care about her and her forgotten justice. He supported Peggy, he went the extra mile, yet he was not welcomed with open arms at the May 25, 2008 memorial service. It was very sad.

Kathryn and I talked throughout the summer, but it was strained. She directed most of her attention toward her non-profit organization and I tried to be objective. We discussed the case and we also discussed her new introduction to her daughter. It was over-due and exciting. "Oh, Michelle this is just so wonderful! She is talking to me and she has children. I have grandchildren I have never met and I can't wait to meet them. I don't even know how to thank you. This is the victory and justice for me. I have my daughter back" I was thrilled by the fact Kathryn finally had a connection with the child she birthed in 1968, but I never lost sight of her 14-year-old sister being brutally murdered in 1968.

I gently approached Kathryn about the subject of Peggy and her justice. "Michelle I don't care what you tell about him, but I don't ever want my children, or my grandchildren, to know anything about it. I don't want them to know the way mom really was or the things I did. I will sit in a court room and tell the truth from back then, but I won't say anything to change the way my children, or grandchildren, look at me. I want him to pay for what he did to my sister and he should have paid a long time ago. You can tell everything you want about him and that wife of his, oh and don't forget his best friend, Ronnie. I am just happy to have my children and grandchildren in my life"

"Kathryn, your children will forgive anything you did back then. Truthfully, you were an abused child. You were a victim, too. Please just tell the truth" I pleaded on behalf of Peggy.

"I will never sit in a court room and tell the truth about how we lived back then. I won't disrespect my mother like that and I won't let my children know some of the things I did back then"

"Kathryn, I don't think Peggy can get justice without your truthful testimony"

"Michelle, it's been a long time. My sister was killed a long time ago. My children are here and God knows I put my boys through some rough times, but I finally have a chance with my daughter. I need to get to know her and my grandchildren. They don't know about how life was back then I don't want to tell them. I just met them for the first time" she was almost pleading with me. "Michelle, I will do everything I can to discredit myself. I won't allow a jury to take me seriously. I loved my sister, but I don't ever want my children or grandchildren to know how it was back then. I don't want them to know about my mom's activities, or mine. I am sure Peggy can get justice without my help."

She couldn't hide Peggy's truth and challenges from 1968, yet in 2008 she was trying to give her children and grandchildren a false sense of history. Peggy Reber was the murdered aunt of any child Kathryn birthed. Kathryn could look into the eyes of her teenage granddaughter and celebrate her life, her innocence and future, but not at the cost of turning her back on her own past. Peggy's life and death was a part of Kathryn's life and history, like it or not. Mary Alice Reber and her scandalous conduct during the 60s was also part of her history, and Peggy's.

Kathryn and Mary Alice were always free to go on and make new lives, while Peggy never had that opportunity. The truth of the past was not easy for either one of them, yet it was devastating to Peggy. The trio embarked on a new life after Herman Reber divorced Mary Alice in April1967. The family he divorced clearly suffered hardships. He remarried by the year's end and by that time a man was charged with ravishing 13-year-old Peggy and Kathryn was pregnant.

Prior to the divorce initiated by Herman they were a typical family. It was not a perfect family, it was not a totally biological family, yet it was a family nonetheless.

Mary Alice tried hard to take care of her children, her family and her home. She dressed her children with care, put dinner on the table like-clock-work and tried to keep her husband happy. She knew she was not the ideal wife because she had twin daughters her husband didn't father, yet he married her when she was pregnant, and they loved each other. She did everything she could to make up for not being the traditional virgin bride.

People still like to focus on the last year of Peggy's life and the compromised woman her mother had allegedly become. Oh, the talkers tell all about a divorced woman and the things she might have done to pay her bills and support her children. Nobody ever bothered to look at the man that divorced her. She was naturally accused of cheating and that was the alleged cause of divorce, yet no one looked at the details or dates. It was acceptable for him to divorce one family and make another within seven months. Herman Reber divorced Mary Alice in April 1967. He walked out on her, twin girls he embraced since before birth and he took a child they created. He married again in December 1967. He married another woman with a young daughter. He was a dad again, while his ex-wife and "last" daughters struggled to find their way in just a mere seven months.

Guess we can all assume he divorced Mary Alice and then met a great woman. Yep, it was like a Disney happily-ever-after, or was it? Mary Alice would tell most anyone he cheated on her and he certainly didn't waste any time in getting married after he divorced her. It was extremely difficult for a divorced woman in 1968. After fourteen years of marriage the woman struggled to find employment, affordable housing and to put food on the table for her girls. She was a social outcast due to the stigma attached to divorced women at the time.

■■■

Early in the summer of 2008 I was contacted by the new lead detective on Peggy's case, County Detective Michael Dipalo. He was a deep-voiced man with a professional demeanor. I was still feeling the sting of Officer Snavely's firing when Detective Dipalo first contacted me and I wasn't sure how I felt about his "new" investigation into the murder of Peggy Reber, but it was the only game in town. I respected Officer Snavely and I hated the price he was paying for picking up Peggy's file, but I could not shun any chance Peggy had at receiving justice. Detective Dipalo and I had a mutual understanding we both had our own reservations about each other from the onset. I had little knowledge of the office of county detectives beyond the fact they appeared to be the DA's investigators and obviously after the firing of city officer Snavely, the file finally got the attention of county officials. I didn't know if the efforts were sincere, or a horse and pony show staged to appease the many people looking at officials with a critical view.

I knew I wasn't winning any popularity contests at the Lebanon County court house and that was not an accident on my part. Officer Snavely's superiors foolishly thought Officer Snavely taught me about the Reber case, so it was only natural Detective Dipalo would entertain the same theory, but he quickly realized otherwise. He did not fire questions out like bullets, instead he carefully asked me about facts I knew and where I located the information. I didn't hesitate or back down from his questions, rather I could answer honestly and thoroughly because I wasn't handed anything. I got down in the trenches and researched and studied the case more than most would ever know or understand. "Michelle you appear to know the names of the tenants of the Maple Leaf Apartment Building, yet you claim you were never there, you didn't know Peggy, and you were only five-years-old when Peggy was killed. Oh, there is that other little matter of the building being destroyed in 1969. Basic math indicates you were only 6-years-old then. So, how did you end up with this list of names and occupations of the tenants all these years later?" I didn't hesitate for a minute "Oh detective you can't be serious" I started to giggle. "I will offer you two little words – city directories. I hope that question isn't indicative of your investigative skills. You opened a file and had the tenants listed for you, but I had to work for it decades-after-the-fact, so I did. It is no secret each public library hosts an annual directory of residents listed by address. I simply went to Lebanon's library, went to the resource section and utilized the wealth of information sitting there. It's kind of funny because Detective Snavely asked me the same question" Once again, I was forced to prove the legitimacy of my efforts to another doubtful cop, but if Peggy benefited at all from my efforts it would be worthwhile.

"Miss Gooden you claim there are other items used in the assault against Peggy beyond the bow. Why would you think such a thing?" I returned the volley "Let's keep it simple for starters. The county coroner, Dr. Tanner, testified at the trial of Arthur Root JR that other items were used in the assault. You can find that in the news reports at the time of the trial" The local news reports could be researched by anyone. "Miss Gooden you do realize newspapers sometimes make mistakes with their reporting" He was correct. "Well, if you aren't satisfied with that point, and I don't fault you, I would suggest you look at the F.B.I. reports and the evidence provided to the Pennsylvania State Police Crime Lab for testing" He almost sounded snide. "YOU have police reports?" I gave into a chuckle. "Yes, Detective Dipalo I have the State Police reports that are sitting right there in a public office in the same building you work in and they are available for purchase by anyone. I also have F.B.I. documents available to anyone upon request from the F.B.I. under The Freedom of Information Act. Oh, and by the way, I have an email from the lead detective-at-the-time confirming what I saw in those reports. Peggy Reber's killer did not limit his assault against Peggy to the bow. No Detective Dipalo the general public was never told exactly what was done to poor Peggy's lifeless body. He was a sick bastard and she was just a kid. The public still has no idea how sick that son-of-a-bitch was, do they? You know detective. We both know. The killer knows, too. It's terrifying to me to think that monster is someone's neighbor. I certainly don't want to raise my little girl next to such a beast and I am certain you and the district attorney wouldn't raise your children next to such a freak either. Let's not fool ourselves detective if Peggy was the daughter of a lawyer, a police officer or a judge her case wouldn't have gone ignored for 40 years and the bastard wouldn't have gone unidentified"

I almost think Detective Dipalo wanted to dismiss me with a brief interview or two and determine me to be spoon-fed with information or ill-informed about the murder of Peggy Reber, but instead he realized my efforts in researching Peggy's murder were my own. He never encountered a layman that devoted such research to a case and in that regard he was no different than Officer Snavely. He never investigated such an aged unsolved homicide, so again he was not much different than Officer Snavely. Unlike Snavely, Detective Dipalo had the support of the district attorney, yet the district attorney still had an issue of his own personal baggage on the fringe of the case. Detective Dipalo could investigate Peggy's murder, strive for truth and justice, but he could not change the fact the district attorney could never really prosecute the case. Naturally, my concerns were dismissed as invalid, but a blind man could read the writing on the wall.

Early in our exchange, I provided Detective Dipalo information collected from my tip line, the email address I dedicated to Peggy and a copy of a 1969 detective magazine featuring Peggy's murder. I made him aware of any names or events that even remotely crossed someone's lips. In many ways it was a déjà vu for me because it was the third time in eight years a member of Lebanon's law enforcement was supposedly carrying the torch of justice on Peggy's behalf. I had to repeat the details of my efforts and obvious facts regarding Peggy's lost justice. It was almost tickling the point of utter frustration, yet I reminded myself Peggy deserved another day in a court of law. The forty years presented more than enough obstacles and if there was any chance the data I collected along the way could be useful in his investigation I had to go the extra mile.

Detective Dipalo and I spent countless hours discussing the murder of Peggy Reber, the many aspects of the case, the witnesses and the challenges each offered. Peggy's justice was not an impossible dream, but it would require complete and uncompromised honesty on the part of every person with the slightest bit of knowledge about Peggy's life and death. There is no question first-hand witnesses failed Peggy in 1968 and they embraced their silence far too long.

I shared information I possessed reporting the Reber home was the point of a brutal home invasion just a few months before the crime against Peggy. It was an alleged savage and bizarre attack against everyone present in the Reber home at the time. The victims supposedly endured many of the acts committed against Peggy during her murder. It didn't make local headlines, but that didn't make it any less true and it definitely broadened the list of suspects. Detective Dipalo managed to confirm the incident was a reality. It confirmed witnesses failed to be completely honest about Peggy's life and death throughout the many years. Perhaps witnesses were scared at the time, perhaps they simply didn't want to get involved, but after 40 years it was time to put Peggy, and her justice, over their personal concerns and silent comfort.

I told Detective Dipalo about a rather strange caller to my tip line that boasted he would refuse to testify before a grand jury. "Michelle you can't refuse to testify before a grand jury and that's why we have grand juries. Oh, one can invoke the 5th amendment offered by the constitution, but no one is simply refusing to testify before a grand jury once they are subpoenaed" Detective Dipalo failed to recognize individuals could lie to a grand jury, they could twist the truth, they could discredit themselves and their testimony. Yes, our legal system is armed with laws regarding perjury, yet laws only get enforced if prosecutors enforce them, and Peggy wasn't faring too well in that arena.

Detective Dipalo devoted the better part of six months to his investigation of the murder of Peggy Reber. He wasn't much different than original investigators because they arrested an imprisoned Arthur Root JR almost six months after her murder in 1968. Detective Snavely also came to conclusions within a six-month period. Lebanon's crimes did not simply stop while Dipalo reviewed the 14-year-old's execution, so his plate was definitely on overload. I empathized with the county cop, but I was relentless in my support of Peggy. "I hate every crime on the books, but Peggy's spilled blood has screamed for justice for too many years. I don't want any crime victim ignored, any murderer to walk free, and the first 48-hours of Peggy's crime robbed everyone, to include Peggy, of rapid results. It is not a cake walk case, but it's time to give Peggy the benefit of a grand jury" I refused to apologize or feel guilty that Peggy's investigation was an additional investigative burden to the county detective. Peggy's murder was an investigation in Lebanon before Detective Dipalo completed first-grade, so it wasn't personal toward him, rather justice for Peggy was long overdue."I don't expect you or anyone else to understand, but I grew up in that same town, I felt safe there and I was a poor kid, too. I curse every detective that retired from Lebanon's police department these last 40 years because they started their careers, ended their careers and Peggy's file sat ignored. Enough is enough.

Is Peggy Reber's killer really that much smarter than every cop Lebanon has employed for over 40 years? You can dismiss me as being unreasonable, but isn't that the bottom line? Peggy's killer is either a criminal genius or Lebanon has a history of employing slack-ass, doughnut-eating Keystone Kops. Gee, let's not forget the multiple district attorneys the residents of Lebanon elected into office over the decades and paid them their hard earned taxes to enforce the law throughout the county. Justice for the only unsolved murder of a child within the county escaped every damn one of them. It is obvious the unsolved murder of Peggy Reber has just been an acceptable norm for Lebanon law enforcement for forty years. Dear God where else in the United States of America does a community actually have to sign a petition to get a district attorney to seek justice for a murdered child? I will hold on the thought this crime is unsolved and ignored because officials are incompetent, indifferent or corrupt. I don't believe for a minute Peggy's killer was some kind of criminal mastermind. To be quite honest with you detective I think he was probably as dumb as a bag of rocks, mean as a rattlesnake and right there watching everybody the entire time. I don't believe for a minute it was some stranger in the night. Unlike you, I grew up there and folks paid attention to their neighbors AND strangers back then. It's hard to picture a stranger entering the building unnoticed, accessing the Reber apartment without any sign of forced entry and then exiting the apartment and the building without ever being seen by at least a couple people. I stand convinced a stranger would have caught the attention of somebody, beyond Peggy. No detective it appears folks didn't see anything out of the norm that day because Peggy's assailant wasn't out of the norm. It looks like he was part of the fabric and he just didn't generate a lot of attention by being there because he was always there. Folks were trying to recall if they caught a glimpse of a murderous monster, while failing to realize the monster was a mere man, and quite possibly a man they all knew. We can debate this all day long, but given the fact the crime is not solved there isn't a cop around that can factually say otherwise"

"Ms Gooden I believe several folks recalled seeing Art Root there that day"

"Yeah detective they did. I know the details, too. Beyond the fact a jury didn't convict Art Root let's explore that just for a moment. Art Root admitted to seeing Peggy in the apartment at 6 PM. He didn't run from that fact and he told detectives how she was upset because she couldn't locate her mother. He also told detectives how she was packing because of their pending eviction by the landlord. I simply love the part about the witness that testified to seeing him there late that afternoon. Detective the witness was Betty Wenzler and she owned the laundry mat Root allegedly robbed. See, he was at the Reber apartment that day trying to get that stolen money because supposedly Mary Alice was holding it for him. Seriously detective, just how objective was Betty Wenzler as a witness against Root? Not to mention Wenzler was a good distance at the time she saw him. There aren't too many locals that won't tell you that was also crossing into Betty's happy hour. She and her husband owned the beer distributorship on Maple Street and she did a pretty good job of sampling the goods. I am not being mean detective. I am simply taking you on a trip down memory lane. Please feel free to believe good old Betty, but there were a few other witnesses that testified at Root's trial. Two employees of the local comfort station testified to seeing Peggy at the public restroom at 8 PM. Sir, they were not at a distance and they certainly were not under the influence of alcohol. They had no personal grudges against Root and they had nothing to gain by their recollection of Peggy's presence in the evening hours. The prosecution insisted Root killed Peggy at 6 PM that afternoon, yet multiple other witnesses squash that theory, so it looks like somebody else killed Peggy after 8 PM. We just went full circle and we are right back at Peggy's killer being such a norm at The Maple Leaf Apartment Building his presence didn't cause anyone to blink an eye"

"Ms Gooden there was expert testimony at the trial about a substantial exchange of fibers between the victim and Root" I fought the urge to laugh. "It sure would be nice if we could see exactly what those experts testified to, but considering the testimony wasn't transcribed you and I are both at the mercy of The Lebanon Daily News, aren't we? Detective Dipalo, years ago I listened to a seasoned detective tell me the jury was confused by the complicated nature of forensic testing, so I set out to learn if he was correct. More than one juror was almost insulted by that ridiculous statement. The jury understood the testimony. Personally, I believe them, but what I don't believe is that the Lebanon Police Department knew how to collect such items of evidence back then. They couldn't even collect fingerprints properly, so how in the hell were they going to handle collecting fibers? I wouldn't be surprised to learn they put Root & Peggy's clothing in the same evidence bag and the exchange of fibers took place in transporting the evidence"

"They didn't collect fingerprints correctly?" he was being coy. "No detective they did not collect fingerprints correctly. There was an empty bottle of beer on the coffee table in Peggy's apartment and almost a dozen of the prints identified belonged to the detective collecting evidence. They didn't know enough to wear gloves when processing fingerprints. I really don't mean to be rude to you, but I am constantly explaining things to members of Lebanon law enforcement and quite frankly I think it's time law enforcement gets out there and gets in the trenches themselves. Oh, that's right Officer Snavely did that and look where it got him. You better be careful detective because it looks like any cop that touches this file in the name of justice just might get a slap on the nose or find a place in the unemployment line"

"Ms Gooden I am making every effort to investigate Peggy's murder to the best of my ability and the district attorney is supportive of my efforts. I am not sure how much more you can ask of us, or that we can do, but Peggy's file is not sitting around collecting dust" I wanted to believe in the new investigation, but I was skeptical. I prayed during the investigation of 2001, I prayed during the investigation of 2006 and now it was 2008 and I was praying once again for yet another investigation being conducted by a cop in Lebanon. Peggy's file collected a lot dust for over thirty years, but the last few years it was getting dragged through the mud. Detective Dipalo was patient with my unwavering desire to see Peggy's case go before a grand jury, but he struck a raw nerve with me several months after our first conversation.

Detective Dipalo emailed me a link about the unsolved murder of 5-year-old Brittany Locklear. Brittany was abducted from her school bus stop on the morning of January 7, 1998 outside her home in Raeford, North Carolina. Her raped and battered little body was found in a drainage ditch a few days later not far from her home. The state of North Carolina was shocked, disgusted and angered by the murder of the small child. The governor of North Carolina did not hesitate to quickly offer a $20,000 reward for information resulting in the capture and conviction of the child's killer. Brittany's murder remains unsolved. The Lebanon County detective sent the link with a mention that Brittany's case was a little bit closer to my home in Fayetteville, North Carolina compared to Peggy's case in Lebanon, Pennsylvania. What was he trying to prove by sending me a link for little Brittany's murder? Sure it was close to my home in North Carolina and I was familiar with the tragedy, but what did that have to do with a Lebanon County detective investigating the forty-year-old murder of Peggy Reber? He was overworked by his current case load and the addition of Peggy's case, yet he had time to look into North Carolina's unsolved murders? I understood his unspoken message only-too-well and I was far from impressed. He stood as a county detective investigating Peggy's murder after a public outcry for justice, after the community petitioned the district attorney for a grand jury investigation into Peggy's murder and he proclaimed the support of the district attorney with his investigation, yet clearly he wanted me to direct my attention closer to my home in North Carolina.

He reminded me of that backwards-southern chief of police collecting a paycheck in Lebanon, Pennsylvania. The chief really didn't understand the upset when he sat in his office in Lebanon, ready to proudly display his Confederate flag in what he deemed to be a respectable format. Guess you could say you could take the boy out of the south, but you couldn't take the south out of the boy.

I lived in North Carolina, gave birth to my children on Fort Bragg, North Carolina and I paid my taxes in North Carolina, but Lebanon, Pennsylvania was always going to be home. I moved my mother to North Carolina after my Dad passed away and when she died she was buried in Pennsylvania. Oh, that detective might have thought he was being cute with an email about a child's murder closer to my home in Fayetteville, but I was military and home is different for every military family. My home will always be Lebanon, Pennsylvania. The detective was wasting his time and mine if he thought he could make a point of children dying near me or since the time Peggy was murdered. His email was a poor representation of the efforts of his investigation. I had to wonder if he was going to try to distract the general public, too. Peggy's murder was not current or easy for any detective to investigate or solve, but if legal convictions were being limited to the easy cases our society was in trouble.

Civil rights cases from the 60s were hitting the courtrooms at a record pace. Racial killings were finally getting the justice they deserved from over forty years ago. The mayor of York, Pennsylvania was not spared from being held accountable for his actions resulting in a death in 1969. I held onto hope that Peggy, too, could see justice after decades of nonsense.

****

"Michelle, I read the police report and it is just amazing the things that insurance man gave in his statement" I listened to the woman on the phone and I sat utterly baffled. "He knew the type of scotch he drank that night at Pushnik's bar, I think he said it was J&B, and he remembered how many drinks he had and then he drove by Peggy's house and remembered some guy running across the street forcing him to slam on his brakes. I can't remember what I wore last Tuesday, but that guy just seemed to remember everything. I thought it was really weird when he got down to describing the socks of the guy that was crossing the street. Who remembers crap like that? A guy runs out in front of your car, you slam on the brakes and yell at the jerk, but you don't remember his socks. I can see why you call this whole thing strange. It's strange to me and I wasn't even born then"

"You saw a police report?" I was at a loss.

"Detectives wanted to talk to my father-in-law because he was married to Peggy's twin back then. Anyhow, last year after Detective Snavely talked to him he got a lawyer. I don't know all the details. I just know after Snavely talked to him he called a family meeting. He was pretty upset about the whole thing. He didn't mention it after that and I just thought it went away. Michelle, it all sounded pretty crazy to me and I had never even heard of Peggy Reber. It just made sense to tell him to get a lawyer. Anyhow, I thought that was the end of it. I really just didn't give it too much mind after that. You don't think he did this Michelle, do you?"

"I don't know. The truth is nobody knows who killed Peggy Reber because the case is unsolved, but I'd like to hear more about this police report you read. Where did you get it?"

"The cops sent it to my father-in-law's lawyer. He's pretty nervous about this whole thing and I guess he is scared they are going to try and frame him. Anyhow, the cops contacted his lawyer asking to talk him and his lawyer gave him this police report that was included in their request. It's the weirdest thing I ever read" I hung on her every word. "It is just unbelievable the things in that report. I can't believe some of the things it says and I guess it's pretty weird they sent it to my father-in-law. I mean Michelle, if they want to question him, why are they sending him the report from that night? Are they trying to refresh his memory? I don't understand, and it is just the weirdest thing"

"It is strange indeed" I just couldn't imagine the reasoning behind such a move.

The young woman went on to explain to me that her father-in-law's lawyer wanted him to have a press conference. The lawyer wanted his client to stand up and deny any involvement with Peggy's murder. Her father-in-law did not hold a press conference and he allegedly terminated the lawyer's services in regards to this particular matter. However, her father-in-law then contacted his real estate attorney for some advice and he said he couldn't help him at all. Ultimately, her father-in-law agreed to meet with detectives on his terms and at a location of his choosing. It was almost horrifying to learn he met with detectives within a stone's throw of where Peggy took her last breath.

I dialed a familiar phone number and asked the dumbest of questions. "Could someone please explain to me how any suspect in the murder of Peggy Reber is in possession of the police report from the night of the crime?" I went on to list the details recanted to me by a young woman that wasn't even alive when Peggy died, yet she read the police report from that night and knew details of witness statements. She had no desire to seek out such documents, no means to infiltrate an unsolved murder file, yet she knew things only police would know. How did that happen?

"I guess my desk was full and it got included in the envelope accidentally when we were contacting the attorney. I made a mistake, alright? I made a damn mistake!"

I hung up the phone. I bowed my head and cried. I didn't cry because a detective made a mistake. I cried because it was just one more mistake made by a Lebanon cop while handling Peggy's justice. Yeah, after a good cry I started to wonder if that mistake wasn't deliberate, but I pushed the thought out of my mind. I simply had to believe Lebanon officials were finally seeking truth and justice for Peggy.

■■■

Peggy's email address continued to receive countless letters filled with support for her justice, tips about the crime and questions. Oh, folks still had many questions about the young girl killed so many years before. I continued to provide every bit of information received to the investigating officer. Granted, the detective was monitoring the DA's dedicated tip line and email set up for Peggy, so much of what I passed on was repetitious. I was slightly surprised by an email I received from a warden of a prison in a western state and his unexpected request that I contact him. The gentleman explained to me he had been contacted to talk to one of his inmates about a murder in Lebanon, Pennsylvania in 1968. He identified the inmate by name and it was not a name associated with Peggy's case, but it was indeed the man charged with her death. The warden was housing Arthur Root Jr. I explained to the warden Root's true name and he said "Michelle I think he changed his name legally years ago"

Oh, I knew Root was using the alias for many years. He married, had a family and used the alias, but I just couldn't see Art Root Jr taking the time to make the name legitimately legal. I was pleased authorities were reaching out to Root because he was a key witness to the events of May 25, 1968. The Constitution prohibited Root from ever being charged with the crime again because he was protected under double jeopardy, yet he was still a wealth of information regarding 770 Maple Street and the spring of 1968. It really wasn't in the warden's place to interview Root regarding Peggy's death, but I rested well knowing investigators knew his location and they knew he needed to answer some questions. Art Root Jr was going to be a very valuable witness when Peggy's case went before a grand jury.

I was beyond delighted when I was told Peggy's case was going to be presented to the highly respected Vidocq Society in Philadelphia. The Vidocq Society is a group of professionals from around the world that meet in Philadelphia and review unsolved cold case files. I was optimistic their professional objectivity would be just what Peggy needed. I was having lunch in a local eatery not far from my home in North Carolina when a city detective stopped in to grab lunch as well. He sat down at my table and we engaged in light conversation. I told him about my excitement regarding The Vidocq Society looking at Peggy's case. "Well, look at you go. You brought that case a long way now, didn't you?" he winked at me with a broad grin on his face. "Me? I didn't do this, but I am glad it's happening just the same" His tone went from playful to serious "Of course you did this and don't you forget it. I remember years ago when you were struggling to learn about this case and I will bet you there isn't a cop up there that's put as much time in this thing like you have these last several years. Oh, sure when it happened those guys weren't getting any sleep and I have no doubt a lot of investigators busted their tales, but just look at the last few years Michelle. You are the constant in the investigation. Oh, I'm not picking at my brothers in blue, but unless a department has a task force set up for cold cases it's a challenge. How many cops picked up this file since you first started looking at it?" I put my sandwich down. "Well, in 2001 a female cop was fired for touching the file, then a county detective took a shot at it, Officer Snavely tried a few years later, but he got fired and now it's sitting in the office of county detectives" In a matter of seven years Peggy's case was getting a lot of attention, yet few results. "That's my point Michelle. What was the constant all those years? You, my dear, and I'm not saying you set out to make this big splash, but until you picked up a little bit of confidence in yourself it looks like there was just some wheels-spinning-in-the-mud.

It's a good thing when average citizens get involved and don't you let anybody ever tell you otherwise. Watch your television and you will see exactly what I mean. The minute a child is missing you see that child's family on every news channel begging for help, information and witnesses to come forward. I spent enough years on the force to know my investigations are only as strong as the witnesses willing to talk"

I interrupted the southern sleuth. "I am not a witness. I never saw anything, I don't know anything and I think that's part of the frustration. I know there are people that saw things, know things and I just can't understand their perpetual silence. If it was their daughter or granddaughter they'd want justice, yet it's Peggy and nobody wants to admit to knowing a damn thing. I just don't get it. I listened to people brag to me that they will not testify or they will discredit themselves on the stand and they don't want their own personal poor conduct exposed to their children and grandchildren. It is the epitome of selfishness and once again at Peggy's expense. Peggy never got the opportunity to have children or grandchildren. Peggy didn't even get to finish 9th grade" My passion was evident.

"Hey look, it's hard for you to see all the progress you made because you are still standing in the storm, but someday you are going to realize you made all the difference in the world. You might not be kin to that girl, but like those parents I just told you about you gave the case a voice" the waitress interrupted him with an offer to refill his drink.

"What if my efforts killed her chance at justice?" I was sincere.

"Oh, you silly, silly girl!" He started to laugh at me. "You still don't see the beauty of your involvement with the case, do you? You can't control justice and you can't change the truth, but what you did do was kick up a bunch of dust and get people talking and get people listening. I don't know exactly why, but you decided this young girl mattered to you. I don't mind telling you I am not sure I would ever want to be the detective you call out for answers to your questions because you're hard-core and you got some damn good questions. I have listened to you talk about this case. I guess there's going to be at least one dumb skunk out there that might try and tell you that your efforts sabotaged justice. I can't recall exact years, but it seems to me this girl didn't have too much justice for quite a long time. How can you sabotage something she never had? How could you have any effect on the events, witnesses and the truth when this crime was taking place"

I jumped in at rapid speed. "What if I made it harder for investigators?" I picked up a pickle from my plate and waited for his response.

"Michelle, investigators met that little girl before you ever heard about her. Don't let yourself forget investigators were at that crime scene. Those fellas investigated the crime and they didn't deliver justice. You're voice is not that of an investigator and that's not your job, but you obviously did a mighty fine job of getting this loss of justice some overdue attention. I think you're concerned over nothing. A little kid remembers something from her childhood and that's great, but it doesn't change a damn thing about the crime, the witnesses or what actually happened. You're the bleeding-heart cheerleader, Michelle. You are a witness because you remember her, period. You are actually a pretty good reflection of the times. It's clear the murdered girl left an impact on many people, so you aren't alone in remembering her, but you are alone in keeping a steady vigil on her lost justice. I can't speak for another police department, but evidence is what it is and witnesses either know something or they don't. Girl, I like you, but you can't change physical evidence and each witness is responsible for their own statement, so get the weight of the world off your shoulders. It's not yours to claim" I tried to smile.

"Listen that review by the Vidocq Society is pretty impressive, yet I hope you realize one thing" I looked at him with a questionable gaze. "The Vidocq Society doesn't investigate cases. They review cases submitted by investigators. They are going to look at the file the investigators provide them and they are going to give an opinion based on that information. You just have to hope they are handed a file they can work with after all this time. They are some sharp folks, so it's a great thing happening there and you just have to hope they are given all the facts and players in an objective format. Those guys aren't mind readers, so they don't know if something's missing in the case. Hey, it's always great seeing you, but duty calls" the man in front of me looked at his pager, paid the waitress and left in a flash.

I sat there for quite awhile thinking about the law enforcement officer's words. I encountered more than one critic that would tell me I was exhausting all chances of Peggy ever receiving justice. Oh, I would beat myself up after each and every claim, yet I never lost sight of how Peggy's case sat ignored for so many years. Hell, even when cops did pick up her file they either failed to talk to witnesses or they got shut down by the administration. Peggy's case was unsolved for over thirty years before I ever read the first news article reporting the crime. It was a far stretch to accuse me of obstructing Peggy's justice. It sounded good "Michelle Gooden is contaminating any hopes of Peggy Reber receiving justice" Sadly, few realized, it was my efforts that pulled the aged case from the shadows. Occasionally, a do-gooder would say "We appreciate Michelle's efforts, and we are grateful for the support of the administration and we trust their efforts" I smiled at such statements because they were usually made by Peggy's family members, excluding Herman Reber. Herman had a far different view on things.

"Hey, Mr. Reber, what privilege has you calling my phone on this beautiful day?" I saw the caller identification on my phone and greeted a kind spirit in my life. "Michelle, you know I will always appreciate what you did for me and my daughter Peggy. There ain't never been anybody that cared so much about this other than me and you. Well, Detective Snavely was a good guy until they fired him. I tried. God knows I tried. I used to walk into that police department every day, every week and later every year. I wanted to know what they were doing about the murder of my girl. I just wasn't gonna roll over and let them forget about her. You know that happens sometimes. Police forget. No boy, I wasn't going to let them forget about Peggy. I don't know who did this terrible thing, but he shouldn't have gotten away with it. I got family crawling out of the woodwork that wants to talk to the mayor and the district attorney like they are some-damn-body important. Everybody wants to be a hot-shot, but they forget that's my daughter they're talking about and I don't need anybody else doing any talking for me. You and I know who really needs to be talking, don't we? I am still just sitting back and scratching my head. I just want you to know I appreciate you taking the time to give Peggy your attention.

I thought for sure Officer Snavely was doing the right thing. I just knew in my heart he was going to get the guy that did this to Peggy. I don't believe all the things they are saying about him right now. I just don't believe it. That young man showed up on my doorstep and he talked to me. He wasn't like those others cops. Michelle, he really talked to me. He wanted to learn about my daughter. I still can't begin to thank you or Officer Snavely enough for that service you made happen. I am still amazed by all those people coming and all those flowers. I just want you to know I appreciate all that. I don't mind telling you that was one of the nicest days of my life. You know, I like that lady on the radio, too. She talks about Peggy a lot these days and sometimes I call in to her show and thank her. I don't care what anybody says but if it wasn't for Kevin Snavely, you, that lady Laura on the radio and the folks at the Lebanon Daily News my Peggy still wouldn't be getting any attention. Nobody made a difference like this before and it's been a lot of years Michelle. I ain't a young man anymore and when my girl was killed it broke my heart. I just never understood how somebody could do that to her. I knew I wasn't a rich man either, so I kept walking into that police station. Yeah, now everybody wants to talk to politicians, but they don't know nothing about what's really gone on all these years.

They want to treat me like I am stupid. I'm old, but I ain't stupid and I ain't dead. I just hope I live long enough to see them put him behind bars" It was the second time in my life I listened to one of Peggy's parents express a desire to see justice for their daughter before taking their last breath.

∎∎∎

November 2008 the first person to shatter the silence surrounding grand jury proceedings was none other than Peggy's identical twin, Kathryn. She testified before the grand jury and visited the local newspaper office immediately after her testimony. Granted, Kathryn worked there for years, but she didn't enter the doors as a former employee visiting co-workers from the past. Kathryn exposed the fact there was a grand jury investigating her sister's murder and she expressed gratitude and optimism toward the proceedings. Her revelation of the proceedings met mixed responses. The law itself sheltered the proceedings to offer every attempt at untainted justice, yet Peggy's twin was the first person to expose the silent proceedings of the grand jury. Perhaps Peggy's twin was so overwhelmed with joy at the proceedings she wanted the world to know her sister was finally getting the justice she deserved? It was queer that an individual that supposedly waited so long in silence for justice didn't remain silent just a little while longer out of respect for the process. Kathryn told news reporters she sat before the grand jury for ninety minutes. The cat was out of the bag.

In the blink of an eye after Kathryn's public revelation of a grand jury reviewing Peggy's murder former police officer Kevin Snavely filed a lawsuit against a handful of local government officials to include the district attorney. The lawsuit was poorly written, lacked accuracy and facts, and it indirectly identified Richard Boyer SR as a suspect in the murder of Peggy Reber. It was an unprofessional and sloppy act that danced on the ethics of not only the terminated officer, but his lawyer as well.

The terminated police officer and his attorney had every right to file multiple lawsuits in excess of six months, yet they opted to file a suit and publicly identify a suspect in Peggy's murder within days of Kathryn revealing there was a grand jury investigating the case. The identity of a suspect in Peggy's murder had no legitimate or necessary place in the lawsuit filed by the terminated officer. The suit addressed Officer Snavely's rights under the First Amendment, while infringing on the rights of others in the process. It was almost a "bitchy" action. Peggy's justice was bound to suffer.

It didn't take long for the media, local lawyers and the general public to question the timing, inaccuracies, content and filing of the lawsuit. There was no reasonable explanation for the lawyer, former law enforcement officer or the lawsuit to taint the investigative efforts of the grand jury by identifying any suspect in the murder of Peggy Reber. It just wasn't fair to Peggy. It appeared to be a weak, disorganized, legal effort for Snavely to take first-claim to identifying a suspect in the Reber murder case, while he couldn't be a part of the judicial process.

Most of us that knew and respected Kevin Snavely stood dumbfounded. No one believed the allegations made against Kevin Snavely during his firing and he was clearly in a desperate place, but the details of the lawsuit he filed were not only unreasonable, but inaccurate, wrong and unethical.

John Latimer, the reporter from the Lebanon Daily News, and I read the lawsuit miles apart, yet both sat exasperated. We joked a bit about the part of the law suit where Snavely claimed I approached The Lebanon Daily News out of my own frustration with the Reber case.

"Please tell me you remember how this went down" I half-heartedly waited for the newspaper reporter to respond.

"I remember Michelle".

"Kevin wanted you to report something on the anniversary of Peggy's death, you told him there really wasn't a new twist to the aged story and he gave you my name. He is now saying I approached you on my own and he had no knowledge of my efforts. That's a blatant lie. What the hell? I hate what's been done to him, but does that give him the right to throw me under the bus, or throw Peggy's chance at justice under the bus, or recklessly involve other individuals without a care? I speak out publicly all the time, but I would never name a suspect! Cops don't identify suspects. Prosecutors identify suspects in crimes; grand juries identify suspects, but not fired cops with a personal ax to grind. It was a complete mockery of the whole process being devoted to Peggy's justice. That lawsuit could have been filed professionally and accurately without half the nonsense it hosted. The junk in this filing is supposed to be what people testify to in a court of law. It's not so much a legitimate filing of a lawsuit, but a monologue of junk placed on public record for shock factor. Sadly, it's a pretty twisted and inaccurate monologue coming from Kevin. I don't see Kevin's lawsuit ever seeing the inside of a court room. It's just one more kick-in-the-teeth to Peggy Reber's justice" I was at a loss. I was disgusted when the administration chose to fire Officer Snavely when they knew it would shatter all his investigative efforts with Peggy, yet he was proving he was no better than them.

Once again, the impact of the law suit filed by the wrongfully-terminated police officer did not register with the majority. The lawsuit exposed the name of a suspect beyond Arthur Root JR. It was the first time since Root's trial the public had an additional suspect identified in the murder of Peggy Reber. One must never forget identifying a suspect does not identify a killer. One must also remember investigators, to include Detective Snavely, never put all the suspects in Peggy Reber's crime to the test of forensics, alibis, dental comparisons or basic common sense. The mention of the Boyer name in the lawsuit was not fair to the Boyer family and it certainly wasn't fair to Peggy Reber.

Several days later, I opened my email and it sported a subpoena to appear before the grand jury convened to investigate Peggy Reber's murder. I opened another email and it sported a second subpoena to appear before the grand jury convened to investigate Peggy Reber's murder, yet on an alternate date. I was beyond confused, so I called Detective Michael Dipalo.

"The grand jury wants to hear from you, and you are at a distance, so I sent multiple subpoenas for you to pick a date to appear before them" I didn't quite understand. "Why would a grand jury want to hear from me? I have zero to contribute to a legitimate investigation into Peggy's murder. After all I didn't know Peggy, I never stepped foot in the Maple Leaf Apartment building and I was little more than a healthy 5-year-old on the other side of town. I am not a detective, an expert witness or a family member. The jurors need to hear from the individuals that can actually testify to first-hand knowledge and first-hand accounts of Peggy's life and death" I waited for the detective to respond. "Michelle the jurors have heard your name and they want to hear from you personally". I wasn't buying it. "Shouldn't the jurors devote their time and their effort to hearing facts from the individuals actually qualified to testify on the events that matter? There are still quite a few witnesses alive from Arthur Root JR's trial, new witnesses located within the last two years and between your testimony and Kevin Snavely's testimony the jury will have a legitimate foundation to base a decision. Any lawyer with a cracker-jack law degree would laugh at the mere suggestion of having me testify"

The detective was reassuring, but I had my doubts and I was stunned after reading the legal verbiage of my multiple subpoenas delivered via email. Oh, they didn't just seek my presence, but a multitude of other items in my possession and I almost choked when I saw the grand jury was requesting my bank statements. They couldn't be serious! I was 5-years-old when Peggy Reber was killed, I never knew her and this grand jury wanted to see my bank statements? I certainly was not a suspect and my bank statements forty-years-after-the fact had nothing to do with a child's murder in 1968! Oh, they didn't just want my bank statements, but my calendars, computer hard drives, faxes, etc. It was a mind-boggling list of things.

I fought long and hard for Peggy to get the benefit of a grand jury and I was not about to make too many waves, but I most certainly was not going to provide anyone the ridiculous list of items requested of me.

I prepared my young daughter, contacted her school and arranged to have her absences classified as an educational field trip. My ex-husband bid us farewell "Michelle I believe Peggy Reber needs a voice, but I do not agree with this email subpoena they issued to you, yet I understand what this grand jury means to you. I just don't trust this crap. I really think you should stand firm and make them force you to testify. It just doesn't smell good Michelle" He hugged our daughter and said. "Stay safe" It was two weeks before Christmas and the timing was less than convenient, yet I tried to convince myself it was in the interest of Peggy's overdue justice.

Friday December 12, 2008 I entered Lebanon's local AM radio station WLBR. Morning talk show host Laura LeBeau and her listeners were definitely the wind behind the sails of Peggy's justice, so I didn't hesitate to accept Laura's invitation to join her on air. The perky radio personality offered me a seat in the studio while pre-recorded news reports played to her audience. "Welcome to my world" I smiled and scanned my eyes across the small hub of Lebanon's talk radio. Laura handed me a headset so I could hear the incoming calls from her listening audience and moved the microphone closer to my face so my responses could be heard. It was not my first time of being a guest on Laura's show, but it was the first time I was an in-studio guest. Normally, I was in the comfort of my own office as I talked to Laura and her listeners on the phone. I squirmed in my seat a little bit and battled nervousness. Laura must have sensed my apprehension because she definitely put me at ease with pleasant conversation before she returned to her live-on-air-program. I genuinely liked Laura LeBeau as a person outside the radio station. Off air Laura was pleasant, charming, soft and engaging, but on air Laura didn't tiptoe around too much. Laura was a quick-witted and sharp-tongued burst of energy. Occasionally Laura's bold approach would offend some of her listeners and that was part of her charm. Laura certainly didn't go to any great lengths to avoid upsetting local politicians. She didn't stalk them for scandal, but she wasn't afraid to call a skunk stinky. Laura's listeners seemed drawn to the fact she had the guts to say what many thought, but few would dare say. Oh, there was always some old tick-in-the-folds that would try and discredit her, yet that was the beauty of Laura. The haters were free to hate and Laura was still getting paid to talk, so one just had to take it for what it was worth.

"It's a pleasure to announce Lebanon native Michelle Gooden is in the studio with me today. Most of you know Michelle from her efforts with the unsolved murder of Peggy Reber and Michelle lives in North Carolina, so this is a rare visit for her to be here with us. Michelle what brought you to Lebanon on this cold December day"? She wasn't wasting any time at getting to the heart of things.

"Well Laura it is no secret due to the huge public outcry of your listeners, and beyond, Peggy Reber's murder is finally getting the benefit of an investigative grand jury. I received a subpoena to appear before them yesterday, so here I am" Naturally, Laura knew why I was in town.

"You received the subpoena yesterday and you are already here in Lebanon? Wow! That's quite a distance for you to travel in such a short period of time and the weather was pretty wicked the last 24-hours. How long did it take you to get here?"

"The weather was horrible! I didn't waste too much time getting on the road because I knew the roads were clear of snow and snow is such a staple this time of year in Pennsylvania I was hoping to avoid it. I avoided snow, but the torrential rain throughout the drive was so bad visibility was almost zero. I had to pull over several times, so it extended the normal 8-hour drive to just under 11-hours" We offered her audience a general recap of the story of Peggy and the milestones the case covered in the last year or so.

"Michelle talk to me about that lawsuit former Lebanon police officer Kevin Snavely filed earlier this month. I don't mind telling you I was aghast when I read it. Is that going to have an impact on this grand jury"?

I took a deep breath "That's a good question. The grand jury is not sequestered, so they aren't sheltered from events or content of the lawsuit. I don't want to throw stones at Officer Snavely and I certainly don't want to take the focus off of Peggy where it really belongs"

"Michelle I think you are attempting to be diplomatic, but he certainly didn't present you in the best light with his filing and I was appalled by the fact the suit attempted to identify a suspect in Peggy's murder. I don't think anyone blames him for suing, but was that really necessary? I don't mind telling you my station and I will not be repeating the name Snavely mentioned because we do not think it is morally correct to do that to any individual that has not been charged with the crime." I agreed with the decision of Laura and her station 100%.

Laura reminded her audience of the laws sheltering grand jury proceedings. "Now we know you are not breaking any laws by being here in the studio today because witnesses are allowed to talk about their testimony provided to a grand jury. We also know you are not the first witness to speak out about the proceeding because Peggy's twin, Kathryn, admitted to testifying before the jury several weeks ago. When will you be in court?" I told her I would was scheduled to be sworn in the following Monday. "How do you feel about all of this Michelle? I mean we all called for district attorney Dave Arnold's attention to this matter and we petitioned for a grand jury, so how are you feeling now that it is actually taking place"?

"I am optimistic and very hopeful Peggy will finally get the truth she deserves. I have not been silent with my criticism of local officials for ignoring this case for so many years and I won't be silent in expressing my sincere appreciation for giving Peggy's case the benefit of an investigative grand jury. I am grateful Dave Arnold respected the voice of the people and a jury of the people will decide what is reasonable and what is not. It's been a remarkable year or so and I am simply amazed at the difference that's been made with the support of the public"

"Michelle what if the grand jury doesn't deliver an indictment and Peggy's case remains unsolved? Will you be disappointed? Will you continue to fight for her justice?"
"This is it, Laura, this is the last battle line in the long fight for justice for Peggy. I will be disappointed if the grand jury does not deliver an indictment, yet we must respect what is transpiring within Lebanon's court system. I have great faith that once the jury hears the accounts of the witnesses they will understand better the facts of Peggy's case. Right now it is up to the prosecutors to present the witnesses, the witnesses to give truthful testimony and the jury

to give a fair and objective review of the information presented to them. Let's celebrate one victory at a time. I really can't stress enough how amazing it is that we pulled Peggy's case from the shadows and got it this far. It is the community that made all the difference with Peggy's case and that is powerful stuff" I choked up a little bit. "If I could reach out and hug each of your listeners or every sweet soul that signed the petition on Peggy's behalf I would. I can't help but think back to the first hundred times I mentioned Peggy's name and the way she was a forbidden subject. I am so touched by the way all of that has changed. Peggy Reber was a 14-year-old child that needed us then and we were not there for her, but the tide has changed. This beautiful community is not willing to forget her or ignore her horrific murder and that in itself is justice. I am damn proud to be a native of Lebanon and I am so touched by the compassion of your listening audience"

Laura and I shared some brief personal chatter before I exited the radio station and headed toward the office of The Lebanon Daily News to talk with reporter John Latimer. I owed him the benefit of an interview, too. Upon entering the building, I extended my hand toward the compassionate newspaper reporter and stopped midway to embrace him. "How can I ever thank you?" I could feel the tears running down my face. "You breathed life into this story and with the support of your editor Paul Baker and the many other wonderful people here at The Lebanon Daily News you made such a difference for Peggy" He gave a light chuckle.

"We simply reported the news, Michelle" I wiped the tears from my face. "You and your team supported the news and I am not quite sure a 1968 murder even qualifies as news. I know that without the compassionate decision of this publication to feature Peggy's story we would not have seen the many wonderful events of the last year. I simply can't thank you enough" The soft-spoken modest man motioned for me to follow him to a nearby conference room. "Michelle the events of 1968 were horrific and our paper devoted a tremendous amount of time, effort and print space to the case. We were here every step along the way. Well, not me personally" He smiled at his attempt at humor. John Latimer, himself, was a child in 1968. "But The Lebanon Daily News covered this story every step along the way" I nodded in agreement.

"You did not have to feature this case 39 years after Peggy was killed, yet you did, and I can't thank you enough" My tears started to flow again.

"Michelle" he waited for me to regain my composure. "We were still reporting news, granted, a human interest aspect of the Reber case, but your research made the difference. You and I discussed this case a lot more than I think you realize before anything was ever published. It became apparent the long-arm of Peggy's murder and the impact it had on the community was so strong it managed to touch you at the time it happened, and we all know you were only 5-years-old in 1968. We now know many people vividly recall the crime and were touched by it because public response is record-breaking, but you took it to the next step and came back to Lebanon decades later and researched Peggy. The core of the story will always be the unsolved murder of Peggy Reber, but you were the new twist to the case and that is what Kevin Snavely said when he wanted me to report on the anniversary of the crime last year. He was right. There really aren't too many 40-year-old unsolved murders that have an unrelated 5-year-old child grow up and study the case in such detail. Michelle I listened to you enough to know you didn't just remember Peggy and read the news reports from the time. It's pretty obvious to anyone that talks to you about this case. The news we reported didn't offer a headline identifying Peggy Reber's killer and we didn't focus on the fact her murder is unsolved; rather we shared with our readers your efforts, your memory and your passion regarding Peggy. How could anyone know it would spark such an emotional chord throughout the community and with so many? One thing is certain, Michelle, you weren't the only resident of Lebanon to remember Peggy's murder, but you are the only one that went out on a limb to pull it from the shadows" I cried a little more.

On the record, I repeated much of what I said on Laura LeBeau's radio show. I was always aware of the speed of radio reporting compared to printed press. Newspapers are at such a disadvantage compared to the rapid delivery of airwaves and internet, yet without the printed press, reporter John Latimer and The Lebanon Daily News on a whole Peggy's case would still be a dusty file.

I walked out the front doors of The Lebanon Daily News and gazed at the Lebanon Municipal Building. I knew it was home to the offices of the district attorney, Detective Michael Dipalo and the courtroom hosting Peggy's grand jury. I threw caution to the wind and decided to enter its doors. After going through standard security checks at the front door of the structure I scanned the building directory to locate the office I wanted to visit. I entered the elevator and pushed the button for the ground floor. I questioned my decision to introduce myself to the detective before offering testimony to the grand jury, but the elevator chimed and I knew I was at the ground floor. I stepped out of the elevator feeling like a fish-out-of-water, but I looked to my right and saw some people gathered behind a desk, so I approached the glass doors to their work place, and as I pulled the door open I saw the sign "District Attorney". My heart started to race and I really started to question my decisions.

"Excuse me, but I am looking for Detective Michael Dipalo"

"Ms Gooden!" a pleasant voice found itself attached to one of the men standing behind the counter. "I am glad you could fit us in today. I heard you on The Radio Laura Show this morning" I smiled and extended my hand, things were moving fast, but I caught the sarcastic tone about my radio appearance earlier in the day. "I am happy you stopped by. I am guessing you got my text message" I had not slowed down enough to look at my text messages throughout the day, so I was unaware the detective had actually invited me to meet him. I showed up on his doorstep on my own accord. We exchanged pleasantries at the reception area of the Lebanon County District Attorney's office and moved toward his office down the hall. I was slapped with a blanket of reality. Never in all my years of researching Peggy's death did I think my efforts would lead me, personally, to the offices of county investigators, the DA or a courtroom on the cusp of testifying before a grand jury investigating Peggy's murder. I knew in my heart any testimony I offered was not a first-hand account regarding the investigation of Peggy Reber's murder. I looked at the sterile hallways as I approached the detective's office and I took a seat in a chair in front of his desk. He had multiple files stacked upon his desk and a corkboard on the wall. He caught my eyes when I spotted a postcard with a weak attempt at humor on his corkboard "I eat cats" was the comedic caption on the picture.

He laughed and told me it was a something he received from a college intern. My nervousness did not allow me to enjoy the questionable humor sported. I certainly wasn't sure about my environment or any man that thought "eating cats" was comical.

However, Detective Dipalo was pleasant-to-a fault and I absorbed his environment. His office didn't boast degrees, awards or a flood of family photos. Detective Dipalo's office was generic and simplistic in nature with one exception. It sported a statue-of-sorts from the Vidocq Society dated 2008. His little trophy came courtesy of Peggy Reber's murder. I reminded myself that Officer Snavely was fired before he had the opportunity to take Peggy's case before the Vidocq Society.

I liked Detective Michael Dipalo, but I had to question many things. Officials could give credit to his new efforts with Peggy's case, but nothing changed the fact local investigators and the local administration failed to give the unsolved murder of this child legitimate effort for decades. I couldn't sing praises for Detective Dipalo single-handedly giving Peggy his investigative efforts. I had to wonder if Kevin Snavely twisted the lid of a jar and Detective Dipalo got credit for opening the jar. We discussed the Vidocq Society's review of Peggy's case. We discussed a lot of aspects of the Reber case. After an hour or so Detective Dipalo took me to a neighboring office and opened a door to the "war room". The room was similar to scenarios one would see on television crime dramas. I stood in the doorway and saw a banker's box on the desk and it hosted Peggy's name, a huge leather binder containing jail logs from 1968 sat in view and various pictures hung on the wall. One particular picture caught my eye and I shook my head in disgust. No, it wasn't a graphic crime scene photo, rather a simple picture of the dress belt used in the assault against Peggy.

"Isn't that amazing"? The detective looked confused. "All the confusion about an orange dress, a green belt, what exactly was she wearing that day and yet that belt isn't like anything ever recorded" He simply nodded. "So Peggy finally earned her own little spot in the court house?"

He closed the door "This is for your benefit Miss Gooden" We continued down the hall to a large conference room where he introduced me to Deputy District Attorney John Ditzler. Mr. Ditzler was a small-framed man in his mid-thirties and he came equipped with a sarcastic tongue and dry wit. I could see where others might find him to be a smart ass, but I almost liked his approach. I was still not comfortable in my surroundings, and the three of us were never going to be friends, but we shared a civil exchange for an hour or so before I excused myself to return to my daughter.

The day before I was scheduled to testify before the grand jury my loved ones and I visited a historical tunnel. We walked the path and marveled at the mild December weather. I knew my child wanted nothing more than to experience a Pennsylvania snow storm. I sheltered my little girl from the details surrounding Peggy's death, but she understood Peggy was killed and her killer was never identified. We left the historical landmark and traveled to Grand View Memorial Park to pay our respects to Peggy Reber.

I approached the young girl's grave and squatted down on my heels to run my fingers across the letters on the child's headstone. It was my first visit to Peggy's grave since she was exhumed. I looked toward the statue of Christ looking over her resting place and I said a prayer. I stood up and took my child's hand "Look Mommy" she reached down to the ground and picked up a small piece of purple fabric laying on Peggy's grave. "Wasn't this Peggy's favorite color"? She handed me the small piece of cloth. I started to smile and said "Why yes it was, sunshine. Peggy's favorite color was indeed purple" I put the small article in my coat pocket and we set out to find a fabulous Pennsylvania Dutch dinner.

Sleep would not come the night before my court appearance. I tossed and turned for hours before finally giving up. I lit a cigarette and stared into space as I replayed so many events over and over in my head. I knew in my heart my testimony had no place of importance in a legitimate investigation surrounding the events of May 25, 1968.

Equally, I was only 6-years-old when Arthur Root JR stood trial for Peggy's murder and I had no connection to that either. I was not a witness to anything, yet I was being called to testify as a witness. I knew enough about court room proceedings to know anything said to me by anyone was considered hearsay in a court of law. I also knew each actual eye witness was required by law to testify truthfully before the grand jury. I had to trust Peggy's family, friends and other witnesses would deliver her truth.

The sun came up and I made a cup of tea, but my nervous stomach was not going to allow me to keep the tea down too long before I had to run to the bathroom. My eyes watered as my body convulsed and I wasn't sure I would be able to keep my date with a jury. I pushed myself to put on my favorite navy blue suit and a light blue sweater. "Great, I have a tear in my stockings and I don't have time to get a new pair. Hell, if I don't get out of here now I will be late" I was way beyond stressed.

"Honey, you need to relax or you are going to make yourself sick again" my dear friend Allecia offered words of support. "I brought you a little something and I want you to put it on before you leave. I want you to know how much we love you and everything is going to be alright. You just need to go in there and tell Peggy's story. I don't blame you for being nervous, but Peggy needs those people to understand what happened and you can tell them" Allecia removed a beautiful butterfly necklace from a small box and placed the jewelry around my neck.

I pulled into the parking lot of the local municipal building when my cell phone started to ring "Miss Gooden we are waiting for you" It was Detective Dipalo. I was running late and I guess they thought there was a possibility I was not going to show. I walked across the parking lot in the early morning light and for the first time ever I was almost afraid of that unidentified monster that killed a young girl so many years ago. I knew I was a prime target for any madman that wanted to silence me as I walked across the open lot.

I entered the court house and emptied my pockets to clear the security at the door. When I removed my cell phone from my pocket I noticed the small piece of purple fabric my daughter retrieved from Peggy's grave. I took the tiny item and placed it in my undergarment and over my heart.

I entered a room filled with coats and ties and the Honorable Judge Brad Charles had me swear to tell the truth, the whole truth and nothing but the truth. The reality of the formalities was taking hold and I started to cry. I cried because I was nervous, I cried for Peggy and I cried because I knew how very important it was that the grand jury truly understands everything about Peggy.

Sitting on the witness stand the court room looked huge. Deputy District Attorney John Ditzler and District Attorney David J. Arnold JR were seated at a long table to the right along with Detective Michael Dipalo and a few other people. The twenty-nine jurors were seated in the back of the court room. Judges are not present for grand jury testimony, so the high-backed chair slightly above my right shoulder remained vacant.

Mr. Ditzler began to question me and I struggled to find my voice between my tears and my nerves. Mr. Ditzler was professional and tactful as he asked me a wide range of questions. Sensing my nervousness he made a sincere attempt to put me at ease. I answered his questions honestly and thoroughly. He questioned me about my memory, my research efforts, interviews I conducted and almost every aspect of my knowledge about Margaret "Peggy" Lynn Reber. He asked me why I thought Peggy's case was unsolved and I took a deep breath before responding to his question.

"Mr.Ditzler it is no secret Peggy's mother entertained a large amount of men in the home she shared with her daughter. I refuse to call her a prostitute because I am not convinced that is the case and she was never charged with such a crime. Mary Reber was the subject of rumor and gossip long before Peggy ever took her last breath. I will not defend many of her choices because I tend to agree with the majority in thinking she should have been at home with her teenage daughter instead of running the roads. I curse the choices she made not just that day, but the year or so before Peggy's death as well. Peggy lived a hard life because her mother exposed her to the wild lifestyle of the 60s. The Reber apartment was a very busy place and police knew it, yet they never made an arrest there until the day Ray Boyer was apprehended for delinquent child support; the day Peggy died. Isn't that odd? The whole town seems to know Mary Alice Reber is a prostitute and Lebanon's finest is in that group, yet they don't arrest her. Prostitution was illegal in 1968. Local law enforcement never hesitated to call Mary Reber the worst of names and all the while claiming they knew she was committing a crime, yet they did not stop her. Could it be they didn't stop the activities in her apartment because they participated in the parties taking place in the Reber home? We know somebody forgot a set of handcuffs because they were taken into evidence when Peggy was killed"

"Are you suggesting a member of law enforcement killed Peggy?"

"No sir I am not, yet we must not forget the crime is unsolved, so we don't really know who killed Peggy Reber, do we? You asked me why I thought Peggy's murder remained unsolved all these years and I am answering your question".

"Well, forgive me, but you made special mention of handcuffs"

"Yes sir I did because there was a set of handcuffs taken into evidence from Peggy's apartment the night she was killed. It's on public record, but it was never reported in the news. I am not a professional investigator, but even I know that matters on some small scale. Given the public's perception of the Reber apartment, the supposed police knowledge of illegal activities taking place there, yet never an arrest…" I allowed my voice to trail off. I sat up straight, cleared my throat and started to say the unthinkable. "Mr. Ditzler all eyes were on the scandalous Mary Alice Reber in 1968. She wasn't going to win any awards for mother-of-the-year, and while the women of this community stoned her in their minds and with their mouths, the men in this community were rolling through her door. It has always fascinated me how everyone could call her a whore and rant about the outrageous number of keys she gave out to the apartment she shared with Peggy, yet her lovers go unidentified with the exception of Arthur Root JR. The news reported multiple times about the keys to the Reber apartment and it always reported six keys. Mary Alice, Peggy, and Peggy's twin Kathryn, were the females that had keys to the Reber apartment. Arthur Root JR – Mary Alice's married lover had a key, Ray Boyer – Peggy's married lover had a key and Kathryn's husband had a key. I always found those news reports so fascinating".

"How so Miss Gooden"?

"Mr. Ditzler common sense would tell anyone the landlord had a key, too. I guess he got overlooked after the murder because he was an officer of the court, yet that doesn't change the fact, does it? Mary Alice allegedly gave out so very many keys to her apartment, yet investigators could only ever confirm six keys? That's pretty sad. Did I really have to grow up and come back here to point out to everyone, including investigators; common sense dictated the lawyer that owned the building had a key to the Reber apartment, too. It seems so. In 1968 investigators still spun controversy and drama about the tremendous amount of keys Mary Alice gave to men, yet they could never identify the men and they didn't identify the landlord either. That's queer. I realize I am looking at things 40 years later, but I don't see any proof of Mary Alice giving out all those keys that supposedly challenged investigative efforts into her daughter's murder. I am seeing documented proof of officers of the court sheltering officers of the court from this crime scene and this crime. I don't know if that's conspiracy, corruption or incompetence, but it is a fact".

"Perhaps investigators did recognize the attorney that owned the apartment building had a key and you simply didn't have access to such information".

"Perhaps they did Mr. Ditzler and perhaps they failed to include him with providing dental impressions, too. Actually we know they did not include him in the group that provided dental impressions. They didn't include Peggy's brother-in-law either and we know he had a key to the apartment also. You asked me why I thought this murder went unsolved for so many years and I am attempting to explain to you the isolated subject of the keys to the apartment. I don't know if it would have solved the crime, but common sense would suggest investigators test all the men they knew to possess a key to the Reber apartment in 1968. We know for a fact they failed to publicly identify and test the lawyer that owned the building and then they failed to test a brother-in-law they clearly knew had a key. Perhaps if investigators focused their efforts on the actual keys they knew about instead of rambling about rumors of Mary Alice giving out so many keys we would not be here today, Mr. Ditzler" My nervousness was rapidly being replaced with confidence and knowledge. I suddenly realized exactly why I was there and I was prepared to meet the challenge.

"Mary Reber was throwing one hell of a party on the third floor of The Maple Leaf Apartment Building and all the locals knew it, but I think they missed the most scandalous party taking place in that same structure. Mary Reber's visitors ranged in age, social status and marital status, but she wasn't the only one entertaining those men. The truly scandalous parties were taking place on the second floor of that building.

Lloyd Hassler was the male version of Mary Alice Reber. It is suggested he enjoyed the company of many of the same gentlemen that frequented the Reber apartment. Investigators didn't identify an attorney with a key to the Reber apartment and they sure as hell were not going to identify the activities of a gay man on the floor below, or his visitors. I am not saying for a minute Lloyd Hassler killed Peggy Reber.

I am simply pointing out some of the activities taking place in that building at that time. There were certain men in this town that could never have their visits with Mary Reber OR Lloyd Hassler known. Much like Mary Reber, Maple Leaf resident Lloyd Hassler had a wide range of visitors, but not one of them wanted to take claim to knowing him publicly either. Sadly, while investigators sheltered the officer of the court that owned the building it appears they might have sheltered other officers of the court with dirtier secrets. There is a distinct possibility Peggy's killer was never arrested because he knew too much about the activities taking place not in Mary Reber's apartment, but in Lloyd Hassler's apartment.

Picture it… Peggy's killer gets arrested and while on trial he tells the scandalous tales of the officers of the court. I don't think the identity of Peggy's killer was ever the challenge, but I do think the investigators battled demons beyond their wildest dreams, and the stability of a community hinged on the truth of Peggy's murder. If Peggy's family testifies truthfully you will know exactly what I am saying. Remember I was not there, but they were and they are responsible for their own testimony. Peggy is no longer here to tell the truth, so her justice is dependent upon others to tell the truth for her.

Some would consider the late Judge G. Thomas Gates the patriarch of Lebanon County, yet beyond the respect bestowed upon him we must recognize he failed to grant a change in venue to the murder trial of Arthur Root JR. If ever there was a case in Lebanon's history that was worthy of a change in venue it was the trial of Peggy Reber's 1968 murder. Seasoned residents know only too well the reputation of Judge G. Thomas Gates, yet it just isn't discussed publicly.

Even today it is almost considered disrespectful in some circles to mention known facts about the man on the bench, while others continue to snicker not only about his life style, but his questionable professionalism. He was a colorful man to say the least. He certainly did not want a fraction of his dirty little secrets mentioned in a court of law.

His legal thumbprint on the trial of 1970 is public record and it kept the details of Peggy's crime, the investigation and court proceedings under his jurisdiction. His decisions are not geared toward an objective legal process for a child's murder or her accused killer. His rulings are highly questionable even today.

The community was outraged by the crime and hungry for truth and justice, but the judge wasn't hosting a game show. He had a legal, moral and ethical responsibility to give the case a fair and objective trial. Judge G. Thomas Gates was far from a stupid man, Mr. Ditzler. Even back in 1968 he knew residents of Lebanon County could not muster the objectivity needed for Peggy's case.

It was almost impossible to find anyone in Lebanon County unfamiliar with the news reporting 14-year-old Peggy's brutal murder. If we agree on nothing else let it be clear Judge G. Thomas Gates did not let go of this case by his own judicial choosing. Why? Why did he insist on keeping this case and its jury in his county, his courtroom and under his control?

He certainly didn't do that in the interest of an untainted judicial process. He didn't do it to guarantee justice for a murder victim either. A conviction was not secured, the trial was not transcribed and that stands as facts within Lebanon County history. Gates is not responsible for a jury's verdict, yet he is responsible for failing to allow this case to be heard by an objective jury in a neighboring community. He is responsible for not surrendering his power to oversee the case and allowing a judge from a different county to preside over the judicial process. Why? Was it ego or was there something else influencing the judge's highly questionable decision? He clearly was not acting as an unbiased officer of the court.

Let me guess….it's just one more little human error on the part of an officer of the court attributing to Peggy's lost justice. There seems to be a lot of that with Peggy's murder past and present.

I don't think anyone would begrudge the authorities forgiveness for making a few human errors, but I do think it is questionable that so many men in power made so many errors with this one case. The questionable acts are not limited to officers responding to a horrific crime scene and the accidental mishandling of evidence, or the oversight of a sleazy lawyer with a key to the apartment. The questionable acts of investigators, the DA and the judge run a little bit deeper.

The judge's court ordered decisions are questionable.

The investigative efforts were challenged, faulty and questionable as well.

The attorney/landlord was rumored to have peepholes throughout the apartment building to watch his female tenants, yet again that wasn't something the legal community wanted to discuss publicly, but perhaps Root's jury deserved to know that at the time. We know the building was destroyed before a jury could ever see it with their own eyes.

"What are you saying?"

"I am saying if Peggy Reber's killer could "out" the extra-curricular and perverted activities of an officer of the court, to include a judge, or especially the judge, there was no way in hell he would ever be put on trial. Peggy Reber's killer wasn't a stranger to The Maple Leaf Apartment Building and maybe he knew a little too much about somebody in power"

"Isn't that speculation on your part Miss Gooden?" the young attorney appeared to be irritated by my suggestion that Peggy's killer escaped being charged with her murder because he could expose the scandalous activities of Lebanon's elite.

226

"Isn't everything speculation with a 40-year-old unsolved murder, Mr. Ditzler. Last time I checked Lebanon's investigative body was baffled by this case and the identity of this child's killer. The local government you represent hasn't done too well with this case for over 40 years. Much like the community you are paid to serve I am tired of excuses. I want a child's killer identified and removed from society. Peggy's killer does not deserve the rights of American citizens. He should not have the freedom of watching his dogs play in his yard, his team play for the Super Bowl or his grandchildren strive to be quality citizens. Nobody cares about any secrets he might expose about the police, lawyers or judges in this town. He wouldn't be saying anything half of us don't already know"

"Ms Gooden you seem to think Peggy Reber's killer is still alive"

"Gee, Mr. Ditzler do you know otherwise?" The cocky young lawyer almost stopped in his tracks. I held firm. Peggy Reber's murder remains unsolved, so the feisty and youthful officer of the court was on weak ground.

My turn to ask a question or two "So, Mr. Ditzler does your knowledge of Peggy's murder suggest you know her killer is dead? Do you have that much insight? Are you aware of facts the community and courts do not know regarding this child's brutal killing? Are you prepared to tell the world the identity of Peggy Reber's killer? If you aren't...." I waited. "I suggest you entertain the fact her killer could be YOUR next door neighbor, yet we know that's unlikely....No you, the DA and a judge or two can see inside Peggy's file and live accordingly. You can raise your children at a distance. What about average people in Lebanon, Pennsylvania? They do not have the benefit of seeing the list of suspects for this child's unsolved murder. They don't want to live next door to a suspected child killer either. You and I both know there were a lot of suspects in this case, but Art Root Jr was the only name ever offered publicly"

"Yes Ms Gooden after a six-month investigation he was charged with the crime"

"Yes, Mr. Ditzler he was indeed and a jury came back with a verdict in less than two hours. Art Root Jr was not convicted of killing Peggy Reber. If we are going to respect the judicial system then we must respect that verdict. We might also want to respect the fact his dental impressions did not match the bite Peggy endured, he admitted to seeing Peggy alive in her home at 6 PM that afternoon and several others will stand up today and tell you Peggy was still alive as late as 8 PM. Actually, two people testified at his trial to that fact. That timeline matters greatly, Mr. Ditzler. Those are two very important hours in the life and death of Peggy Reber. Prosecutors insisted Root killed Peggy at 6 PM on that fateful day and a jury didn't believe them. I don't believe them either"

"Are you certain the jury didn't make a mistake, Ms Gooden?"

"Juries are made up of people and people make mistakes, but don't forget prosecutors are human, too. Investigators, attorneys and judges make mistakes all the time. It's no secret somebody made a mistake because the case is unsolved. I guess we can sit here today and blame a jury in 1970, but that's a little extreme considering all the things we know today. I also think it's highly hypocritical of the judicial process"

"Well Ms Gooden that's why we are here today. We want to give this case every benefit of the court and every opportunity at justice"

I ran out of the house in such a rush I did not slow down long enough to grab my purse. I started to laugh at myself when Detective Michael Dipalo approached me. "May I buy you lunch?" I looked beyond the generous detective and smiled at the young college intern in his company. We drove through town in the government vehicle as the radio blared reports about Lebanon native Michelle Gooden testifying before an investigative grand jury researching the murder of Peggy Reber. "Where would you like to eat Miss Gooden? Do you have any preferences"? It mattered not to me. It was a break from the stress of sitting in a court room. The detective drove to a nearby restaurant and I had to smile. We took our seats and I ordered a burger while trying to engage in light conversation.

"Did I just testify to the likelihood that good old Gates didn't want to get caught with his pants down?" Detective Dipalo smiled "I was waiting for the walls of the courtroom to come crashing in around us, but yes you did"

We chatted, ate and got up from the booth when a waitress approached me with open arms "You really showed them, didn't you? You stood up against them and I waited on you the day before you did it. I am so proud to know you" I embraced the woman and I remembered her, too, but I knew she didn't recognize the company I was keeping. We returned to the vehicle and Detective Dipalo made a weak comment about the waitress that approached me.

"I don't think you or the administration realizes just how much Peggy Reber's justice matters to average people" I could see Detective Dipalo was surprised by the response of the waitress, but he was a cool pickle and moved forward.

We returned to the court house and I was instructed to wait in the law library on the third floor while another witness gave testimony. I paced the library floor and looked out the window. I laughed and shared with the college intern in my company how I was probably crazy, but I had a silly piece of purple fabric tucked under my shirt. The youthful college intern looked at me and said "You're too hard on yourself" I smiled at her and turned my attention back toward the window. I might have been too hard on myself, yet little did the youthful spirit in my company realize, but Peggy Reber had touched her, too.

I visited the restroom during my wait and I gave into a hearty laugh when I saw a coin-operated machine offering feminine hygiene products for a mere ten cents. Somehow I just knew the price had not changed since Peggy's first case in Lebanon's courts in 1970. I returned to the library and my place by the window. I never knew Peggy, yet I could feel her presence. I knew she was aware of her last opportunity for her truth to be told. I also knew Peggy understood I couldn't tell her truth. Peggy's truth and justice hinged on the testimony of her family, friends, witnesses and members of law enforcement. Her lost justice still rested on the shoulders of the same people from 1968. Peggy needed each and every person that failed her in 1968 to right-the-wrong over 40 years later. She didn't get a second chance to change the events of May 25, 1968, yet the voices that could tell her truth were granted a second chance to be heard in a court room on her behalf. The fourteen-year girl that had five holes in her heart during her autopsy forty years earlier needed a select few to step out of their comfort zone and tell her truth. I could sense Peggy knew I did everything I could for her and the rest was up to a few others.

■■■

The testifying witness exited the court room in less than an hour and I was called back to the witness stand. I couldn't believe it. I knew exactly who I was watching exit the court room and I stood floored that he managed to testify in under an hour.

Former Detective Clifford Roland was present at the crime scene, the autopsy, the extensive man hunt for Peggy's killer and Root's trial. How did he manage to testify about so much in under an hour? Granted he was tickling ninety-years-of-age, but he was either a qualified witness, or he was not. I just couldn't see any one with such a depth of information testifying within an hour, while I was on the stand for several hours.

I embraced my belief in the legal process and I trusted the grand jurors to realize he had so much more to offer   than an hour of testimony would allow. I was reminded of the fact Peggy's twin testified a mere 90 minutes. How on earth did she fit her wealth of knowledge about Peggy into 90 minutes of testimony? She was her identical twin, she lived next door to Peggy until the day before the crime, she was married to an individual on the list of suspects and she managed to give a thorough a detailed testimony in only 90 minutes. Was that even possible?

Given my nervousness and the goal of Peggy's justice I didn't have the time or energy to ponder what was taking place, but I was losing faith in the motives of the prosecutors.

I resumed my seat on the witness stand and I realized District Attorney David J. Arnold JR was not present in the court room. Mr. Ditzler wanted to address the issues regarding the district attorney's possible conflict of interest with Peggy's case. I explained the details as I understood them to him, and the jurors, to the best of my ability.

"So Miss Gooden you believe David Arnold had a marital dispute with his former wife and you further believe police officers were called to his home, but what does that have to do with this case?"

"Given the fact we do not know who killed Peggy Reber and equally noting her brother-in-law was listed as a suspect I think it matters greatly. The district attorney's wife did not spend Thanksgiving with him on November 25, 1999 and one should also note that was his birthday as well. She was having dinner with the Boyer family" Mr. Ditzler was not surprised by my statement, yet he challenged me, while he completely disregarded a violent disturbance at the Arnold home that day. The police report detailed the events in question.

"Miss Gooden how do you know for a fact Mrs. Arnold was with the Boyer's on Thanksgiving day in 1999?"

"Because I talked to the hostess of the dinner party and she confirmed Mrs. Arnold's presence in her home. I have an email from the hostess of the dinner party and it details not only the fact that Mrs. Arnold was present for the festivities at the Boyer home, but she went home to a hostile David Arnold JR"

"Miss Gooden I am looking at the documents you provided my office and I don't see any such email here" the feisty attorney was not pleased.

"Mr. Ditzler I apologize if you did not receive a copy of that email, and I will gladly provide you a copy before I return to North Carolina" The young lawyer and I locked eyes and exchanged a civil nod of our heads.

"So is one to understand that any defense attorney representing this case would call such events into question. Is that what you're trying to say Ms Gooden?" I didn't hesitate with a response 'Wouldn't you, Mr. Ditzler? If you were the defense attorney for any suspect ever charged in this case wouldn't you question the district attorney's personal involvement attached to the case? If Mr. Arnold ever attempted to prosecute a member of the Boyer family a good defense attorney would accuse him of grinding a personal ax in a court of law. On the other hand, if Mr. Arnold attempts to prosecute anyone else for this crime an equally sharp defense attorney could point all fingers at Boyer and accuse the district attorney of sheltering a family friend. I have nothing personal against the district attorney, but this is one case he can never prosecute and the proof is right there in your hands" The court took a brief recess.

I entered the law library to find District Attorney David J. Arnold JR kicked back in a chair with his feet propped up on a table. His demeanor was cocky, yet I uttered an apology just the same because I was sincerely sorry I had to reveal his compromised conduct from years prior. Divorce is not easy for anyone, yet the entanglements of a young district attorney and his former wife could not be allowed to compromise a murdered child's justice. Peggy's justice was the priority far more than the secrets of lawyers from yesterday or today and David J. Arnold Jr was no exception.

The young man was arrogant when I spoke to him. I was not about to be intimidated by any individual ever charged with domestic harassment no matter the circumstances. I really had to wonder how seriously he took cases of domestic violence considering his own history. No, he was not convicted of the charge, but in a town where a child's killer walked free that really wasn't surprising.

When I returned to the witness stand after the brief recess the District Attorney was seated at the prosecutors table once again.

By the time my testimony ended, the December sun was starting to set on Monday December 12, 2008. I spent an entire day on the witness stand testifying about a crime and crime victim I never knew first-hand. I never imagined my childhood questions would lead me to the threshold of a grand jury, but I knew one thing for certain and that was Peggy Reber didn't want to be forgotten, and she wasn't.

The following morning my daughter and I woke up to the most beautiful sight. It was snowing in central Pennsylvania. Lady Justice was eluding us, but Mother Nature was batting for the home team. We entered the court house so I could provide the prosecuting office with copies of any documents I missed. Detective Dipalo joked with my child and his softer side was in full display. "Here you can make copies of this" I handed the investigator a few sheets of paper.

"Copies? Miss Gooden I am not even sure you should be in ownership of such documents" I said nothing. The detective and I both knew I didn't obtain the documents illegally. He made copies and returned my original documents to me. He handed my daughter a cloth uniform badge for Lebanon County Detectives as a souvenir of her time in Pennsylvania and walked us toward the door. We encountered Deputy District Attorney John Ditzler on our way out and he smiled and joked with us as well. There was a dart board on the wall and I made a few playful comments. I didn't walk out of the court house liking those men or hating those men, instead I accepted the fact we all had a job to do. In an ideal world we would all be striving to give Peggy justice, but at a minimum I knew I gave Peggy truth as I knew it.

Evening approached and my daughter and I gathered with family and friends to celebrate the beautiful snow storm. She squealed with delight as she hopped on the back of a 4-wheeler to tackle snow-covered hills. We enjoyed a winter wonderland with the very best people. "Shelly you did the right thing" I directed my attention toward a man I loved my entire life. "It's up to the jury now, but Peggy couldn't ask any more of you. You did everything you could and then some. I was an adult back then and who would have thought you would be the one to help give Peggy another day in court? You were just a kid"

I picked up a handful of snow and started to pack it within my hands. "Yeah, well back then I didn't know how to make a snowball either, but I do now, so look out" I broke the serious mood and enjoyed the pleasure of the snow and the company of my loved ones.

■■

Six months later my mail carrier knocked on my front door with a certified package "Girl it ain't never good when I need you to sign for something" My delightfully southern mail delivery person was holding a huge envelope in her hand. I scribbled my signature on the return receipt and ripped open the package.

I had a copy of the grand jury report and a letter from the judge telling me I could defend myself. I read it again just in case I misunderstood something. The grand jury viewed me in a negative light and under Pennsylvania statutes I was being given the opportunity to provide a formal response. I stood stunned. I tried to laugh. I just kept reading the same words over and over. The grand jury was given the task of investigating Peggy Reber's murder and I certainly did not kill Peggy, but I had to defend myself. They did not hand down an indictment for the murder of Peggy Reber, but they didn't hesitate to put me on trial.

After reading the first few pages of the grand jury report I wanted to scream. I called Detective Michael Dipalo "You can't be serious" I was at a loss.

"Michelle this is the decision of the grand jury. You wanted a grand jury and you petitioned for a grand jury" I fought the urge to pound my phone against my desk.

"Yeah Mike the grand jury prepared this report and they used legal words like scintilla when they did it. Who REALLY prepared the report? I realize the jurors were given a secretary to assist them, but this document appears to reach beyond the scope of assistance. Which one of you composed this nonsense? Twenty-nine average residents did not write this report. The grand jury claims to know Peggy Reber was NOT pregnant when she was killed even though she was NOT tested in 1968 and her exhumation did NOT allow any testing in 2008. I stand accused of implicating a man, yet the report says I never identified a man. Gee, how did I do that? The report states Detective Randy Edgar went to Oklahoma to interview Art Root JR in 2000, yet we know he did NOT go to Oklahoma in 2000, or ever for that matter" I was on a roll.

"That's a typo" he was dead in his response.

"A typo? It is not factual information" I was livid. "Is that how you handled the grand jury? Were they fed a bunch of information that wasn't factual? I see in the report where former District Attorney Deirdre Eshleman and you were swapping emails at my expense"

He interrupted my ramblings. "Michelle I hope you understand the only reason Deirdre is involved is because you don't trust Dave Arnold and she was his political opponent, so her endorsement of me should put to rest any questions you have about me and my professional skills regarding this investigation" I listened to the detective and I had to chuckle because in the former DA's email she boasts Detective Dipalo was not political in any way, yet he was seeking a recommendation from Arnold's political opponent. It was almost a contradiction.

I recalled she was the district attorney that paid to fly detective Randy Edgar to Arizona to interview Root in 2001, NOT Oklahoma the way the grand jury report read. The investigation under her administration didn't manage to interview Peggy's family in Lebanon or locate physical evidence in a police storage area, but it picked up the bill for plane tickets to interview a man already judged by a jury. They spent money in hopes he would confess, while they didn't bother to actually investigate the case. She was hardly a good job reference for any detective working the Reber case. She didn't get it right during her own administration, so who in the hell was she to utter an opinion after the fact? Did her endorsement of Dipalo make Arnold feel better, or Dipalo? It was self-serving for one or the other, and it didn't do a thing for Peggy's justice.

The Grand Jury expresses knowledge that I was writing a book about the case which I claimed to be factual. They mentioned in their report I did not provide Detective Dipalo a copy of my manuscript upon his request. My manuscript was not a key to Detective Dipalo solving the crime. My manuscript didn't even deserve mention in a grand jury report.

"Detective Dipalo, I see where the jury mentions my subpoena required me to provide them things and I failed to do so. Let me guess detective....you and the prosecuting office failed to tell the grand jury none of you bothered to formally serve me with a legally binding subpoena. Oh, I am sure you provided the jurors a copy of the subpoena you sent to me, and the jury probably trusted you, but they were fooled, weren't they? The grand jury was deceived by none other than the officers of the court. Yeah, no corruption or conflicts here folks"

Two employees of a local public restroom testified in 1970 to seeing Peggy alive at 8:00 PM that same day. One of those witnesses is alive, well and living blocks from the Lebanon Municipal Building. She thought for sure detectives would contact her to testify before the grand jury in 2008, but they failed to even talk to her. A bona fide eye witness to the timeline of Peggy's last few hours was not included in this "thorough" investigation of Peggy's murder, but prosecutors didn't hesitate to put various other people on the witness stand with no connection to Peggy or the crime whatsoever. What was really being investigated? Furthermore, the current detectives still couldn't manage to get out from behind a desk and talk to a confirmed witness from 1968. History continues to repeat itself.

Peggy's girlfriend, Ruth, was with her until 8:15 PM the night of her murder and she was excluded from grand jury testimony. My questions about her absence met a response of "What was she going to tell Michelle when Peggy was last seen alive"? I couldn't believe my ears. Yes, that would be exactly what she would tell and perhaps Peggy's mindset and concerns that fateful night. Most investigators and investigative grand juries want to hear from all eyewitnesses known to be with a murder victim the last twenty-four hours of the victims life, but that isn't the case with Peggy Reber.

Years later I talked to that woman and she expressed a total dislike for Detective Dipalo. "Michelle that guy really pissed me off. I told him where Peggy and I walked together that night and what time my mom picked me up. We were a few blocks from Peggy's house. He kept trying to tell me I was confused and it was the weekend before. I have a memory like an elephant and you just don't forget the details of seeing your friend hours before she was killed. I will never forget anything about that day. Who in the hell was he to tell me it was the weekend before? What does he know? He wasn't there. I know where I was that night. I told him what she was wearing, too, and it wasn't that orange dress everybody talks about. She had this really cute little outfit on and I remember complimenting it. She was a really pretty girl. That detective didn't want to hear anything I had to say" I simply shook my head in amazement.

Whether the detective liked her or not the jury deserved to hear from Peggy's girlfriend to form their own opinion of her recollection. No, this first-hand witness was not presented to the grand jury. Instead, radio host Laura LeBeau received a hand-delivered subpoena.

Considering Laura was only a year old in 1968 and living in Michigan at the time of Peggy's death she was hardly worthy of being considered a witness to the crime they were assigned to investigate. However, Laura spent the same amount of time on the witness stand as Peggy's identical twin. One really had to wonder what the prosecutors and / or the grand jury were truly investigating. They mention in their report they did not set out to investigate Gooden, yet it is obvious that's exactly what they did. The fact remains I did not kill Peggy Reber and they were wasting time, resources and man hours attacking my character instead of focusing on the details of a child's murder. The jury was being entertained with various witness testimony dedicated to little more than character assassination while actual eye witnesses of Peggy's last few hours never even made it into the court room.

A 10-year-old child came forward for the first time after forty years of silence and told all of them what she saw that day, yet the investigative body, to include the grand jurors, refused to really listen to what she was saying. Prosecutors were so busy throwing stones at every damn thing Kevin Snavely ever did they overshadowed the witness testimony. Peggy's 10-year-old neighbor saw Peggy open the door that fateful night.

Clearly there is reasonable doubt about the claims of Art Root JR being the last person to see Peggy alive at 6:00 PM on that fateful day. God forbid! That would suggest former District Attorney George C. Christianson was wrong in the case he presented against Root in 1970. We're right back to the officers of the court.

The case Christianson presented against Root did not render a conviction, but for some unknown reason investigators past and present refuse to reach out beyond the timeline Christianson presented even with eye witness testimony. Not one, not two, but three women will attest Peggy was alive after 6:00 PM on May 25, 1968, two were never called to testify before the grand jury and the third got silenced as prosecutors staged an attack on the credibility of Kevin Snavely. If this does not summarize the twisted priorities of Lebanon prosecutors nothing ever will.

The jury considers me to be a corrupt source of information, while the prosecuting office failed to provide them with an honest, thorough and ethical representation of facts.
The jury reports "Gooden went so far as to influence witnesses and the stories that they told"

The nerve of the grand jury to dump the integrity of others on my lap! I am not responsible for the testimony, recollection or first-hand knowledge of anyone beyond myself.

I am credited with being a primary source of information like it was a negative thing. I did step up publicly on behalf of Peggy's justice, I did give media interviews, I did set up a My Space page in Peggy's honor, and I made every effort to educate the public on the aged unsolved murder of a child. I encouraged the general public not to accept me as their source of information, but to make the effort to research the public records on their own.

The case was not used to generate controversy as the grand jury states because the case itself has been controversial since Peggy took her dying breath in 1968. No one has to generate controversy about the Reber case because it continues to breed controversy even four decades later.

"Given the passage of more than 40 years since the murder and the pervasive taint associated with the investigation, we firmly believe that only a detailed and corroborated confession and/or the existence of compelling forensic evidence could lead to a final resolution of the case". So, not only did this grand jury not identify a suspect worthy of an indictment, but it projected its opinions onto further efforts of justice for the slain child. Unbelievable!

The report tells us "experts believed the body of Peggy Reber would be well preserved even after 40 years provided it was not exposed to water". Any resident born in Lebanon County before 1965 would have some recollection of the horrific flooding of 1972. Experts were probably right, but residents of Lebanon knew only too well about Hurricane Agnes in 1972. I just couldn't imagine over two dozen residents of Lebanon County composing that statement in a grand jury report.

To see the jury mention the investigative man hours devoted to the investigation is questionable to say the least. Man hours? Twenty-nine residents of Lebanon were selected to pass judgment on a 40-year-old unsolved murder of a child, and they were concerned about man hours? Is that really what investigative grand juries think about? Or report about? One can only hope these jurors realize they were called into order to investigate an aged and unsolved murdered of a child and their concerns were to be directed toward justice, not the prosecuting office's operating budget. Again, it really makes one wonder who exactly authored the investigative grand jury report? Obviously it was someone concerned with a government budget.

An unidentified witness appeared before the court to attest to her departure from the Justice for Peggy movement and my alleged obsession with the case because *"it was getting too vigilante for me"* this testimony is not directed toward investigating Peggy's murder. It has nothing to do with solving the crime at all. The subpoena of this witness and the testimony mentioned is geared toward little more than assassinating my character, yet my character did not kill a defenseless child.

The list of witnesses subpoenaed to testify before the grand jury is sheltered under the law, but Lebanon, Pennsylvania is a small town. Witnesses with no knowledge or connection to Peggy's crime, yet identified in the lawsuit filed by terminated Officer Kevin Snavely, testified before Peggy's investigative grand jury. Why? Surely the elected officials named in the lawsuit weren't utilizing Peggy's jury to question potential witnesses in the pending lawsuit against them? One thing is certain and that is the witness pool was not dedicated toward the effort of investigating Peggy's murder.

The grand jury report repeatedly accused me of implicating Richard Boyer, yet the report states I did not publicly identify a suspect. The jury accused me of speaking out of both sides of my mouth, yet that's what they were doing in their report. I simply could not implicate any individual I did not identify. I simply could not implicate an individual as a suspect that was already a suspect in 1968. Further in the report the grand jury says "The lawsuit filed by Snavely publicly identified, for the first time, Richard Boyer as the "suspect" in the Reber murder"

The grand jury verified Richard Boyer was the first person named on a suspect list in 1968.

The jury confirmed after forty years the suspect at the top of the list finally provided dental impressions for a child's unsolved murder. It took forty years. I couldn't even take the sentence seriously that said he was excluded as having inflicted the bite to Peggy's breast. I was still fixated on the fact investigators skipped over a name at the top of a list of suspects, an individual that had a key to the apartment and it only took forty years, and a public outcry for investigators to obtain a dental comparison. What in the hell were investigators doing all those years?

On page twelve of the grand jury report it states "Bite impressions were secured from Richard Boyer in 2008. Richard Boyer was excluded as having inflicted the bite to Reber's breast" Could that be due to all the dental work he had within the months prior to giving his impressions? Could it be the fact no one has the same dental impression after forty long years? Or could it be because in the tiniest of print in a footnote at the bottom of page eight of the grand jury report it says "It is not possible to definitively match the bite mark with dental impressions given the limitations associated with photographic comparison" Per the grand jury report no one is ever going to match, so therefore the only thing to do is exclude Richard Boyer and anyone else submitting dental impressions.

Investigators overlooked Richard Boyer in 1968 for whatever reason and forty years later investigators took his impressions knowing there wasn't a possibility of a match. That sums up the investigative effort surrounding Peggy Reber's murder.

"With the exception of Snavely, Gooden was harshly critical of each and every investigator, past or present, who played any role in the Reber investigation" A grand jury investigating the brutal murder of a child had more important things to consider than public approval of investigators, but I don't mind telling anybody I am disgusted by the mockery investigators made of this little girl's murder investigation. I'm still amazed it took investigators forty long years and my big mouth to test a man with a key and on the top of the list of suspects. Yes! I AM critical of investigators. The grand jury is correct.

The Grand Jury mentions how some of the original investigators and former DA George C. Christianson theorized more than one person was involved in Peggy's murder. Root's mystery accomplice may have inflicted the bite on her breast according to information provided the grand jury.

There was only one man put on trial for the murder of Peggy Reber and that was Art Root JR. His dental impressions did not match the bite mark Peggy endured. He was acquitted by a jury in February 1970. Prosecutors did not identify or charge anyone else for the crime against Peggy.

Now 40 years later, original investigators and the former district attorney theorize it was Root's mystery accomplice that inflicted the bite mark on her breast. If they had any knowledge of an accomplice why didn't they charge him?

If they had any suspicions of an accomplice why didn't former DA George C. Christianson have Root's trial transcribed to preserve the expert testimony while pursuing that accomplice? After Root's trial Lebanon officials slammed the book on Peggy's justice. There was no preservation of court testimony, no further investigation of the brutal murder and no other arrests.

It's pretty simple for people of average intelligence. If there is an accomplice you charge him. If you do not know his identity or lack sufficient evidence to make an arrest you transcribe the trial and work until you put a child killer behind bars. You don't just lose a case, close the books and allow a murderer or his imaginary accomplice to walk free. It all starts to smell bad after awhile. It's equally upsetting to find Christianson and former investigators refuse to let go of their theory regarding Root's guilt. A jury decided they were wrong. Perhaps if they respected the original jury's decision that they were in error and continued to investigate the child's murder, instead of being so egotistical and insisting they were right and the jury was wrong, they could have correctly identified and convicted Peggy's killer generations ago.

The grand jury report reads "Given the intense public focus on Richard Boyer, we subpoenaed him to testify". That is a ridiculous statement! The jury was convened to investigate a child's unsolved murder and an individual at the top of the list of suspects earned a subpoena with or without "intense public focus". Richard Boyer was a member of Peggy's immediate family when she was killed, he was a tenant of a neighboring apartment and he saw her within the last 24-hours of her life. Of course he was worthy of a subpoena. It almost sounded sympathetic on the part of the grand jury "Given the intense public focus..." Did they not understand what they were assigned to do? Public focus did not have anything to do with questioning witnesses and suspects named in the police file.

However, Richard Boyer did not testify at Root's trial in 1970 either and he was just as much a neighbor, a relative, a witness, and a male with a key back then. Public records show he was subpoenaed and he received $17.52 for three days time and thirty-six miles of travel. He never testified.

Richard Boyer and his wife testified before the grand jury to being harassed since the investigation was reopened in 2006. They told of anonymous phone calls and mailings accusing Boyer of the murder. Richard presented various cards he received in the mail. Two of the envelopes hosted a North Carolina postmark and I admitted to the jury I sent the two items, but the jury does not tell my entire testimony. Richard Boyer was Peggy's brother-in-law, a member of her family, and I showed his intimate relation to her the same respect I did her Daddy and sent him a Christmas card in 2007. There was nothing anonymous about it because I signed my name. I also included him on the list of individuals on the mailing list for Peggy's memorial service, a list of seventy-five other individuals as well. It was a respectful gesture. He may be remarried with a new family, yet he is still the father of Peggy's niece and his teenage sister-in-law was savagely murdered when he was married to her twin. My mail was sent to a man approaching 60-years-of-age that experienced the horrific death of a teenage family member in his younger years.

I found it beyond queer that he held on to a Christmas card I sent two years prior. I don't know if it is reasonable, flattering or just downright creepy. I had nothing to do with any other mail, calls or harassment the couple mentioned.

Per the report Boyer's third wife, Linda, testified to being harassed, yet Boyer's harassment is not the focus and purpose of the grand jury. The prosecution is almost tickling the role of defense because they aren't presenting the horror Peggy endured, rather they want the grand jury to understand the hardships endured by the Boyers.

However, the Boyers are NOT the victims in this case. Peggy Reber is the victim and the jury was supposed to be investigating her 1968 murder.

The Boyers testified Officer Snavely frequently parked near their home and even followed them on occasion. The grand jury does not bother to mention that Officer Snavely was still a Patrol Officer for the city of Lebanon at the time. Perhaps the Boyers are exempt from being monitored by city police officers for traffic violations. Perhaps Lebanon City Police Officers need to be informed they are not permitted to park anywhere near the Boyers residence. (It's a good thing the Boyers don't live on Walnut Street in Lebanon because city police officers routinely park there to enforce city speed limits and issue traffic citations)

Mrs. Linda Boyer had much deeper insight to offer the grand jury than complaints about a patrol officer in her neighborhood or the possibility of receiving an unwanted traffic citation.

Mrs. Linda. Boyer is not exactly ignorant of events in 1968. She gave birth to Richard's child seven weeks before he married Peggy's pregnant twin in February of 1968. Peggy's twin was 6-months pregnant with Richard Boyer's child at the time she exchanged vows with him. It was Richard's second marriage and Kathryn's first. Mrs. Linda Boyer shared her baby's father, and her man, with the murdered victim's sister. He did not marry her until several years and a few children later.

••

The minimal word-for-word testimony of Kathryn Reber included in the grand jury report is devoted exclusively to discrediting me, Michelle Gooden. The grand jury report shares a dialogue between the prosecutor and Kathryn Reber that doesn't even include poor Peggy's name being mentioned. Peggy's injustice waited many, many years for an investigative grand jury, yet even during the testimony of her identical twin she took a backseat.

The Grand Jury report quotes Kathryn Reber telling how I offered to send her money for envelopes and postage to stage her own mail campaign and to hide efforts coming from North Carolina. I stood up publicly and alone in May 2007 on behalf of Peggy's justice. I didn't hide behind Kathryn Reber, or anyone else. I did countless interviews, set up a tip line at my expense, an email account and designed a My Space page in honor of Peggy. I certainly did not shy away from identifying myself or the fact my efforts were stemming from North Carolina.

I talked to and briefly met Kathryn during one of my first trips home to research Peggy's files in 2001. I did not talk to Kathryn Reber again until she and I were at Grand View Memorial Park the day of Peggy's memorial service on January 25, 2008. She did not assist with any of the public efforts associated with generating attention to her sister's injustice. She did not assist with the distribution of the petition requesting the District Attorney convene a grand jury. She did not participate in the planning of Peggy's January 25 memorial service. In fact, it was only after Ray Boyer repeatedly assured her he would offer her personal protection that she even agreed to attend her sister's memorial service. The Lebanon Daily News published a letter authored by Kathryn admitting as much a few weeks following Peggy's memorial service.

I did encourage Kathryn, her family, friends and supporters to call the District Attorney, chief of police and mayor daily. I repeatedly asked many people to write letters to the local newspaper and get involved. I did not invent that concept. The Grand Jury report details how Peggy's dad was the only layman to enter their office on a weekly basis for years seeking information about his daughter's murder. Herman Reber believed the squeaky wheel would get oil. I followed his lead and encouraged others to do so as well.

The Grand Jury went on to dismiss much of Kathryn's testimony, beyond her assault on my character. They still gave her original statement to police credibility as part of a corroborated alibi for Richard Boyer in 1968. It was again an example of them speaking out of both sides of their mouth. "Boyer's then-wife, Kathryn, and mother both confirmed Boyer's alibi in their statements to police in 1968" The Grand Jury is referring to Richard's mother and his 14-year-old suicidal, abused and vulnerable teen bride that just learned her identical twin was murdered. Her suicide attempt alone should render her 1968 statement questionable and unworthy of being part of anyone's alibi, yet it stands until this day.

The grand jury report offers portions of Kevin Snavely's investigative report where a much older Kathryn told him she was "coached" by Richard Boyer and his mother to tell investigators a particular story in 1968. She told Snavely how she witnessed Boyer's bloody clothing on the washing machine and Boyer's mother burned and/or washed it. After Kevin Snavely was fired and Kathryn Reber appeared before the Grand Jury she changed her testimony, yet she danced between the aisles of being "coached" and receiving "input" when giving her statement to police in 1968. One really has to wonder what the difference is between the two.

Did Kathryn lie to Officer Snavely? Everything indicates Officer Snavely trusted the statement Kathryn Reber provided him. Her recollection had considerable impact on his efforts to piece together details of May 25, 1968 in an attempt to give her sister justice. Did Kathryn contaminate the detective's investigation of her sister's murder by spinning a wild tale about her ex-husband or did she lie to the grand jury?

Kathryn had a moral and legal responsibility to give Peggy the truth during her grand jury testimony. If she lied to Detective Snavely because she was a bitter and jilted wife she owed Peggy, Snavely and the grand jury that truth. She needed to admit she lied. If her statement to Snavely was true she owed Peggy's justice and the grand jury that testimony as well.

The grand jury report states Kathryn never implicated Richard Boyer in her sister's murder until Michelle Gooden became involved in the case.

Kathryn spoke with a Lebanon news reporter in 1973 and told him all about her suspicions regarding her husband's involvement in Peggy's murder. I was 10-years-old in 1973 and had never met Kathryn Reber. That particular reporter read the grand jury report and called me."Michelle she lied on you. She's trying to tell everybody you told her Richard Boyer was a suspect, but she told me the exact same thing she told Kevin Snavely and that was back in 1973 " The veteran news man offered to publicly share his knowledge and documented proof of his conversation with her from thirty-five years prior. I declined the offer.

Kathryn's known her share of hardships, yet she knows the joy of her children and grandchildren wrapping their arms around her neck. Sadly, her 14-year-old sister had something else wrapped around her neck. Peggy never had the pleasure of having children or grandchildren, but she still deserves truth.

The grand jury wasn't exactly objective regarding Officer Snavely. They admit knowledge of his firing, his lawsuit against city officials and the district attorney. They make it a point to mention the fired cop was the only witness that invoked his Fifth Amendment rights while appearing before them. They thought it necessary to point out the terminated police officer would not assist Detective Dipalo with his investigation of the Reber case. I don't know too many people that get fired, publicly humiliated and then assist their replacements. In fact, it appears to be an absolutely outrageous request on the part of Detective Dipalo and unworthy of any mention in a grand jury report.

The grand jury faults Snavely for an affidavit he prepared mentioning an injury sustained by Richard Boyer where blood was dripping from his hand. Oddly, the grand jury does not bother to mention the altercation was between Richard and Ray Boyer the night before Peggy's death. Kevin Snavely documented an argument involving Peggy within the 24-hours before her violent death and the grand jury attempts to suggest he was impartial in providing such facts. Peggy's killer was filled with rage and any dispute surrounding her in the hours leading up to her death is highly relevant. Sadly, the jury seems more concerned with attacking the credibility and motives of Officer Snavely than studying what was going on around Peggy in the last hours of her life.

Again the grand jury speaks out of both sides of its mouth regarding Peggy's boyfriend Ray Boyer. The report states the grand jury learned Ray Boyer reached his conclusion about his brother's involvement in Peggy's murder only after speaking with me. The very next sentence of the report says Ray Boyer claimed that he always knew his brother had committed the murder.

Ray Boyer testified his brother was violent toward women and otherwise ornery and ruthless. The very next sentence the grand jury says "Interestingly, we learned from other witnesses that Ray Boyer was frequently in the company of his brother and was known to have a similar reputation" If it made the jurors feel better to slap Ray on the nose in the report that was their prerogative, but it didn't change the fact Ray Boyer was in jail the night of the murder, and Richard was not. The jury just could not seem to grasp the fact their focus was supposed to be on the events of May 25, 1968 and the murder of Peggy Reber. Their mention of Ray Boyer's socializing with family members and even his reputation is off-point.

I stand utterly perplexed by the revelation that the investigators of 1968 focused on Ray Boyer as a suspect and questioned him extensively about how he got out of jail to commit the crime against his youthful girlfriend. I cannot fathom how investigators, grand jurors or anyone else can actually think he escaped jail, walked the streets of Lebanon, entered the Reber apartment without knowing exactly when Peggy would return from the comfort station, savagely killed her, walked the streets again and returned to his jail cell without a single person seeing anything. There was no jailbreak, no jailbird witnesses to this fantasy, no law-abiding citizens outside the jail saw him and he had no blood on his clothes. Investigators then and now seriously entertain this as a possibility and we wonder why this case isn't solved.

Ray Boyer testified he did not see lawyers at the apartment, yet we know the building was owned by an attorney, and we know the attorney kept an office on the third floor to collect rent on Friday afternoons. Peggy Reber lived on the third floor. Ray Boyer bragged about having to run that landlord off because he was making advances toward Peggy. Ray Boyer's testimony is odd.

The grand jury makes reference to a movie-like conspiracy regarding the sheltered dirty little secrets contained within the walls of The Maple Leaf Apartment Building. The Maple Leaf Apartment Building had quite a reputation back then and that has nothing to do with movie-like conspiracy. Conspiracy comes into question with a lawyer holding a key to the apartment being excluded from forensic testing or a judge with a few-too-many secrets insisting on keeping the case under his thumb.

The grand jury boasts the various local, state and federal agencies that contributed to the original investigation in 1968. What the grand jury does not mention, or perhaps understand, is the Lebanon City Police Department was the reigning agency over the investigation. The state and federal agencies merely assisted the LPD. The Lebanon City Police Department was always the agency calling the shots.

The grand jury stands convinced Root and Richard Boyer would have been privy to the same information about illicit activities taking place at The Maple Leaf Apartment Building. Simply sharing the same apartment or the same address does not make any two people privy to the same information. Doubt me? Please just ask any divorce attorney. Root only returned to the Lebanon area three months before Peggy's murder. Prior to February 1968 Root lived in Illinois with his wife and two daughters. By the time Art Root JR returned to Lebanon, Kathryn Reber was six months pregnant with Richard Boyer's child, so clearly Richard had a longer history and far more exposure with the Rebers.

Richard Boyer was a rent-paying tenant of The Maple Leaf Apartment Building and Art Root JR was a married man that randomly shacked up with Peggy's mother in the three months before her daughter's death. They are not as equal in opportunity and availability as the jury suggests.

The jury details Root was not a "patsy" to avoid focus on a true suspect. They go on to list easy targets original investigators could have pinned the murder on in 1968. The grand jury mentions the two men that committed suicide in the weeks following the crime as well as two Hispanic males present at the apartment during the apprehension of Ray Boyer the day of Peggy's death. Did the jury forget they already noted all four of these men were cleared after extensive F.B.I. forensic testing of hair, fiber, and each one of them provided dental impressions that did not match? They weren't exactly easy targets. The grand jury is in error because all four men were cleared of committing the crime.

Attorney Walter Graeff was an easy target. He owned the building, had a key and he was known to have peepholes throughout the structure to watch his young female tenants. Granted, he was still a lawyer, but he was known to be a notoriously creepy man. Peggy's killer was far from a normal man.

Richard Boyer was an easy target. He had a key, a reputation of violence toward women and he had a fight with Ray the night before over providing Peggy boot-legged electricity. If there is an ounce of truth in the divorce papers filed by his first wife Ruth Trompeter he was on probation prior to their marriage in 1965. She also mentioned he served time in jail for corrupting the morals of minors due to events that took place during sex parties in Annville, and all of that was three years before Peggy was murdered. Mary Alice and Herman were still married and raising their children in a traditional home during that time. Mr. Boyer apparently had quite a reputation long before he ever met the Reber girls. Officials weren't blind to the facts mentioned in Ruth's divorce because those divorce papers were prepared by the private practice law office of the district attorney, Lewis, Christianson and Beaver.

Boyer and Graeff had alibis courtesy of their wives. Art Root Jr's wife testified her husband was with her, too, that night. His wife didn't stand as a respected member of the community like a lawyer's wife and she also didn't just attempt suicide like Kathryn Reber, yet investigators accepted statements from Francis Graeff and Kathryn, while they ignored Root's wife, Virginia. I guess it was a frightening thought for officials to even consider putting Graeff on trial. Oh, the sleazy testimony that could generate within the court room was more than the local Bar Association could handle. In some ways it was just too convenient to keep the focus on the scandal and flaws surrounding Mary Alice than to face the skeletons lurking in the closet of the county court house.

Kathryn Reber told me her husband was a frequent visitor of Llyod Hassler's apartment on the second floor of The Maple Leaf Apartment Building. It's likely Richard Boyer knew other visitors Mr. Hassler entertained, too. Late in 2008 a county detective shared with me that Richard Boyer admittedly lived with Mr. Hassler for a brief period following his separation from Kathryn in 1968. It appears they were more than just two men unbeknownst to each other living in the same building where Peggy lost her life. Kathryn told me in the months before Peggy's murder she saw a local government official, also an attorney, enter Hassler's apartment. Again, any court testimony of that nature would be enough to bring the small town's local government to its knees.

The grand jury report mentions in a footnote "Michelle Gooden made much of the fact that Richard Boyer 'escaped' bite impressions in 1968. She concluded from that fact that Richard Boyer must have been involved in the murder and that investigators were covering for him. However, a review of the evidence indicates that investigators worked diligently to investigate Boyer's alibi, going so far as to direct authorities in South Carolina to interview one of Boyer's co-workers who was in boot camp at Paris Island. Because Boyer's alibi 'checked out', it was reasonable for investigators to conclude that he had not been involved in the murder"

Investigators *diligently* went so far as to pick up a telephone and make a long distance call to authorities in South Carolina to ask them to talk to a third-party to confirm Boyer's alibi. Keeping in mind the remainder of his alibi is little more than a statement provided by his mother and his suicidal teenage wife. That's the diligent efforts of investigators exploring the possible involvement of Richard Boyer as a suspect in a 14-year-old child's murder. The fact remains he had a key to the dwelling and investigators did not secure his dental impressions in 1968.

Ray Boyer didn't need an alibi because he was sitting in jail the night of the crime, yet he was subjected to dental comparisons.

Investigators did not exercise the same diligence of making a long distance phone call to contact authorities in Illinois to talk to a third-party when attempting to confirm Art Root's alibi. They sent three Lebanon police officers to do it personally; one of them being Lebanon's current sheriff Michael Deleo. Root also submitted dental comparisons.

The only three men reported to have keys to the Reber apartment and the diligence applied to investigating Richard Boyer and his alibi is very different than the other two men.

Why? Officials didn't send three police officers to South Carolina to talk to Boyer's alibi personally, yet they did that with Art Root.

Officials still don't accept Ray Boyer's alibi and he was in the local jail.

Officials rejected the statement given to police by Virginia Root offering an explanation of her husband's activities the night Peggy died. Virginia Root was not a likely candidate to lie on her husband's behalf because it was just weeks before she showed up on Mary Reber's doorstep to retrieve her cheating husband.

No, the statement from the wife Root betrayed was not enough to secure an alibi for him, yet the statement from Richard Boyer's suicidal teenage wife and his mother was sufficient. It does not represent the investigative diligence the grand jury suggests, it does not represent a thorough investigation and it breeds questions as to why investigators handled Richard Boyer differently than the other two men with keys to the Reber apartment.

The grand jury is correct in recognizing my criticism of the investigative procedures applied to Richard Boyer in 1968. I am the source of such questions because I am the first noted layman to realize the details surrounding the standards of Root and Ray Boyer compared to Richard Boyer.

My efforts toward Peggy's justice were recognized and supported by a considerable portion of the Lebanon community. I am the source of public awareness, but I am by no means to credit with the compromised investigation of Peggy Reber's murder, or the inconsistency investigators applied toward reasonable suspects. One must never forget the way investigators complained about the challenges of the investigation given the amount of keys given out to the Reber apartment, yet investigators only managed to identify three men with keys; Root and the Boyer brothers. Investigators never mustered the intelligence or willingness to recognize the attorney that owned the building had a key to Peggy's apartment, too.

Evidence is only as good as the means by which it is collected, stored and processed. Root demands consideration because of the excessive amount of fibers exchanged between his green leisure suit and the orange dress Peggy was wearing upon the discovery of her body. However, more than one investigator has wondered if the articles of clothing were placed in the same container when they were collected by original investigators. We scoff at such an idea because today's general public realizes the absurdity of such a thought, yet it was the Lebanon Police Department that collected the evidence, not the F.B.I. and it was 1968.

The small town police department was definitely challenged with the crime, collecting evidence and processing everything correctly. To better illustrate the point there was a glass quart beer bottle on the coffee table in the Reber home. Detectives submitted the bottle for fingerprint testing and eleven (11) prints were identified as coming from the detective that submitted the item for testing. Most people know enough about crime scenes that the collection of evidence requires gloves, yet that was not the case with the detectives processing the crime scene in 1968. If the simplistic factor of donning gloves escaped them it is not unreasonable to doubt the collection and handling of fiber evidence as well.

The grand jury mentions the fact that the district attorney and his staff took Peggy's case before the highly respected Vidocq Society in Philadelphia. However, much like 1968 when all the local, state and federal agencies assisted with Peggy's investigation this was no different. The Vidocq Society reviewed the information provided by the hosting law enforcement agency. The Vidocq Society does not conduct an actual investigation of its own. The trip to Philadelphia was little more than a field trip and trophy for the district attorney and his staff courtesy of the taxpayers in Lebanon County.

The grand jury doesn't mention The Vidocq Society determined Ray Boyer to be a person of interest. Didn't investigators bother to tell the group of experts Ray was in the Lebanon City Jail when Peggy was killed? It is an injustice that Ray wasn't removed from consideration, so the seasoned professionals could direct attention on the men outside a jail cell that night.

In 2008 Lebanon investigators weren't much different than the investigators of 1968. Oh, there were rumors about how inmates could bribe a jail guard to buy a little free time on the outside, but it was never proven Ray did any such thing. If that's an illustration of the integrity of government employees in 1968 it says a lot about the free-for-all taking place by men-in-authority, and that was just guards at the jail working for hourly pay.

Lebanon Daily News reporter, John Latimer, was in receipt of a subpoena to appear before the grand jury and a very natural and legal process took place. The grand jury report makes it a point to mention not once, but twice legal documents were filed on behalf of Latimer seeking a Motion to Quash his subpoena on the basis of journalistic privilege. Latimer's employers and guardians of the right to free press objected to the subpoena issued under The First Amendment. The effort was not an attempt to avoid Peggy's grand jury, rather it was a formality dedicated to the preservation of The First Amendment.

The jury included in its report John Latimer wrote twenty-three articles about the Reber murder and they heard from others that he believed Richard Boyer was responsible for Peggy's death. The jury didn't actually hear from John Latimer so they had no first-hand knowledge of his beliefs on any level, yet they dedicate part of their report to hearsay regarding the newspaper reporter's unconfirmed opinions. They practically damn him if he ever reported on their integrity or conflicts attached to the Reber case and referred to it as the "height of hypocrisy". The unexplainable bitterness continued when they said it was consistent with what they learned through their investigation. It was evident the author of the grand jury report wanted to shut John Latimer down from ever reporting on the Reber case again.

It was hard to believe twenty-nine objective citizens could stage such a vicious verbal assault against any individual for simply doing one's job. The grand jury had no reason to be concerned about a reporter writing twenty-three articles the last twelve months, or the last twelve years for that matter. They were supposed to be investigating a murder that occurred forty years earlier. Speculation on Latimer's personal opinions was again of no importance regarding their assignment.

The voice of the true author of the grand jury report could be heard loud and clear. The grand jury proceedings were not utilized for investigative purposes. Instead, there was a deliberate effort to fault and discredit anyone associated with public criticism of Lebanon's administration, or anyone offending Richard Boyer. It was becoming increasingly obvious somebody in power wanted to put Peggy back under the blanket-of-silence and they were willing to use a grand jury to do it.

The First Amendment is one of the keystones of American freedom and it needs to be handled with the utmost care. Once it was realized there would be a hearing to challenge Latimer's subpoena the grand jury decided they didn't really want to hear from him after all, so the hearing never came to fruition.

It is no secret at the same time and in an unrelated case Lebanon County was generating national attention due to controversy surrounding an alleged violation of The Second Amendment. In the weeks prior to the assembly of Peggy's grand jury a resident of Lebanon had her conceal and carry permit revoked by Lebanon County's sheriff department under the most questionable of circumstances. The story made news reports throughout the world while activists and supporters of The Second Amendment looked at Lebanon's local government with a watchful eye. It's almost too convenient that the grand jury withdrew its request to hear from John Latimer because it spared the local administration the scrutiny of challenging not only The Second Amendment, but The First Amendment as well. It could be a real attention-getter and highly alarming to find one small local government accused of challenging the core of American freedoms.

The Grand Jury wanted it known "At no point was our investigation thwarted by the District Attorney or any member of his staff. To the contrary, we were given the opportunity to conduct a thorough, fair and objective investigation as to any issues or allegations relating to the murder or its associated investigations". The jury could criticize any efforts made by Officer Snavely, fault reporter John Latimer for reporting anything less than the administration's praises and I took my share of insults, but they were definitely on board with the District Attorney and his staff.

The grand jury report states "We were also requested by the District Attorney to investigate longstanding as well as current allegations of corruption, cover-up and conflicts of interest associated with the investigation into Ms. Reber's murder"

In their report the grand jury recognizes Officer Kevin Snavely returned to his position as a member of the Lebanon City Police Department during their seven-month investigation of Peggy's murder. What the jury does not mention is that Officer Kevin Snavely was reinstated after a union arbitrator rendered an opinion that Officer Snavely was fired due to controversy surrounding the Reber case.

That one objective opinion did the grand jury's work for them. Obviously, the administration within Lebanon had a conflict with the Reber case. They fired Kevin Snavely because of it. The arbitrator was not part of any network in Lebanon, he had no affiliation with the case, Officer Snavely or Michelle Gooden. He managed to see how the administrative powers had such a conflict regarding Peggy's case they were willing to destroy a man's career.

However, the grand jury assigned to investigate "longstanding as well as current allegations of corruption, cover-up and conflicts of interest" simply ignored the message delivered by the arbitrator that overturned Officer Snavely's wrongful termination.

Officer Kevin Snavely wasn't fired for stealing anything or disobeying a court order. It was determined Kevin Snavely was fired due to controversy surrounding Peggy Reber's case. He struggled professionally, financially and emotionally in excess of a year due to the wrongful termination. He was a victim of poor management, poor judgment and the abuse of power by his superiors.

Office Kevin Snavely dropped his lawsuit against government officials not long after returning to the police department. "I am just grateful to have my job back. I don't know that it's a career anymore because of everything that's happened. I can't be sure how far I will be allowed to move up in the ranks, but I love what I do and I am glad to be back on the force"

A footnote on the bottom of page ten (10) of the grand jury report: "We were made of aware (sic) of a variety of allegations as they pertained to District Attorney David Arnold. We were never dissuaded by anyone from investigating these allegations. To the contrary, we were invited to investigate any and all allegations. At times, District Attorney David Arnold left the Grand Jury room so as not to influence our discussions or the testimony of certain witnesses. In fact, we met privately, outside the presence of the District Attorney and his staff on multiple occasions to discuss the direction of our investigation. We voted to issue subpoenas to potentially controversial witnesses, to include members of the local media and those who had been close to Gooden"

The Grand Jury expresses an understanding of their power to subpoena witnesses. Who could better explain the questions surrounding the allegations pertaining to David Arnold than the District Attorney himself?

Why didn't the grand jury subpoena Dave Arnold? Instead, they voted to subpoena the local media and anyone close to me, yet unlike David Arnold I was not being investigated, or was I?

According to the laws governing and protecting grand jury proceedings throughout the Commonwealth of Pennsylvania individuals being investigated by a grand jury are not present during witness testimony, yet we can see in this grand jury report allegations pertaining to David Arnold were part of their duties and he was indeed present during witness testimony.

The bottom of page twenty-six of the grand jury report states they requested the District Attorney leave the court room during my testimony about his potential personal conflict with the case.

Witness testimony given before a grand jury is to be given out of the ear shot of other witnesses.

Why was District Attorney David Arnold present during any witness testimony? How did he know the grand jury would not issue him a subpoena, so they could hear from him directly? Did he have a crystal ball? Perhaps he is psychic.

While investigating allegations about David Arnold the grand jury wanted to hear from the local media and those close to me, yet it made more sense to hear from David Arnold and those close to him.

Why didn't the jury subpoena the former Mrs. David Arnold? She had an open, public and documented relationship with the Boyer family and it clearly continued during her marriage to the DA. She is still friends with Boyer family members. She had valuable insight to offer the jurors regarding the night her former husband, the District Attorney was charged with domestic harassment. She knew first-hand where she was that evening and why she and the District Attorney had police summoned to their home.

Why didn't the hostess of the Boyer family gathering testify? She stepped out of the shadows in the interest of a murdered child receiving untainted justice. She provided an email to be presented to the grand jurors. I provided it to prosecutors when I testified. The grand jury was aware of her identity, provided her statement, yet they didn't subpoena her.

Richard Boyer JR was not only named in Snavely's lawsuit, but quoted in a local paper after the filing of that court document. He seemed to have some knowledge of Arnold's possible conflict with the case and he also told the news media about his father's activities the night of Peggy's death. Why didn't he testify to his knowledge?

Two local police officers responded to the Arnold home after receiving a call about a domestic dispute. Those officers were witnesses to the situation in question. North Lebanon Township Police Officer Duane Koons filed the offense report charging David J. Arnold Jr with domestic harassment. I provided the jury a copy of that report, so they knew who to subpoena.

The police report identifies the district attorney's former sister-in-law and three other individuals present during the dispute.

Why didn't the judge presiding over the grand jury testify? The Honorable Bradford Charles was the District Attorney at the time a citation was filed against fellow officer of the court David J. Arnold. In the statement provided to the grand jury the hostess of the Boyer family gathering said "Dave got in trouble the next day and was told by Brad Charles that if anything like that ever happened again, he was going to lose his job"

One must almost wonder if he should he have been a part of the grand jury proceedings at all? How could one know the grand jury wouldn't want to hear from him, or even his predecessor former district attorney Deirdre Eshleman for that matter? There is no disputing David Arnold was charged with domestic harassment, yet not convicted of the charge. Who was to say that instead of issuing subpoenas to the media and those close to me the jury might actually want to understand the details and events surrounding the allegations about Arnold's potential conflict with the Reber case? Unless The Honorable Brad Charles also has a crystal ball or psychic powers he could not be ruled out as a potential witness either.

Events surrounding David Arnold and the charges filed against him in November 1999 were in question and anyone with any knowledge of those events could be called by an objective grand jury to testify. I am not to blame or to credit for the domestic challenges within the Arnold home in 1999. It was not front-page news, yet it is not a secret throughout the community. In fact, in the big picture of David Arnold's life it is a small blemish, and it does not define him as a person or an attorney, yet it could matter greatly if he attempted to touch the Reber case. It mattered greatly during the investigative grand jury process.

Questions surrounding any personal conflicts on the part of the District Attorney are illuminated by the actions of the prosecuting office during the grand jury proceeding.

Sadly, the jury didn't bother to subpoena Arthur Root Jr either. He certainly had information to contribute regarding Peggy, visitors to The Maple Leaf Apartment Building and the questionable investigation of 1968. Lebanon investigators did not talk to Root in 2008; instead they had a prison warden talk to him for them. The grand jury tells us Root told the warden he had no interest in testifying before a grand jury and indicated he would refuse to cooperate.

It was Detective Michael Dipalo that told me early in our relationship one cannot simply refuse to cooperate upon receiving a grand jury subpoena. Failure to honor a grand jury subpoena places one in contempt. It didn't matter if Root "had no interest in testifying before a grand jury" the grand jury had the power and responsibility to subpoena him, and they failed to do so.

He was one of the only first-hand eye witnesses to everything they were supposedly investigating. Granted, it was going to require a little work on the part of the DA's office because they weren't going to get away with issuing his out-of-state subpoena via email like they did mine. There was also expense attached to enforcing the subpoena. Are we to understand the grand jury's investigation was limited to keeping the prosecutor's job easy?

It was easy to subpoena the employee working at the comfort station that night, she lives within two miles of The Lebanon Municipal Building and she wasn't subpoenaed either.

"Gooden continues to question the integrity of our investigation and claims that we have not been provided with pertinent information about the case". The Grand Jury is in grave error if they believe me to be the only person that questions their investigation. Residents throughout Lebanon and beyond have scoffed at the legitimacy of the grand jury's investigation into Peggy's murder and the other issues assigned to them. Their report, the witnesses subpoenaed and the absence of certain witnesses subpoenaed does not reflect the thorough investigation to which they take claim. They are either fooling themselves, or they have been fooled, but the general public is not fooled.

I like to think there is at least one juror…maybe two….that had a little good old-fashioned common sense and devoted some thought toward Peggy instead of the circus the prosecuting office paraded in front of them. I realize the jury foreman's signature legally represents the unanimous voice of the twenty-nine jurors, yet I struggle to accept the fact they were all so naïve. I believe in my heart the jurors trusted the prosecuting office to guide them in their journey. I believe Peggy trusted them, too.

The grand jury actually started with thirty members, but one of the jurors passed away during the proceedings. I know that only because Detective Dipalo attempted to make me feel guilty by saying that person missed valuable time with loved ones by sitting on that jury.

Peggy Reber missed valuable time with her loved ones, too.

The most upsetting statement in the grand jury report referred to the late Lester White. The grand jury reported he was charged with attempting to "ravish" Peggy in the days prior to her murder. I guess the grand jury was not correctly informed again.
Lester White was charged with "ravishing" Peggy in April 1967 and that was thirteen months before her murder. His case went before the courts in February 1968 and attorney/landlord Walter Graeff was his public defender. Lester White did not kill Peggy Reber. He was cleared through forensic and dental testing. Again, he was indeed charged in April 1967 with "ravishing" the 13-year-old child.

However, April 1967 is hardly "the days prior to her murder" the way the grand jury reports.

The grand jury makes it a point to say I claim they have not been provided pertinent information about the case, yet they make a statement relating to "days prior to the murder" and one really has to wonder. There is a tremendous difference between "the days prior to her murder" and thirteen months before she was killed. Did they truly understand this "pertinent" piece of information and simply choose to misrepresent the facts in their report, or were they deceived again? If they willfully and knowingly misrepresented that fact in their report – shame on them. However, it's hard to imagine twenty-nine reasonable people agreeing that an event that transpired over a year before Peggy's death could be classified as occurring "the days prior to her murder" yet that is what all twenty-nine agreed upon.

■■

There are integrity issues with the investigative grand jury proceeding and they are the result of the District Attorney's office failing to provide the jurors truthful, factual and unobstructed information. The timing regarding Lester White's crime against Peggy is just part of the abstracts.
"We also learned Gooden was writing a book about Reber's murder which she claimed to be factual. However, when Detective Dipalo requested a copy of her manuscript during his investigation Gooden refused to provide it. She provided a copy only in response to her grand jury subpoena. Gooden's subpoena also required her to provide us with any and all documents she had acquired relating to the Reber case" – page twenty-eight of the grand jury report sums it up pretty well.
The jurors believed they issued me a subpoena and I did not show the document or them the respect owed. The District Attorney's office failed to tell the jurors they were too lazy to

have me formally served with an official subpoena. Contrary to what the jurors believe and reflect in their report I was not "required" to provide them anything and I did not have to travel a thousand miles to appear before them. I showed them greater respect than they realized by choice, yet they condemned me for not honoring their subpoena… a piece of junk paper the district attorney's office used in an attempt to discredit me and deceive the grand jury. Oh, someone should definitely be condemned for not honoring that subpoena and it should be the District Attorney.

One almost has to wonder about the ethical issues in place regarding that matter. Did the District Attorney ignore an investigative grand jury's request to subpoena a witness? It looks like he did. Page twenty-six of the grand jury report states "We subpoenaed Michelle Gooden to testify on December 15, 2008" The grand jury wanted me subpoenaed, believed they subpoenaed me, the District Attorney and judge signed a subpoena for me, and I am sure the jury saw a copy of the subpoena signed by the DA and the judge, but prosecutors failed to have me served with the subpoena, so it wasn't worth the paper used to print it. Several years later and the prosecuting office still defends the means by which I received not one, but two subpoenas – via email.

Interestingly, the grand jury's claim about how the District Attorney would leave the grand jury room so as not to influence the jury's discussions weakens. He obviously influenced their discussions in a different manner. He allowed them to believe he honored their request to subpoena me. He allowed them to believe per their order I was legally required to provide them many documents and I did not comply to their demands. He clearly influenced them with deception surrounding a subpoena he failed to properly execute.

It is impossible to expect any jury to make a reasonable assessment of the case when they have been provided such distorted information. This jury couldn't even trust prosecutors to issue a subpoena to witnesses they wanted to question. Prosecutors made a mockery of the judicial process.

The District Attorney's office and the grand jury report devoted more time and effort to discrediting me than directing their focus on the lifeless body of a child in the morgue. I was merely an advocate for Peggy's justice. I generated attention toward the child's unsolved murder. I had no business testifying as a witness and I certainly didn't have any business testifying for five-hours. It's a damn shame. While I am but a mere advocate for a slain child robbed of justice and jurors were average citizens devoting their time and energy to Peggy's case it is the District Attorney and his staff that show their true character or lack thereof through the grand jury proceeding. A court room is supposed to be a respected and sacred host to our judicial system; the prosecuting office used it and abused it to silence anyone that criticized the local administration. I am saddened by the blatant lack of respect the senior officers of the court extend the court rooms, citizens and victims they are trusted to serve within Lebanon County. Lady Justice needs a blindfold, so she doesn't have to see the massacre of justice for all taking place in Lebanon, Pennsylvania.

The District Attorney posted the grand jury report and my formal response on his web site the better part of a year for all to see. I was ashamed for him. The ridiculous slaughter of the grand jury process and the indifference towards Peggy's murder was nothing for any District Attorney to proudly publicize. Though the grand jury report was intended to discredit me, insult me and shame me into silence I am not the one that needs to be ashamed. I am amazed by the effort and disgusted by the fact even forty years later Peggy cannot obtain the mere opportunity of an objective court proceeding within Lebanon County.

What is it about this child's murder that causes Lebanon judges, lawyers and prosecutors to squirm in their seats and deny Peggy every benefit of the judicial process and possible justice? Judge Gates demanded control in 1968, George Christianson failed to transcribe the trial in 1970 and in 2008 a grand jury is deceived about a subpoena signed by the DA and judge, while the grand jury report was used to silence the masses once again. There are far too many errors to call any of this coincidence. Lebanon's court system has denied Peggy Reber justice since the day she took her last breath.

Why? The grand jury says "We categorically reject the multitude of conspiracy theories attendant to this case" They are at liberty to reject anything they choose, but their words do not change the actions of the investigators, prosecutors and judges attached to this case. Actions speak louder than words.

I will not be ashamed of any of the character assassination I am subjected to in the grand jury report. Third-party emails composed almost forty years after the crime and taken out-of-context had NOTHING to do with Peggy's murder, or identifying her killer, but it made for a wonderful distraction from what truly mattered and juicy gossip. It wasn't a pursuit of truth and justice for Peggy, but a circus the DA and his staff staged in front of the grand jury, not at my expense, but at Peggy's expense. The grand jury report hosts more questions pertaining to me than it does the victim, the crime or the suspect. Prosecutors and jurors were not focused on the unsolved murder of Peggy; they were hell-bent-and-determined to shut Michelle Gooden up once and for all. The nerve of me to step on the toes of any cop, lawyer, district attorney or judge! The accusations that I was responsible for influencing the testimony of other witnesses that provided statements to police in 1968 is pathetic. Those witnesses took an oath and they were responsible for their own truthful testimony, but it sounded really good to blame Michelle Gooden.

While on the subject of oaths there is a little oath a few men attached to the grand jury report need to be reminded: "I do solemnly swear (or affirm) that I will support, obey and defend the Constitution of the United States and the Constitution of this Commonwealth and that I will discharge the duties of my office with fidelity." Lawyers take an oath, too, and a few need to be reminded of the true definition of fidelity more ways than one.

It's rather obvious Peggy Reber was not going to receive justice in Lebanon in 1968 or 2008. Officials practically issued a "Get out of jail free" card for her killer. The sadistic bastard will never be identified or sentenced for this crime. Peggy's true justice rests with a Higher Power than the men wearing black robes within Lebanon's Municipal Building. Her killer will face a much more powerful judge with Peggy's blood still on his hands and each individual that failed to honor their oath will stand in line behind him.

The court issued the grand jury report and ultimately that was supposed to close the book on Peggy Reber, and put the subject to rest. I sorted through my disappointment, sadness and confusion for years. I cried, I cursed and I prayed about the total betrayal of Peggy's last chance in a court of law. Peggy's supporters continued to reach out to me and ask "What can we do now?" I was at a loss.

Repeatedly, I was asked about the manuscript I composed about Peggy Reber. I didn't see the importance of publishing a book until one of Peggy's supporters in Lebanon asked me the strangest question "Michelle, what do you think Peggy would want you to do now? You carried her memory through your childhood and you gave her your voice when no one else would speak out on her behalf. The court failed her, witnesses failed her and justice escaped her, again. She just might need your voice one last time. You, personally, can't convict a killer or clean up a compromised court process, but you can tell her story, Michelle. Tell her story through your eyes and your experiences because you were such a small and innocent child when she left her mark on your memory. It looks like she wanted you to remember her. She had an impact on you and you followed through with so much effort on her behalf decades after her death. It's hard to call that an accident. Michelle, you were only five-years-old when she died. Please give that fact alone some serious consideration. It's a question for angels more than lawyers. The grand jury can call you a corrupt witness, but Peggy knows the truth about her life and her death. She knows who the true witnesses are in her tragedy and you aren't one of them. Maybe that's why you were compelled to remember her, Michelle. Maybe Peggy knew even back then the people around her would fail her in death the same way they failed her in life. Maybe Peggy gently touched your youthful heart so you could grow up and carry her torch when no one else did. You do realize you did that Michelle, don't you? Your voice ignited a fire within the community decades after she died and it made a difference, but I will ask you again....what do you think Peggy would want you to do now?" I didn't have an answer.

"Michelle, what do you think Peggy would say to the witnesses that failed to tell her truth? Peggy didn't want to lose her life, who does? She wanted to grow up, get married, have children and grow old. She never had the chance to learn how to drive a car. God knows her teenage body was tortured. She didn't pass in her sleep or due to disease or tumors. She was murdered. The forces of evil robbed her of her life and a handful of selfish people robbed her of truth and justice. What would she really say now? I don't think she is holding grudges, but I do think there is a possibility she still needs the truth to be told. Tell her truth through your eyes and your experiences since you were five-years-old. Like I said, she just might need your voice one last time. Peggy didn't get justice and that grand jury report doesn't come close to telling her story. Consider telling her story beyond the few public records that record her life, death and injustice"

I listened to the gentleman with a sharp ear and a heavy heart. I seriously pondered the question "What would Peggy want me to do now?" I remembered her, I studied her and I stood up for her. I knew in my heart Peggy would never obtain justice in a Lebanon County court of law. Peggy's justice and not only my efforts, but the voice of a community stood defeated. I heard the caller's message. Without a book, Peggy's only recorded truth rested among The Lebanon Daily News reports scanning decades, flimsy court records from an aged trial and the grand jury report issued in July of 2009. Peggy deserves better.

Oh, countless people talked about writing a book, so I waited for someone to tell Peggy's story. I waited and I waited and I waited. It was apparent no one was going to make the effort to step beyond the investigative grand jury report of 2009. Sadly, that report does not accurately detail the life and death of Peggy Reber. The report doesn't mention her childhood friend that saw her late that evening, her empty stomach during her autopsy or even all the items used to mutilate her body. The report is not dedicated to Peggy, her murder and her lost justice. It misrepresents some facts, omits other facts and dedicates a tremendous amount of attention to things of no importance to solving her crime.

The 38-page investigative grand jury report of the murder of Peggy Reber sits on public record for anyone to view; my twelve-page formal response is in addition. Keeping things in perspective Peggy's grand jury report is 50-pages in length with no indictment rendered. Recently former Penn State football coach Jerry Sandusky was investigated by a grand jury and their report including addendums is only 28-pages in length.

The detailed witness testimony of the grand jury is protected by law and will never see the light of day. The individual named at the top of the list of suspects from the aged unsolved murder of a child is mentioned seventy-five (75) times throughout the report. Me? Well, I was only 5-years-old when Peggy Reber was killed and mutilated, yet I was mentioned sixty-seven (67) times in the investigative grand jury report. I spent more time on the witness stand than her family, friends and investigators. The fact remains I did not kill Peggy Reber. I did not have the power, influence or desire to obstruct her justice in excess of forty years either.

In fact, I fought long and hard to get Peggy the attention, respect and justice she deserves.

■■

Not surprisingly, Margaret "Peggy" Lynn Reber's murder remains unsolved.

■■

I continue to include Peggy in my prayers and I apologize to her not merely for her tragic death, her lost life, but the absence of her truth. I apologize to her for the decades her murder went ignored, I apologize for the compromised legal system in Lebanon, Pennsylvania and I apologize for the true witnesses that failed her, yet again.

Peggy Reber was a 14-year-old kid.

She didn't care about lawyers, politicians or court room drama. She did not commit a crime or owe a debt worthy of her life, yet she was brutally executed on May 25, 1968.

The helpless teenager was alone and vulnerable that fateful day. Her twin sister moved out of their apartment building, her married boyfriend was jailed leaving her alone and her scandalous mother was nowhere to be found.

Peggy Reber was only fourteen-years-old, but that was her reality the last day of her life. She was alone, she was scared and she was in danger. She was still just a kid.

The beautiful 14-year-old child with so much future ahead of her was dead within hours.

She died with no food in her stomach, no electricity in her home and the last person to look into her youthful eyes, her killer, was consumed with evil. The government responsible for delivering her justice had its own questionable and self-serving agenda, then and now.

■■

My daughter is a little older now and each day I pick her up after school. I watch her prance toward my car smiling, giggling, with the sun bouncing off her hair. She struggles to carry her purse, a book bag, and her viola we playfully refer to as "Violet". Even on the most ordinary days she oozes with excitement over the strangest of things. She loves music, puppies, chocolate and Jesus. She is vibrant, she is beautiful, she will soon be fourteen-years-old. Every now and then I pause and think of 14-year-old Peggy, the little girl that was denied her childhood, her life, her truth and her justice.

■■

The following pages are a few of several public records mentioned throughout the book. They are not the public records in their entirety, but a collection of random pages to provide each reader a better understanding of documents mentioned.

I.   INTRODUCTION

On November 10, 2008, we, the members of the Investigating Grand Jury of Lebanon County, were convened and tasked by the District Attorney of Lebanon County to investigate the 1968 murder of Margaret "Peggy" Reber. We were specifically requested to make a recommendation as to whether any person should be charged for the murder. The Court provided specific instructions to us as to the concept of probable cause which is the level of proof necessary to institute criminal proceedings. We were also requested by the District Attorney to investigate longstanding as well as current allegations of corruption, cover-up and conflicts of interest associated with the investigation into Ms. Reber's murder.

In conducting our investigation, we were given the opportunity to meet privately, outside the presence of the District Attorney and his staff, to discuss the direction of our investigation. We were given the authority to subpoena witnesses to testify before us. During our investigation, we heard from thirty (30) live witnesses and met on eleven (11) occasions. We reviewed investigative reports summarizing interviews with others and listened to audio-taped interviews. We reviewed physical evidence and records. At no point was our investigation thwarted by the District Attorney or any member of his staff. To the contrary, we were given the opportunity to conduct a thorough, fair and objective investigation as to any issues or allegations relating to the murder or its associated investigations.

Given the controversy surrounding this case, real or perceived, we know that this report may not be well received by some. However, we hope that the issuance and content of this report will help to bring public controversy and allegations of conspiracy to an end. In drafting this report, we cannot begin to distill all of the information that we have obtained in a cogent

4

written report. This report will discuss the highlights of what we learned and set forth our conclusions.

II. DISCUSSION

The body of fourteen (14) year old Margaret "Peggy" Reber was discovered at approximately 0300 hours on Sunday May 26, 1968 in her third-floor apartment at the Maple Leaf Apartment Building. The Maple Leaf Apartment Building was located on the southeast corner of the intersection of 8th and Maple Street in the City of Lebanon. Peggy Reber resided in Apartment #22 with her divorced mother, Mary Reber. Mary Reber discovered Peggy's body when she returned to the dark apartment upon returning from a trip to New Jersey. The electricity in the apartment had been shut off at least one day prior at the direction of the landlord, Walter Graeff.[2] Graeff was in the process of evicting the Rebers from the apartment.

Upon discovering the body, Mary Reber immediately notified neighbors who contacted the Lebanon City Police Department. According to Mary Reber's statements to police in 1968, she originally thought someone was passed out on the floor of the bedroom. However, when she reached for the body, Mary Reber discovered that it was cold and in a state of rigor mortis. At the time of her death, Peggy was dating nineteen (19) year old Ray Boyer. Peggy's twin sister, Kathryn, was married to Ray's twenty-one (21) year old brother, Richard Boyer. Kathryn and Richard Boyer had moved out of an adjacent apartment days prior to the murder, and Kathryn had recently given birth to Boyer's child. Mary Reber forced Richard Boyer to marry her daughter in lieu of pursuing rape charges against him.

---

[2] The lack of electricity in the apartment is an important fact. Because the apartment was so dark, investigators past and present theorized that the murder may have occurred in the evening hours of May 25, 1968 when it was still light outside. Investigators returned to the scene following the murder to evaluate the lighting conditions. They concluded that it would have been very difficult for one to have perpetrated this murder in total darkness.

5

Mary Reber was known to be very promiscuous. She entertained many men at the apartment and is believed to have also engaged in prostitution. At the time of Peggy's murder, Mary Reber had reportedly traveled to New Jersey to "work" a migrant camp. She located her daughter's body upon returning. Multiple men were known to have keys to the Reber apartment, including the Boyer brothers, Arthur Root, and others. The investigation of the murder was undoubtedly complicated by the fact that a very large number of men regularly frequented the Reber apartment.

Dr. Leonard Tanner conducted an autopsy of Reber's body at the Good Samaritan Hospital on the morning of May 26, 1968. Dr. Tanner concluded that the cause of death was asphyxia due to ligature strangulation. He also located multiple internal perforating wounds, including 10 perforations of the diaphragm, 11 perforations of the lungs and respiratory tract, 9 perforations of the cardiovascular system, and 16 perforations of the gastrointestinal tract. These internal wounds were caused by a post-mortem rectal assault with a recurve hunting bow. At autopsy, a human bite mark was located on Peggy's left breast. The bite mark will be discussed in detail below. The breast was excised and sent to the Armed Forces Institute of Pathology. No evidence of semen was located on/in the child's body. Despite recent allegations to the contrary, Peggy Reber was NOT pregnant at the time of her murder. At least two (2) present day forensic pathologists have indicated that Tanner's autopsy report was very thorough.

Investigators collected one hundred twenty-one (121) questioned items and eighteen (18) known items of evidence; including the clothing of potential suspects, the clothing of the victim, fingernail scrapings, blood evidence and bite impressions. The evidence was analyzed by the Pennsylvania State Police, Federal Bureau of Investigation, and the Armed Forces Institute of

6

been at the apartment at least two (2) times on May 25 looking for Mary Reber. He even removed a stereo from the Reber apartment as collateral for the missing money. A jury acquitted Arthur Root of the murder after a ten (10) day trial in 1970.

Little, if any, further investigation was conducted following Root's acquittal. No witnesses came forward to police with information relating to the murder. Herman Reber, Peggy's adoptive father, was the ONLY layperson who maintained interest in the case. According to Clifford Roland, one of the original investigators, Herman Reber came to the police department every week to ask if police had developed any other leads relating to Peggy's murder. We heard from surviving investigators and the prosecutor, George Christianson. To date, all firmly maintain that Arthur Root was involved in the murder of Peggy Reber.

In 2000, Detective Randy Edgar (retired) of the Lebanon City Police Department reopened the investigation after obtaining information concerning the alleged involvement of John Ebling in Peggy's murder. Investigators discussed the prospects of exhuming Ebling's body to secure his dental impressions to compare them to the bite mark on Reber's breast.[6] Ultimately, it was decided that Detective Edgar would travel to Oklahoma to interview Arthur Root who was incarcerated there. Investigators believed that Root might be willing to confess to the crime given that he could not be retried for the murder. Root denied his involvement in the crime, and the case was again closed.

In 2006, Detective Kevin Snavely of the Lebanon City Police Department requested permission to reopen the investigation and to investigate the case on his own time. Snavely

---

[6] We also discussed the prospects of exhuming Ebling's body which is buried in Texas. However, as will be mentioned herein, there is no objective evidence linking Ebling to the murder but rather only suspicion generated by his ex-wife and others. Thus, there is not adequate legal basis to exhume Ebling's body. If Ebling's body were to be exhumed, his dental impressions could be compared to photographs of the bite mark on Reber's breast. However, because there is no scale in the photograph, Ebling could only be excluded as having made the mark. It is not possible to definitively match the bite mark with dental impressions given the limitations associated with photographic comparison.

8

initiated an investigation and, according to his reports, almost immediately developed Richard

Boyer as a suspect. In 2008, Snavely was terminated from his position with the Lebanon City

Police Department.[7] Prior to his firing, Snavely had been removed from the Reber investigation

by his superiors amid allegations that he had released confidential investigative information to

sources outside the investigation.[8] We were also made aware of the lawsuit filed by Snavely

against city officials and the District Attorney in which Snavely claimed that he was fired due to

his involvement in the Reber case. We began our investigation before Snavely filed his lawsuit.

Nonetheless, we are cognizant of claims questioning the objectivity and integrity of our

investigation given the controversy relating to Snavely's firing.

We subpoenaed Kevin Snavely to testify on December 19, 2008. Snavely appeared with

his attorney. After approximately one hour of testimony, Snavely invoked his Fifth Amendment

rights against self-incrimination and refused to answer further questions. Snavely was the only

witness to appear before us who invoked his right against self incrimination and refused to

testify.[9] Even after Snavely was awarded his job back with the Lebanon City Police, he persisted

in refusing to testify as evidenced by a letter from his counsel indicating that Snavely would

invoke his Fifth Amendment rights if recalled to testify. Detective Dipalo told us that he

telephoned Snavely on August 7, 2008, well before Snavely filed his lawsuit, to interview him

concerning his knowledge of the Reber case. Snavely refused to cooperate with Detective

Dipalo in providing information or insight to the investigation. Dipalo quoted Snavely as stating,

---

[7] Snavely, the then evidence custodian for the city police, was reportedly fired for falsifying evidence forms relating to a DVD player.

[8] Following Snavely's removal from the case, the investigation was undertaken by Detective Michael Dipalo and Detective Sergeant Richard Radwanski of the Lebanon County Detective Bureau. Detective Dipalo told us that he was given complete autonomy by the District Attorney with respect to his investigation of the case.

[9] One other requested witness, John Latimer, a reporter from the Lebanon Daily News, filed a Motion to Quash his subpoena on the basis of journalistic privilege.

9

Gooden. However, it quickly became apparent to us that Gooden was the primary source of information on which others had relied in implicating Richard Boyer.

As to Richard Boyer's alleged involvement in Reber's murder, we heard absolutely no competent, credible, or reliable evidence from which to conclude that Richard Boyer was involved in Reber's murder. In fact, evidence obtained in 1968 led investigators to conclude that Boyer was not involved in the murder. This evidence has never been disproven. Although Gooden and others have claimed that Boyer was never considered a suspect during the initial investigation, we learned that Richard Boyer was the first person named on a "suspect list" of 84 individuals prepared by investigators in 1968. Thus, Gooden's allegation that Richard Boyer had never been a suspect, like many others, was simply not true.

Investigators in 1968 learned that Richard Boyer worked second shift at Reading Alloy in Robesonia and that he was working on the night of the murder. Investigators obtained Boyer's time card which confirmed that he left work at 11:05 p.m.[12] Boyer reported that he went home after work and learned of Peggy's murder the following morning. Boyer's co-workers and supervisor corroborated his alibi. More importantly, Boyer's then-wife, Kathryn, and mother both confirmed Boyer's alibi in their statements to police in 1968. Bite impressions were secured from Richard Boyer in 2008.[13] Richard Boyer was excluded as having inflicted the bite to Reber's breast.

---

[12] Snavely testified that he was not aware that investigators had obtained Boyer's time card in 1968 in spite of the existence of a report in the file reflecting this fact. Those that claim Boyer was not at work theorize that another employee must have clocked his time card for him. There is absolutely no evidence of this. To the contrary, witness statements from 1968 and today do not support this theory. Moreover, not one witness provided any evidence as to how Richard Boyer allegedly got from his job in Robesonia to Lebanon to commit the murder. Boyer did not have a car and relied on others to get to and from work.

[13] Michelle Gooden made much of the fact that Richard Boyer "escaped" bite impressions in 1968. She concluded from that fact that Richard Boyer must have been involved in the murder and that investigators were covering for him. However, a review of the evidence indicates that investigators worked diligently to investigate Boyer's alibi, going so far as to direct authorities in South Carolina to interview one of Boyer's co-workers who was in boot camp

In identifying Boyer as a suspect in Reber's murder, Kevin Snavely testified that he relied primarily on statements made by Kathryn Meador. Snavely reported that Kathryn told him that she was "coached" by Richard Boyer and his mother as to what to tell investigators in 1968. During her grand jury testimony, Kathryn Meador denied that she was "coached" to tell investigators a particular story in 1968. However, she acknowledged that she relied on input from others given her age and shock associated with of the death of her sister. Snavely also reported that Boyer was observed with cuts on his hands and that Kathryn Meador had witnessed Boyer's bloody clothing on the washing machine and that Boyer's mother had burned and/or washed it.[14] Meador's sworn testimony was inconsistent with Snavely's reports relating to his interviews with her. Furthermore, investigators learned that Richard Boyer was involved in an altercation at the Maple Leaf Apartments on the night before Peggy's murder. In 1968, at least two independent witnesses observed Boyer with blood dripping from his hand in the hallway of the Maple Leaf Apartment Building. This altercation occurred on the night prior to the murder and was corroborated by a number of witnesses at the time, including Ray Boyer. In spite of this, Snavely included this fact in an affidavit implicating Richard Boyer.

Those who focused on Richard Boyer ignored potentially exculpatory evidence and instead focused only on evidence which tended to incriminate him, regardless of whether it was corroborated by or consistent with other known facts. We learned that some of this alleged evidence was fabricated or tailored to support the theory that Richard Boyer had committed the murder. We learned that many of the people who claimed to know something about Reber's

---

at Paris Island. Because Boyer's alibi "checked out", it was reasonable for investigators to conclude that he had not been involved in the murder.

[14] We heard multiple rumors relating to others who were alleged to have washed or burned bloody clothing at various locations following the murder, none of which were consistent or corroborated. We also heard testimony as to persons who were allegedly observed to have blood on their clothing at or near the time of the murder. We concluded for a multitude of reasons that this testimony was not at all credible.

13

murder obtained that information from Michelle Gooden and relied on it as factually accurate. As time progressed, some who had been close to Gooden and supported her efforts grew concerned about her apparent obsession with the case. One witness commented about her departure from the Justice for Peggy movement: *"it was getting too vigilante for me, and I decided that this wasn't what it was supposed to be about"*.

Ray Boyer, the brother of Richard Boyer, told us that he believed that his brother was responsible for his girlfriend's murder. Despite being given repeated opportunities, Ray Boyer offered absolutely no objective facts to support this allegation. Boyer offered that his brother was violent towards women and otherwise ornery and ruthless. Interestingly, we learned from other witnesses that Ray Boyer was frequently in the company of his brother and was known to have a similar reputation. Otherwise, Boyer offered no facts to support his conclusion. We also learned that Ray Boyer reached his conclusion regarding his brother's involvement in Peggy's murder only after speaking with Michelle Gooden. Although Ray Boyer claimed that he always knew his brother had committed the murder, Richard Boyer provided us with recent photographs of Ray Boyer at Richard's home on holidays and special occasions. We find it hard to believe that Ray Boyer would have played Santa Clause at his brother's home if he always knew, as he claims, that his brother killed Peggy Reber.

Ray Boyer also acknowledged that he had been unwilling to provide information to the Lebanon City Police or the District Attorney's Office relating to his alleged knowledge of his brother's involvement in the murder. The following exchange occurred during Ray Boyer's testimony:

> Q. Okay. When you met with - - do you recall meeting with John Ditzler in our office back in I think February of this year?
>
> A. Yeah. Um-hum.

14

caused such a serious injury to the breast. Boyer claimed that he gave Peggy a hickey on her breast but did not bite it. Ray Boyer was consistent, however, with the positioning aspect of how he delivered the hickey. In viewing photos of the bite mark on the breast, it is difficult to conceive of one causing such serious injury during consensual lovemaking. To this end, we investigated the prospects that Ray Boyer had gotten out of jail and was involved in Peggy's murder as we heard stories that security at the Lebanon County Prison was somewhat lax during the period in question.

Ray Boyer had been arrested by Constable William Kimmel on the afternoon of May 25, 1968 for an outstanding child support warrant and was in jail at the time of the murder. According to police reports and the testimony of Ray Boyer, investigators initially focused on Ray Boyer as a suspect in 1968 and questioned him extensively as to how he got out of jail to commit the murder. Despite the issues relating to the bite mark, we heard no evidence from which to conclude that Ray Boyer was involved in the murder. That being said, Ray Boyer's statements to the police in 1968 are not at all consistent with his current opinions.

Ray Boyer was repeatedly asked whether he had any objective information to substantiate his claim that his brother had committed the murder. Again, the following exchange occurred:

Q.   You talked about this idea that Dick, your brother, committed this crime and that you knew and Detective Snavely knew and all these other people knew, right?

A.   We just - - everything comes back to him. I've been trying to tell everybody this for years. If you sit down and look at his demeanor and what he did, what I stopped him from doing.

Q.   But beyond those things, Ray - -

A.   He jumped out of a car, convertible, at 60 mile an hour just because he didn't want to go somewhere and broke his arms. He has plates and pins. He just got up and jumped out of the car down the highway. What person in their right mind does that?

17

Q.   Okay. But beyond those types of things, this idea of about you know who, you know how he is, you don't know how he would have got from work to the apartment that night to commit this murder; is that a fair statement?

A.   He has friend. He has friends.

Q.   But you don't have any independent knowledge of how that would have happened?

A.   No.

Q.   Okay.

A.   No, I do not.

Q.   That's what I'm asking. Do you know if anyone else would have had that type of information given that there's this focus on Dick?

A.   Information like what?

Q.   Objective information about him actually committing this crime. We know that because x, y and z, other than we just know what kind of guy he is?

A.   No...

Ray Boyer was also asked about repeated allegations that authorities have no true interest in solving the Reber murder. He also responded to questions concerning the involvement of "influential" people in Reber's murder.

Q.   What facts do you have — what evidence do you have to suggest that ...we don't have a true incentive to solve this crime?

A.   I just – I believe you do now. I see it. You got the jury here. You got a Grand Jury. Now I believe you, but you's got to remember where I'm coming from. I'm coming from, like I said, it ain't the detectives from back then, but I had them detectives screwing my head over for months. You understand what I'm saying? How can I—yes, it's a different era. You's are not them detectives, but you are still detectives.
                                    * * *

Q.   There have been accusations by some different folks that one of the reasons this case went the direction that it went back in the 60's and 70's was that there was prominent local people who were frequenting that place and didn't want to be known for that?

18

A.	No prominent people came to that apartment. Now, I'm not saying what she did other places and when she went for five or six days, came back with a pile of money, but they never came to that house.

Q.	You didn't see doctors, lawyers, police officers?

A.	No. No, I did not.

Ray Boyer's statement in this regard is of critical importance when evaluating one of the most widely and firmly held conspiracy theories relating to this case. It has been alleged that investigators and prosecutors in 1968 implicated Arthur Root in the murder of Peggy Reber so as to avoid implicating Richard Boyer, the alleged killer. According to conspiracy theorists led by Michelle Gooden, "prominent" persons involved in the investigation frequented the apartment of Mary Reber and the Maple Leaf Apartment Building for illicit purposes.[16] Consequently, these "prominent" people knew that Richard Boyer could disclose their "dirty secrets" if he were implicated by virtue of his involvement with Mary and the Reber girls. Conspiracy theorists claim that Arthur Root was implicated because he was an easy target and unaware of the secrets investigators and prosecutors hoped to keep secret. Ray Boyer's statement that no prominent people visited the apartment would appear to eviscerate this theory. We find it virtually impossible that such a movie-like conspiracy could have existed given the number of individuals from various local, state and federal agencies who were involved in the original investigation. Conspiracy theorists also ignore the fact that Arthur Root maintained an intimate relationship with Mary Reber and would have been privy to the same information available to Richard Boyer.

---

[16] This theory was adopted in an editorial, Don't Lose Focus, published in the Lebanon Daily News in 2008.

Meanwhile, conspiracy theories that have been floating around even before Reber's body was buried continue to circulate. (There's not space here to explore these theories. They have to do with the idea that powerful people—past and present—have a personal interest in keeping a lid on the story. The person of interest, by the way, is not a powerful person. But it is not too much of a stretch to think that he may have powerful information to share about them.) (emphasis added).

19

Given the intense public focus on Richard Boyer, we subpoenaed him to testify. Richard Boyer appeared before us without counsel and agreed to testify. He denied that he was involved in Reber's murder. He testified that he had been at work on the night in question and had gone directly home thereafter. There is no reliable evidence to refute this claim. Boyer said that he and his wife, Linda, have been harassed since the investigation was reopened. Richard Boyer and his wife both testified that they had received anonymous phone calls and mailings accusing Richard Boyer of having committed the murder. Richard Boyer presented various cards and envelopes that he and his wife had received in the mail. Two of the envelopes contained a postmark from North Carolina.

Michelle Gooden resides in North Carolina and acknowledged during her testimony that she had sent cards to Boyer. Richard Boyer and his wife also told us that Kevin Snavely frequently parked near their home and even followed them on occasion. In an e-mail, Kathy Meador claimed that Michelle Gooden wanted her to send harassing letters to the Boyers.

> *And she told me she wanted to mail a couple dozen letters each week. She told me these letters would be to the DA's office, accusing them of coverup and hounding them to do something. And she said she would send letters for dick, hounding him about giving himself up. And for Linda to put a guilt trip on her. Then she said she would send money for envelopes and stamps. All I would have to do is mail them weekly to the DA's office and to Dick. That way they wouldn't suspect anything if they didn't come from NC.*

Richard Boyer testified that Kevin Snavely interviewed him in July, 2006. He told us that Snavely immediately accused him of having killed Reber and alleged that he had located Boyer's DNA on the cloth belt used to strangle Reber. Despite Snavely's ruse, Boyer continued to deny that he had been involved in the murder. However, Snavely did not believe Boyer and told others he knew Boyer to be lying during the interview. We learned that Snavely repeatedly

20

communicated with individuals outside the investigation.[17] This served to further foster the controversy relating to this case.

Snavely's reports reflect that he spoke with Kathryn Meador and that Meador told him that she believed that her then-husband had killed her sister. Snavely also spoke with Ray Boyer who also allegedly indicated his belief that his brother had killed Peggy. Neither Meador nor Ray Boyer had ever implicated Richard Boyer in the murder until Gooden became involved in the case. During her sworn testimony, Kathryn Meador testified as follows concerning Gooden's influence:

> Q. Ma'am, do you know a woman by the name of Michelle Gooden?
>
> A. Yes.
>
> Q. At any point in time has she suggested to you what you should tell the police in the investigation?
>
> A. Yes.
>
> Q. What sort of things has she suggested to you?
>
> A. I don't know. There was so many different things she would say about the time that he come in, are you sure that it wasn't earlier or later or this and that. And that's why it was so confusing for me. I wanted to try to get my own memory back. She'd be calling and saying, Well, what about this person or that person? Wasn't he involved with this person? I don't know, but basically she — I mean, she wanted to show that it was Dick as the killer, but not that I really wanted that, but I believe that, and I guess because I believed that she really wanted me to say different things about different time periods. And I said, I can't swear to anything I don't remember, you know. If I say something one time, I might remember. I blocked a lot of things out. If I get home, I remember something, but there was so many things she was asking. And she went to the point of saying that he was living in the apartment somehow, and all the time, you know, and as far as I knew we didn't have the apartment at all, just different things like that. I don't know why. It was very confusing.

---

[17] One witness refused to answer a question concerning what Snavely had told him about Richard Boyer's alleged involvement in the murder. The witness claimed that Snavely had told him the information in confidence and that he knew Snavely should not have released the information to him. Given his loyalty to Snavely, he did not believe he had an obligation to answer the question. The Court compelled the witness to answer.

21

Q.   Okay. So she indicated to you that she believed that Dick was the killer?

A.   Yes.

Q.   And when she would ask you questions, if you didn't give her the answer that she wanted you to give, what would her response be to that?

A.   Well, that would be an hour. She'd say, Well, I think you're wrong. I think you should remember this or I think you should say this. I think you should go back and remember this or that, and I don't know. Just she wasn't happy when she didn't get an answer she didn't want.

Q.   And again, the information that you've given us today, is that information based entirely upon your own personal recollection of what happened?

A.   Yes, that's why I basically stayed away from her for months because I didn't want anybody's influence as I was beginning to remember things more. I wanted my own memories to come back.

We learned that Kathryn Meador has given many different statements to police concerning her sister's murder. In 1968, Meador gave statements to police that were corroborated by other witnesses. Meador does not remember making any of those statements. Over the past several years, Meador has given inconsistent statements concerning her recollection of events.

Q.   Do you have a concern in your mind, Kathy, about what you truly remember as your own independent thoughts versus what you've come to believe over time by virtue of things people have told you?

A.   Well, I started to believe that, and that's why I kind of got myself away from people.

Q.   You separated yourself from that?

A.   Yes, too much was coming at me as I was remembering things because I blocked out a lot for a long time, and I didn't want to mix that with what, oh, okay they said that, so it must have happened. The same thing with Mary. So I tried to stay away as much as I could to make sure they were my own memories.

22

While we appreciated Ms. Meador's candor in acknowledging that she has been influenced by others, we also realize that Ms. Meador has little if any independent recollection of the time or events associated with her sister's murder. Like Ray Boyer, Kathryn Meador was not able to provide any objective facts in support of the widely held theory that Richard Boyer participated in this murder.

Following her grand jury testimony, Gooden provided an e-mail to Detective Michael Dipalo that had been forwarded to her from radio talk show host Laura LeBeau. The e-mail reflects messages exchanged between Kevin Snavely and Laura LeBeau on the heels of Snavely having filed a lawsuit against City officials and District Attorney David Arnold. The lawsuit filed by Snavely publicly identified, for the first time, Richard Boyer as the "suspect" in the Reber murder. In her e-mail which she also sent to Gooden[18], LeBeau chastised Snavely for identifying Boyer as it exposed others who had backed efforts to implicate Boyer.

> *Kevin, I feel that you violated some bonds or trust by naming so many names and inside information when vague generalities would have served your purpose just as well. Again, with the errors in the timeline of events........ it really looks shoddy, and if this is an indication of your work-product as an officer, what is a person to think about your professionalism?*

***

> *I know you have to concern yourself with all of your issues, but I think you've screwed a whole bunch of people in the process......and it calls your credibility into question. I would have hoped that you could prevail in your case against the city, because I believe they clearly screwed you over in retaliation for their public embarrassment. But by naming (although indirectly) the suspect you identified......while a grand jury is convened on the matter and the DA is trying to secure an indictment against him......may have just given him his "get out of jail free" card. He can say you tried to frame him, and unless you have the corroboration of Michelle, John Latimer, Mike Mangano, Doris Belanger and others whom you've outed....the DA might not be able to make anything stick against him, particularly if those folks choose to turn their backs on you.*

---

[18] LeBeau wrote to Gooden; "*I sent this to Kevin this evening. I do want some of those defendants he named to fry....such as Harvey, Anspach, maybe even Carpenter. But, he should know that he screwed you over, too. Laura.*"

23

In Snavely's e-mail to LeBeau generating the above response, Snavely made the following statement:

As always I ask that you do not mention this info came directly from me.

Prior to invoking his right against self incrimination, Snavely denied that he had exchanged e-mails with LeBeau or others. We learned that Snavely released investigative information to various sources throughout the investigation. Ray Boyer told us that Snavely was his "source" of information throughout the investigation. Michelle Gooden told us that Snavely provided her with crime scene photographs and even police reports relating to the investigation. Kathryn Meador told us that Snavely was operating of the mindset that Richard Boyer was responsible for the murder when he first interviewed her shortly after reopening the case. Other witnesses testified that Snavely announced to them that he knew Boyer was responsible for the murder and that he was going to prove it.

Given the fact that Peggy Reber was murdered in 1968, we would expect witnesses to have a lack of specific memory concerning events 40 years ago. However, in this case, multiple witnesses testified that Snavely's police reports were not consistent with what they had told him. By way of example, Snavely reported that one witness, who was ten years old at the time of the murder, told him that she observed Richard Boyer outside the Reber Apartment on the night of Peggy's murder. Snavely described this witness as being hysterical about coming forward with this information for the first time after almost forty (40) years. However, the witness told us under oath that she told Snavely that she saw two (2) people in the hallway that night and that she believed one of those people to be Ray Boyer and one to be Richard Boyer. The witness said that Snavely convinced her that she could not have seen Ray Boyer because he was in jail at the time. She explained that Snavely talked her out of that portion of her statement relating to the

24

second individual. In his report, Snavely makes no mention of the second individual and reported only that the witness saw Richard Boyer in the hallway outside the Reber apartment.

The witness also denied that Snavely's report was accurate concerning her alleged demeanor in providing this information. Snavely characterized the witness in his report as being hysterical when he spoke with her. The witness denied that this was true. We learned that this witness initially told Snavely that she had not seen or heard anything on the night of Reber's murder. She later changed her story. When Detective Dipalo sought to re-interview this witness, she was reluctant to cooperate. In fact, upon being contacted by Detective Dipalo, the witness reached out to Michelle Gooden in an internet posting.[19]

During her testimony, the witness was specifically asked as to her opinion concerning Richard Boyer's involvement in the murder.

> Q.   Let me ask you this if I can. Do you have an opinion today as to whether or not Dick Boyer was involved in the murder of Peggy Reber?
>
> A.   I don't know. I mean, I don't really know.
>
> Q.   Because at least from Kevin Snavely's reports he seems to indicate that you believe Dick was the killer?
>
> A.   Well, I asked Kevin – before I knew – before Kevin told me who he thought it was or whatever, like he didn't name any names, I mean, but I knew what I saw back then. So I said to Kevin when he said about he has a suspect and before I even told Kevin about what I saw back then, I said to him, "Are you sure that this person, who your suspect is or whatever, are you sure that he did it?" I mean, I was thinking maybe it was the same person I saw so. And he was like, "Oh, there's no doubt in my mind." And I said, "I mean, are you really sure because I can't be positive. I mean, I would hate for somebody to go to jail that didn't do it." But then he said he was -- there was no doubt in his mind, and then he said he couldn't talk to the person anymore because they lawyered up or something like that; but then of course in my mind I had seen Dick at the door.

---

[19] The internet posting contained the following message: *"Michelle, It's *****. So sorry I have lost touch with you. My work has taken most of my time and so much is going on. Moving on...I need you to please e-mail me. There are detectives calling me and I need your advice"*. We learned that other witnesses reached out to Gooden, particularly upon receiving subpoenas to testify before us.

25

So I mean, you know, you put two and two together, but I don't know for sure of course. I didn't --

Q. Are you aware of any other facts other than you seeing Dick at the door that night that could lead you to conclude that he was involved here? Anything else that you can think of?

A. No.

We subpoenaed Michelle Gooden to testify on December 15, 2008.[20] In spite of her harsh criticism and alleged expertise concerning the Reber case, Michelle Gooden did not provide us with one objectively verifiable fact to support her conclusion that Richard Boyer killed Peggy Reber. Gooden testified for over five (5) hours. Gooden was asked repeatedly to provide us with facts and evidence in support of her conclusion that Richard Boyer had committed the murder. She provided long, rambling speeches which were not responsive to the question(s) posed. She acknowledged that all of the conspiracy theories relating to the case were only theories and had no factual foundation. She also acknowledged at the close of her testimony that she had been given a full opportunity to provide us with facts and to explain her theories and conclusions.

Q. At any point today have I treated you unfairly in here?

A. No. I'm (not) going to ruin your reputation.

Q. At any point did I not give you an opportunity to explain whatever you wanted?

A. You've been very fair to me. There goes that reputation.

Q. Thank you.

A. Oh, my God, did we just find a government employee I am not going to criticize and pick on, say it isn't so.

---

[20] Given Gooden's accusations relating to District Attorney Arnold, we requested that Arnold leave the courtroom during portions of her testimony.

MR. DITZLER: Thank you very much, Michelle. I believe we are prepared to excuse you from your testimony.

Despite the extensive questioning of Ms. Gooden during which she was provided with the opportunity to provide us with all evidence known to her about the case, we gleaned very little about the case from her testimony. Gooden's skepticism and paranoia persisted even when confronted with objectively verifiable facts that conflicted with her conclusions. Gooden explained that she was not a trained investigator and that she could not be held to the same standard as one. With respect to the current investigation and her focus on Richard Boyer, Gooden testified as follows:

> Q. I think it's probably a good time to take a break..., but let me end with this. Do you think it is a fair inference that we're going to impute all of this knowledge to Dick Boyer but nobody else?
>
> A. No, that's not true. I am still receptive, as Detective Dipalo knows, there is a possibility that a fruit loop went in that apartment, killed her, walked away, and we never see them again. **I live in a land where you're innocent until proven guilty, and I believe in that. You have the skills and the qualifications to do this, not me, and I will accept whatever you come up with.**

(emphasis added).

Despite this, Gooden continues to question the integrity of our investigation and claims that we have not been provided with pertinent information about the case. Gooden also continues to claim that politics is the driving force behind our investigation. We obtained e-mails that Gooden exchanged with former District Attorney Deirdre Eshleman. Gooden wrote to Eshleman after being initially contacted by Detective Michael Dipalo:

> *I wanted to offer you a little sideline entertainment. Detective Mike Dipalo contacted me a couple weeks ago. It is safe to say he was apprehensive about communications with this crazed lunatic, and quite surprised when he learned I did extensive research and know the case rather well. Yesterday, I decided to enlighten him a little bit in regards to my knowledge of his fearless leader.*

* * *

27

I remain silent about the Arnold because timing is everything, and it's just not time, but the good DA should realize time is on my side not his. Oh to be a fly on the wall in the DA's office today, Michelle.

In reply, Eshleman wrote to Gooden:

Michelle

I was the DA when we hired Mike DiPalo. He is without a doubt the most talented investigator in Lebanon County. If he is handling Peggy's case, you can be sure the investigation will be well handled. If I were you, I would cooperate with him in every way possible. If you want justice for Peggy, you should send him any written statements from witnesses, and tell him everything you know about any leads you've discovered. He is tenacious – he will track down anything and everything. He is not political in any way, and has never been influenced by anything other than a sincere desire to find out what happened.

I am pleasantly surprised that he's been assigned to the case. It's a hopeful turn of events.

Gooden did not heed Eshleman's advice.

We also learned that Gooden was writing a book about Reber's murder which she claimed to be factual. However, when Detective Dipalo requested a copy of her manuscript during his investigation, Gooden refused to provide it.[21] She provided a copy only in response to her Grand Jury subpoena. Gooden's subpoena also required her to provide us with any and all documents she had acquired relating to the Reber case. In response, Gooden provided us with a small stack of miscellaneous papers relating to the case which was not at all commensurate with the length and scope of her alleged investigation. We subsequently obtained many documents and e-mails from other sources that had originated with Gooden but which she had failed to provide to us.[22] During her grand jury testimony, Gooden stated, "*Wouldn't I be the hypocrite to*

---

[21] In an e-mail dated August 10, 2008, Gooden wrote to one of her supporters: "*The DA's office wants my notes, files, manuscript, etc. I am accused of "stone-walling" I am not guilty of that in the least. I am not a detective, I was never "investigating" and the professionals are much more qualified to produce accuracy over my efforts.*"

[22] A third-party provided Detective Dipalo with over 800 e-mail messages from Gooden. Gooden provided none of those e-mails in response to her subpoena.

28

be for the Grand Jury and then refuse to give you what you want to see? That's talking out of both sides of my mouth." That is precisely what Gooden did.

We unanimously question Gooden's true motivations and veracity given what we know about her involvement in this case. We are also troubled that so many loyally followed her in her efforts to implicate Richard Boyer and to publicly smear those who questioned her true motives or who otherwise attempted to remain objective. We reviewed numerous e-mail messages authored by Gooden which were turned over by a third-party to Detective Dipalo in May of 2009. Those messages even contained references to the utilization of fabricated information to further the case against Richard Boyer. By way of example, in referring to Ray Boyer, Gooden wrote:

> *Let me explain Ray to you...this is in the strictest confidence. If someone tells Ray something he immediately takes ownership as the source.*
>
> *Example – I talked to Ray 7 or 8 years ago, and our communication faded. I shared some information with him at that time-remember that ******, I shared WITH him. Years later Snavely gets involved and one day he told me about Ray sharing some information Ray picked up with him. *****, it was the info I gave Ray, and he looked very stupid when I shared the emails with Kevin to prove his egotistical lie. **We never exposed Ray because it served no purpose, but we both had a better understanding of him.***

(emphasis added).

Given the passage of more than 40 years since the murder and the pervasive taint associated with the investigation, we firmly believe that only a detailed and corroborated confession and/or the existence of compelling forensic evidence could lead to a final resolution of this case. With respect to forensic evidence, we learned that only limited items of evidence from the original investigation remain. Evidence maintained by the Lebanon City Police Department was damaged and/or destroyed by flood waters from Hurricane Agnes in 1972. Certain items of evidence that had been introduced as evidence at the trial of Arthur Root were

29

preserved, although most were subjected to flood waters. The hair and fiber evidence which formed the basis for the original prosecution of Arthur Root is no longer in existence and could not be re-examined using modern techniques.

All remaining items of evidence were forensically examined using the most advanced forensic techniques available. No forensic evidence, to include DNA, was located on any item of evidence. We should also note that the District Attorney and his staff presented the Reber murder case to the Vidocq Society[23] in Philadelphia on October 16, 2008 in an effort to generate input and ideas concerning further investigation. Vidocq members agreed to assist with further forensic analysis, to include teeth impression comparisons.

All remaining items of evidence were ultimately sent to National Medical Services, a private forensic laboratory in Willow Grove, Pennsylvania. A forensic scientist from NMS told us that he attempted to extract and isolate DNA material from a variety of items, to include the bow, the belt used to strangle Reber, bottles purportedly containing fingernail scrapings from Reber, and various other items. His efforts were unsuccessful. In cataloging the remaining evidence[24], Detective Dipalo sought out and obtained microscopic slides containing Reber's breast tissue from the National Institute of Pathology which had maintained custody of the slides for 40 years. Those slides contained tissue at the site of the bite mark on Reber's breast. They were also examined for foreign DNA material with negative results. Richard Boyer and others voluntarily submitted DNA samples for purposes of potential comparison.

---

[23] The Vidocq Society is a non-profit organization made up of "forensic professionals and motivated private citizens who, as a public service, donate deductive, scientific and other talents for the common good. A long-unsolved homicide or death is the focus of a Vidocq Society meeting during which the case and its evidence are dissected for members and invited guests, all with an eye towards rekindling or refocusing the investigation". (www.vidocq.org) Presentation of a case to the Vidocq Society is by invitation only following an appropriate request from law enforcement sources.

[24] When county detectives undertook the handling of this case, they discovered evidence, to include pill bottles labeled as containing Reber's fingernail scrapings, in a cardboard box in the city police evidence room. These items were repackaged according to modern standards and submitted for forensic analysis.

30

We also learned about the exhumation of the body of Peggy Reber which was conducted on April 29, 2008. In conducting the exhumation, it was hoped that the body of Peggy Reber would be well preserved for advanced forensic examination. Experts believed that the body would be well preserved even after 40 years provided it was not exposed to water. We saw photos of the exhumation process and learned that the concrete liner protecting Reber's casket had failed over time. Reber's wooden casket had disintegrated and her remains had decomposed. We observed photographs of Reber's skeletal remains and learned that no forensic testing could be performed.

Last, we investigated the bite mark located on Reber's breast. As previously stated, photos of the bite mark depict a severe bite impression surrounding the nipple. Although Ray Boyer took credit for the bite mark in 1968 and specifically described his positioning in making it, he now denies that he made it having seen the photo for the first time. Ray Boyer could not be excluded by experts as having made the bite. However, many others, past and present, were excluded as having made the bite. Richard Boyer's dental impressions were secured in 2008 and he was excluded as having made the mark.

We are perplexed by the bite mark. It appears to us to be a severe bite inflicted at or near the time of death as opposed to one made during consensual lovemaking[25]. It was undoubtedly an important piece of information in defense of Arthur Root as Root was excluded as having made it. George Christianson and some of the original investigators told us that they believed that the bite mark was an important factor for the jury in acquitting Root. They theorized that more than one person was involved in Reber's murder and that Root's accomplice(s) may have

---

[25] At the trial of Root, experts disagreed as to the timing of the bite mark. Multiple experts consulted by Detective Dipalo believe that the bite mark was inflicted at or near the time of death as opposed to hours or days earlier.

inflicted the bite. Regardless, we did not reach any firm conclusion as to the maker of the bite mark.

In conducting our investigation, we learned about many other potential suspects in the case. John Ebling, deceased, was viewed by some as a potential suspect. Ebling's former wife told us that she believes Ebling committed the murder because he had told her that he had committed a terrible crime and had not been caught. She also claimed that Ebling's friends referred to him as "the Bow". We heard from at least one of Ebling's friends who denied that this was true. Although Ebling was on the suspect list created in 1968, investigators were unable to speak with him because he left town shortly after the murder. Although an aura of suspicion surrounds Ebling, we heard no credible facts on which to rely to support the conclusion that Ebling was responsible for the murder.

Walter Graeff, deceased, the owner of the Maple Leaf Apartment Building, was also considered a potential suspect. Graeff was an attorney and had a colorful reputation as being perverted. It was alleged that Graeff had installed one way mirrors in the building through which he was able to view female tenants. Although Graeff was a lawyer, he was not considered by most to be a prominent member of the community. Investigators in 1968 learned that Graeff was with his wife at the time of Reber's murder and he was excluded as a suspect.

We also learned that (2) two individuals committed suicide shortly after Reber's murder. Marlin Jones provided a statement to police in the days following Reber's murder that he had observed an individual running from the Maple Leaf Apartment Building at 11:45 PM on May 25, 1968. Jones described driving past the apartment building when an individual ran out from between two parked cars. Jones said that he had to skid to a stop to avoid hitting the man. Jones provided an incredibly detailed description of the individual down to the color socks the man

32

was wearing. The detail of the description was uncanny considering the time of day and the seconds Jones had to observe the man. Police even created a sketch based upon Jones' statement. Jones committed suicide in the Cold Springs area on June 7, 1968. His statements to police as to his own whereabouts on the night of the murder could not be corroborated by investigators in 1968. However, Jones was excluded as a suspect largely by virtue of the fact that no forensic evidence linked him to the crime. Jones' bite impressions were found not to have matched the bite mark on Reber's breast.

Likewise, another potential suspect, Morris Purcell, committed suicide at the Lebanon County jail in the weeks following Reber's murder. Purcell was found hanging in his cell. Purcell initially fled from investigators when they attempted to speak with him concerning the murder. Investigators located stolen items in his apartment and believed this was the reason Purcell fled. Again, no physical evidence, including bite impressions, linked Purcell to the crime.

Suspicions about others, living and dead, continue to circulate. In 1968, investigators spent considerable time investigating two men, Carlos "Chico" Reyes and Jose Rivera, who had been at the Reber apartment in the days prior to Reber's murder. Investigators extensively investigated these subjects and spent considerable effort attempting to corroborate their respective alibis. We learned that Lester White, deceased, was also investigated as he had been charged with attempting to "ravish" Peggy Reber in the days prior to Reber's murder. White was referred to by investigators in 1968 as a "known sex offender". White's alibi, however, was also confirmed by investigators.

As to Arthur Root, Jr., the only person charged with Reber's murder, we learned that he is incarcerated in Oklahoma. Root's criminal history is extensive and includes a conviction for

33

276

the rape and sodomy of his 12 year old step-daughter at knife point. Even if Root were to confess to participating in Reber's murder, he could not be retried. Root was interviewed in 2001 by Detective Randall Edgar of the Lebanon City Police. Root denied involvement in the murder. In 2008, Root was interviewed on at least (3) three occasions by the warden of the correctional facility where he is incarcerated. During the recorded interviews, Root consistently denied knowing anything about the murder and was unable to remember anything concerning his whereabouts and activities on the night of the murder. He specifically stated that he had no interest in testifying before a grand jury and indicated that he would refuse to cooperate.

Of all those who have been cast under the shroud of suspicion, mentioned herein or otherwise, we found no compelling direct or circumstantial evidence to link any particular person to this crime. Speculation, suspicion and rumor do not equate with the legal standard of probable cause, nor do wild accusations unsupported by even a scintilla of fact.

As to wild accusations, we investigated the long standing allegations of cover-up, conspiracy and conflict of interest associated with this case. We found absolutely no evidence to support the allegations made by some. Some claim that the initial investigation and the prosecution of Arthur Root were orchestrated by "prominent" people so as to hide their alleged relationship with Mary Reber and others. Not one witness provided a single fact to support this accusation. In fact, witnesses who resided in the Maple Leaf Apartment complex or who were within the inner circle of the Reber family, including Ray Boyer, denied that prominent people were involved or connected with Mary Reber. Despite the availability of objectively verifiable information which would tend to disprove such a theory, it has continued to survive.

34

We heard no facts to support the claim that Arthur Root was a "patsy" and was sought after to avoid focus on the true suspect.[26] If investigators in 1968 needed an easy target, they could have pinned the murder on one of the two men who committed suicide soon after and were known to have a connection to the apartment building. Likewise, Carlos Reyes and Jose Rivera were two transient Hispanic men who had been in the apartment on the day of the murder and who would have made easy targets for conspiring investigators in 1968.

The logical, reasonable and factually supported conclusion to be drawn from all of the facts that we obtained is that investigators in 1968 firmly believed that Arthur Root, Jr., participated in the murder of Peggy Reber. This conclusion was supported by the most advanced forensic evidence known to investigators at the time. Even Kevin Snavely told us during his abbreviated testimony that he found no evidence of conspiracy or cover-up during his investigation. Ray Boyer, part of the Reber inner circle in 1968, offered no evidence in support of any conspiracy or cover-up.

We subpoenaed John Latimer of the Lebanon Daily New to testify concerning his knowledge of the Reber murder and the conspiracy theories attendant thereto. Latimer wrote 23 articles about the Reber murder and witnesses told us that he too believed that Richard Boyer was responsible for the murder. Latimer's attorneys filed a Motion to Quash our subpoena on the basis of the First Amendment and journalistic privilege.[27] In one of Latimer's recent legal filings which we reviewed, he too challenged the integrity of our investigation and claimed that it should be turned over to the Attorney General's Office. We provided Mr. Latimer with the opportunity to testify and to tell us anything he knew about the Reber case and the alleged

---

[26] Michelle Gooden and others insist that Richard Boyer was the suspect intentionally ignored in 1968.

[27] We withdrew our request to hear from Mr. Latimer so as not to further delay our investigation and because we concluded that he received information about the case from Gooden and Snavely.

35

scandals associated with it. He refused that opportunity. For him to now claim knowledge of facts relating to a conflict of interest or to make allegations challenging the integrity of our investigation represents the height of hypocrisy. It is however, consistent with what we learned throughout our investigation. Those who alleged that they knew the most about this case and demanded a prosecution had little interest in appearing before us.

We categorically reject the multitude of conspiracy theories attendant to this case. Not one witness provided a factually supported or otherwise cogent analysis of any conspiracy, cover-up or conflict of interest. Witnesses were openly invited to provide us with such information. One witness went so far as to suggest that the Republican Party could be responsible for some cover-up associated with the case. Not one fact was presented by any witness that would lead us to such a conclusion. As Grand Jurors, we were never asked or requested to provide our political party affiliation. The ignorance and absurdity of this comment was offensive to all of us, particularly where there is not one shred of evidence to support it.

III. CONCLUSION

The murder of Peggy Reber was a horrific crime. The investigation of the crime was complicated by the unfortunate and dysfunctional environment in which Peggy was raised. We are disappointed to conclude that some who were the most vocal advocates of "Justice for Peggy" were motivated by interests wholly unrelated to legitimate interests of justice. Some chose to use the case for political purposes while others used it to draw attention to themselves and/or to generate controversy. In doing so, we believe that they exploited surviving members of the Reber family and this community.

We voted to conclude our investigation after exhausting further investigative opportunities. We provided those who claimed to know the most about the case with the

36

COURT OF COMMON PLEAS OF LEBANON COUNTY
COMMONWEALTH OF PENNSYLVANIA
COUNTY INVESTIGATING GRAND JURY OF NOVEMBER 2008

SUBPOENA NO.

DOCKET NO. CP-38-MD 245-2008

INVESTIGATION NO. 003

TO: MICHELLE GOODEN

1.   You are ordered by the Court of Common Pleas to appear as a witness before the County Investigating Grand Jury for the County of Lebanon in Courtroom No. 3 in the Lebanon County Municipal Building on **Monday, December 15, 2008 at 8:30 a.m.** to testify and give evidence in regard to alleged violations of the laws of the Commonwealth of Pennsylvania and remain until excused.

2.   You are further ordered to bring with you the following:

Any and all documents and manuscripts regarding Peggy Reber. (Documents" in the broadest sense possible includes, without limitation, any tangible thing upon which any expression, communication, information, data, or representation has been recorded by any means including, but not limited to written, printed, recorded, taped, filmed, videotaped or in computer, digital or magnetic memory or storage, however produced or reproduced, and also includes originals, drafts, and non-identical copies wherever located. "Document" or "Documents" shall include, but not be limited to, books, contracts, agreements, correspondence, electronic mail, computer tapes, computer discs, computer files, computer printouts, CD-ROM's, computer hard drives, magnetic memory, printouts and keypunch cards, memoranda, diaries, notes, reports, bulletins, printed forms, telegraphic communications, pleading and other legal papers, notes, records of any sort of meeting, invoices, financial statements, bank statements, cancelled checks, telexes, telegrams, telecopies, facsimile reproductions or "faxes," actual compilations, data compilations, statistical compilations, plans, diagrams,charts, journals, change orders, studies, surveys, sketches, art work, graphics, checks, ledgers, catalogues,brochures, pamphlets, press releases, advertisements, invoices, minutes, photographs, microfilms, microfiche, films, personnel files, quotes, stenographic notes, working papers, preliminary, intermediate or final drafts, telephone records, schedules, bids, voice recordings, reports of telephone conversations, desk calendars, appointment books, audio or video tape recordings, transcriptions, and all other writings and recordings of every kind that are in Your actual or constructive possession, custody or Control. The term "Document" further means any document now or at any time in the possession, custody, or Control of the entities to whom this document request is directed (together with any predecessors, successors, affiliates, subsidiaries or divisions thereof and their officers, directors, employees, agents and attorneys).

Failure to attend may cause a warrant to be issued for your arrest and will make you liable to the penalties of law for the contempt of court.

_____
District Attorney

_____
Assistant District Attorney

President Judge
Court of Common Pleas

Issuance Approved:

_____
Supervising Judge

Date: 12/10/08

IN THE UNITED STATES DISTRICT COURT FOR THE MIDDLE DISTRICT OF PENNSYLVANIA

KEVIN SNAVELY   CIVIL ACTION LAW

    Plaintiff   NO.

    VS.

DAVID ARNOLD, ROBERT
ANSPACH, WILLIAM HARVEY,
DANIEL WRIGHT, ROBERT
McALLISTER, the CITY OF LEBANON
and WILLIAM CARPENTER,   JURY TRIAL DEMANDED

    Defendants

COMPLAINT

Introductory Statement

1. This is a complaint brought by a police officer whose first amendment rights to speak out on matters of public concern and for seeking a redress of grievances was violated by the defendants. In addition the plaintiff was defamed pretextually as an act of retaliation.

JURISDICTION AND VENUE

2. Original jurisdiction to hear complaints of constitutional violations by state officials, under badge of state authority, employing the remedial statute 42

1

21. On or about April of 2006 the plaintiff developed a suspect in the case.

22. Ms. Gooden contacted plaintiff in May of 2007 and indicated that she had developed the same suspicions about the suspect and further that she was very unhappy with the progress of the investigation and that she intended to contact the Lebanon Daily News. Plaintiff played no role in her thinking or decision, neither encouraging nor discouraging her.

23. On May 27, 2007 the Lebanon Daily News published an article postulating that the killer might still be living in Lebanon.

24. This article kicked off a storm of controversy creating a major public issue for a long period of time.

25. Plaintiff suffered harassment at the hands of his superiors, particularly chief William Harvey who persisted in referring to Ms. Gooden as plaintiff's "girlfriend"

26. On or about December 2007 Michelle Gooden contacted plaintiff and expressed her belief that Dist. Atty. David Arnold should recuse himself from the case. She went on to claim that she possessed a police report from North Lebanon Township PD indicating that Arnold had previously been arrested in a domestic violence case against his previous wife (Louisa). Gooden claimed she had gotten the report from a local news reporter. She said the charges had later

5

been reduced to a summary offense but that the reason for the report was that Arnold had struck his wife over his belief that she had been unfaithful with a man named Richard Boyer Jr. This person was the son of the murder suspect. Gooden believed Arnold was fearful that this information would be publicly disclosed and would be biased against investigating or prosecuting properly.

27. At this time the plaintiff advised Gooden that he had "no desire to be part of anything political and wanted no part of this". Gooden then told plaintiff that she intended to speak to Arnold and if he did not move forward she was going to report him to the Attorney General. She later did so.

28. Plaintiff then went on medical leave which required him to be out of work for six weeks. Just before going on medical leave plaintiff was advised by the defendant Wright that although he would still be allowed to actively work the case and if he needed to conduct any interviews he could bring them into the Lebanon Police Apartment "after hours" but that he "would not be compensated for any of this time". Plaintiff agreed.

29. Plaintiff went on medical leave in January of 2008. In late January 2 material events occurred. The murder victim's father delivered a petition with roughly 2000 names on it signed by local citizens urging DA David Arnold to convene a grand jury for his daughter's case.

6

30. On January 25, 2008 a memorial service was held at the United Methodist Church in Lebanon for Peggy Reber. Plaintiff attended the service on his own time in civilian clothing, while he was still on medical leave.

31. Shortly after plaintiff returned to work in mid February the defendant Wright and Lieut. Breiner invited plaintiff to a meeting to discuss the case. This meeting took place on February 27, 2008 beginning at 7:45 AM immediately after plaintiff came off the midnight shift. Plaintiff was instructed to bring any notes that he had compiled on the case to this meeting.

32. The following occurred during the aforementioned meeting:

a. Wright opened the meeting by attacking plaintiff for attending the memorial service for Ms. Reber. Wright began "you made us all fucking look bad". Wright indicated plaintiff had done so intentionally to make "them" look bad because he attended the service without telling "them" and therefore they had not set a uniformed representative to the service. Plaintiff responded he had no idea he was supposed to notify "them" and that he had done nothing further on the investigation in which they had no interest anyway and therefore had not stopped in.

b. Wright continued yelling that "he was fucking pissed off" but that if Kevin thought Wright was pissed off he should "see the Chief (William Harvey), the Mayor (Robert Anspach), and the District Attorney (David Arnold).

7

284

c. Right then ask plaintiff had taken his "report" home on medical leave and plaintiff responded that indeed he had. Plaintiff also reminded Captain Wright that he was free to take his report from the very beginning because he was doing everything on his own time at his own expense as per the official disinterest in the investigation at LPD.

d. The defendant Wright then accused plaintiff of providing his homicide report to Michelle Gooden. Plaintiff responded that that was totally untrue and expressed that he had no idea why Wright would think such a thing.

e. Wright then said he had been reading Gooden's "MySpace" page and she had mentioned the word "police report".

f. Wright then told the plaintiff that this was an "internal investigation".

g. Wright then confiscated the report.

h. Wright then began making accusations about a North Lebanon Township Police Department report indicating that David Arnold had been arrested. Wright also indicated that plaintiff went to the NLT PD and retrieved the report. Additionally, Wright indicated that plaintiff went to Good Samaritan Hospital and acquired Louisa Arnold's (previously Arnold's wife) medical records. Wright went on to accuse plaintiff of giving these records to Gooden in North Carolina. Plaintiff demanded to know if Wright had gone

8

to NLT PD and/or to Good Samaritan Hospital to verify these outlandish and false accusations. Wright had no response.

i. Plaintiff insisted on being able to take a lie detector test waiving any and all objections. Both Wright and Breiner called plaintiff a "liar" a number of times and Shortly thereafter plaintiff was permitted to leave the office. Plaintiff had endured three hours of false and accurate accusations including being called a "liar" and "incompetent" several times.

33. Plaintiff had never given his "report" to Michelle Gooden or anyone else nor had he ever retrieved any records having to do with David Arnold from anyone.

34. A few days later the defendant Capt. Wright called plaintiff into his office and said "that meeting went that way for a reason". Wright said that plaintiff had "said all the right things" and that "no disciplinary action was going to be taken".

35. About three days later plaintiff witnessed his former fiancée Kelly Heilman in Capt. Wright's office and became aware that she was there for at least an hour while plaintiff was in the police department.

36. On May 6, 2008 plaintiff was called into Capt. Wright's office where the defendant Robert McAllister (human resource officer) was present along with a union representative (Sgt. Thomas Hirschbock). At this meeting Wright told

9

plaintiff views conducting a new "internal investigation" into an item that was given to him "from two years ago". Plaintiff was being used of misappropriating disposable evidence.

37. Wright told plaintiff he was being placed on leave pending an investigation to determine if any other items had been taken by plaintiff.

38. Plaintiff responded that he had never taken anything that didn't belong to him when informed of the fact that he was being, in effect, subject to a total criminal investigation using the so-called "internal investigation" as a cover.

39. On May 16, 2008 plaintiff went on vacation. When he returned he was ordered to be in Chief William Harvey's office on May 24, 2008 at 9 AM for a meeting.

40. When plaintiff entered the room he was met by the defendant Anspach, the defendant Harvey, and the defendant McCallister. Plaintiff was told that he was terminated immediately.

41. Later that same day, plaintiff learned that Kelly Heilman had turned the DVD player over to DA David Arnold indicating it was just recently, and that she wanted to know "if Kevin Snavely was going to be fired". Plaintiff called Heilman shortly thereafter who denied she had turned the DVD player over to Arnold at all.

10

42. In early April plaintiff applied for unemployment which was opposed by the City of Lebanon.

43. It has been common practice for many years, well known to and approved by plaintiff's superior including the defendants Harvey and Wright, that items identified for disposal as unused or expired evidence, could be taken by police officers for their own use. This includes confiscated alcohol that was taken home by the defendant Wright among others (before he was made Captain).

44. Plaintiff has been unlawfully deprived of more than $40,000 in lost wages and emoluments as a result of the defendants unlawful actions.

45. These defendants violated plaintiff's right to speak out on matters of public concern when they permitted him without objection conduct a private investigation into the death of Ms. Reber.

46. When that investigation drew the attention of a private citizen who was investigating on their own, and had been for years, matters were revealed that indicated not only criminal misconduct by the Dist. Atty. of Lebanon County David Arnold but also indicated conflicts on Mr. Arnold's part.

47. Subsequently, these defendants acted to create exaggerated and false accusations of misconduct against the plaintiff in retaliation for his speaking out in the form of conducting a private complaint and expressing himself thereon (not in violation of *Garcetti*).

11

288

48. The defendants blamed the plaintiff for Arnold's exposure on matters which were public facts but embarrassing to him.

49. These defendants then came together and used their official power and positions to conjure up false charges against the plaintiff which were not based upon fact at all but were used as a pretext by these defendants to deter the plaintiff from the exercise of his 1st Amendment rights.

50. The plaintiff, upon being terminated from his employment, filed an unemployment compensation claim which, in retaliation, knowing the defendant had done nothing wrong, and thus in further violation of the plaintiff's First Amendment rights, was opposed by the defendant" City of Lebanon".

51. After listening to the evidence presented by both sides the Unemployment Compensation Referee the Honorable Brian L. Parr Referee. concluded that the employer (City of Lebanon) by and through its witnesses, which include some of the defendants here, failed to sustain its burden of demonstrating that the plaintiff's ("claimants")... "violation of employer policy constitutes willful misconduct in connection with the work". (Appeal--08-09-F-2278).

52. Plaintiff was awarded his Unemployment Compensation benefits sometime on or about August 2008. The City since appealed this decision to the Workers Compensation Review Board, who reversed the referee, abusing its discretion. Plaintiff is now appealing to the Commonwealth Court.

12

53. Plaintiff was able to acquire some part-time police force work after being wrongfully discharged by the defendants and the City of Lebanon.

54. On or about July 18, 2008 the defendant Arnold wrote a self-serving and pretextual letter to plaintiff's employer, the Township of Annville Pennsylvania. The purpose of this letter was to retaliate against the plaintiff, in a hateful and vindictive manner, because the plaintiff had spoken out on matters of public concern, and because he sought a redress of grievances.

55. The letter indicated that Mr. Arnold would not accept criminal cases filed or signed by Mr. Snavely. It also contained a disingenuous threat of investigation.

56. On or about March 28, 2008 the defendant Carpenter told a Lebanon citizen that David Arnold had approached him about the "cost" of the Reber case. Carpenter also told this person (Doris Belonger) that plaintiff was dismissed from his job for "stealing". Carpenter said "Detective Snavely's termination had nothing to do with the Peggy Reber case", indicating his personal knowledge of the issues in this matter. Carpenter was aware of intimate details of the so-called investigation including the use of bite marks which had been in the case file for approximately 40 years. Carpenter's misrepresentations that Snavely "was caught stealing" were false, inaccurate, and misrepresented the

13

circumstances, even those which were pretextually conjured up by these defendants, which led to the unlawful discharge of Kevin Snavely. Snavely stole nothing from anyone at any time. For Carpenter to so cruelly and inaccurately represent that Snavely had stolen something presented Snavely in a false light and is actionable. Carpenter made the same unlawful comments to Mike Mangano, a local businessman on April 7, 2008.

Wherefore plaintiff demands judgment of the defendants Arnold, Anspach, Harvey, Wright, McCallister and the City of Lebanon for the deprivation of, and for conspiracy to deprive plaintiff of, his federally guaranteed rights under the First Amendment. Plaintiff seeks punitive damages against the individual defendants together with damages for pain and suffering, humiliation and embarrassment and for damages in excess of $40,000 in a more exact amount to be determined at trial for lost wages and benefits due to the outrageous and injurious acts of these defendants. Plaintiff also complains under Pennsylvania law alleging injuries for unlawful wrongful discharge. Plaintiff complains of all individual defendants for participating in a civil conspiracy under Pennsylvania law and he complains that the defendant Carpenter defamed and/or otherwise misrepresented facts about the plaintiff placing him in a false light, all together with costs, fees, interest, attorney's fees, and such other relief as the court may deem appropriate.

14

FREEDOM OF INFORMATION
AND
PRIVACY ACTS

SUBJECT: Death of Margaret Lynn Reber

FEDERAL INVESTIGATION BUREAU OF

CLOTHING OF ROOT:

Q60-Q61 Pair of shoes
Q62   White shirt
Q63   Green trousers
Q64   Green sport coat

Q65-Q66 Fingernail scrapings of victim
Q67-Q68 Fingernail scrapings of [   ]   b7C
Q69-Q70 Fingernail scrapings of
Q71-Q72 Fingernail scrapings of

ITEMS FROM SCENE:

Q73   Piece of linoleum
Q74   Cardboard box
Q75   Bed slat
Q76   Mop
Q77   Bow
Q78   Dress
Q79   Handbag
Q80   Hair from wound
Q81   Scrapings from wall
Q82   Scrapings from under bed
Q83   Scrapings from bed
Q84   Shirt
Q85   Panties
Q86   Hairs from left armpit of victim
Q87   Hair from wastebasket
Q88   Green belt
Q89   Bottle of deodorant
Q90   Spoon
Q91   Linoleum from hall
Q92   Material from east end of hallway
Q93   Material from door of apartment
Q94   Material from stairway
Q95   Material from fire escape
Q96   Girdle
Q97   Sweater
Q98   Pair of handcuffs
Q99-Q100 Two tubes of lipstick
Q101 White button

Page 3
PC-A6913   JM JV HB

(continued on next page)

ITEM Q-98 shows the handcuffs taken into evidence

ITEMS FROM VICINITY OF APARTMENT:

Q102 Panties
Q103 Tissue paper
Q104 T shirt
Q105 Hair from victim's left thigh
Q106 Orange pajama top

K1   Head hair from victim
K2   Pubic hair from victim

Also Submitted: Nine latent lifts from bow
                 Wastebasket
                 Photographs from scene

b7C Specimens personally delivered on 6/12/68, by Trooper [   ]
                                                  PC-A6988 JM JV

     Q107 Yellow shirt
     Q108 Trousers
     Q109 Coat
     Q110-Q111 Pair of shoes

     K3   Pubic hair of [   ]
     K4   Arm hair from
     K5   Leg hair from
     K6   Head hair fro[   ]

Specimens personally delivered on 6/19/68, by [   ]
City Detective, PC-A7119 JM JV

     Q112 Purple blanket
     Q113 Toy stuffed animal
     Q114 Necktie
     Q115 Schmidt's beer bottle
     Q116 Towel

     K7   Head hair clippings from [   ]
     K8   Head hair clippings of
     K9   Pubic hair clippings o[   ]
     K10   Leg hair clippings of
     K11   Arm hair clippings of [   ]

Also Submitted: Nine fingerprint cards
                 Three latent lifts
                 Individual fingerprints of [   ]

Page 4   (continued on next page)
PC-A6913 JM JV HB

ITEM Q115 is the Schmidt's beer bottle from the coffee table in Peggy's home

294

ARTHUR McKINLEY ROOT, SR.   MURDER
alias ANTHONY WINSTEAD, JR.   Action No. 44, 1969

COURT ROOM No. 1 - Hon G. Thomas Gates P.J. Presiding
Trial Begins Monday, February 9, 1970 - 10:10 AM
Court Reporter Sworn 10:14 A.M.
Juror No. 1 Sworn - 11:52 AM
Recess For Lunch - 11:53 AM
Trial Resumes - 2:05 P.M.
Jurors No. 2 Thru No. 11 Sworn - 5:00 P.M.
Adjourn For The Day 5:01 P.M.
Trial Resumes Tuesday, February 10, 1970 - 10:05 AM
Juror No. 12 and Alt. No. 1 and Alt. No. 2 Sworn 11:30 AM
Jurors - See Sheet Attached
Recess For Lunch - 11:33 A.M.
Trial Resumes - 2:34 P.M.
District Attorney Makes Opening Statement To The Jury 2:50
Adjourn For The Day - 5:08 P.M.
Appearances: District Attorney George Christianson
For The Commonwealth, Attorney Thomas A.
Ehrgood and Attorney Robert Rowe For The
Defendant
Trial Resumes Wed. February 11, 1970 - 10:10 A.M.
Recess For Lunch - 12:01 P.M.
Trial Resumes: 2:03 P.M.
Adjourn For The Day: 5:16 P.M.
Trial Resumes Thursday February 12, 1970 - 10:03 AM
Recess For Lunch: 11:52 A.M.
Trial Resumes 2:01 P.M.
Adjourn For The Day: 5:05 P.M.
Trial Resumes Friday February 13, 1970: 10:09 AM
Recess For Lunch 11:56 A.M.
Trial Resumes 2:00 P.M.
Adjourn For The Day: 4:48 P.M.
Trial Resumes Saturday February 14, 1970: 9:33 AM
Adjourn For The Day: 12:00 Noon
Trial Resumes Monday, February 16, 1970 - 10:04 AM
Commonwealth Rests - 10:07 A.M.

(over)

MONDAY FEBRUARY 16, 1970
~~ATTORNEY FOR THE DEFENSE MAKE~~ OPENING STATEMENT TO THE JURY 10:47AM.
RECESS FOR LUNCH - 11:55 A.M.
TRIAL RESUMES 2:04 P.M.
ADJOURN FOR THE DAY - 4:50 P.M.
TRIAL RESUMES TUESDAY FEBRUARY 17, 1970 - 10:01 AM
RECESS FOR LUNCH - 12:00 NOON
TRIAL RESUMES - 2:03 P.M.
DEFENSE RESTS 2:20 P.M.
ADJOURN FOR THE DAY 4:34 P.M.
TRIAL RESUMES WED. FEBRUARY 18, 1970 - 10:14 AM
RECESS FOR LUNCH - 11:58 AM.
TRIAL RESUMES 2:03 P.M.
~~COMMONWEALTH RESTS ON REBUTTLE 3:52 P.M.~~
ADJOURN FOR THE DAY 3:54 P.M.
TRIAL RESUMES THUR. FEBRUARY 19, 1970 - 9:30 AM.
ATTORNEY THOMAS A. EHRGOOD MAKES SUMMATION TO
THE JURY 9:31 AM.
DISTRICT ATTORNEY GEORGE CHRISTIANSON MAKES
SUMMATION TO THE JURY 11:29 A.M.
RECESS FOR LUNCH 12:24 P.M.
TRIAL RESUMES 2:03 P.M.
COURT CHARGES THE JURY 2:04 P.M.
JURY RETIRES TO REACH A VERDICT - 4:15 P.M.
JURY RETURNS A VERDICT 7:06 P.M.
VERDICT - NOT GUILTY
FORE LADY - JANET E. GANTER
VERDICT SLIP FILED FEB. 19, 1970

Commonwealth Witnesses

2-10-70	Mary Reber
2-11-70	William Kimmel
	Blanche Kling
	Barbara J. Gardner
	Phyllis Copenhaver
	Phillip Sciotti
	James Rucco
	Harry Baumgardner
	Louise Lawson
	Pauline A. Shay
	Joy Annette Wagner
	Joseph Wida, Jr.
2-12-70	Betty Wenzler
	Jewel Beard
	Earl Wike
	Anthony Verna
	Marion Parsons
	Dr Leonard Tanner
	Linda Schneider
	James Sagan's
2-13-70	Bernard Reilly
	Clifford A. Roland
	Mark Kristovensky
	James Smith
	Thomas Kelleher, Jr.
	Paul M. Stombaugh
2-14-70	" " "
2-17-70	REBUTTLE
	Robert Cortright
2-18-70	Gus Zeppos
	John Robert Brown
	Grace Conrad
	Clifford Roland
	Ray Boyer

DEFENSE WITNESS

2-16 GARY MATTHEWS
      WALTER RAPASH
      GLORIA M. MILLER
      RICHARD MILLER
      GEORGE H. GREEN
      EVELYN WHITE
      DASIEY HAAGY
      MABLE GERNISHNER
      HARRY GREENAWALT
2-17 KATHY REBER BOYER
      CHARLES HARTMAN
      EMANUEL HAITOS
      FAYE EBY
      MRS DONALD LIGHT
      ARTHUR MCKINLEY ROOT, JR.
      VIRGINIA ROOT (MRS.)

The handwritten public records detailing the February 1970 trial of Arthur Root Jr

298

PENNSYLVANIA STATE POLICE
LABORATORY DIVISION
2191 & HERR STS., HARRISBURG, PA. 17103
TEL: 717 284-4081

LABORATORY EVIDENCE RECEIPT

DATE RECEIVED:	LAB. NO.:
May 29, 1968	

OFFENSE:	LOCATION (CITY, BORO, TWP/COUNTY):	INCIDENT NO.:	DATE OCCURRED:
Murder	City of Lebanon, Lebanon Co., Pa.		May 25, 1968

VICTIM:	SUSPECT:
Margaret Lynn Rober	

ACCUSED:	RECEIVED FROM:	DATE REQUIRED:
	Det. James F. Smith, P.D., Lebanon, Pa.	

SUBMIT REPORT TO: (INCLUDE ADDRESS)
Chief of Police, A. Corbin, City Hall, Lebanon, Pa.

IF LABORATORY RESULTS ARE NEGATIVE, THE LISTED
EVIDENCE MAY BE DESTROYED BY THE LABORATORY.

SIGNATURE

ITEM NO.	QUANTITY	DESCRIPTION
1.	1	One piece of linoleum from floor at scene of crime. Containing a stain.
2.	1	Large cardboard box with stains on bottom.
3.	1	One bed slat with possible blood stain.
4.	1	One mop.
5.	1	One bow.
6.	1	Dress and handbag of the victim.
7.	1	One bag containing clothing off the victim.
8.	1	One plastic container with hair that was attached to neck wound.
9.	1	One plstic container with scalp hair of the victim.
10.	2	Two plastic containers with fingernail scrapings of rt. and left hands of suspect. Jose Rivera.
11.	2	Two plastic containers with fingernail scrapings of rt. and left hands of suspect. Carlos Reyes.
12.	2	Two plastic containers with finngernail scrapings of rt and left hand of victim.
13.	1	Container of HUMPHREYS 11, for Irregular or Delayed Menses.
14	3	Three envelopes containing scrapings from iron frame of bed, left side bottom, from floor under bed & wall west end of corridor.
15.	1	One plastic bag containing Man's torn shirt found at scene.
16.	1	One box of fingerprint lifts from Bow.
17.	1	Pink panties with lace found at scene. — CHECK LIPSTICK.
18.	1	One plastic bag containing hairs found under victims left arm pit.
19.	1	One plastic baog containing hair found on victims thigh.
20.	1	One white paper bag containing pubic hair of victim.
21.	1	One plastic bag containing scalp hair of the victim.
22.	1	One plastic bag containing hair found on waste basket in bedroom.
23.	1	One plastic bag containing belt found around victims neck.
24.	1	One plastic bag containing "Buttons & Bows" deoderant.
25.	1	One plastic bag containing one small silver spoon found on living room floor.

CHECK HAIR, BLOOD, SEMEN.

ALL ITEMS RETURNED TO TPR. STRMA, + S.
+ DET SMITH ON JUNE 7, 1968.

RETURNED TO: (SIGNATURE)	DATE:	RECEIVED:
		J. Sagond, Sgt

LABORATORY EVIDENCE RECEIPT

PENNSYLVANIA STATE POLICE
LABORATORY DIVISION
2101 & HERR STS., HARRISBURG, PA. 17108
TEL: 717 334-4081

		DATE RECEIVED:	LAB. NO.:
OFFENSE:	LOCATION (CITY, BORO, TWP/COUNTY):	May 29, 1968	
Murder	Lebanon, Lebanon County, Pa.	INCIDENT NO.:	DATE OCCURRED:
VICTIM:		SUBJECT:	May 25, 1968
Margaret Lynne Reber			
ACCUSED:		RECEIVED FROM:	
		Detective James F. Smith, Lebanon P.D.	
SUBMIT REPORT TO: (INCLUDE ADDRESS)			DATE REQUIRED:

IF LABORATORY RESULTS ARE NEGATIVE, THE LISTED
EVIDENCE MAY BE DESTROYED BY THE LABORATORY.   SIGNATURE:

ITEM NO.	QUANTITY	DESCRIPTION
#26	2	white paper bags containing lipstick found on floor in bedroom of victim
#27		white paper bag containing white button or stocking holder found near body of victim
#28		blue suitcase containing clothes of Jose Rivera
#29		box containing a blue shirt and a green shirt, property of Carlos "Chico" Reyes
#30		brown case containing clothes of Jose Rivera
#31		man's grey hat - owner unknown
#32		brass wastebasket from bedroom of victim
#33		coat, trousers, shirt and shoes owned by Arthur Root, Jr. and worn night of crime
#34		box containing clothing of Carlos Reyes, which he said he wore the night of the crime
#35		One vial of blood from the victim. ▓▓▓▓▓▓▓

My name is Richard R. Boyer; and I reside at 711 Chestnut
Street, Lebanon, Pennsylvania. I am 26 years of age, and I am presently employed as a laborer.

My wife, Katherine R. Boyer, is 19 years of age; and I do not
know if she is employed. She resides at the O'Yes Hotel in Ono, Pennsylvania.

We were married on February 21, 1968, in Hagerstown, Maryland;
and this was the first marriage for both of us. There was one child born
of this marriage, Samantha Lynn, who has been adopted by my parents.

I believe our marriage started out wrong from the beginning.
My wife was only 14 years old and was pregnant. I feel she was not
mature enough to accept her responsibilities as a wife and especially
as a mother.

Our marriage was fairly smooth up until our little girl was
born. At this time, my wife started to neglect our child completely.
Her whole attitude towards our little girl was a complete disregard for
her safety and wellbeing.

We had many arguments during this time, mostly about her
care of our child. On one occasion, in fact it was my birthday, I
wanted to go out with some of my friends to celebrate. My wife said
she did not care to go. At this time, we were living in an apartment.

-1-

301

She started to rant and rave and scream. She called me vile names and started throwing things. I left the apartment and she actually threw things through the window, breaking the glass, which flew all over our little girl. I came back to the apartment and said I was taking our little girl to my parents since she had no regard for her safety. This made her even worse and finally, I called the police, who let me have the child. This caused me much embarrassment and humiliation; because of course, it drew quite a crowd of people. This was typical of her behavior during our marriage.

We reconciled after this but the situation only got worse. We lived with my parents for some time, and she constantly -- and I might add unjustly -- accused me of infidelity.

Again, thinking it might help the situation, we moved into an apartment. This only made things worse, since we lived near her mother and she spent most of her time there. Whenever we were with her mother, she constantly degraded me, calling me vile names and acting as though she hated me.

At this time, I discovered that my wife had been dragging our little girl all over the place. She was taking her to places where no child should be. She was constantly drinking and carrying on. We had many arguments about this, because I felt it was no way for a mother to be treating her child. She acted as if she didn't care about our daughter's safety.

All these things occurred within about a three month period. The final incident which really ended our relationship happened approximately in May of 1968. I was working steadily and one day I finished work earlier then usual. I came home and the doors were locked. I left and came back a short time later. As I was coming in the door, three or four Puerto Ricans were leaving the apartment by the back entrance. Earlier I had heard, through friends and relatives, that illegal things were going on in our apartment while I was at work, but this time I saw it for myself. We, of course, had an argument. I again took our child and sent her to my parents.

At this time, my wife left me. A few days later, she and my brother, who lived in the apartment upstairs, came to me and told me that they had been having an affair and that they intended to live together. I found this most embarrassing and humiliating since my parents, of course, knew all about it, along with my friends.

My wife never came back after this. She was constantly seen with my brother and they were openly living together.

One day she came to me and said she no longer wanted to have our child. She said the child was tieing her down and that she could not do anything that she wanted because of our little girl. At this time, the Court stepped in and gave full custody of our daughter to my parents, who later adopted my little girl. I feel this was for the best, since they could give her the kind of love and care she needed.

-3-

303

My name is Ruth Ann Boyer, and I am the plaintiff in this divorce action. I am represented by my mother, Mrs. Betty Jane Trompeter, whose address is 1402 Willow Street, Lebanon, Pennsylvania. I am twenty (20) years of age, having been born on July 30, 1946, in Lebanon County, Pennsylvania, and am a factory worker.

My husband, Richard Robert Boyer, is the defendant in this action, and he is represented by his sister, Mrs. Rosemary Davis, who resides at 726 North 7th Street, Lebanon, Pennsylvania. My husband is nineteen (19) years of age, having been born on March 28, 1947, in Lebanon County, Pennsylvania. His usual occupation is that of a factory worker.

I first met my husband in 1962. I met him at a dance. We did not start dating until 1964. We dated until February of 1965 when we became engaged. We were married on June 5, 1965 at the Trinity E. U. B. church in Lebanon, Pennsylvania.

After we were married we went to live in a trailer at the Green Acres Trailer Court. We both worked; he at Bowman's Tree Service and I at Bogene Plastics. We were both on day shift. For the first two weeks of our marriage things went well but then trouble started. We had money problems and also we had arguments over my child which I had had single. It was during this period of time that he also started hitting me. I don't remember why he hit me the first time but

LAW OFFICES
WIE, CHRISTIANSON
& BEAVER
PALMYRA, PA.
LEBANON, PA.
RICHLAND, PA.

- 1 -

he did it often. He didn't need much excuse and usually it was when he didn't get his own way. As I said, he particularly resented the fact that I had to care for the baby. One time he even threw the dinner all over the floor because he felt he should be fed first.

Another problem was his friends. Over most week ends he had some fellows there and they drank heavily. This was in a small trailer and it was bad. He was too young to drink anyway.

In July, 1965, I got sick and couldn't work. I have a bad heart. Then he quit his job which had paid $1.35 per hour for a job that paid $1.00 an hour. We didn't have enough to eat and I couldn't afford to go to the doctor, despite the fact that he always had enough money to buy paint or parts for his car or go drinking and skating with the fellows. I remember one time he took our last two dollars to buy paint two days before pay day and we didn't have any food in the house.

My husband has a terrible temper. Also he is not too bright. He was a special education student but I didn't know this before we were married. He was also in trouble with the police. In fact, he was on probation before we were married. He didn't tell me this either.

It got to the point that we were arguing all the time, and since he had a terrible temper it always ended up by him hitting me. He knocked me down to the floor several times but usually just slapped my face or knocked me against the wall.

Finally he mistreated the baby and threatened to take him away

2

from me. I couldn't stand that so I left him and went home to my parents. That was in August of 1965. After I left he came around to the house with his friends and made trouble. One of his friends got in a fight with my father when he told them to leave.

Shortly after I left, he went to live with his parents. Then he started dating a lot of different girls. The first one was a Cheryl Hess, also Jean Dunlap. He now has Jean pregnant and another girl by the name of Janice Clay, with whom he now lives according to a friend of mine who knows him.

Since I left he has been in trouble with the police again. He was charged with burglary and loitering. I don't know what happened to the case.

He was also in jail for corrupting the morals of minors. This arose out of drinking and sex parties at a place in Annville.

Just two nights ago, he and his Puerto Rican friends came to the house and tried to get in. I called the police.

My marriage was a mistake but I am glad we had no children who would be hurt, so I feel a divorce is the only solution.

Ruth Ann Boyer
Ruth Ann Boyer

Made in the USA
Lexington, KY
05 June 2012